HANDS THROUGH STONE

How Clarence Ray Allen Masterminded Murder from Behind Folsom's Prison Walls

James A. Ardaiz

CRAVEN STREET BOOKS

B O O K S

Fresno, California

Published by Craven Street Books
An imprint of Linden Publishing
2006 South Mary Street, Fresno, California 93721
(559) 233-6633 / (800) 345-4447
CravenStreetBooks.com

Craven Street Books and Colophon are trademarks of
Linden Publishing, Inc.
Cover image © Benjamin Howell

ISBN 978-1-610353-99-1

Printed in the United States of America
on acid-free paper.

Library of Congress Cataloging-in-Publication Data on file

Dedication

This book is dedicated to the men and women who wear law enforcement badges. They place themselves between us and those that would hurt us. They do this every day and they keep doing it until they finish the job they have been given. The officers depicted in this book are real people, but they represent all of those men and women: Willie "Bill" Martin, Art Christenson, Tom Lean, Ernie Duran, Harry Massucco, Ken Badiali. Each of them saw their job through to the end, and that end came long after they had retired. They stood their watch. I am proud to count them among my friends. And to my friend and investigator, Bill Martin, when the final moments closed in this case we all drank a toast to you. You were there in spirit and you will always be there in our hearts.

I would also like to acknowledge the courage of a young man who has borne the scars of a crime victim from youth to middle age. Joe Rios survived this crime by the grace of God and his own quick thinking. He stood his ground as a witness, as did others who gave their lives because they were witnesses. He was a hero and he stood up in court for his friends. And so did Jack Abbott, whose courage helped us track down a killer.

I would also like to dedicate this book to citizens who walk into court every day, raise their right hands, and swear to tell the truth. Seldom have witnesses who performed this duty paid with their lives. Bryon Schletewitz did, and he deserves to be remembered for doing his duty as a citizen.

Finally, I would like to dedicate this book to the district attorneys and attorneys general who bring these cases to trial and sometimes, as in this case, spend their entire careers to help give justice to those who have been victimized, like Ray and Fran Schletewitz. Ray and Fran didn't see justice in their lifetimes for the crimes against their family, but I think they knew that others would make sure that justice was delivered. I would like to think that they knew I kept my word. I tried to see it through to the end. That is what this book is about.

Acknowledgments

I would like to thank the many men and women in law enforcement who assisted me in ensuring the accuracy of this book. I would also like to thank my editor, Barbara Gordon, for helping me make this a better book and my agent, Andrée Abecassis of the Ann Elmo Literary Agency, for encouraging me when I needed encouragement.

To my friends who read this book and not only offered their insight, but also stayed my friends when I asked them to read it again and again, I thank you. Justice Betty Ann Richli, Nic and Nancy Boghosian, Tom Lean, Art Christenson, thank you.

And most of all, thank you, Pam, my wife, for putting up with me writing things down at all hours of the night. Thank you for constantly encouraging me to keep at it. When I first ran for office you pulled our kids along in a little red wagon, going door to door to tell voters about me. No matter how long I live I will always think of you pulling that wagon and I will know that, as with almost everything in our lives, you did it for love of me. There is no greater gift.

Contents

PART III: A WHISPERING VOICE

PART IV: RETRIBUTION

Author's Note

This is a true story. The characters are real. The names are real. The events are real. It is not a figment of my or any other's imagination. It is written from the viewpoint of a person who has been a prosecutor, a trial judge, and an appellate judge over the span of thirty-three years. This case and its participants traveled through almost all of those years. I have written about the effect of that journey on me and many others. It is written from the perspective of one who was there and saw it all.

Prologue

July, 1974
Fresno County, California

The great San Joaquin Valley of California spreads itself out into foothills that rise against its edge. In the heat of summer, the foothills glow golden by day, and by night they shine silver on spring grass dried by the sun. The yellowed blades sway in the summer breeze, their swishing music lost by day to the sounds of birds, rustling leaves, and man's traffic. It is by night that the symphony of the grass plays out to those who listen as the air moves gently. But on some nights the air lies still. On those nights, there is only silence. On those nights, the only sound is made by the hunters of the darkness.

On that summer night, the air of the great valley barely moved the high grass, which had been dried by the searing daytime heat to the brittleness of straw. A rabbit sat quietly in its burrowed-out hole, waiting to move for forage. The slightest movement would bring the rustle of the grass, breaking the silence, and with it a signal to the predators the rabbit knew were waiting.

The sound of tires on gravel brought the rabbit and nighttime predators to a frozen silence. Even feral minds knew enough to hide themselves from foreign sounds—sounds that might mean death even to those who were accustomed to being the hunter. It was the law of survival. Sometimes the hunter could become the hunted. Eyes meant for the night watched and waited.

The silver moonlight danced off the car as it rolled to a stop at the side of the Piedra Bridge, twenty miles outside of the city of Fresno. The two men's faces were alternately cast blue by the moonlight and black by the shadows as they got out of the vehicle and moved to the truck bed. They pulled at the limp heaviness of the bundled form rendered shapeless by the blankets which wrapped it. Stepping stones wired tightly around the form added to their burden. Grunting at the weight, the men carried the bundle to the edge of the bridge, balancing it on the retaining wall as they looked down at the canal. The water below ran deep and black, sliding along cement banks slick with moss, shimmering as its ripples caught the thin light.

"Push her over, goddamnit. Let's get this over with. We got to get back to the old man."

The other man didn't respond. He slid his end, the feet, over the cement wall of the bridge and let gravity do the rest. They both watched as the body slipped through the air. There was no scream. There was no sound left to be made except the splash of rushing water as it parted and accepted her into its cold embrace.

The men watched for a moment, waiting to see if she might surface. The swirls left by her last journey closed over her. The water resumed its course into the night, now with one more thing to pull along in its current and dissolve into the flotsam carried by its rushing mass.

The sound of tires on gravel receded into the darkness. The night hunters waited silently for the rustle of grass to make them dominant again. Their world was returned to moonlight and the newly stirring sounds of their prey. They were once again the hunters, left with the night. The rabbit stayed silent. It was not its time.

PART

I

MEMORIES PAST

1

Murder at Fran's Market

Six Years Later
7:30 P.M., Friday, September 5, 1980
Fresno, California

It was almost closing time at the small country store. The last customers had either left or were leaving with what they needed for another day. Fran's Market was a convenience store for people who wanted life's necessities and were willing to do without twelve choices for the same product, accompanied by background music. For that, they needed to make the twenty-minute drive into Fresno, the city whose lights were beginning to glow in the distance.

The sun was dropping in the sky, drawing out long shadows across the parking lot. It was after 7:30 in the evening. The dusty, gray-black asphalt in front of Fran's Market would hold the heat of the day long past the last glimpse of the sun. But at that moment it was still absorbing heat within its graying blackness, emitting small, radiant waves that rippled the air if you looked out toward the road that ran in front of the store.

The dust from the surrounding farmland and from the passage of cars going to and from Sequoia National Park settled on everything in the last days of summer, coating the parking lot, the store, and the nearby road with the thick grime that would stick until the first rains. The rains would not come for at least another month. Any drops of early moisture would only dimple the dust and leave muddy smears baking in the last vestiges of valley heat.

In the parking lot, a thickly muscled man sat in an aging car and pulled a bandanna around his head. During the few days since he had left dimly lit rooms, his fair complexion, unadapted to prolonged exposure to the sun, had quickly taken on a burned ruddy hue. He rubbed the rough stubble on his face, smoothing the heavy mustache that hung over the edges of his mouth, and felt the thin slick of perspiration and body oil. He looked out the car window toward the store. He had parked on the far side of the parking lot, away from the front of the market. His eyes flickered for just a moment on the radiating waves of heat and the brown hills just visible in the distance. It had been a long time since he had been able to look straight out at land that wasn't surrounded by high walls and concertina wire, and he still felt uncomfortable in open space. It was a feeling experienced by most men who had spent long periods in confinement and then walked out into the world. In fact, it had been little more than a week since he walked out the gate of Folsom Prison and took the bus to Fresno.

He looked over at the woman seated in the rear seat of the burgundy 1962 Mercury Comet. The car ran rough but it was all he had been able to get. The passenger side bucket seat was missing. The woman sitting in the car with him was little more than a stranger, but he had already slept with her. He knew her body better than he knew her. It had been years since he had any woman and she had been willing, more than willing. And now she was with him. It was the way of things as he knew them.

He slid his hand over to the sawed-off shotgun lying on the floorboard where the passenger seat would have been before it had given way to time and neglect. He pushed the weapon into his pants, the rough end of the sawed barrel catching at his clothing. With the cut-down stock, it was almost like a large pistol, but much more deadly. His windbreaker would conceal it as long as he held it with the inside of his arm. The woman also wore a bandanna. She held a small silver pistol nervously in her lap. He nodded at her. "Put the gun in your pocket. Just do what I do, babe. Like we talked about."

He could tell she was highly agitated by the way her hands were shaking and by how she kept rubbing and scratching at her face. The meth she had taken to calm herself down had only gotten her more worked up, but at least she was still with him. He opened the car door, got out, and waited for the woman to follow him.

4

They waited until the store appeared to be ready to close. Through the window he could see that some of the lights at different counters had been turned off. Paper signs, advertising prices for sale items, concealed parts of the store interior. That was good. The beer signs were beginning to glow in the lengthening shadows of dusk. He could see people moving around, but he had seen them the night before and he knew they were only store employees, not shoppers. Two of them had helped him when he and the woman had gone in to case the store.

The man paused, adjusted the sawed-off, and glanced around the almost empty parking lot. Good, he thought; it was now nearly empty, with only one car parked in front. The few other cars were over on the far side of the lot, most likely belonging to employees. He would weigh his options when he got inside. He patted his windbreaker, fondling the hard, cylindrical shotgun shell casings in the pocket. There were enough for what he had to do, and for what he might have to do.

The woman came around the car and looked at him. He had a moment's reflection, not about whether it was right to have brought her, but about whether she would hold up. He hadn't told her everything that would likely happen. She would find out soon enough. She touched the hard muscles of his arm. He could already feel the tautness of his prison muscles starting to soften. Two weeks ago, all he had to do was lift weights and wait. That and talk to the old man about the market, the safe, and how it would go down. He realized that he hadn't lifted any weights since he walked out of those steel doors. He pushed that thought aside and grabbed the woman's arm. "Let's go."

He treaded slowly across the hot asphalt, his footsteps picking out the ground like a feral animal; it was the walk of a man used to being around others who would prey on any weakness, and he had learned to show none. With each step he could feel the heat through the thin, rubber soles of his shoes. His senses were heightened; the clarity of the scene made an impression on him: the vividness of the colors, his sense of smell, and the vibrancy of his touch. It was like being hyper alive. He could feel the adrenalin course through him and the rush of a growing sense of power. It had been a long time since he had felt any real power, but now it began to take control; it calmed him and sharpened his senses. In his mind, it was a slow walk, but in reality he was moving more quickly with each step, leaving the woman to hurry behind him. He paused at the door of the store. They would enter together. They needed to appear to be just a shopping couple to those in the store. He opened the glass door and was greeted by a burst of cool air crashing against the outside heat, the bright fluorescent light glowing white on the rows of shelves.

Joe Rios was working his way down the aisles, moving the big dust mop from side to side to pick up the detritus of the day's business. Ray Schletewitz, the owner, and his wife, Fran, had gone home earlier. Doug White, an eighteen-year old junior college student, was working in the back and "Phina," Josephine Rocha, a senior in high school, was working near the front counter. Joe wanted to get home, but he had to clean up and then help Bryon, the owner's son, lock up. When the man and woman walked in, Joe looked up. They were both wearing windbreakers and bandannas, but that fact wasn't what caught his attention. He had seen them the night before. He hadn't forgotten the man's face; it still gave him shivers, but he shrugged it off. When Joe first saw him he noticed the man's arms, first with envy, and then with a sharp coldness in his stomach which he couldn't understand. The corded veins and the narrow waist were those of a man who had spent a lot of time pumping iron, a man who held his body like sculptured intimidation. On this night, Joe realized something else—he was thinking that the man looked like he had been in prison or, at least, what Joe thought somebody would look like if he had been in prison, although maybe his reaction was a result of the rough tattoos he had spotted on the man the previous night. The woman was shorter than the man, dark-haired, with an almost pretty face, but one that was hard-edged, like she had seen the underside of life. Her windbreaker hid the slightly full-figure that he remembered from the previous evening. He had felt relief when the couple left the night before and the store had been locked up, but now they were back. Joe looked over his shoulder toward Bryon, who was distracted, performing his closing chores.

The woman looked at Joe. "You got chuck steak? You know, for shish-ka-bob? We want a roast so we can make that." Rios looked at her blankly. He was no expert, but shish-ka-bob was usually made with lamb. *Maybe they just wanted to make some kind of skewered beef*, he thought. He called to the back of the store where Bryon was standing behind the meat counter, talking to the only other customer. "Hey, these people want a chuck roast to make shish-ka-bob."

Twenty-seven-year-old Bryon Schletewitz, used to customers who had to make the most of their money, looked at the couple, just as the other customer left the store. "That's a tough piece of meat. You're going to have to marinate it to make it work." Bryon flipped on the meat counter lights so the people could see the meat.

The woman hesitated. "That's okay. It's for this Sunday, for a birthday party." She looked over at the man next to her, who merely nodded.

Rios shook his head. "Take the top sirloin. It's $3.98 a pound. It'll work better."

The man stared at Joe for a moment, his eyes hard and flat. Then he looked back at the woman. "I don't know, babe. Maybe we should get the better meat?"

She shook her head. "I don't want to pay that much. Give me the chuck roast."

Rios shrugged, moved behind the counter, and began cutting up the thick roast. Bryon looked on as Joe cut the meat. He directed his comments to the couple. "You marinate it and it will probably be okay, probably come out tender."

The woman looked at Bryon and then back at Joe. "Oh, yeah, and I want a chicken." Rios nodded as he wrapped the meat. He heard the couple talking about other things they wanted to get. It seemed to be idle conversation. As soon as they were done, he could lock up and go home. He wrapped the whole chicken and set both packages on the top of the counter. "Here you are."

She turned around and looked at Joe. "Oh, I wanted a chicken too."

Joe put his hand on the wrapped chicken. "It's here." The woman looked distracted, a little confused. Joe tilted his head to one side and stared at her, wondering if she was loaded on drugs.

The woman shook her head as if she wasn't sure what she had been thinking. She stared at Joe for a moment. "Oh, yeah. I wanted some paper towels, too."

Joe pointed toward the paper products. He watched the two of them walk down the aisle, but he could see that the woman's purse seemed empty. He looked around for Bryon and Doug, thinking *maybe they're trying to steal stuff.* He could hear her saying the same thing over and over about the party. *She's on something.* The man kept pointing at different things, saying, "Let's get this, babe." Joe could hear the strange inflection to the man's voice, different than he had heard before, like a white man with a Mexican accent. It didn't fit, and it had a harsh edge to it, like someone who was used to talking to rough people.

The man said to the woman, "Let's get this. Just hurry up, grab some things. These people, they want to go already and it's a quarter after eight." He looked over his shoulder toward Joe. "I thought you closed at nine."

Joe shook his head. "No, eight. But we'll wait." The man nodded. Joe walked back to the dust mop and started pushing the dirt toward the back of the store where the stockroom door led to the side parking lot and the garbage bins. Doug, the tall, husky young man he worked with, was in the back stocking shelves near the walk-in cooler. Joe signaled to Doug to catch his attention. "That guy out front? Maybe I'm crazy, but he looks like he just came out of prison."

Doug nodded, keeping his voice low. "Yeah, and that girl? She must be on drugs or something. I saw her grab for something, and she looked like she was freaking out."

Joe pushed the dirt over toward the side door. "I know. I'm telling you, Doug, that guy just looks like he's done time." He walked over to the dustpan and reached down to fetch it.

"ALL RIGHT MOTHERFUCKERS, DOWN ON THE FLOOR."

Joe stopped abruptly as his eyes caught the expression on Doug's face. The man's voice grated against the shelves and walls of the small stock area. The harsh, clipped sound carried the snapping menace of a whip. Doug froze, staring at the open door from the stockroom into the store. Joe turned his head. The man in the bandanna and windbreaker was holding a short-barreled shotgun and standing behind Bryon and Josephine as he herded them into the stockroom. The woman was to his right, holding a silver pistol. She was looking around, her arms moving back and forth. The man stared straight ahead. There was nothing in his eyes except blackness. Joe looked at the gaping hole in the end of the shotgun; the rough-sawn end of the barrel glinted as the man slowly swung it across the space of the store room.

The man waited while Joe, Josephine, Doug, and Bryon got down on their knees. He pointed the shotgun at Doug. "You, big guy, open the freezer. Open the fucking safe."

Doug looked at the gun pointed at him. "What are you talking about?"

"OPEN THE FREEZER."

Douglas White got up from his knees and walked over to the walk-in cooler. He turned toward the man, who gestured with the shotgun for Doug to go in. As Doug walked in, a look of confusion clouded his face. The man followed and looked over his shoulder. "Where's the safe?"

Joe barely moved, his eyes focused on the black barrel pointed at Doug. The silver pistol in the hands of the woman glinted in his peripheral vision. *There's no safe in there. What's he talking about?* Joe could see Josephine next to him, her big blue-gray eyes glistening, but she was quiet. He wanted to tell her everything would be all right. *Maybe if we just do what they say.* Ray had always said nothing in the store was worth getting killed for.

Doug lifted his hands. "There's no safe in here." Doug was starting to shake, his voice beginning to show the strain as he stared at the black hole at the end of the short barrel pointed at him, like a single, unblinking eye holding all his focus.

"I know there's a safe in there." The man brought the sawed-off up and thrust it out toward Doug. His voice carried both a tone of menace and a crack of uncertainty.

Doug's raised his voice. "Honest, honest. There's no safe in here." He remained standing inside the walk-in cooler, looking around at the others, who he could see through the door.

The man gestured with the shotgun. "Get the fuck out, Bryon." Doug's eyes narrowed in confusion.

Bryon Schletewitz was kneeling on the floor. The woman had the pistol pointed at him, Joe, and Josephine. Bryon raised his voice so he could be heard. "I'm Bryon."

The man stared at the thin, brown-haired young man still kneeling on the floor. He looked back at Doug, his face showing the realization that he had made a mistake. He pointed the shotgun at Bryon. "Get up. Where's the safe?"

Bryon pointed toward the back of the storeroom, to an area hidden by several floor-to-ceiling shelves of food stock. "It's way over there."

The man gestured at Bryon with the shotgun. "Let's go." He waited until Bryon got up and walked behind him until they were in the back of the storeroom, concealed from the view of the others, who were watched over by the woman. Doug was back on the floor. Josephine was next to Joe. He could see her trembling out of the corner of his eye.

Joe raised his gaze to the woman holding the gun. Her hand was shaking. As the man marched Bryon to the back of the storeroom, she said, "Keep an eye on these guys." Joe shifted his weight and the woman pointed the gun directly at him. A cold, tingling sensation of fear rippled up from his stomach. He was thinking about running into the bathroom. She stared at him. "I hate to do this."

Joe looked around, afraid she was going to shoot. "I ain't doing nothing. I ain't doing nothing."

The woman stared at him a moment longer. "You all just stay on the floor."

Although Joe couldn't see anything, he heard the sound of somebody being pushed around, thudding against the wall. He could hear the man's voice, raised and angry. "I KNOW THERE'S ANOTHER SAFE. THERE'S ANOTHER SAFE, MOTHERFUCKER. A BIGGER ONE."

Bryon stood with his back to the wall between the desk and a small safe up against the storage shelves. The entire area in the backroom was only five or six feet wide, with just enough room for the small desk and chair. A compact steel safe sat on the floor just behind the chair and up against the wall, next to a locked metal box. Bryon had no room to move, no place to run. The man pushed him against the wall with the barrel of the gun, prodding him in the stomach, screaming. "I KNOW THERE'S ANOTHER SAFE."

Joe heard Bryon's voice; he could hear the fear in it. "These are the only ones. These are the only two. I'll open them." Joe heard Bryon's voice rising. "I'm going to open them. I'll open them."

"Give me the fucking keys, the store keys. Which one is for the doors?" Bryon fumbled with the store keys, singling out the one to the front door as he held the key ring out to the man glaring back at him, his eyes narrow and drawn. Bryon stared at the shotgun and back up at the eyes of the man holding it. All he could see was anger. The man was thrusting the shotgun into his stomach, pushing him back against the wall, yelling at him, insisting that there was another safe. Byron could hear the pleading sound in his own voice. He stared at the gun and then back up at the man's eyes. Only blackness in the eyes.

Joe heard the booming sound reverberate off the walls in the small storeroom. There was a crashing sound as something hit the wall. For a moment, the room shook—and then there was silence. Joe smelled the sharp acrid odor of burnt gunpowder in the confined space of the storeroom. The man in the bandanna backed up. Now Joe saw him, the shotgun held loosely in his hands. Wisping smoke curled from the short, black barrel as the man turned and walked back toward them.

The man snapped the shotgun open, pulled the expended cartridge from the breech of the gun, and put it into his pocket. He kept his eyes on the three people on the floor. They kept their eyes on him, watching the thin strand of white vapor oozing from the breech as the man shoved in another cartridge and snapped the shotgun closed. Joe felt himself flinch at the metallic sound as the breech closed. The man's eyes never left the three people on the floor, and Joe's eyes never left the shotgun and the man holding it. Joe could tell that Josephine and Doug were staring, frozen with fear, their eyes widening. His own eyes were wide and unblinking. In that moment, Joe knew it. He knew they were all going to die.

Joe felt his eyes suddenly blinking rapidly as he tried to focus on what was happening. The man walked slowly from the back area where the desk was. Joe couldn't see Bryon, couldn't hear him. The sound of the shotgun blast was still ringing in his ears.

The man held the weapon out in front of him as his eyes moved across the faces of the three young people kneeling on the floor before him. The smell of fear soured the air, overwhelming the mustiness of the storage area and the tincture of burned gunpowder that now added to the mélange of odors filling the room. The shooter slowly moved the barrel of the sawed-off in front of the faces staring back at him, their eyes wide, tracking his every move. He could feel the control, the rush. He paused and pointed the gun at the face of Doug White, who stood six-foot-six, although he still carried the softness of his eighteen years. "All right, big boy. Where's the safe at?"

Out of the corner of his eye, Joe watched Doug, whose eyes were locked on the barrel positioned just inches from his face. Joe moved his eyes back up at the man holding the gun. He could smell the pungent odor of fear seeping from the two people kneeling next to him and rising up from his own body. He could feel himself swallowing nothing but dry air, his mouth devoid of any moisture. Joe heard the tremor in Doug's voice, the pleading tone of his explanations, knowing that each word carried the ebb or flow of his life. "Honest, honest, there's no other safe. Those are the only two."

The sharp explosive burst was deafening, as a blast of hot, buffeting air rocked Joe's head. He couldn't hear. He couldn't think. But he could see. Doug's entire body unfolded from the floor, slamming backward as if some unseen force lifted him off the cement and flung him flat against the wall. A red bloom sprayed from Doug's throat, spreading out from a gaping black hole. Doug made no sound, except for a soft gurgling noise that was lost in the reverberation of the shotgun blast.

Joe's mind filled with one all consuming thought: *My turn is next!* He didn't think anymore; he could feel panic consuming him. He didn't look anywhere; he jumped up and bolted for the store's bathroom door, stumbling past Doug's body lying spread-eagled on the cold cement, while Josephine still kneeled, frozen in fear. *The door, lock the door.* He fumbled with the simple latch and desperately locked himself inside. The inner door to the toilet was half open—another door, another barrier. Joe pushed it open, scrambling to find a place to hide, trying to make himself small, to make himself safe, pushing the privacy lock, turning in the small space, hoping to find one more place of concealment. But there were only walls.

Josephine's knees were rooted to the floor. She couldn't move. She had seen it. She had seen Doug's body slam against the wall. She was only seventeen years old. She had not seen death before and now Death stood in front of her, his face an emotionless mask. He broke the shotgun open, his eyes never leaving the wide-open, blue-gray eyes staring back at him. He slipped the expended shell from the breech, the hot brass casing plugging the smoke inside the barrel until he pulled it out. He cradled the sawed-off and reached into his pocket for another cartridge, wrapping his hand around the hard cylindrical shape, feeling the end rather than looking at it. He slid the new canister of small pellets into the breech, closed the gun, and pointed it at the chest of Josephine Rocha. The blue-gray eyes stared back, unblinking, glistening with the tears of someone who has just seen the horror of the brutality that was certainly destined to come. Fear and shock immobilized Josephine as her mind tried to wrap itself around the surreal reality of her last moments, grasping at the sole refuge of total denial.

His hand pressed against the trigger and the man could feel the buck of the sawed-off as the shortened butt pushed back against the brace of his stomach. The girl's slender body jumped back, almost suspended in the air and then slammed into cardboard boxes stacked against the wall. He watched as she slid down the boxes, coming to rest on the cement floor, her wide-open, blue-gray eyes staring up. The man knew he was the last thing the girl would ever see. Simultaneously, he blocked out the screaming of his woman. What she didn't know before, she did now. He would deal with it later. His eyes moved over to the closed door of the bathroom.

Joe felt the muffled whump of the shotgun blast shake the thin walls of the bathroom. He didn't need to see. He knew he was the only one left.

The shooter stepped over the body of Doug White. He stared at the white door. It was a door that could only lead in. He knew he blocked the path of the only way out. He reached for the knob and jerked the flimsy door, breaking the lock. The five-by-three room was empty, the sink glinting dully in the white light of the single fixture. His eyes fixed on another door just in front of him. He could hear nothing, but he didn't need to hear. He knew.

Joe heard the outer door slam open. The footsteps made a scuffling sound on the cement. He could hear the pull on the door to the toilet room, his room, from which there was no escape.

The man pulled hard on the door, breaking the privacy latch, and the hard, white light outlined the dark-skinned young man who was pushing himself into the corner of the small space, trying to make himself small, trying to make himself part of the wall, staring back at the intruder, his eyes wild with terror.

Joe pushed his body into the corner of the closet-sized room. He folded himself against the painted sheetrock wall, feeling the slight give in the wall, wishing he could slip into the paint and disappear. The man was standing in the door. He lifted the shotgun and pushed down the barrel, filling the room with the whispery odor of gun smoke that was no longer trapped in the breech.

The shooter held the shotgun cradled in his arm. He kept his eyes on the boy pressed into the corner of the tiny room. There was no sound now, except his woman wailing in the other room. His fingernails caught the edge of the expended casing, sliding it back out of the breech. He put it into his pocket and took out another unexpended shell, wrapping his hand around the firm plastic sheath holding more pellets and explosive charge, the brass end casing warm from his body heat. He slipped it into the empty breech and snapped the sawed-off closed. The boy was the last one.

Rios tried to focus on the man's face, the receding dirty-blond hair and the drooping mustache, the dark eyes drawn into slits of concentration, but he couldn't keep his eyes off the black hole at the end of the short-barreled gun. It was like a single black eye rising up from some kind of reptile as its steel body straightened itself with a snapping sound against the blunt wooden tail and uncoiled to its short, deadly length. The boy tried to close his eyes, but he couldn't. What there was left of his life's moments were before him. He would see it. He could not close his eyes at the end. He pushed his body further into the wall, trying to find the last, small space where his life could take refuge.

The shooter stood less than three feet away from the thin, young man staring back at him. He sensed the barrel locking into place as he snapped the breech closed and pulled the butt of the shotgun against his stomach. He tightened his index finger against the trigger and squeezed it.

The explosion filled the small room, shaking the walls and blowing the sound back through the doorway he stood in. The sawed-off bucked against him, his body absorbing the recoil and the sharp jab of the weapon, the explosion of gas pushing the shotgun back as the barrel discharged its deadly bite. The blast hit the boy's left side, his arm and chest shattering from the spray of pellets. The wall became spattered with a mist of blood and tissue as the boy sank down to the floor, the outline of the white space where his body had once pressed against it now painted in the residue of human fluid and flesh.

The shooter stood for a moment, staring at the body crumpled in the corner of the bathroom floor, his ears ringing from the booming sound that reverberated inside the small space. For the first time, the acrid smell of gunpowder reached his nostrils. A smoky haze in the small room slightly misted the still form on the floor. The man let the shotgun drop to his side. This boy was the last of them; the last of those he had seen in the store. The sound of his woman gasping for air, choking and crying, began to fill the silence and his attention turned to her. "All right, baby, let's go." He turned and stepped over the lifeless body of Doug White.

The shooter could feel the adrenaline begin to leave him. He looked around the small storeroom. For the first time, he felt his hand and noticed the warm stickiness of blood and a stinging pain. He looked down at the webbing of skin between his right thumb and forefinger and he realized the flesh was sliced open, welling blood that slicked around the area of the breech where his hand held the still warm weapon. He had caught his skin in the breech when he snapped it shut, slicing his hand open as neatly as with a blade. He looked at the floor and the drops of his blood, blood that made small, perfect circles on the cement, in sharp contrast to the spreading blood pools flowing from the people lying on the floor. He put his hand in his mouth, sucked at the salty, warm fluid, and then causally wiped what was left on his pants. He reached into his pocket for another shell—just in case. He turned to his woman and guided her back through the swinging door that led into the store. He still had to find the safe.

As the shooter walked into the bright, fluorescent light of the store, his eyes were focused on the front door. Nobody had entered the store. His first few steps left a bright track of blood in the stained tread pattern of his shoes, but the marks thinned out as he walked until the only evidence of his passage through the store were the bright, red drops of blood that dripped from his hand onto the beige linoleum pathways between the lines of shelves.

Joe Rios sat on the floor of the bathroom, where he had slid down the blood-smeared wall. There was no clarity to the moment. It was more like he was detached, watching somebody else. Only the throbbing of his left arm and the heavy pressure of his own blood seeping from his shoulder reminded him that he was not watching someone else. Yes, it had happened to him. He sat there, trying to gather his thoughts. The shock of the wound and the adrenaline that had fueled his body began to sweep waves of nausea through him. It was not pain that dominated his consciousness. It was the very real awareness that he was still alive. The man who shot him had left him for dead. He let the relief of life settle before he thought about what to do. The man might come back, might find him alive. There was no doubt in Joe's mind about what would happen if the man returned. There was no choice; he had to leave the small room. He had to escape to have any hope of living. To stay was to die.

Joe struggled up from the floor, using his right arm to steady himself. The inner door to the toilet was still open. He could see into the small sink room. The outside door was ajar, filtering the light of the store-room. There were no sounds outside. The killer had left. Using his right hand, Joe grabbed at the jamb of the outer door, nudging the door fully open. Josephine and Doug were lying on the floor. He didn't kneel down to touch them. Although he had only seen dead people at a few family funerals, he knew they were both dead.

Bryon's body was stretched out on the floor. Joe could only look for a moment at what was left of Bryon's face, and he quickly turned away. Slowly, Joe moved away from Bryon's body, stepping quietly toward the bodies of Josephine and Doug. He could not bring himself to look at them any longer. Joe stepped over Doug's long, still legs and edged toward the swinging door that led into the main store.

The store seemed empty. Joe moved quickly to the freezer, near the meat department. He heard the sharp jangling of keys. The man and the woman were trying to open the front door, fumbling with the keys, trying to find the right one. Joe stared at the backs of the man and woman, sharply defined by the white, fluorescent light shining down on the stillness of the empty market. He backed up toward the swinging door leading into the storeroom. He turned and looked back at the door leading into the parking lot. Doug's body was stretched in his path. He tried not to look at Doug's face, but passing the body was the only way out.

Jack Abbot sat quietly with his wife on the patio of his backyard that looked out onto the parking lot area of Fran's Market, which was separated from his yard by a low wall. While the heat of the day was beginning to draw down, the air itself still wasn't cool; but Jack knew that as the shadows lengthened into darkness, the air would finally lose its warmth. The lights of Fran's Market gave off enough glare that the stars were still obscured. But later, after the store closed, the night sky would not be polluted by the lights, unlike the skies above the city of Fresno, only a few miles to the west. Jack leaned back and spoke quietly to his wife, while he waited for the evening quiet to take control of the countryside.

A slightly muffled booming sound resounded from inside the market. Jack was well aware of the usual sounds of the store and his neighborhood. He also knew the sounds of guns. He could tell the signature bellow of a shotgun when he heard it, as it filled the air with its blast so unlike the sharp crack of a pistol. Jack sat forward. Within moments, he heard a second muffled boom. Something was wrong. He knew it. He looked at the old car in the corner of the parking lot. It was empty. The store should be closed. It was after 8:00. Jack ran back into the house and grabbed his shotgun.

Joe Rios backed away from the swinging door that led from the store-room into the store. The man and the woman were still standing by the front door. Maybe he could make it. He stepped over the legs of Doug White, glancing sideways at Josephine Rocha, lying on the floor. He couldn't help them now. Nothing could. He threw up the bar that was placed across the back door for security purposes. The sound of the bar as he moved it filled his ears. Joe pushed the door open, not looking back into the store, and he ran as fast as he could.

Jack Abbot came out from his house and moved quickly toward the small retaining wall that bounded his backyard and the parking lot. The door to the storeroom slammed open. A dark figure began to run across the parking lot. It was too dark to see who it was, just that the figure was running and that he was male. He raised his gun and heard himself yell, "Hey," and then he fired up and in the direction of the running man. He fired almost from the hip, the blast of pellets streaming up into the night sky.

Joe could barely hear the sound of a man's voice. *Maybe it is the man who shot me.* He didn't stop. He wouldn't stop. He heard the roar of the shotgun. To stop was to die. He just ran headlong into the darkness.

Abbot walked quickly to the rear door of the market. The two young people on the floor lay like tumbled statues in a reflecting pool of blood. He stepped back. He didn't want to touch them. There was no time. If they were to have any chance it would come only with help. He ran back to the fence and yelled for his wife to call an ambulance and the sheriff.

Jack looked back over his shoulder, pulling his shotgun around in the direction of the store. The bright lights of the storeroom silhouetted a man near the door. The figure moved toward him. Jack squeezed the trigger, feeling his shotgun buck. The man faltered and cried out.

The sound of a shotgun blast filled the air around Jack. It wasn't muffled like the other ones. He felt the blast hit him from behind. Jack's knees crumpled.

As Jack fell, he saw a man stagger across the parking lot and get into the old car he had seen earlier. He could hear the sound of the starter grinding as the engine resisted, and then finally it turned over. As Jack sank to the ground, the car moved out of the parking lot, and Jack lost sight of the car, lost sight of everything, as his body fell below the line of the fence.

Joe Rios heard the second shot as he ran, stumbling through the darkness. Fences blocked his way. He pulled himself over, his left arm useless. Dogs were barking. He didn't want to jump over a fence into a yard with dogs. He could feel nothing except fear of the man who was behind him. Someone had shot at him. Someone was still shooting. Suddenly, he felt the sharp drop before he realized where he had run. The shallow ditch took his footing. He could feel himself falling, losing his balance, his knees coming up against his body as he rolled into the ditch. He could feel himself gasping for air. But he couldn't stop. He forced himself up. There was a light, a house. He ran toward the light.

The shooter could feel his left foot throbbing. The person who was outside when he came through the storeroom door managed to get off one shot and he unloaded one when the man yelled at him. He heard the sound of the gravel and pavement as the shot went low but he caught something in the foot, probably pellets. He couldn't tell and he wasn't going to stop to look. He was sure he had gotten the guy who shot him, but how badly he couldn't tell. His woman was still in the store. He wasn't going to go back. It never even occurred to him.

He pulled open the door of the aged Mercury Comet and shoved the keys into the ignition. The starter kept grinding; the engine wouldn't start. He kept turning the key in frustration; the tired engine coughed, but finally caught. He pushed on the accelerator, feeling the pain in his foot as he shoved it against the floorboard. Gravel shot out from behind the tires as the Comet made a feeble attempt at exerting its long-sapped power against the worn surface of the parking lot. He pushed down on the gas as hard as he could, willing the car to speed up, to carry him out onto the street. Darkness and distance were his only safety now. He needed to get rid of the car in case somebody had seen it. And he had to make a call.

2

"We have a triple ..."

Friday, September 5, 1980
8:30 P.M.
Fresno, California

By September, the nights in Fresno can move quickly from the daytime heat of the waning days of summer to the growing evening bite of autumn chill. This happens more quickly than the shortening of the days. When the pager on his belt buzzed, District Attorney Investigator Willie "Bill" Martin grabbed his jacket. He immediately called his supervisor, the chief of homicide in the district attorney's office, at his home. That was me, Jim Ardaiz; I was the chief of homicide. My given name is actually James, but I only use that in court—more impressive sounding. Before you ask, my name is Basque and it's pronounced Ar-daiz, with a long "i" and a silent "a." It rhymes with "lies," but that's a defense lawyer joke that I never thought was very funny.

If you don't know who the Basque people are, then I will tell you that they are the indigenous people who inhabited the Pyrenees Mountains between Spain and France long before there was a Spain and France. They speak Basque, a language without a Latin root. You hear about them now and then, particularly when certain rebellious Basque factions blow up things or people on either the Spanish or the French side of the border. Anyway, that's what I am on my father's side. Besides that, I am a little over six-feet tall and I have green eyes. However, at this particular moment, my attention wasn't focused on what defense attorneys called me, but on the reason I had received an urgent call from the sheriff's office.

"What do we have, boss?" It was an affectation Bill cultivated, calling me "boss." I was his supervisor in title and pay, but we both knew that Bill was the more experienced investigator. I, the "boss", was the legal mind. I treated Bill as an equal out of respect. Bill treated me as an equal out of deference—as for equality of respect, he was getting there. Ours had proven to be a mutually beneficial relationship, with me, the young prosecutor, learning from the older homicide investigator. Over time, we had grown in respect for one another's abilities, and our friendship had grown after the many nights we shared, standing around at murder scenes, spending weeks and sometime months sifting through evidence and, later, savoring beers with other detectives at our favorite bar after we had finally brought our man down. In some aspects, our job was like that of hunters, but our prey walked asphalt and concrete and usually carried a gun.

"We have a multiple murder at Fran's Market. Just got the call from sheriff's dispatch. Get on the horn, Bill, and find out what's going on. They didn't seem to know much, just asked for us to respond." We knew Fran's Market was a small rural market, located on the outskirts of Fresno. We had been there before, almost three years before, during another murder investigation. I knew Bill would call in and then fill me in the details on the way.

"I'll pick you up, boss."

"I'll be outside, Bill. We have to move."

I knew what Bill was thinking as soon as he put down the phone. *Like the kid needs to say "we have to move." When do we not?* We always have to move when we get a call. Bill put down the phone and walked into his home office to get his service weapon, a nine-millimeter automatic. He never carried it anymore unless he was going to a homicide scene or to an arrest. Most people think cops carry their service weapons all the time. Some do, usually the young ones and always the ones in uniform, but with detectives, the older they get, the more most of them just put it in the glove box when they are driving or they use a small revolver or automatic that can be carried in an ankle holster or, more comfortably, in the small of the back.

Bill always laughed at the television cops who pulled out some cannon they carried in a shoulder or hip holster. You only had to sit in a car with a gun stashed somewhere on your body to realize how uncomfortable it could be. Besides, a gun on your hip or in ruined your clothes. And Bill liked his clothes to look good. "For the ladies," he would say. As for the shoulder holster, we had all heard stories about the guy who pulled his gun out of his shoulder holster and shot his partner standing next to him as he swung the gun around. Bill would leave the shoulder holster to Dirty Harry. But this was a homicide—Bill's service weapon would be with him at all times on his hip, as would the .380 Walther PPK in his ankle holster. Bill always carried a backup when he went into the field. Old habits die hard. "So do cops who don't carry a backup," Bill would add with a small smile.

"In my forties," Bill liked to say if someone asked. A tall, African-American man, he looked younger than his years, and he was definitely older than he would admit. He would never tell his exact age. Bill had coffee-colored skin and a well-formed mustache that he liked to rub when he was thinking. His given name was Willie, but nobody called him that except guys with whom he had ridden patrol with as a young man. Now he was "Bill." For some reason, the younger guys hadn't liked calling him Willie. It seemed to make them uncomfortable, political correctness being what it was, even back then. They assumed that his given name was William rather than Willie, so they just made him Bill. He knew they were trying to be respectful and had grown accustomed to Bill. If you asked him his name, he would size you up and decide whether he was a Willie or a Bill. Although I had reached the point where I could call him Willie, I called him Bill.

Before he became a D.A. investigator, Bill had been a member of the sheriff's department homicide unit. After a while, he realized that working nights and weekends was taking a toll on both his marriage and himself. That's why he had come to the D.A.'s office, for regular work hours and weekends free. But that had its downside, too. It could get pretty boring just interviewing witnesses. When he was offered the chance to work the D.A. homicide unit as primary investigator, he jumped at the chance, although it meant he still had to work some nights and weekends. But it was a good compromise. And I knew he had decided I wasn't bad to work for. Actually, he thought I was pretty good for a young guy. At least that's what he told others behind my back. He also said I was a little cocky—all right, a lot cocky—but with cops that fit right in. Anyway, I didn't think I was all that cocky. I did think I was good, but that was different. At least, I thought it was different.

Bill pulled the heavy automatic from its holster. He dropped the clip and pulled back the slide. He always carried one in the pipe and a full clip. The chambered-round ejected. He slipped the clip back and chambered another round. Then he dropped the clip and loaded the round that had been ejected and shoved the full clip back in the butt of the automatic. He opened his briefcase and checked for his extra clip, his cuffs, and his flashlight. He was ready. He already knew it was going to be a long night.

Bill pulled up, watching me pace back and forth in my driveway. He would have been disappointed if "the boss" wasn't outside waiting. He knew there was no point in telling me to wait in the house until he got there; I would never do it. I was always outside pacing and looking at my watch.

Bill smiled. It was a homicide. The victim would be on the floor waiting for us. He or she wasn't going anywhere. Besides, there would be homicide investigators at the scene when we got there. The D.A.'s job was to assist the homicide investigators at the scene. We weren't the primary investigators. Still, there was always a little adrenalin surge when you rolled into a homicide scene.

The first time Bill called me "boss," I laughed. I knew what he thought of me. When I first arrived at the D.A.'s office, I didn't know anything, just like most young deputy district attorneys fresh out of law school. But I listened and I learned.

I remember the first time I went down to the Identification Bureau. The "I" Bureau we called it. These days, there are whole television shows built around the people at the "I" Bureau. They call them "Crime Scene Investigators" or "CSI." I guess "CSI" sounds more exciting, but as far as I'm concerned it's the "I" Bureau. If they had a television show called the "I Bureau," people would probably think it was about the local department of motor vehicles. I can hear it now, "I work for the 'I' Bureau," and people will wonder if they can get their driver's license photo fixed. I told one of the "I" Bureau techs, Jessie, to "run the print for a match." She had a big stack of fingerprint cards, a magnifying glass, and a latent print card with the unknown perp's prints. That was how they did it back then; they would take out a stack of print cards with some common characteristics and compare them by hand and eye to the latent print lifted at the scene. I remember that Jessie looked at me and smiled the way you do at a child who still believes in Santa. "Well it might take me a little while—what did you say your name was again?" That's the first time I realized I had made an ass out of myself with seasoned investigators. Lesson learned. This wasn't like television.

Things were different now. The difference for Bill was that now I was no longer fresh out of law school. I still listened and I knew I still had things to learn, but I also had come to know things he didn't know, and he tolerated that. There was even his grudging concession that took me by surprise one morning when over a mug of coffee he observed that for a lawyer I might not be totally useless. When I told him to do something, it was usually after he had either politely and obliquely suggested it or we had discussed it. In a way, it had become a game between us—I would occasionally say the right thing before he suggested it, and this was happening more and more frequently. We had become a team. In law enforcement parlance, "a team" means that you take turns buying donuts, but it also means a lot more: like the unwritten rule that the other guy is the one who watches your back and you watch his.

Becoming chief of homicide for the district attorney was my dream. It was the top of the line for a trial prosecutor. Oh, you might be *the* district attorney, but when you were the chief of homicide you were at the top, as far as trial prosecutors were concerned. You got the biggest cases and you tried the toughest ones. And, while you always represented "The People," who you really spoke for was the victim.

As far as investigators were concerned it was the same thing. "Homicide Investigator" was more than a title; it was the top of the line for cops. It was where all the other cops wanted to be. Whoever watched a show on television about the burglary division?

For me, well, I was never the high school quarterback, but he never became the chief of homicide either. Besides, my stories were a lot better. So, to put it mildly, I liked my job. After I graduated from law school, I briefly considered going to work at one of the big law firms. A lot of money was out there if you did it right. But me? I wanted to be a real trial lawyer. I wanted to try cases all the time. I didn't want to sit in an office listening to some client pissing about what had been done to him or what he wanted to do to somebody else or how much it was going to cost in legal fees. No, I wanted to be exactly what I was.

There was that one moment at the beginning of a big case when the judge would slowly look at everyone gathered, all of those who waited pensively, the jury, the defense team. Then the judge would focus on me. That was my moment at which all the nervousness disappeared, the great beginning when the curtain went up and I was alone on the great stage of human drama. I liked standing up and saying, "Ready for the People."

Bill flipped on the dome light and got on the radio. He wanted to know which investigators were at the scene. He lowered the window on our undercover car. I always laughed at the idea of his car being under-cover. Who drove a blue Dodge with a whip antenna except cops? Of course, that was back then. Nobody has a whip antenna anymore, but the blue Dodge hasn't changed. It still looks like a cop car and doesn't fool anybody, especially since the blue color is one that nobody would really pick for a car, and there were also the cheap hub caps to always give it away. I think automobile makers must have a selection of paint just for police undercover cars, or maybe it's just the paint that is left over after all the other colors are picked.

"Boss, it's a triple. We got some witnesses and I guess a neighbor tried to play John Wayne with the shooter. Got himself shot in the ass. You ready?"

"Yeah, yeah." I slid into the front seat beside him. A triple? Not "three dead," not "three people murdered"—we called it a "triple." If it had been two, it would have been a "double." If it was a single, it was a "dead guy" or, depending on the part of town where the homicide occurred, "a stiff." When you said it, everybody in the business knew what you meant; "I worked a triple last night." That was enough. Besides, when you said it, you didn't need to swagger. Those on the inside knew what you did and those on the outside just knew that you must do something special. Bill gunned the engine. He never did that in his own car, a Cadillac. Oh, well, it wasn't his gas.

"What else we got?"

Bill glanced over and frowned. "Three down in what looks like a robbery, but Kenny says there's something not right." Kenny was Kenny Badiali, the on-scene sheriff's detective.

"Not quite right? How?"

"They got some woman who was at the scene when the first officers rolled up. She was in the bathroom, covered in blood and hysterical. They took her to the hospital. Ross Kelly talked to her. Kenny thinks there's a connection. Said she wasn't hurt and she looks like she's loaded, maybe on meth. Says he doesn't want to talk more over the radio. Too many people are listening." Kelly was another on-scene investigator. He was built like the stereotype version of a truck driver: curly, reddish hair, thinning in the middle of his head, with the rest of him spreading out around the gut. A really good guy.

"Kenny spends too much time worrying. Wired too tight. Tell him that we need to draw blood from her at the hospital and run a drug screen," I said.

"Well, wired too tight or not, he knows what he's doing. He says we need to get there yesterday. If Kenny says something's wrong, then something's wrong. And, I'll bet he's already asked for the drug screen."

"Just make sure, Bill. I want that blood before she starts to realize something's going on."

Bill didn't give me his usual comment about the investigators knowing what they were doing, which meant he wasn't sure either. He got on the radio while I sat back and stared out the window. I had a bad feeling. Not something I could put my finger on—it was just a bad feeling. Years before, I had handled another murder that came out of a burglary at Fran's Market. I had gotten to know the owners, the Schletewitz's, good people, Ray and Fran. I hoped they weren't lying dead in the market. It may seem kind of crass of me to hope the bodies in the market weren't my friends, because whoever was lying there was somebody's friend or son or daughter or husband or wife. I guess I have been to too many homicide scenes. After a while, you get kind of jaded. The victims stop being human beings, lying on the floor or on the street or in the dirt, their aspirations unfulfilled and their dreams ended. They become pieces of evidence.

That wasn't true for me if the victim was a kid. I still couldn't handle the kids. You kept thinking that they had a whole life ahead of them and some asshole had stolen that away from them. And if it was a woman, well, I guess there is a double standard. It still bothered me more if it was a woman and, especially, if it was a woman who had been raped.

For a while, I had been in charge of sexual assault crimes and crimes against children. I couldn't handle it. Sometimes, you get to the point where you start to hate the "perps." When you get to that spot, you don't have any objectivity. You can't step back. I just couldn't handle those middle-of-the-night talks to women spitting blood out of holes where their teeth used to be, or trying to get some little kid to tell me what some pervert had done to him. No, homicide was the right fit for me. For some reason, murder never became as personal with me as did sex crimes. I guess it had something to do with the fact that I never got to really know the victim. Maybe that says something about me, maybe not.

Bill was moving fast. There was a red light that we could put on top of the car, but it wasn't an emergency and we didn't need it. Even in an unmarked car, a cop will always take liberty with the traffic laws. If you don't get stopped, no problem. If you do get stopped, the traffic officer will see our exempt license plate and know it is another cop.

It was almost 9:30 P.M. when we got to the scene. I hadn't been to Fran's Market for over three years, not since the earlier homicide investigation. The long, rectangular cement block building looked the same, a quasi-country market, painted paper signs in the window advertising whatever was on sale, a beer sign glowing. Fran's wasn't far enough outside the city to be in the "country." In fact, its location was just right—if you were a robber. Sheriff's officers' cars filled the lot, and the obligatory yellow crime scene tape was already up. People had gathered around to look. Sure, some were there out of concern, but most just came to gawk. Blood and death always draw people who want to see it and then tell everybody how awful the scene was. That's why traffic always slows down as people drive by an accident. Everybody wants to see the horror and then shudder when they describe to their friends just how terrible it was.

Some news media reps were already there and the cameras turned on me as I got out of the car. There was a time when I would pay attention. Now, I just moved past them to get to the deputy trying to control the crime scene and keep people out of the area. At the other side of the parking lot, I saw Ray and Fran. I didn't go over. I was relieved to see them outside the store. But their son, Bryon, also worked there on some nights. As I said, I had a bad feeling.

Kenny was waiting outside the back door to the storage room. I had been in it before when I worked the first homicide, a burglary that turned out a lot worse. There was a certain degree of irony in going into a place on a 187—that's the California penal code for murder—when you'd been there before on another murder case. There were some places where it seemed like every year we were making a visit, usually a liquor store or the local "stop and rob," where some poor soul trying to make some extra money was working the night shift and got stuck up. You'd just shake your head every time because the clerk would be dead on the floor, usually with a gun in his hand that he didn't know how to use. I doubted that was going to be the case this night.

The door was partially closed and a beam of light cut across the parking area. Kenny didn't wait for me or Bill to say anything. He just got right to it. That was Kenny. All business, but it always seemed like he had too much coffee in his system.

"Jim, Bill, how ya doing? This is bad. We got two kids down just inside the door. A third one is over on the other side of the storage room. There was a fourth victim who the shooter left for dead in the bathroom. He ran out after he thought the shooter was gone. How that kid made it, I got no idea. He was hit pretty bad—shotgun blast almost took his arm off."

"So who got here first?" Bill asked as he looked around the area.

"Deputy Humann was dispatched...." Kenny looked at his notebook, "at 8:15 in response to a shots fired call. He said he was here within five minutes. There was one man down by the corner over there." He pointed to a lawn area near the northwest corner of the market. "He says the guy down was a Jack Abbott, a neighbor. I'll say this for him, the guy's got guts. He yelled at the first guy he saw and then he saw the second one. He fired a shot and thinks he hit the second guy. But the guy turned toward him and Abbot saw he had a gun, so he started to run for cover, but the shooter got him in the ass. When Humann got here, that's where he found Abbott, down on the ground. He went inside and found the other victims, a white female and two males."

Bill was already looking around. "Any description?"

"Not much. Just a white male adult, maybe six feet tall."

"What about the kid that got out? Anything from him?"

"Yeah, Deputy Mendosa talked to him before the ambulance got here. He ran to a house where he knew the people. He told Mendosa that a white male, about six feet, 170–175, wearing a bandanna on his head, and a white female adult, approximately five feet, five inches, 125 pounds, brown hair, also wearing a bandanna, robbed them. He says the male was the shooter and the female was armed as well."

"So you think the woman that they found in the bathroom could be involved?" I asked as my eyes were panning the scene, taking it all in.

Kenny shrugged. "Maybe. Who knows. She had blood all over her and she was in the bathroom in hysterics. We won't know until we talk to her. We've asked for the hospital to do a drug screen." He looked over at me. "Like you asked."

So Bill had told him that I asked. That's it, the way it always was; dump it on the lawyer. Cops always stick together. No matter what you do, they never forgive you for being a lawyer. At least I had reached the point where they were willing to overlook it most of the time.

Bill and I headed to the door. "Let's take a look."

Kenny slowed me down. "Take it easy. There's a lot of blood."

I was used to blood, more used to it than I ever wanted to be, but I wasn't prepared for this. Just inside the door there were two people, a young man, maybe nineteen or twenty, and a young girl, maybe sixteen or seventeen. There were only a few dry spots on the cement floor. Blood was everywhere, thickening as it began to congeal. On television and in the movies, the blood is always bright red. I guess that's so you will know it's supposed to be blood. But in the real world, that isn't how it looks. It doesn't take very long before it starts to turn dark red, and by the time it dries it is a dark reddish-brown. Sometimes it is almost black, especially when the sun has dried it. So, when a television program shows the bright-red puddle on the floor, or the guy they find out in the woods three or four hours or even days after the homicide has a crimson stain on his chest—that isn't what it really looks like.

Right now, less than two hours after the incident, it was just pooled blood that spread out into a dark red stain across the floor, only it was thick and the edges were dark where it had begun to dry. Bill and I moved carefully around the blood. Bright light flooded the storeroom, and we had no problem seeing. The problem came when we had to actually look at what was there to be seen.

The girl was lying on her back, with her head propped against the wall next to what I guessed was the bathroom door. A plastic plug from a shotgun shell and shotgun wadding lay near her head. The boy was lying near her feet. If you didn't know better, you would think that it was the way two kids would look lying on the grass at a picnic. If you didn't know better.

Nobody looks very good when they are dead and lying on the floor. But she was a pretty little thing—somebody's baby girl. Somewhere a mom and dad were going to go through the worst moments of their lives and it was going to happen in the next few hours when they learned what had happened to their little girl. I've seen a lot of bodies and most of the time I just looked at them and then started to examine them to see what would be important for evidence. But this time I paused for several moments. It was her eyes—they stayed with me. She had gray-blue eyes, and they reflected nothing more than a vacant stare. I can't describe it any better than that. She just had these pretty gray-blue eyes. One thing you discover about people who have just died is how their eyes look. You can just see those eyes and you know they are dead. The color is there and the shape is there but the shine isn't there anymore. There is a light in a person's eyes that tells you they are alive. When they are dead, that light is gone. The light was gone from her eyes. In the movies, when people die, they close their eyes. In real life, when people die, their eyes are almost never closed. They just stare sightlessly. I resisted the temptation to reach down and close her eyes. As long as I live, I will see those gray-blue eyes. She had a large wound to her upper left chest—it looked like a shotgun wound. I remember thinking, so little of life lived; so much of life taken. She was just a kid.

The boy lying near her had his eyes almost closed. He had on a brown knit shirt. There was a hole about the size of a half dollar in his throat— shotgun blast, probably a twelve-gauge at close range. There wasn't much of a spread pattern, and you could see the powder tattoo on the shirt left by bits of burning powder as they hit him. Sometimes, those burns are on the skin if the gun is fired from a close enough range. This shotgun was fired from very close range, probably no more than two or three feet at most, or else the pellet spread would have taken his head off. These kids knew what was coming after the first shot. So why did they just stand there?

Fortunately, neither the responding officers nor the paramedics had made much of a mess of the crime scene. Usually, they rush in and do what they're supposed to do, which is save lives. They don't pay attention to moving things around that might be evidence. That isn't their job. This time they hadn't made any quick gestures. They, or the first deputies on scene, had turned the bodies to check for vital signs. It was obvious both kids were dead. The blood from the two bodies spread out all over the floor. It always amazed me how much blood there is in one human being.

Bill was standing behind me. "Look over here behind the shelves. We have another one. Maybe a little older, but still a kid." Bill had been around a long time but I could tell that even he was shaken. They were just kids and I could hear him muttering "Goddamn" over and over again. When you have your own kids and you see something like this, it really brings it home.

I looked over and could see the feet sticking out from behind the shelving that was along the back wall of a walk-in freezer. The body was lying on its side, the back to a desk along the wall. The room was obviously used as an office area. His face, or what was left of it, was turned in the direction of a small safe. It was a young man in his mid-twenties. Even though the top of his head was gone, I knew him. It was the owner's son, Bryon. He had been a witness for me several years before in the other murder that came out of a burglary of the store. Now, he was a murder victim. I looked up at the shelf. His brain was sitting up there like somebody had just casually placed it there. The rest of his head, the top of the skull and the hair, was splattered all over the wall. There was a fine mist of blood that had traveled up the wall. Pieces of skull and bloody tissue were splashed on the desktop and the adding machine sitting on the desk. Blood, tissue, and bits of bone were spread over so many places that it was hard to envision the impact of the shot. The shooter had obviously intended to kill the boy. But why? This was just a country store. How much money did the killer think he would find? Besides, these kids didn't have any weapons. They weren't a threat.

The crime scene didn't make any sense. People don't just stand around waiting to get shot if they have a chance to get away. For some reason, these kids just stood there after the first one got shot. And the shooter's actions made no sense. Most of the time, a robber will shoot in a panic and then run. They don't usually intend to kill anybody when they walk in, even though they have a gun. Most robbers just intend to use the gun as a threat. This was an execution. But why? Whoever did this was way beyond being just some two-bit, punk robber. Kenny was right. There were too many questions, and there was something very strange about the crime scene.

When you've seen enough homicide scenes, you get a sense of what happened. Most of the time, murder follows a pattern, and so, when something doesn't fit, you can sense it. Regardless, whoever did this was a really bad guy. Shooting someone in a panic or without thinking is one thing, but pointing a gun at a kid and deliberately killing him or her? For that, one had to be a cold-blooded killer, and those kind of people are a breed apart. Most murders happen because people get angry or panic or are intoxicated. I had investigated a lot of homicide cases, but it wasn't often that you saw a real premeditated murder, the kind where the killer thought about it in advance and then did it just like he was killing a bug. Those guys are scary, but even *those guys* usually don't kill kids. This guy was more than scary. Somewhere out there we had a real killer.

The coroner joined us. Unlike what a lot of people think or what is shown on television, the coroner called to the crime scene is usually not a doctor and is there to check for information and control disposition of the deceased. The coroner looked down at the boy with the head wound and said, sadly, "I pulled his ID out. We'll need to make a positive identification later. I can't tell from the ID if it's him. I hate it when people have to see their kids like this, and I'm always the guy who has to tell them."

Bill glanced at me. I spoke first. "Don't bother. I can make ID. His name's Bryon Schletewitz. I saw his parents outside. I know him. He was a witness in an old case of mine involving this store."

The coroner looked up. "Do you want to tell his parents or should I?"

He looked relieved when I said I would do it. I had done it before with other parents or husbands or wives. It was never easy, but at least this time it would be coming from somebody they knew and not from a stranger. "The names of the other two kids?"

"I don't have an ID on the girl yet. The boy's driver's license says Douglas White."

Kenny interjected, "We don't know yet whether they were working here or just happened to be in the wrong place at the wrong time. Right now, we got two witnesses and maybe a third, depending on whether the woman in the bathroom is a witness or a perp. The kid in the bathroom knows what happened I'm guessing, but he's in the hospital right now. We'll have to wait on the woman. She's over at county medical center at the moment, but I got a guard on her." Kenny stared at me for a few seconds. "You going to talk to the parents?"

31

"Yeah, Bill and I will take care of it." I looked over at Bill for moral support. He was shaking his head. He wasn't happy about being dragged into informing the parents, but he knew it was something that needed to be done and he too had done it many times before.

I stepped back out of the storage room, being careful not to open the door too much. The television camera lights were on and the glare was directly in my face. The cameramen were trying to get the camera eye into the storage room, and I wasn't going to give them a chance to catch any part of the victims or the blood on the floor. It was bad enough that several parents were going to get the worst possible news tonight about their kids. I wasn't going to make it worse by having family and friends see their loved ones bleeding on the floor of a storage room. People deserve better than that.

Bill and I walked past the news crews, shouting questions at us. The deputy holding the onlookers back lifted the crime scene tape. He took the lead, putting his arm in front of the lunging cameramen. "Not now, please. Just step back." We moved around them and for once they didn't follow. If they had known the family was over on the other side of the parking lot they would have been there trying to wring the last ounce of emotion out of the scene; asking the questions that they themselves would never be able to answer if they were on the other side of the lens: "Is your son in there?" "Do you know if your daughter is alive?" "How does it feel? How does it feel?" What is it about the need for human misery to be portrayed on the news at 11:00? Some moments obviously need to be private, but not much is private anymore. Misery is big, I guess. Decency goes on the afternoon news—must be the family hour.

Ray and Fran Schletewitz watched as Bill and I walked across the parking lot. Fran stepped back as we neared. They both knew me from the previous case and we had seen each other occasionally over the years. Fresno isn't so big that you don't cross paths with people you've met before. Ray just stood there looking at me. I could tell he knew what was coming. He had already prepared himself. There is no easy way to tell somebody their child is dead. About the only thing you can do is get it over with as clearly and as gently as possible. I reached out to him. As he took my hand, I looked at Fran and then back at him. Bill stood off to my side. Ray was staring directly at me, and it was all I could do to hold his gaze. A man deserves to be looked in the eye when you are about to tell him the one thing no parent ever wants to hear and is never prepared for.

I opened my mouth and then closed it, measuring my words and thinking what to say and how to say it. I looked at the mother and father waiting for me to tell them what they already knew but wanting to hold onto that last sliver of hope that they were wrong. There is no good way, I guess. I finally just let it out. "Bryon is in there, Ray, Fran. I'm sorry; he's dead. I wish there were something different I could tell you."

Fran started to cry and Bill went to her. A group of women, family friends I suppose, began to gather around her. Ray's eyes hadn't turned their gaze from me. He looked at me with an expression on his face that was beyond description. It was like watching a man's body just drain itself of everything but grief. I recognized the moment all too well: those fleeting seconds of shock and screaming denial when a loved one is caught between the reality of what they are being told and the flood of emotion that is coming. Somehow nothing came. Ray just stood there with age showing in every line on his face.

"Jim, I knew it when I saw you walk over. Bryon wasn't even supposed to work tonight. We had somebody off. Who else is in there?"

"A young girl, looks to be around seventeen or eighteen, and a young man who has an ID that says Douglas White. They work for you?"

"They both work in the store. They're just kids. The girl, must be Josephine Rocha, she's just a kid. Doug isn't much older. Their parents—this will kill their parents. There was another boy working tonight, Joe Rios?"

"We have another boy that was shot. He got away. He's at the hospital. We're sending somebody over right now to get a statement. I'm sorry, Ray. I just don't know that much yet."

I know some people think it's insensitive to ask questions of a person under these circumstances, but solving a homicide is a race against time. You have to ask. If you are going to identify the killer, you probably have your best chance within twenty-four to forty-eight hours. After that, things start to get cold. Some people are initially so emotionally overwrought that they can't answer your questions. However, it always surprised me how many people are fairly calm. Ray was calm. We needed a statement from him and besides that I needed to protect him from his own parental instincts. All parents are the same. They want to see their child. It's not something that you can allow, not because of rules or regulations, but for their sake. I knew what he was going to say before he said it.

"Jim—my boy—I want to go in. I want to see my boy."

That was something I couldn't allow. First of all, it was a crime scene and he wouldn't know what to do. More importantly, if I let Ray go in there, he would never get the image out of his mind. He would see it for the rest of his life when he closed his eyes at night, every time he thought about his son. That wasn't going to happen if I had anything to say about it. Some people resent it, but later most people realize it was the right thing to do.

"Ray, I'm going to tell you something and you need to listen and trust me. There is nothing you can do to bring Bryon back. I don't want you to remember Bryon the way he is right now. You stay here with Fran. One of the detectives will be over to take a statement. Then you go home with your friends. I'll have one of the deputies drive you. We'll call you. Trust me on this, Ray. This is best. I won't let you go in there. I'm sorry."

I walked over to Fran. Bill had his arm on her shoulder. She was shaking her head. The sound that was coming out of her was a low, keening moan. What could I say? All I could do was let her know that I cared. "I'm sorry, Fran. There's nothing else I can say. I'll let you know things as we figure them out. Right now we just don't know anything."

I'm not sure she really heard anything I said. For her, all that was important was said when I told her I was sorry. Her friends looked at me and then surrounded her in a circular compassionate embrace. I saw Ray, standing still and erect, staring at the store. I patted him on the shoulder and walked back toward the crime scene. There was a long evening ahead and I was already emotionally drained.

There is a symmetry to the chaos of a crime scene, especially a murder scene—things that should be there and things that shouldn't. What is there and what isn't tells you a lot about the perpetrator. This scene was no different. It just took a little longer to adjust to the reality of it. Even seasoned investigators have a hard time when three innocent young people have had their lives ended so abruptly and so violently. Almost all of us had been to triples before, but they were normally drug shootings or barroom brawls that turned into combat zones. These were kids and they didn't do anything except be in the wrong place at the wrong time. It was going to be hard explaining it to their parents.

Bill and I walked back toward the crime scene tape and started to
go under it when a young man grabbed at me. He said he was Bryon
Schletewitz's brother-in-law. He wanted to go inside. I removed his hand
from my arm while Bill stepped behind me. The man kept saying that
Bryon was in there and he wanted to see what had happened to him. I
didn't have time for this, but I also didn't want to turn my back on him.
I told him "No" as firmly and as gently as I could and then I nodded to a
deputy who guided him away. I had done this enough times that I knew
if it were me, I wouldn't have felt any different than these people. I often
thought that I probably wouldn't behave as well. Maybe that's because
I knew what lay ahead and they didn't. We all depend on the system to
bring us justice. The problem is that to most people the only justice in
crimes like this—the murder of children they love—is seeing the son of
a bitch who ruined their lives taken out and shot. Well, while I knew that
wasn't going to happen, they hadn't figured it out yet. And even when
we got the killer, and I was sure we would, prosecution would be a long,
slow grind. That night I had no idea how long it would be. That's the final
part—the long, inexorably slow, grinding process of the law. By the time
the perpetrator gets what the law says is coming to him, the system has
worn the victims out, worn the attorneys out, and worn itself out. The
only one who isn't worn out is the one who started it all. Those types
never seem to wear down.

Bill and I walked carefully back inside. The bathroom door was open
and the light was on. The room was divided by a sink on one wall and
a door that separated the sink area from the toilet. The back wall of
the room with the toilet was covered with bits of flesh and bone, and
blood had splattered all over the corner, outlining a blank space where
something had blocked the spray of blood and tissue. Kenny offered his
thoughts. "I'm guessing the shooter stood at the door and fired at the kid,
the one that got away. From what we can piece together, the kid must have
shoved himself into the corner and turned away from the shooter. His
left arm took most of the blast. The shooter must've thought the kid was
dead because he left him there. Then, later, I guess the shooter heard him
leaving through the storeroom door that led to the parking lot and chased
after him." The bathroom was only a few feet square, and with the toilet in
it there wasn't much room to move.

When you look at a crime scene, you try to visualize what happened. It
helps you to think about where evidence might be located, and it will be

of invaluable help when the time comes to interrogate suspects or to question witnesses. This one wasn't hard to figure out. The shooter stood at the toilet room door, pointing the shotgun at the kid. The end of the barrel was no more than three or four feet away when this guy pulled the trigger. The kid must have been terrified, looking at the end of that gun and the face of a man who intended to kill him. In a macabre way, he was probably fortunate. My guess is that he went into shock and collapsed on the floor when he was hit. With all the blood and gore, the shooter figured he was dead and left him. The kid was the lucky one.

When a shotgun is fired, the ejected buckshot spreads in an inverted-cone shape from the barrel. The farther away the barrel is from the target, the wider the spread of the pellets. At almost point blank range, there is a very limited spread pattern, but at three or four feet, there is a noticeable spread. Assuming he has the weapon or knows what weapon was used and the kind of ammo, a forensic expert will look at the spread pattern and be able to determine with fair accuracy how far the shooter was from the victim when he fired. The two kids on the floor showed almost no spread. The shooter was probably no more than a foot or two away, and he was likely three or four feet from the kid in the bathroom. For Bryon, well, that was something that we would have to evaluate later. He had fired at Bryon, but he had aimed high. Whatever the precise distance, this guy was so close that he didn't have to be careful with his aim.

The surviving witness said the gunman was a man, but it had never occurred to us that the shooter wasn't a man. Maybe it isn't politically correct, but there are distinct differences in the way women kill and the way men kill. First, women aren't usually as violent, at least not as violent in the same way as men are. It is pretty unusual to see premeditated violence from a woman. Oh, a woman will kill, but when they do it they usually are really pissed. I mean, a woman will unload a gun if she's going to shoot you. She'll keep firing until she hears the click. A man will usually just shoot you. Another thing, a woman is unlikely to kill kids this way. She might kill her own kids, but then she will usually try to kill herself, or else she's plain crazy. No, this was a guy. Some things you just know.

Bill kept looking around. "No shells." He looked back over his shoulder. "Kenny, has anybody found any shells?"

Kenny shook his head. "Nope, haven't seen any. Of course, they could be under the shelves or somewhere around here. But I don't think there are any."

That meant one of two things. Either the shooter used a single-shot shotgun and removed the empty shells each time he fired, or he picked up the ejected shells. When you fire a single-shot shotgun, you need to open the shotgun at the breech, remove the expended shell casing, put in a fresh shell, and then close the breech. Most people who fire once will then turn and run. They don't stand there slowly reloading and placing the empty casing in their pocket. If the shotgun carried multiple shells and they ejected as rounds were fired, the alternative was that the shooter had picked up the ejected shells, which meant he had the presence of mind to pick up a casing, which would have extractor marks on it from the ejection mechanism or a firing pin impression. Either way, this guy was cold-blooded. But people don't just stand still and let somebody shoot them. Almost always they'll fight or they'll try to run. It's instinctual. But these kids didn't run. That meant that most likely there was more than one person involved. It also meant that the second person had a gun on them, too. These kids didn't move. They knew they had no chance. The boy in the bathroom had been conscious enough to tell us a woman was also involved, but if it was the woman in the bathroom, then the shooter left her behind, and no gun had been found on her. Her being in the bathroom, covered with blood, didn't fit either. It was too soon to tell for sure who she was, but right now I had stopped giving her the benefit of the doubt. None of it made any sense, except for one thing that was clear: This wasn't just a robbery.

Bill came to the same conclusion almost at the same time as I did. Probably, he came to it *before* I did. "The woman in the bathroom, the one they have over at the hospital. The first officer on scene finds her in the bathroom where the Rios boy was. She's covered with blood and screaming hysterically, so she was in there when it happened and she wasn't shot." Bill looked over at me, his eyes narrowing. "She's the second one or at least one of them."

The lack of shells on the floor and the fact that there were no bloody footprints where the shooter would have walked to pick up the expended shells pretty much told the story. We could look for shells on the floor, and we would look, but we weren't going to find any. This guy had used a single-shot shotgun. He had methodically pointed the shotgun at each of the kids, pulled the trigger, and then broke the shotgun open, removed the expended shell, put it into his pocket, and reloaded. All the while, a second and maybe a third person held a gun on the remaining kids while the shooter performed his role as executioner. If Rios, the kid who got away, was coherent enough to give us a straight story, then the second person was a woman and we probably already had her under guard. But we hadn't found a gun on her. If she had wielded a gun, where was it? And, if the shooter took the gun, why did he leave her behind?

It didn't fit together. Not only were these just kids, and there was no point in shooting them, but most robbers don't have the stomach for this kind of bloodshed. This was intentional. This had been contemplated before the killer even walked in the door.

Like I said, I had been to Fran's Market before. I had been in that back room before. I had also talked to Ray and Fran before and I had talked to Bryon before, and now he was lying on that worn floor and his parents were looking to me for answers. Ray and Fran had once stepped up before as citizens. They cooperated with me and law enforcement to help bring a murderer down. They testified when another parent's child was a victim and now it was their child who was a victim.

Nobody knew that earlier case better than me; I had been the prosecutor, three years away from the job I held now. Now, these same people were depending on me to do something—to make it as much right as something like that could be made right. The memories of that earlier case surrounded me as Bill and I walked around the store. Yes, we both had been to Fran's Market before and, yes, we both had made promises to Ray and Fran—and to Bryon, their only son, not to worry, we would take care of them. That case, those promises, were now reflected in the faces of Ray and Fran. I could see them still standing in the corner of the parking lot, surrounded by friends, but I felt like they were looking right through me.

They were calling in the promises I had made in that other case when they had trusted me. And they had every right to do so. I couldn't help thinking back, and I could tell from his silence that Bill was doing the same thing.

3

A Cop's Worst Nightmare

September 5, 1980
10:00 P.M.
Fresno, California

While the Identification Bureau techs worked inside the storeroom, Bill and I stood outside the door. Kenny left to talk to the boy who had been shot. It was after 11:00 P.M. by the time Kenny got to Valley Medical Center to talk to Rios. The kid was in horrible pain. They were prepping him for surgery but he could still talk. A brave kid, he was talking through a lot of agony, and the condition of his shattered arm had to terrify him. I'm not sure he realized yet how lucky he was to have survived, considering the wound he had suffered.

Ross Kelly had gone with Kenny to talk to the boy. It hadn't taken Rios long to tell them enough to conclude that the woman who had been found in the store was with the shooter. Now she was in a different part of the same hospital. As Ross listened to the kid, he realized that if the woman in the bathroom had been the one who held the gun, then most likely the gun must still be in the store. "The woman in the bathroom, Connie Barbo, there's a connection all right." Kenny's voice came over the radio confirming Bill's and my own suspicions. "Ross said her purse was still in the bathroom when our boys found her. He's guessing that if she was with the shooter, then maybe the gun is still there, probably in the toilet tank. I think we should check it ASAP."

Over time, a good detective, just like a good street cop, develops instincts, a sort of sixth sense, although sometimes they can't tell you how they knew someone was carrying a gun or why something didn't seem right. Kenny immediately got on the radio to the I Bureau techs still processing the scene. The techs were back in the store bathroom within minutes. Sure enough, there was a loaded .38 caliber revolver in the water tank behind the toilet.

Bill and I were still at the scene when they pulled out the gun from the toilet tank. So Barbo was with the shooter and she had used a gun. Now we had something to go on. The first rule in a homicide investigation is to use common sense and the "Rule of Ockham's Razor." If you don't know what I mean by Ockham's razor, it means the simplest explanation is most likely correct. I always laugh when I watch television shows and movies with all their elaborate plot schemes. If criminals were that smart, we probably wouldn't catch most of them. No, most of the time the explanation for why somebody does something is pretty simple. Stick with the simple explanation and common sense. In this case, common sense and the simple explanation meant backtrack on Connie Barbo. She was one of the people holding a gun while the shooter did his work, but when the shooter fled the scene, she got left behind; so much for chivalry among thieves. We needed to find out who she had been associating with; we'd then probably find a group of names that included the killer or, if not, would point us in his direction.

From the state of her emotional condition, the combination of blood and violence had pushed her over the edge. When he let us know what Rios had said, Kenny didn't hesitate. "I'll put an arrest hold on her at the hospital." *Well I guess so.* I didn't say anything. Kenny didn't have my kind of sense of humor. Like I said, he was wrapped too tight.

Bill and I walked back through the storage room door to reexamine the floor. The cement showed through the pooled blood like gray islands. There were tracks on the dry parts of the floor left by someone stepping through the wash of blood. One person, wearing tennis shoes, had walked through the blood and then through the storage room door into the store. The shooter had left his footprint etched in the blood of his victims. But he also left something else. Along side the bloody shoe tracks there were well-defined circles of blood that had dripped onto the floor. This guy had been bleeding himself. Not enough blood was on the floor to indicate a serious injury, just large, round blood drops every few feet.

"My best guess is that he caught the webbing between his thumb and fingers when he snapped the shotgun closed after he reloaded it," said

Bill, keeping his eyes fixed on the floor. "It's easy to do if you're not careful. Almost every cop has done it at least once. At least, we'll know his blood type and that he'll have a wound on his hand when we get him."

Catching the webbing of your hand between the barrel and the breech wasn't that hard to do with either a single-shot or a double-barrelled shotgun. The barrel is on a hinge attached to the wooden stock. To load it, the barrel is released from the stock and snaps forward on the hinge, exposing the barrel for a round or rounds to be slipped in. The barrel is then closed, seating the rounds against the breech plate and the firing pin. A lot of people forget where their hand is when they snap the barrel closed. It didn't take much for me to hear the sound in my head of a shotgun closing on fresh rounds. The sound is as loud and distinctive as a bone cracking. It also didn't take much for me to think about the fact that the last sound those kids heard was the sound of the killer sliding a fresh round into his shotgun and closing the breech.

We stepped into the storage room. The blood drops were over by the walk-in freezer and in the bathroom, near where Bryon's body was still lying on the floor. More drops were near some boxes next to the door into the store. We walked back inside the store and found still more spots around the corner and by the dairy case and also at the door to the beer cooler. The cooler door handle was stained by a bloody smear.

Inside the beer cooler there were more spots on the floor. The tracks seemed to lead in the direction of the meat counter, which made even less sense. I said to Bill, "He went into the freezer and the beer cooler." We left the door closed in case there were any prints on the handle.

Bill looked at me with a puzzled expression, which was unusual, coming from him. "What the hell did he think was in there?"

Something was stirring in the back of my mind, but I couldn't put my finger on it. At least not yet. Clearly, the shooter had been looking for something and he must have thought it was in the freezer or the walk-in cooler. Bill went over to the forensic techs and told them to check for prints on the beer cooler. The techs were already busy, taking swabs from the blood drops on the floor and placing a ruler next to the bloody foot-print for photographs. The ruler would allow us to get an exact perspective of the shoe size. If we were lucky, maybe there would be some type of wear pattern in the shoe that we could match if we nabbed him with the same shoes on. If we were even luckier, maybe there would still be blood on his shoe. Most people have no concept of how hard it is to get rid of all traces of blood, particularly on the bottom of a shoe.

Like I mentioned earlier, there is a symmetry to homicide scenes. This guy was a shooter and he was a cold-blooded killer. This guy was no cherry; this certainly wasn't his first crime. Anybody who could do this had been around and had gotten used to violence. Most likely, he was a convicted felon. And, most likely, he had done something earlier that had involved violence. As usual, it was Bill who said it: "My guess is this asshole just got out of the joint."

"And that woman they found in the bathroom?" I asked.

"Connie Barbo?"

"Yeah. What do we know about her?"

"I talked to Kenny; he said the docs say she's loaded, most likely meth."

Bill and I walked out of the store. We had seen it. We knew what was there. There were witnesses that needed to be talked to. Hopefully, our people had gotten what they could from the Rios boy before he went into surgery. And, we needed to get a statement from the neighbor who had shot and been shot.

In a homicide investigation, the fewer people trying to take a statement the better. Unless you are recording the statement, what is said becomes a combination of the memory of the investigator and perception of what was said. People are not designed to remember exact words quotes and they almost never repeat a statement in exact quotes. What is reported is what people *think* they heard. The more people taking the statement, the more muddled it can become, even for professional investigators. But the opposite is true when it comes to checking the crime scene; the more people who look over a crime scene the better the results, as long as they aren't all tromping around at the same time. Kenny had gone to do his thing and we had stayed to do ours. My job was to make sure that I had a complete idea of what had happened at the scene. And so we surveyed the store one more time. We had three kids dead and no idea who the shooter was. All we knew was he was out there and he had to be brought in quickly. For him, killing was obviously an easy thing. At this point, there was absolutely no reason to believe he would hesitate to kill anybody who got in his way, including a cop.

I vividly remember walking out of the store. I didn't look to see if Ray and Fran were still there. I certainly hoped not. A small crowd was still milling around, waiting, I suppose, to see the coroner bring the bodies out. The television news crews were gone and the only newsperson still there was a photographer who stepped in front of us. I remember that a sheriff's deputy waved him off, and Bill and I stood for a moment outside of the shaft of light coming through the slightly cracked open door to the storage room. This is the moment when your mind begins to filter through all of the observations and statements, trying to come up with a coherent theory. For the first time that night, my mind began to focus on Bryon Schletewitz as a person. So far, I had stayed detached, but on murder cases as soon as you slow down your emotions can catch up with you real fast. Especially when you know the young kid whose blood is still slowly seeping out onto the floor.

Both Bill and I were smoking a cigarette, reviewing the entire scene in our minds. Sometimes your mind can be working on something while you are asleep or while you are concentrating on something else, and then the thing you are trying to remember just slips forward. I suddenly remembered why going in the freezer had touched a nerve with me. The first time I had been in Fran's Market was for a murder case involving one Clarence Ray Allen, a case where Bryon Schletewitz had been a witness to a burglary involving the market. "Bill, it just came back to me. There has always been a rumor that Ray Schletewitz kept a second safe in the walk-in freezer, with lots of cash in it. I remember from the Clarence Allen murder case that his gang was convinced Ray Schletewitz had a safe with twenty-five thousand or more stashed in it. Ray always insisted that wasn't true, but maybe that's what this guy was looking for."

Bill shook his head. "There wasn't any safe in there, never was. I hope those kids didn't die because of some rumor."

I blew out the last draw from my cigarette. "You know that Bryon was a witness in a major murder case and now he's a victim in a major murder case. There's a real irony there."

Bill wasn't given to philosophical introspection. He looked at me and I'll never forget his words. "It would be something if that case and this one were connected." I realized that it was going to be a very long night. During the ride back to the office, I leaned back against the headrest and closed my eyes as Bill drove. I could feel my mind compartmentalizing as I went through what I had seen. I couldn't close my mind on the old case and I couldn't seem to open my mind and just focus on the new one. I began to draw mental lines across the page between the facts of the two cases. Somewhere, deep in the back of my mind, a voice was whispering that there was a connection here, but logic told me that a connection was not realistic. I didn't have time to waste running down motives that didn't make sense. But *this* case didn't make sense.

I couldn't help thinking about the facts of the first murder. It had been the first really big murder case of my career. You promise witnesses that nothing will happen to them. You mean it. If there was a connection between that case from over three years ago and the deaths of those three kids, then we were dealing with something that was the worst nightmare of any cop or D.A.

PART II

A MOTHER'S VENGEANCE

4

A Gun Definitely Gets Your Attention

Four Years Earlier
December 8, 1976
Sacramento, California

The clerk looked up as the customer walked into the store. The clerk hadn't seen him before. The customer wasn't a local boy and not that old, maybe fifteen or sixteen, but he looked different, like he had seen a lot more than your usual sixteen year old. It was his eyes, tired, like a man who had seen life from the bottom side. He was dark, probably Hispanic, thought the clerk. The boy looked nervous; his eyes darted around the store as if he was looking to see if anyone was there. The clerk could feel himself getting edgy, and it wasn't long before the clerk knew why the kid made him nervous. It was when the kid pulled out the gun. The pointed gun instantly got this clerk's attention, and it also caused him to hit the silent alarm.

There is something about a .45 caliber automatic that you have to be aware of, especially when you pull it out: The old Army issue .45 is a touchy weapon. You carry it half-cocked; that is, if you are planning on using it. Most people who aren't familiar with guns tend to put their finger on the trigger when they pull a gun. This usually isn't a problem because most guns won't go off with just a little pressure on the trigger. I wouldn't recommend that you try that because I said "most guns." But there is one gun which you never want to put your finger on the trigger of unless you are ready to fire, and that weapon just happens to be a .45 automatic. Many people have learned this the hard way, and the kid in the

Sacramento convenience store became one of them. He pulled the gun, and before he could say it was a stickup, the gun went off. Oddly, it was the second time he had made the same mistake. The first time he shot himself in the leg. Robbery was definitely not his strong suit.

The next thing Raul Lopez knew, he was surrounded by police officers, and he quickly came to a new revelation: He was alone. The man who brought him to the store, his getaway driver, had left him. As he was handcuffed, it seemed that everyone around him was talking at once. The cuffs hurt like hell—but they did not cause Raul as much discomfort as the thought of telling his mother what had happened.

The clerk watched from behind the counter as the police pulled the kid up from the floor. His heart still hadn't slowed down. The smell of burnt gunpowder was now added to the smell of stale coffee and the jumble of odors that made up a convenience store.

5

Never Piss Off a Mother

Two Days Later
December 10, 1976
Fresno, California

Detective Sergeant Art Tabler sat at his desk in the office of the Fresno County Sheriff Detective Division, Crimes Against Persons. In the trade, that basically meant robbery/homicide/rape, not to mention the usual non-fatal Saturday night knifings. One could describe Tabler by saying his face was eminently forgettable. But that wouldn't reflect the reality of the man. He was one of those people who looked like he worked some regular job, nothing distinctive or special, the kind of guy that you would walk by on the street and never notice. He wasn't fat but he wasn't thin. His face was fleshy but not round. What hair he had was dark but not gray. In fact, he was basically bald. That much you would remember; Art was definitely bald. If it weren't for the fact he was bald, you wouldn't remember much of anything about Art Tabler—unless, that is, he was asking you questions while you sat in a chair. Then you would remember Art Tabler forever, because you would most likely be under arrest for murder and he would be reeling you in like a fish. He had that way about him. Nobody ever really saw it coming until they heard the click of the cuffs.

Tabler picked up the report in front of him. It was about a call from the Sacramento sheriff's department. Officers there had a robbery suspect in custody and, believe it or not, like most criminals, he had a mother. The reason the Sacramento S.O. contacted Fresno was because they had talked to the mother. Not only was she angry that her boy was in custody, she had a story to tell. Somebody had put her boy up to a robbery and then abandoned him, leaving him to fend for himself, and she wanted to get even.

You never want to piss off somebody's mother by mistreating her kid. Even lousy mothers are, at some point, protective about their kids. Must be instinct. Yes, some mothers beat their kids half to death and then cry when the cops take their kids away from them. This mother was no different—with a few minor exceptions. Barbara Carrasco was in prison in Alderson Federal Penitentiary in West Virginia, and Barbara Carrasco wanted to talk about a murder. She wanted to name names. Like I said, never piss off a mother by hurting her kid.

The name that Carrasco gave up was Clarence Ray Allen. Tabler thought about it. This was the kind of case that his old partner, Art Christensen, should handle, and that thought reminded him of one of the downsides of being a sergeant; you no longer had a partner, now that you were a supervisor. He missed the field and he missed sitting around with Christensen, telling each other lies, but he had made his choice. You had to know when it was your time to come in out of the field. And, ten months ago, his time had come. Now he made a note and stuck it in Christensen's box, telling Art to see him as soon as he came in. It wasn't long before Christensen was at the door, along with his new partner, Tommy Lean.

There are many ways I could describe Christensen but all of them would start with the word "gaunt." He was tall and he was thin. Actually, thin isn't quite how you would describe him. Thin would mean that there was some beef on him but not much. With Art, there was skin on him and that was about it. Christensen's nickname was "Blade," but that was not because he carried a knife. It was because he was about as thin as a knife blade and the name distinguished him from his former partner, Art Tabler. Otherwise it would have been Art and Art so nobody would know who you were talking about. Blade didn't mind what you called him, although Art Tabler did. Christensen was one of the last of the old-time sheriff's officers, part cowboy, part good ol' boy, and part wolf. One of the first things I learned about Art Christensen was that however he perceived the person he was talking to would dictate the role he would play in responding to that person—cowboy, good ol' boy, or wolf. Most people were misled by his demeanor. They underestimated him. It was a serious mistake. His teeth weren't straight and his light brown hair was always slicked back with Brylcream or something else that held it in place like Elmer's Glue. Brylcream used to be big back then with people over forty, but you have to remember, "back then" was over thirty years ago. Yes, Blade was definitely a good ol' boy. He liked his friends, he liked his wife, and he liked his horse. He always made it clear that he liked his wife best—but he liked his horse a lot.

Standing next to Blade was Tommy Lean. The contrast was clear. Blade favored cowboy shirts, jeans, and boots. Tommy looked like a poster boy for surfers. Lean was just like his name, tall and with the leanness of a college athlete, which he had been. He had blond hair that fell over his forehead that he routinely pushed back with his hand. He liked Hawaiian shirts and loafers. Unlike Christensen, during most of the year he carried his nine-millimeter automatic in a shoulder holster, which made his Hawaiian shirt bulge and look a little out of place, but in the winter he covered it with a coat. In the summer, Tommy conceded that a shoulder holster made people nervous, so he would wear a hip holster and drop his shirt outside his pants.

There was a difference in the way the two partners carried on their interrogations. Blade approached interrogation like he was circling his prey. Lean approached interrogation in a very laid-back manner, and he kept the intimidating demeanor to a minimum. By any stretch, they were an odd pair, the seasoned and cynical homicide detective who could look right through you and the younger detective who would ask how you were doing right after he slipped the cuffs on.

It takes a long time to develop a good partnership. And to make a good homicide detective takes even longer. A homicide detective, or any detective for that matter, has a different way of thinking than a street cop. The ability to size people up and slip inside their heads is more of a character trait than a learned skill. But it also requires experience and, often, a good mentor. Usually, the way you learned detective skills was from somebody who knew what he was doing, and Blade knew what he was doing. He and Tabler had been partners for twelve years before Tabler moved up to sergeant.

It was a difficult transition, changing partners, after years of getting used to being Art and Art. When Tabler and the captain asked Blade who he wanted for a new partner he remembered a young man who had done some work on a juvenile homicide. Blade told them, "Give me Lean." If it takes a long time to become a good homicide investigator, it can take longer to make a good homicide team, to make a perfect fit, where each man knows what the other man is going to do before he does it. Blade was a plainspoken man and he didn't pull his punches or worry about diplomacy or politics, nor did he have concerns about keeping his thoughts to himself. But so far, Blade hadn't said anything bad about Lean, which for Blade was good. Lean had learned the first lesson—to keep his mouth shut, and he followed it most of the time. But he wasn't one of those guys who could follow the lesson all the time. And he had a tendency to view regulations as suggestions, whereas Blade viewed regulations as a necessary inconvenience that you could bend but not ignore. Blade taught his younger partner restraint and Lean taught his older partner to loosen up. They had found a happy medium in their partnership, not unlike a marriage.

Tabler looked up and motioned for the two detectives to take a seat. "I got a call from an Inspector Leeper in the Sacramento sheriff's office. He said they had a 211 the other day involving a kid named Raul Lopez or Raul Carrasco, depending on what name he wanted to go by at the time."

In cop talk, a 211 is a robbery. The quickest way to show that you weren't an investigative pro was to start referring to a crime as a robbery or a homicide or a murder. That would instantly mark you as some kind of wannabe. At least it would do so with experienced detectives, and these guys were experienced detectives. Part of the reason for using numbers instead of the names for crimes is for shorthand, part because of cop vernacular, and part because it depersonalizes the situation. Good cops and good detectives have to keep themselves separate from both the attitudes of the perps and the emotions of the victims. If you can't do that, you lose your objectivity, and then you lose your perspective. You always have to remain outside the emotional box of the players.

Tabler threw a report toward the front of his desk, nodding for Blade to pick it up. "Anyway, this Lopez Carrasco kid, I guess, pulled a .45 auto out when he tried to rob some convenience store. Damn near shot himself." Tabler smiled. "Just like some guys shoot other people when they try a cross draw with a shoulder holster."

Blade picked up the report while Tabler continued. "Blade, you and Lean call Leeper and find out what he has for us. Could be nothing, but then it might turn out that we got a body we don't know about." Tabler drew out the moment before he said anything further. He knew Blade like he knew his own face in the mirror. "Anyway, you may be familiar with one of the names he gave me, Clarence Ray Allen. I told him Allen ran a rent-a-cop agency here in Fresno. He said the kid fingered Allen as the getaway driver."

Tabler waited for Blade's reaction. Blade had been bumping up against Clarence Allen since he had been out on patrol years before in the late fifties. There had been snitch reports and rumors about Allen, the owner of a local security agency, for years. Word on the street was that he was using the agency to case businesses for burglaries. People were saying that Allen Security offered its services, but if turned down, the next thing they knew the business was burglarized. However, nothing ever amounted to solid evidence. Blade remembered that when he was a patrolman, a liquor store had been cleaned out in a burglary. They took everything except the shelves. The liquor store owner said that he had received a call from Allen Security about protecting his business, but he hadn't thought he would need it. And look what happened next. Ray Allen and his criminal activity had managed to remain nothing more than whispers on the street. Blade and Tabler had come close to getting him a couple of times, but never closer than a good sniff.

Blade glanced up sharply. Allen irritated the hell out of Blade and Tabler knew it. Maybe it had something to do with the fact that Blade could smell a crook, and if he couldn't nab him, he was like a dog chasing a bone. Both Tabler and Blade heard the rumors, but nothing stuck. In any event, they knew rumors were like smoke—somewhere there was a fire. Blade nodded his head in the slow, laconic way he reacted to most news. "Allen, huh? Well, that could be interesting." He picked up the report. It had Leeper's phone number written in pencil across the top. He looked at Leeper's title and then he looked up and leaned back in his chair, carefully balancing on the back two legs. "Says here this Leeper is an *Inspector*," he said with a touch of sarcasm, drawing out the word for emphasis. "Is that what I'm supposed to call him, *Inspector*? How come I'm not an *Inspector*?"

Tabler tilted his head and pushed his mouth to the side in a smirk. "You're not an Inspector for the same reason you're not a sergeant. Anyway, we don't have inspectors in this department but we do have sergeants."

Lean genially slapped his partner on the back. "He has a point. He does have a point, Blade. Anyway, you wouldn't want to be an Inspector.

Sounds too much like a sergeant or some kind of cop who doesn't really work."

Blade nodded. "You do have a point."

Tabler waited until the two were through with their little routine. "Okay, I don't care if he's a lieutenant colonel, just call this guy and see what you can find out."

Lean stood up. "We're on it. We'll get back to you as soon as we know something." Blade stood up and nodded. His ears had perked up for other reasons when he heard Clarence Allen's name. Blade ran horses and Allen often showed horses at some of the same auctions. A bad guy running horses interfered with Blade's image of himself as a modern cowboy.

Blade and Lean walked back to their desks in what passed for the detective division offices. Actually, it was just a large room with as many desks shoved into it as the area allowed. If it was full of detectives, the room would be crowded, but it was rare that more than two or three were there at any one time. Most of the teams were out working and their paths crossed only at odd hours.

Blade picked up the phone and called the number on the report. "Inspector Leeper, please."

Tommy motioned for Blade to put the call on the speaker. "Yeah, Inspector, this is Detective Art Christensen, Fresno S.O. How you doin'? Look, my partner's here. I want to put this on speaker so he can hear. That okay?" He waited a moment and then nodded to Lean. A voice came through the speaker. It was definitely a cop voice, to the point, carrying just a hint of "I've been around." "Here's what I got. Two days ago, we had a 211 attempt at a local stop-and-rob. A kid tried to hold up the place— name Raul Lopez, aka Carrasco. That means 'also known as' to you boys down in Fresno." Both Christensen and Lean gave the little polite chuckle that they knew was expected, rather than the "up yours" that they knew was deserved. It's kind of a cop thing between agencies. Leeper left a little gap in his briefing until he could hear the sphincter tightening at the other end of the line and kept on. "Anyway, the kid used a .45 auto. Lucky he didn't shoot his dick off when he pulled it out of his pants. The clerk hit a silent alarm and when our boys got there the kid was still standing there. He didn't give us any trouble, but the guy who was supposed to be driving the getaway car left him holding the bag. He sped out of there when he saw us rolling up."

"Turns out this kid has an old lady who's doing hard time at Alderson Federal Prison in Virginia or West Virginia, anyway someplace in one of those Virginias. She's in for alien smuggling. The kid tells us that the getaway driver's from your area, name of, ah, of," and there was a moment's pause, "Ray Allen. According to your Sergeant you boys have heard of him. Guess Allen just left the kid to fend for himself. Well, the mother put Allen at the 211, because she had talked to him in Sacramento and to her son right before the robbery. The kid gave us the motel where they had been staying. Anyway, the kid wanted us to call his mama, so we did. It took a while to get her on the phone, but as soon as we ran down what happened she blew up. She talked to the kid and told him to talk to us, and then she got back on the phone with us. Told us that she had been a girlfriend of this Allen and that they lived together for a while in Tijuana. She said that the kid was her adopted son and she brought him in off the streets. Said that when she got popped for alien smuggling—this part's a little unclear—that she either left the boy with this Allen to take care of him or told the kid to go to Allen's house. Apparently, Allen told her that he would help the boy make some real money. She told me that when she got picked up by the feds she was with a white male adult, approximately twenty-five to twenty-six years old, named Lee Furrow. He also goes by Eugene Furrow. Said that before they were arrested, Furrow had some kind of attack of conscience and told her that Allen forced him to kill a female in the Fresno area because she was aware of a burglary and that this Allen and some others had been passing money orders of some kind that they got in the burglary. I don't know much more. She said this whole thing happened sometime in August of 1974. I already called the Fresno police department, and they say they don't have any unsolveds involving the murders of young females.

"All I got on Carrasco is that she is one hard broad. She's got a whole bunch of aliases, Richardson, Picklesimer—there's a name for you, Betty Picklesimer. Also goes by Wood and LaFaye. We're getting a warrant for Allen, with bail set at $25,000 for 211 and conspiracy. I would appreciate some help from you boys in picking him up. That's all I got."

Blade had been writing. So had Lean. Blade put his pencil down. "Okay, Inspector, we'll get on it. It may take us a while. We just got radios down here in Fresno, you know. Appreciate your help. We'll see what we can do on Allen. We been hearing things about him for a while. It won't break our hearts any to bring him in. As soon as you get the warrant out, give us a call. We'll let you know."

Blade hung up and stared at his partner. "Okay, let's run this Furrow guy and see what we get. I'll go down to records and see if we have any unsolveds that fit the description, or any missing persons. You get a Soundex of Clarence Allen to this Leeper and get what you can on Furrow." Lean nodded. "Oh, and run his rap sheet. Let's see what we come up with on Allen and on this Furrow, too."

A Soundex is a telephonic transmission of a photograph. This was way before fax machines, and e-mail was basically a note that you left on somebody's desk. There weren't even any little yellow sticky notes.

When Lean returned, Blade was looking at a report on his desk. Tommy put his notebook down. "Allen's been running a security agency here, probably out of his house. He's listed as living out on East Belmont."

Blade nodded. Belmont at that location was largely rural, with a lot of nice houses in the area on several-acre lots. Lean could sense that Blade had something, and he was pleased to be slowly getting a feel for the way Blade operated. "You got anything as a possible on the woman?"

Blade nodded. "I got two. One, a Kathy Parker, age 17, body dumped. Fits the age. And I got another one, missing person, Mary Sue Kitts, nineteen years, reported missing November 6, 1974. Last seen July 15, '74. Any guesses?"

Lean knew better than to guess. Blade already had something. "So go ahead. What you got?"

Blade leaned back as far as his chair would allow in the confined space. "It took me a while, but I remembered that Tabler and I did a missing persons report two years ago. It was a young woman and it didn't hit me right away, but the girl was last seen leaving her home in July of 1974 with Roger Dale Allen. They were in a security patrol vehicle belonging to Allen Security. Roger is Clarence Ray Allen's kid. It took some scratching through our records until I found it. I couldn't remember her name, but I remembered the missing person report and the connection to Allen."

Lean nodded, "Kitts would be my guess."

Blade leaned his head back and pulled a picture of Mary Sue Kitts from the missing persons file on the table. "Yeah, lucky guess. You got anything on Furrow?"

Lean picked up the picture, a high school graduation picture of an attractive eighteen year old with long, light-brown hair, and stared at it before putting it back down on the desk. "There isn't much. White male, twenty-six, five-foot, ten inches, 150, with brown hair, brown eyes. Has a record. Got popped for alien smuggling down in El Centro, California, so that fits. On parole. But there isn't much else that fits the story. Doesn't have the profile of a murderer, at least not the kind we're looking at."

Blade shook his head. Murder was a unique kind of crime. Most people thought a murderer looked like a murderer, like he would be drooling or wild-eyed. The fact was that Blade had arrested hundreds of men and quite a few women for murder, and most of them didn't look like murderers until you finished with the case. But there were certain kinds of murderers that were always different. Premeditated murderers— murder in cold blood—those kinds of killers are different. You don't see many of them. It takes a special kind of person to think for a while about killing another human being and then do it without anger or without being in the grip of a sudden spurt of unbridled passion. Most murders happen because the killer is angry or drunk or scared or some combination of the three. People who kill in cold blood—well, you don't see many of those, and when you do, you can feel it when you are around them. Some would say that those type of people were crazy, but Blade knew better. People who can kill in cold blood aren't crazy. They know precisely what they are doing. No, those people were missing that thread of conscience that is present in almost everybody else.

Conscience is what Blade sought most when he sat somebody down in a chair. It is the thing he would gently massage until the person broke. All he had to do was bring it to the surface. Sometimes, he had to poke pretty hard, but if he could sense a glimmer of conscience, he would slowly take advantage of it. But if it wasn't there, you had to break them down with evidence, and if they broke, it was because they couldn't see any other way to make a deal, or they had become caught up in their lies. He knew what Lean meant when he said Furrow didn't fit the profile. The kind of person who committed premeditated murder almost always had a record that included violence or something in their background that made you take a step backward. They usually had something missing, that aspect that stopped most people from hurting other people. Furrow didn't have that record, and if Carrasco's story was true, Furrow had a conscience. It didn't mean he couldn't do it and it didn't mean he didn't do it. It just meant that something didn't fit. At least, it didn't fit yet. And that was their job—to find the pieces and make them all fit.

Christensen rocked his chair back until all four legs settled on the floor. "You get Allen's rap sheet?"

"There isn't as much as I would've thought. Born in Oklahoma in 1929, brown hair, brown eyes. Just under six-feet tall, about one hundred seventy-five. Most of what we have is applications for security guard licenses, but he does have a '62 arrest for grand theft, reduced to a misdemeanor. Nothing much came of it. Our office gave him a concealed weapons permit. Can you believe that? He has an arrest for attempted robbery last year, but that apparently didn't go anywhere."

Blade's smile pulled his lips back over his teeth. It gave him a wolfish look, which usually appeared when he had some new realization about a case. "I know that case. Detective Badiali was working nights. Some guy came in; I don't remember his name. Anyway, he said he was a night watchman at a lumberyard. Claimed that Allen wanted him to participate in a phony robbery. Badiali and some of the boys set up a surveillance, and they caught Allen inside the lumberyard, but Allen must have spotted our people. Anyway, we jumped a little too soon. We couldn't make the case. The thing I remember is that the guy who snitched Allen out was threatened by Allen, at least according to the guy's wife. Anyway, he just disappeared. No witness, no case. Sounds familiar doesn't it." He stared at Lean. "What do you think?"

Lean hesitated; he knew better than to have a thought that Blade would think was stupid and then let him know it by blurting it out. "Don't know; I guess first things first. We need to go talk to Mary Sue Kitts' parents and see what we can find out."

The lines on Blade's leathery face grew deeper while he thought for a minute. "No, not yet. First, we need to talk to this Carrasco woman and see if we really have anything. No point in talking to Kitts' folks until we know something."

Lean nodded. He wasn't any more enthused about calling the parents of the Kitts girl than was Blade. The parents had been waiting for two years to find out about their daughter. There wasn't much news, but it was going to be hard to keep them from guessing that their little girl was dead. Even when their child mixed with bad people, the parents only remembered the little girl with a ponytail.

Working homicide is never an easy job, but you got used to many things—the blood and the trauma, the smell of loosened bowels, and the sickly odor left by a body after several days in the sun. What you don't get used to is the grief. Both men knew that there was going to be grief for a family and they would be the messengers of death. Although they hadn't caused it, they were going to bring news of it to parents who had been holding onto hope for two years and were still holding on to hope to this day. It was a hard thing to do when you took away hope. Sometimes, you were taking away all that people had left to keep them going. And there was no point in taking away hope until you are sure.

Blade stood up. "We're going to have to have more than we got now. First, we call that federal prison and talk to Carrasco. If she confirms what she told Leeper, then we got something to go with to get approval to go to West Virginia."

Unlike television, where the supervising detective never asks how much it's going to cost to run a case, in real life the supervisors always ask. Everybody is on a budget. The boss wants to know if the case is going to go anywhere. Tabler would instantly get it—without talking to Carrasco, the case wasn't going to work out. This was a murder lead. You had to at least investigate it to see how warm the trail was. But Tabler wasn't the captain and the captain signed the authorizations. They had to sell the captain. Blade already knew what it would take with Tabler.

It took all day to get Barbara Carrasco on the line. It is never easy to get the feds to do anything, and that includes federal prison authorities. Most state cops think the feds are born with a stick up their ass. They hate to ask them for anything and they know better than to expect much. It's like bank robberies. The feds always take the cases with the picture and the confession. If they don't have that, then they turn it over to the state. No wonder they don't lose many. It's not hard to win when you're holding all the cards.

Getting into the prison to talk to an inmate without providing a long, drawn-out explanation took forever. You would think you could just tell them who you were and give them a number to call back and confirm. But no, that would be too easy. If it was another state agency, you could wrap it up in ten minutes. With the feds, it was an all-day affair.

Finally, they heard a woman's voice that identified herself as Carrasco. You didn't have to see her to know she'd been around. It was a voice that had been burnished by secondhand smoke and a life that hadn't been easy. She got right to the point. Yes, she told Leeper about a murder. She wanted to share that information and she wanted a little help with her boy. But most of all, she wanted a piece of Clarence Ray Allen's ass.

Like I said before, never piss off a woman by hurting her kid.

Blade and Lean walked into Tabler's office without knocking. Blade folded his thin frame into a chair. As usual, he rocked the chair backward. "Okay, Art, this is what we got. This Carrasco woman is in the joint in West Virginia and we talked to her. She says she can give us Clarence Ray Allen for murder. She says we come back there and we'll get what she has. We think maybe the victim is this Mary Sue Kitts, who went missing about the right time." Blade slid the photograph of Mary Sue across the desk for Tabler to look at. "Carrasco wants some help with her kid, who, by the way, isn't really her kid. He's some street kid she picked up in Tijuana, but she raised him. Kind of like a mother wolf, I guess. Anyway, we need approval for two tickets to Alderson, West Virginia, courtesy of the County of Fresno. Also, you could throw in some overtime approval, and a cash advance would help. Any questions?"

Tabler gave them a wry expression that for him passed as a smile. He remembered the missing person report and the reminder about Roger Allen, the son, brought it all back to him. Tabler would go to the captain, but not before they had something more to go on. "Sacramento says they're going to have a warrant for Clarence Ray Allen. Let's wait for the warrant, arrest him, and maybe he can be shaken a bit."

Blade snorted. "Art, this guy isn't going to shake. You know that."

Tabler was unmoved. "Just the same, we have a tight budget. You wait until we have the warrant and then go arrest him. Maybe we'll get lucky."

Blade shrugged. Becoming a sergeant did the same thing to everybody. They forgot what it was like to be picking up momentum on a case. Tabler could read the look on his old partner's face. "Blade, I have to justify things now. I can't just go off and spend department money by myself even if I think it is a good idea. I have to ask and I have to have a good reason. See if you can give me one."

By Monday, the warrant for robbery had come into the office. Blade and Tom drove out Belmont Avenue to serve the warrant. A few years earlier, nothing was out near where Allen lived; it was just citrus groves and walnut trees. Now, expensive houses on large lots were being built between working farms whose owners were holding out for a good price, or else holding on because they didn't want to give up the life they had always known. Houses like Allen's weren't the exception out there—the pools and stables, everything reflected the lives of people who had money. The only problem was neither Blade nor Tom could see Allen's money coming from a nickel-and-dime security agency. No, he wasn't getting his money from wearing a plastic badge and shaking doorknobs.

They walked up to the long, ranch-style home and knocked on the door. Both men stood slightly to the side, with their hands in position to pull their weapons. The man who answered the door was definitely Clarence Allen, but he didn't look like his picture. He had put on some weight and his hair was graying. "Can I help you?" he asked the officers.

Both men shifted position. Over the years, a cop gets a feel for people. Most of what you can see comes from body language, but the real message is the eyes. Some people show fear. Others stare at you and you can tell they are resigned. Still others give you a look that tells you they're going to fight. Some people have dead eyes. When Allen stared at them, what they saw were the eyes of a person who wasn't afraid and wasn't resigned. What they saw were the eyes of a man who would kill them if it was necessary and he wouldn't think twice about it. When you look in a man's eyes and you see nothing but emptiness staring back at you, you can be sure that he'll do whatever he decides is best for himself—and that includes doing what is not good for you. You won't know until he does it. Ray Allen had dead eyes. Both detectives felt the adrenaline surge. They waited a few seconds.

Blade spoke first. "You Clarence Ray Allen?"

"You know I am."

"Fresno County sheriff's office. We have a warrant for your arrest for armed robbery in Sacramento. Please step outside. Keep your hands where we can see them."

Allen stepped out and allowed Lean to turn him around while he was handcuffed. He didn't resist, but he obviously wasn't afraid, either. All he said was, "Oh my goodness." It was like he was just shocked that he would be accused of something like that. Then his voice hardened. "Well, I got nothing to say to you, so let's just get on with it."

They pushed Allen into their car and drove back to the jail and booked him. The only thing that had been impressive about their contact was his lack of reaction. As they walked back to the detective division, Blade muttered, "Told Tabler he wouldn't talk. Now we go talk to Tabler and then the captain. We need to talk to Carrasco."

Captain Bud Lauter asked, "Why can't just one of you go? Just get the interview and then we decide."

Blade didn't hesitate. "Look, Captain—Bud—it all fits. The Kitts girl disappeared at the right time. She was with Allen's son, Roger. It's just too close to be a coincidence. If something happens to one of us or our credibility is questioned, then the other one is there to back up the report. We both need to go."

Captain Lauter nodded. It was part of his job to ask the question. He already knew the answer. "I'll talk to the sheriff. We'll get you approval, but you better come back with this asshole's head on a platter. We don't have the budget for you two to go on some vacation. Get it done."

They left joking about how the captain had made it sound as if he were approving their going on a spree to Paris and not merely 3,000 miles away to the bleak environs of a woman's prison. Still, it could be interesting. Neither had never been to a federal women's prison. At least, it would be different.

6

Even Criminals Have Standards

December 16, 1976
Alderson Women's Prison
Alderson, West Virginia

The Alderson Federal Women's Prison isn't a long way from nowhere, unless you are inside it. It's about 270 miles southwest of Washington, D.C., and is near Alderson, West Virginia, which is back to a long way from nowhere.

The oldest federal women's prison, Alderson was established with the help of Eleanor Roosevelt, while she was first lady. It looks more like a place where you would go for week-long business retreats, except you can't leave. There are no metal fences and no walls, except on the inside. It looks different than what you would expect for a reason. A women's prison *is* different because women are more communal than men. They aren't as violent; notice, I didn't say they weren't violent. They just aren't *as* violent. If you're sent to a place like Alderson and if you've been around, you know what the alternatives are if you don't obey the rules. Given the alternatives, people generally obey the rules.

Most of the inmates are there for crimes involving men they hooked up with or for drugs. Some of them are there for more sophisticated, white collar crimes. Alderson has been home for some celebrated criminals. Axis Sally was incarcerated there after World War II for treason, and so were Squeaky Fromme and Sara Jane Moore for shooting at the same president—but at different times, of course. More recently, Martha Stewart worked in the laundry there. Some of the inmates are there so that law enforcement can make a public point, and when that kind of prisoner leaves, she seldom returns to the system. But some inmates are basically just criminals; it's what they do, and they don't need men to help them. For them, doing time in Alderson is just the cost of doing business and it is sometimes far better than the alternatives. Barbara Carrasco was a criminal. However, even criminals have standards. The question facing Blade and Lean, as they waited to get inside, was what kind of standards Barbara Carrasco had.

You have to be careful when you question a woman. You have to be a little more oblique than you are with men. But the tricks are the same as with any interrogation—keep them talking. Don't confront unless you have to. Wait until they make a mistake and keep massaging that conscience buried down there somewhere. With a woman, you have to watch for just the right moment before you bring up the big question. When talking about their man, they are more loyal than men are to each other. So it can take longer. And the reality is that women will talk for a long time while they are thinking about where they are going to wind up before they get to the point. If you push them too hard, they will just stop talking. Men don't talk as much so you have to push them differently. No one knows better than a homicide detective how different men are from women.

Carrasco was no cherry; she had been through the system. She was used to jail and she was used to cops. A cherry breaks easier and they talk easier because they still have a certain respect for authority—and they are afraid of you. They don't want you to think they are really bad people. That's a funny thing about people being interrogated for the first time. They are concerned about what you think of them, and they don't realize that just because you sound friendly, you don't really care about them. You would think that when a person is in custody, they would realize you probably aren't very impressed with them. But wherever they are, most people still want to be liked—even in prison.

When you talk to somebody who has been through the system, they aren't afraid of you. They know who you are, what you are, and what you can and can't do to them when you sit down in front of them. People like Carrasco know you don't have their best interests at heart. They don't give a damn what you think of them and they know you don't give a damn about them. You want something; they have something. How you talk to a person like Carrasco is entirely different than how you talk to a cherry.

So, for Blade and Lean, the whole issue was Carrasco's motivation: What did she want and what was her reason for wanting it?

Carrasco wanted help for her kid, but most of all she wanted to get even with the man who hurt him. Since she was in the joint, the only way she could get even was by using people on the outside. Basically, she needed cops to do what she wanted—that is, as long as she wanted it to be legal. So Blade and Tommy knew that the key with her was to stay on her good side and to convince her they could help her get even. They would let her use them, but they had to be careful. After all, she was a criminal. She could lie, and most of the time she did during her everyday life. You would take what she said for what it was worth and figure how you could use it. She would give it for what she thought it was worth and what she could get out of it—no more, no less. Blade and Tommy had already decided their MO—give her the opportunity to screw Allen and thus create a mutually beneficial relationship.

When she walked through the door, they knew in an instant that this interrogation was going to be conducted on equal terms. Barbara Carrasco was about five feet, four or five. Her face had the ruddy look of a fair-complexioned person who had worked long hours in the sun, although you couldn't tell what it had once been like, as it had coarsened from hard times. Her hair was beginning to show gray through its original brownish color, and it was pulled away from her face. If it had been brushed, the brush had been her fingers. She didn't bother with makeup to cover up what she was; it was clear she was comfortable with her looks. She was heavyset in a way that told you this was a woman who could do hard work. She was around forty but she looked older, as if she had earned every one of her years the hard way. You had the sense that Carrasco wouldn't be afraid to hit a man, nor would she fear getting into a fight with a woman—or a man. Some people just have that look—like they may not win if you tangle with them but you're going to get hurt if you do. Barbara Carrasco had that look. She didn't extend her hand. She looked at the two detectives, tilting her head like she was sizing them up and sat down. Carrasco understood her world. She knew the ropes and she had a certain amount of stature in the prison; the older inmates usually do if they've been around. Barbara Carrasco had definitely been around. She wouldn't take crap from anybody, including cops. Both detectives knew immediately the usual bullshit wasn't going to work.

Blade and Lean had agreed that Blade was going to do most of the talking until they could evaluate which of their personalities was more effective. Most women liked Lean because he was charming and good-looking, but that wouldn't work with a woman like Carrasco. It didn't mean she didn't appreciate charm and good looks. It just meant she didn't run with charming and good-looking men and she wasn't going to buy into it. She knew what she was and who she was. Her style was men like Blade, who had a little rougher edge. He would start; they would keep the charm in reserve.

Blade smiled. "Mrs. Carrasco, I'm Art Christensen and this is Tom Lean. We're the detectives from Fresno who talked to you on the phone. Thanks for agreeing to talk to us." He waited to see if there would be any response. Carrasco looked at Christensen through narrowed, unblinking eyes, sizing up the two men in front of her. Blade had seen the look before. For her, they were her natural enemy and any alliance would be uneasy and temporary. He cleared his throat and nodded slightly, a demonstration that he understood what she was thinking. "By the way, we wanted you to know that we've been talking to the authorities in Sacramento, and your boy, Raul, is doing fine. He was lucky; he dropped the gun when the sheriff's deputies got there. Whoever gave him that .45 should have thought about how dangerous it was to give a gun like that to a kid. Even men with experience can easily shoot themselves by accident with a .45." He waited. He had scratched the scab a little bit, by reminding her that Allen had taken advantage of her boy. Her mouth opened slightly, showing teeth that were surprisingly white. And then she spoke in a voice that reflected its share of border bars and border men, a voice raised loudly enough to be heard and used to being listened to.

"Clarence Ray Allen is a son of a bitch. He shouldn't have given no gun to a kid. He shouldn't have left him there like he did." She moved her heavy body forward in the chair. "Let's get to it. I only got nine months left before I get out but if it's the last fucking thing I do in my life, I'm going to get a piece of him." Blade nodded, waiting for her to keep talking, wanting to give her a feeling of some control.

"If those cops in Sacramento haven't told him nothin' about me, then it's cool. I got lawyers. I know what it's all about. I know about circumstantial stuff and I don't want any of that circumstantial shit. He knows where my kids are. I want you guys to take him down good."

Carrasco had enough experience with the system to know that if Allen didn't know there was an insider talking, it would be easier to get solid evidence on him. Lean pushed the tape recorder forward so Carrasco could see it. "Mrs. Carrasco, we'd like to record this." He didn't ask it as a question. When you shove a tape recorder in front of most people, it scares them. If you ask their permission, they may say no and that leads to a whole lot of other problems. If they don't say anything, then you're okay. You don't ask for permission. You just assume you have it and they may not think about asking if they can refuse. You want to avoid confrontation. Carrasco knew the drill. She eyed the recorder.

"Whatever. Just call me Mom. Most people in here call me Mom."

Lean squirmed, so Blade replied, "Okay, but we have to type up the report, so how about if I just call you Barbara. I'm too old to be calling you Mom."

Carrasco sniffed. "Okay. Whatever you want. So, like I was sayin', Clarence Ray Allen ain't nothin' to play around with. But if you want me to be buddy-buddy with him to get what I want, honey, then I'll do it, 'cause like I say, nobody messes with my kid. What I got to say is things been told to me. Somethin' about me—people like to tell me things they don't tell nobody else. I don't talk. Never have, not once. But this is different. Nobody'll blame me for talkin' about a man that hurt my kid."

Blade leaned back in his chair. She was talking. You don't interrupt. Just keep them talking. First rule.

"Clarence Ray Allen carries around a big roll. I seen as much as $12,000 at a time he's laid out. Drives a '76 Lincoln Continental and he runs a henhouse security agency out of a little town outside Fresno—Sanger. That business doesn't pump out this kind of money. We been in some shit together along the line but nothin' that turns out the kind of money he throws around. He told me you guys almost got him last year with a shotgun in the back of his car. If you'd a' waited, he was gonna take down a lumber business. He told me you boys got too eager."

Blade gave a slight smile. "We had some young officers out there."

"Yeah, jumped the gun. Anyway, he likes to brag a lot. Like I said, people tell me things. I never say the wrong thing, honey. I'm smuggling aliens, okay. I do something where I believe I'm okay. Ain't got the guts to go in and put a gun to somebody and say give me your money. So I'll do it the sneaky way, 'cause I ain't got that much guts. I don't make that much money from those poor suckers. See, I'm a sucker too, 'cause them fools come over, they got a wife and ten kids in Mexico and then when I get them over, they ain't got no money. I mean it costs me money to bring 'em but I say, shit, what are you gonna do?"

Blade nodded sympathetically. "What are you gonna do?"

Barbara looked at him out of the side of her eyes, weighing whether he was with her or jerking her chain. She decided he understood. "So, that old bastard, Clarence, called me after the robbery in Sacramento went sour. I asked him what did you have my kid up there for? And he says well it ain't important what Clarence Allen says 'cause it don't mean shit. You don't want to fuck with him. So I just kept my mouth shut. Now I'm talking to you guys. Been messin' with your guys for years. Now I'll work with you two—this time I guess."

Carrasco slumped slightly in her chair. "What he done, he got my boy there. Now my boy, he ain't mine, but he's mine. He belongs to me. I raised him, loved him, since he was eight years old. I'm all he's got. I picked him up in a street in Tijuana and raised him 'cause he didn't have nobody. When I got sent here, I told him that Clarence would help him. Just stay at his place until Mama gets out of jail and then we'll be a family again—it will all be okay. So he goes there. I tell Allen that he'll help with the horses. You seen his place?"

Blade shook his head. It wasn't the right time to tell her Allen was in jail for the robbery. She might decide that was enough and she could deal with Allen another way, the way personal grievances are handled by people inside prisons where justice is much more abrupt and very final. "Not yet."

Carrasco nodded slowly, her mouth drawn down into a knowing line. "Well, he's got himself a stable and a big pool out there and everything. He said he'd take my boy and take care of him 'til I got out. He knew I was good for it. Look, I never had nothin'. I don't expect nothin'. My kids, they sent me twenty dollars on my birthday. Allen told him he could help me. He's a con artist, baby. He can sucker you. Like he had these men working for him and suckered them, you know, burglaries and everything. Used his men to knock over places they was supposed to be guardin'. So he tells my boy that I need money to get home on when I get out and the kid believes it. I would'a got the money together; probably be ridin' my ass on the rails or the bus, but Clarence, he tells the kid he can get money to help me and maybe buy me somethin' for Christmas. He's put a story on my kid and then he put a gun in his hands and said walk in that store. I talked to my boy before Allen took him to that store. I asked him what he was doin' and he said he was gonna buy some stuff for me for Christmas. So when the Sacramento police called, I knew what went down. Plenty of older dudes on the street. You don't have to put no gun in a kid's hand."

Blade stepped in. "So Barbara, what happened with Clarence Allen and this Lee Furrow?"

Carrasco stopped. She had a story and she was going to tell it her way. They needed her but she needed something, too. She hadn't had any visitors since she'd been inside, so talking to people from the outside, even cops, was entertainment. "Hurtin' my kid. Look, that's where Clarence made his mistake 'cause otherwise I'd never be talking to you at all; you believe that?"

Lean had been sitting quietly. "Yeah, we do."

Carrasco looked over at the younger detective and nodded. "Good. I want something done for my boy. I want to protect my kid; don't want him going to prison. You get it?"

Christensen nodded. "Yeah, we get it."

"He may have to do some time. I get that. But if I can help him—I'm responsible for him. I'm the one that got him mixed up with that no-good Allen. All I know is I got my one boy, so I want something done for him."

"We can't make promises, but we'll do what we can."

"I been around. I understand no promises, but I'm counting on you boys to do right by me if I do right by you. You understand?"

Blade had put a little edge in his voice when he had asked about Lee Furrow and Carrasco's eyes had flashed briefly. "Okay, so I had these accounts, you know? People owed me money. Now, you aren't going to tell all this shit to the income tax people are you? Those are guys I never want to mess with."

"Income tax isn't our problem." Lean laughed. "We all understand income tax."

Carrasco was opening up more and more, telling the detectives that Furrow and Clarence's son, Roger, had worked for her when she needed some money collected and she sent them out to collect it. She had been in jail on charges different than those that caused her to end up in Alderson and needed bail money. Upon her release, Furrow and Chuck Jones, another boy who worked with Clarence, came down to her house in Mexico. They carried American Express money orders they ripped off of one of their accounts at some joint. She couldn't remember the name. But she could remember one thing that turned out to be crucial.

"Anyway," she added, "when they came down, they had this little, blond-haired girl with them. Just a little thing."

Blade held his hand up to stop Carrasco from going forward. "And can you describe the girl?"

"Well, she was young, maybe seventeen or eighteen. Clarence's boy had been running around with her. Anyway, she had hair just past her shoulders. She was maybe five foot, four or so. Only weighed around a hundred. I notice things like that." Carrasco looked down at her square body. "No time in my life was I built like her. She was built pretty good. But I had other things, you know?" Blade and Lean laughed and nodded, encouraging her to continue.

"See, Clarence wanted to pass these money orders and I told him, if you can get to the money exchanges in Mexico, maybe they can do it. Anyway, nobody would exchange them. They came to my house and my old man—I got one you know, at least before I got in here—he went over to San Diego with Allen, and I went with them in a different car. Furrow was driving me. So, they got some of the money orders passed in San Diego. Then Clarence took all of us to this restaurant, but I left before everybody was finished. I had some runs to make that night. Had to make a living, you know—business."

Tommy broke in. "And what about the girl?"

Carrasco looked over at Tommy. "Don't get ahead of me, honey. I'll tell you everything but you got to let me get to it."

Blade laughed. "Well, he's young. Just go on."

Barbara smiled at the older detective. "See, I was in jail around August. It was after I got out that Eugene Furrow told me about the girl and what happened to her."

"Did you talk to Clarence about this?"

"I asked him about it after I talked to Eugene and he said, 'Yeah, we had to waste her.' I didn't ask him more about it because you gotta know Clarence. He said that she opened her mouth about things, about the money orders, and they had to shut her up. But Clarence was always talkin' shit like that. He would say things like, 'I had to waste this guy'; I did this, I did that. I never paid attention to it because it always seemed like so much bullshit, you know? But this was after I knew about it from Eugene, so I knew it wasn't no bullshit about the girl. Anyway, they bailed me out and Furrow came back to San Diego and started working for me again. But when my kid got sick, Furrow took me and my kid to the hospital. We was waitin' at the hospital for the doctors to finish with my kid. Eugene was talking to me and then outta nowhere, he starts cryin' and asks me to go outside. He's gettin' real upset, so I walked out with him and he starts talking about some robbery and then he says the girl's name. I still can't remember it. And he says, 'We had to waste her, Barbara, the girl that was with us when we was here before.' He says that Clarence made him do it."

"So I said, 'What do you mean, Clarence made you do it?' And he says, 'Well, they said they had to shut her mouth.' Then he said that Clarence was supposed to give her some sleeping pills that were gonna put her to sleep but that it didn't work so Clarence told him to do it and Furrow just started choking her. He said it was bothering him so bad that he couldn't sleep. He said that he was choking her and she just kept looking at him."

"Did you ask him where this happened?"

"Yeah, he said that Clarence and the others said it had to be done and he had to do it, so they did it at Shirley's house."

Lean interrupted. "At Shirley's house? Who's Shirley?"

"Shirley is Clarence's girlfriend. I been to her apartment before. She had red hair, a dye job, 'cause she weren't no natural redhead, you know. Anyway, she's around 35, maybe five foot, six, got a good figure. Works as a secretary for him, but she does more than type, if you get my meaning."

Blade held up his hand to slow Carrasco down. "We get it. So this is in August, in '74?"

"Yeah."

"And Eugene said he choked her? Strangled her with his hands?"

"Yeah, he said he had his hands on her throat and her eyes was lookin' up at him."

"Did he say he used anything else to maybe stab her or shoot her?"

"No, just that he choked her. That's why I remember so well because he kept talking about her eyes. She just looked at him. Eugene said nobody was with him when he started to do it and when he couldn't, they called him from outside and told him he had to do it or else. Clarence said if he didn't he was going to kill him and her, too."

"So he was in fear for his life?"

"Yeah, that's what he said, that it was either her or both of them."

"And it was all over these money orders? She was going to tell on these people?"

Barbara nodded. "She was talking too much and they was afraid that the cops would connect them to it."

"So, when did Furrow tell you all this?"

"It was in November, but he said that all this stuff with the girl happened while I was in jail and that was between August 2nd and August 21st."

Lean reached into his pocket and took out the photograph of Mary Sue Kitts. "Do you remember this girl? Is this her?"

"Yeah, that's her, but she had blond hair, honey. Not like in your picture where it's kind of brown. I mean it was bleached real blond when I saw her. I heard her mother came to ask Roger about her. Did she report her missing? She is missing isn't she?"

Blade nodded. "Yeah, yeah. She was reported missing on November the 6th and she was last seen in July of that year."

Carrasco shook her head. "Like I told you guys from the gate, I ain't no bullshitter, okay? I ain't got nothin' to gain from this except helping my kid. There's no way I can testify to nothin'."

"When Furrow told you this, did he say how they disposed of the body?"

"Furrow said it was Clarence," she explained. "See, I do illegal things but I don't ask questions. People talk but I don't say nothin'; people just tell me things. I might say 'what the fuck you do that for?' But I don't ask because I don't want to know. But Allen told me they dumped her in a creek high in the mountains. They rolled her up in a blanket and I guess put some wires around it and weights and dumped her in a creek in the mountains. But I don't know where."

No matter how the two investigators tried to discover something about the location of the creek, Carrasco couldn't come up with it. She added only that some of Allen's men went with him to dump the body. "I don't think Eugene went, but I'm not sure. I do know that one of the guys who went was a guy who had a missing tooth. I had met him before, but I didn't talk to him."

Blade looked down at his notes. "I know we're going to have more questions, but for now we're just starting."

"Yeah, well you got a long ways to go on this and I ain't got a whole lot more to tell you. But, I can give you one more thing. Eugene Furrow's feelin' real bad about this. This was two years ago and the conscience, well, the conscience is a hell of a thing, honey, and I don't think there's a soul born without it. Except, maybe, that isn't true for Clarence. Hell, I don't know. Anyway, I think Eugene will crack real easy. You get him and you'll get the whole story."

Blade's mouth pulled back into a knowing smile. "So Eugene isn't the hardened criminal type?"

"Nah, he said he couldn't sleep. He said when he went to sleep he could see her eyes open and staring at him and he couldn't get over her eyes looking at him when he was doin' it and he probably never would. I told him, 'What's done is done. There ain't nothing I can do for you, all the talking in the world ain't goin' to change anything. Either you go tell the police or you gotta live with your conscience. You live with it or you do something and try and make it right.' And he said, 'I don't know how I'm ever gonna live with it.' And I told him, 'Then you've got to do something about it, don't you?' So, I guess he never did nothin'—learned to live with it, I guess. But Eugene ain't like Clarence. Eugene may have done it but Clarence is the one. He's the one that *made* him do it. I don't think Eugene would ever do that on his own. He was just like me. I mean I break the law sometimes, but I don't kill people. Guys like Clarence are different."

"Barbara, is there anything else you can remember right now that we need to know?" Lean asked as he reached for the tape recorder

"Well, you get him. I can't help you much with testifyin' and such. I'm an ex-convict, baby. Well, I guess I'm not an ex-convict yet, 'cause I'm still here, right?" She added with a chortle. "Anyway you look at it, somebody's going to be calling me a liar. I haven't talked before to buy myself time, so this is the first time with you guys. Make sure you keep me out of it or I'll have Clarence Ray Allen on me. I know him and you don't fuck with him. You got to put him in jail for good on this. He shouldn't have messed with my kid. If he hadn't of done that, I wouldn't be talkin' to you now. Nothin' personal, you understand, but you guys never did me no good. Hey, maybe you can get me transferred back to Terminal Island in California. I would be closer to my family. Maybe you can do that?"

Blade turned off the tape. "We'll see what we can do."

They waited for Carrasco to rise. Lean walked to the door and knocked for the guard. "We're done."

Blade stuck out his hand. "Thanks for talking to us, Barbara."

Barbara Carrasco stood there for a moment and extended her hand. "Just remember, you take Allen down and you leave me out of it. You don't know him like I do."

"We understand." Blade and Tommy waited until the guard walked Barbara Carrasco out the door. She didn't look back. She had done what she had set out to do. What they had to decide was whether what she said was true or whether she was just trying to bury Allen in a pile of bullshit. Both men had questioned a lot of people, some hard types and some just regular folks. You get a feel for when it's bullshit and when it's true and even when it's somewhere in between. As they walked out the doors of Alderson Federal Penitentiary, they were sure that Clarence Allen was guilty of murder, and that he did it by making someone else do it. They also knew that at least one man was so terrified of Allen that he had been willing to kill a woman for him. There was no question; Clarence Allen wasn't the kind of man who would crack. They had to take him down. To do that, they had to make others crack.

Blade was one of the old breed. It was time to hunt down Clarence Ray Allen. And Blade knew well that the sometimes it takes a wolf to hunt down a wolf.

7

You Don't Break a Horse in One Ride

December 17, 1976
Alderson Women's Prison
Alderson, West Virginia

A murder case takes on a life of its own. People may think that they understand the process, but they really don't. They think that because they've seen some television detective wrap up a murder investigation in an hour, they know how it's done. But life isn't like television. Most of the success in solving a murder or in catching a murderer comes as a result of plain sweat and hard work. You know that murder always has a pattern—you just have to find it.

Assuming you have a suspicion, and even some evidence about who the murderer might be, it doesn't mean that you can prove it. Every detective knows that you can bring a stack of paper to the district attorney and tell him or her that you have a case, but that doesn't mean you *have* a case; all it means is you have a big stack of paper. All a detective needs in order to make an arrest is a strong suspicion and an arrest warrant. But a conviction of murder requires proof beyond a reasonable doubt. And that means evidence, lots of evidence.

Barbara Carrasco was right about her information; it was hearsay and couldn't be used in court against Allen unless the person testifying had actually heard him say it—and without more, it wasn't enough to prove murder. First, there was no body. Without a body, it's very hard to prove a murder has been committed. In most murder cases, the body is the best evidence. Without a body, a pathologist can't determine, and certainly can't prove, cause of death. Without a body, you need an eyewitness to prove there *ever* was a body. Without a body, you can't find physical evidence at the crime scene because you don't have a crime scene. So, without a body, only in the rarest of instances can you prove murder.

Blade and Lean knew that without a body, whatever Barbara Carrasco said wouldn't mean much. They had to have more. In the arcane world of evidence, it also meant that only what Eugene Furrow said about himself could be used against Eugene Furrow and only what Clarence Allen said about himself could be used against him. All Furrow or Allen had to say was that Barbara Carrasco was lying when she testified about what either of them supposedly told her, and then what? After all, who were you going to believe? Certainly, Carrasco had a motive to lie. She hated Clarence Ray Allen for what she believed he had done to her son. And Barbara Carrasco was a proven liar; she admitted that she made her living by lying. She was a proven and admitted criminal, accusing other people of being criminals. She had a slew of felony convictions which would be paraded in front of a jury, whose members would then be asked to accept her word over that of Allen and Furrow. While it wasn't always true that if you had no body you had no case, there was a reason why after Jimmy Hoffa disappeared without a trace, nobody has ever been successfully charged.

The next day, Blade called Tabler to ask him to check with counties near Fresno to see if they had found any unidentified bodies that might fit the description. Blade didn't want to talk further over the phone, and he told Tabler that Carrasco had come through and he would explain when he got back.

It was a long plane ride back to California, but the detectives didn't talk much about the crime. Carrasco had said that the motive had been to remove a woman who talked too much about floating forged money orders. What she didn't know was where the money orders had come from. If the motive for killing Mary Sue Kitts was to cover up a burglary, there had to be proof that there *was* a burglary *and* that it involved stolen money orders. Blade and Lean didn't even know when or where such a burglary might have taken place. It was simple: no burglary, no apparent motive. Without a motive attributable to him or some physical evidence, all Allen had to say was "Why would I do that?" There wouldn't be any good answer other than you thought he "had done that."

Assuming they could prove a burglary, they had another problem. They couldn't prove Mary Sue Kitts was even dead or that she had ever been involved with Allen. The most obvious thing they knew was that Clarence Allen wasn't going to help them prove anything. They didn't even know the names of the people who had been involved with Allen, with the exception of Eugene Furrow. Somebody was going to have to talk—somebody who had been there. Blade and Lean had been partners long enough that by the time they got off the plane, each of them knew what the other was thinking. What they knew was that no district attorney would waste their time writing NCF, no charges filed, across their request for a complaint; he would just use a stamp instead of wasting the ink in his pen.

First things first. They had to be able to convince their captain, Bud Lauter, and, more importantly, their sergeant, Art Tabler, that there was something here that would take them somewhere at the end. Even serious cases have to be prioritized. You can give cases so much time and then you have to move on, because there is always another body, there is always another case.

Both detectives wanted this case. They wanted to close the book hard on Clarence Ray Allen, but from the beginning they knew they had to approach every step carefully and build their case slowly. They had to put a case together before they started to make arrests and interrogate suspects.

When you sit down to interrogate a person for any crime, but especially for murder, there are unwritten rules as to what can be a very intricate dance. Very seldom do people crack just because they are sitting in front of you. You have to measure them and you have to bring them in slowly. To do that, you have to know the facts, because when suspects lie—and they almost always lie—you have to know it. A good interrogator gets into the head of the person in front of him. It's a matter of knowing when to push forward and when to pull back. Unfortunately, right now, Blade and Lean had nothing that would shake anybody.

After sifting through their options, Lean asked his more seasoned partner, "So, Blade, what do we tell Tabler? We both know that this case is going to take hundreds of hours and we may end up nowhere."

Blade grunted, "We tell him that we got something to work with and that it's too hot to ignore but not yet solid enough to make the case. When we got enough to show 'em that we're making progress, then we ask for a little more. If we do it right, soon we'll have enough so that they'll have to give us more. It's like the bank loaning money to the big boys; pretty soon the bank is in so deep with them that they have to loan them more in order to get their money back. What we have to do is convince them that they need to stay with us until we either come to a dead end or we hand 'em Clarence Ray Allen's ass on a platter."

Lean grinned. "All right, should I send the Carrasco tape down to transcription? Or are we just going to go in and tell Tabler that we got some hard-nosed old broad in a federal prison that has a case of the redass for Allen, and we think she's telling the truth and we need to run it out— that's going to do it?"

Every sergeant Lean had ever worked for would ask for the report so he could look at it. You didn't get to be a sergeant just by kissing somebody's ass. You had to have been in the field and you had to know what you were doing. The men wouldn't respect you unless you had been there, done that, and had the T-shirt to prove it. After that, if you kissed a little ass to become a sergeant, well, they understood that too and overlooked it, up to a point. Telling an experienced sergeant that you didn't have time to prepare reports or that this case was special and that regulations should be overlooked wouldn't cut it. Tabler could smell bullshit from a mile away. He would want reports unless there was a damn good reason not to prepare a report.

"No," Blade replied, "we tell Tabler that we got Allen admitting to murder and we need to set up the evidence before we question him. All we want to do is go see the parents of the Kitts girl and establish that she's probably dead. And, we need to find out if there was a burglary that fits what Carrasco told us. We'll find it, I know it, and then we'll go from there. Bits and pieces, boy. You don't break a horse in one ride. And we aren't going to make any reports. We keep our notes with us. This case gets out and people will start talking about it. Anyone asks and we just say that we're running out leads on an old missing person report. All we need is one whiff of this getting out and we may end up with more dead witnesses. Remember, the guy that tipped us once before on Allen disappeared. Now this girl disappears. When we close the door on this, we do it all at once. The only ones we trust are Tabler, the captain, and the sheriff. We let Tabler talk to the captain and the captain talks to the sheriff. As for us, we don't talk at all."

8

Follow the Money

December 27, 1976
Fresno, California

When Blade and Tommy walked into Tabler's office, he was staring at a stack of reports and nursing a cold cup of coffee. He didn't waste time. "So what do you think? And don't be telling me that Clarence Ray Allen is an asshole, so you know he did it."

Blade shrugged. "Well, he is an asshole and we know he did it but we need to work on this some more, try and push it together a bit." They filled him in on Carrasco's statements and the fact that Allen had admitted the murder.

Tabler looked at the pile of unread reports on his desk. "Okay, I don't suppose you have reports do you? Or are you going to blow smoke up my ass about how special this case is?"

Blade was ready. "Tom and I been thinkin' that we do some work on Kitts and see if anybody's heard from her. Just work it like a missing person report that we're trying to follow up on. We stay away from letting anybody know that we think Allen had her killed until we got something." Blade hesitated. "No reports. We'll keep you in the loop so you can talk to the captain, but that's what we think. Remember, Art, this isn't the first time a witness against Allen has disappeared. We had that with the guy who talked to us before and we never heard from him again."

Tabler's face took on a thoughtful expression. He remembered. "Okay, for now, no reports. Work it some more and see what you can come up with, but unless it really starts to come together quick, you're going to have to take your turn in the barrel on the other cases, too."

"Take a look at those other files in the inbox," Tabler called as they hurried out. They heard him. He knew that. If other cases came in, they were just going to have to make room. The trouble was that there were always other cases and there was hardly ever enough time.

It had been a week since their return from West Virginia, and Blade and Lean hadn't had a moment to spend on the case. Instead, they pursued two other homicides and several robberies that had to be worked, with witnesses to be interviewed and suspects to be chased down. Finally, there was a breather after all the other reports had been completed and sent over to the district attorney's office.

Tom handed Blade his fifth cup of stale coffee and waited for him to say something. Blade didn't even look up, merely nodding acknowledgment of the coffee. Finally, Tom broke the silence. "So, what's up with the burglary? We know that Carrasco was in jail in San Diego during at least nineteen days in August, and we know that Furrow told her about the deal only after she got out. So, I'm figuring the killing had to be sometime in July or early August."

Blade looked up from his files. "Yeah, we could be looking at a time period anywhere from May through August. These people aren't all that sure of the time frames, so probably July, but I think we backtrack as far as May. We think we know it went down in Fresno County, but we don't even know if it was Fresno city or county. It could have happened anywhere. The only thing we know for sure is that the money orders were stolen. So we put out feelers to the burglary divisions in each of the departments, but I think we start with ours and then contact the Fresno city police department. Better to start with our people, and maybe we'll get lucky, and it would sure be easier to control having to provide a lot of explanation."

Lean had worked burglary, and he had investigated money order cases before, so he knew there was an effective approach, which he described to Blade. "Money orders are numbered sequentially and recorded against the place where they're sold. So, if any of Allen's people passed them, we should be able to find out where they were passed from the company that produced them, which would have a report of the stolen money orders being passed. So," Tommy said with a broad smile, "we track back on the money orders. We find the burglary, get the sequence of numbers on the money orders, and then get the stolen reports from the money order company."

Blade was out of his chair, "Let's go down to property crimes and see if they got anything for that time period where money orders were taken in a burglary. There can't be that many. Most people aren't going to fool with them unless they have a check imprinter."

There were no computers back then to whiz through countless reports and turn up all matches to a word search. Instead, there were only file clerks who had hundreds of cases to go through, stopping just long enough to check on what was stolen. It could take several weeks. There were thousands of files; burglary was a growth business even then.

It was nearing the end of January, and Lean was waiting for Blade when he walked into the office. Usually, it was the other way around. Tom came from the school of thought where an appointment made for a specific time was merely a suggestion. Blade came from the old school, where a specific time was when you showed up. Immediately, Blade knew that they had something. "So, Tommy, what you got that has you in here before me?"

"I got a call from Yoshio, the modus operandi specialist in records. She found a burglary report at Fran's Market on June 29 or 30th of 1974. Guess where that is?" Lean waited a minute to see if Blade would ask. He knew he wouldn't, but it was always worth a try. Blade just stared at him, puffing his cheeks in and out, waiting until the younger man folded. He only had to wait a few seconds. Lean accepted defeat with a grin. "At Belmont and Temperance Avenue, just down the road from Allen's home. I'll bet the son of a bitch shops there. Somehow the alarm must have been disabled," Lean continued, "and whoever did it hauled off the whole damn safe. They got around one hundred and thirty American Express Company money orders and a check imprinter, which was in the safe."

Blade was listening while he situated himself in his chair and stared at the remains of yesterday's coffee in the bottom of his cup. He hadn't quite reached the point where he was willing to drink what was left over in the cup, but he was close. "You get the check numbers?"

"Yeah, we got 'em. I already got a call into American Express to see what they have. El Cajon, that sound familiar?"

"Carrasco and Furrow were from that area."

"Right. Well, I got a buddy in the El Cajon police department. I called him just to see if we might get lucky. Maybe they passed some in the area. He said they had five of the forged money orders in their evidence file. They got them when the checks came back to the stores as stolen. Anyway, they reported at least five checks floated in their area. Here's the incident report." Lean flipped over a two-page report containing the information from the El Cajon P.D.

Blade picked up the report and scanned it. The checks passed in El Cajon were from the number sequence taken from Fran's Market. The next step was getting the checks and the full report from El Cajon.

"Before you ask," Lean said, "yes, I already called El Cajon P. D. and requested they send up the checks. I told them we were working a murder investigation and that the checks looked like they would be a link to the perpetrator. The detective I talked to said he had lots of hot money orders and bad checks with all kinds of numbers. Said he would be happy to share some of the others if we would take them off his hands."

Blade moved his rear around in his chair. When you didn't have much meat on you, you had to squirm a bit to find a comfortable spot on the thin chair pad. "Well, it won't help us any to get the checks unless we can connect them back to Allen or one of his people."

"Or to Kitts." Lean interrupted. "Maybe we'll get lucky and the checks will have her handwriting or her fingerprints, or Allen's."

The men sat in silence, thinking maybe they had caught a break. It was too soon to tell. A few days would pass before the checks were delivered from El Cajon. No FedEx overnight delivery back then, either. You had to depend on the U.S. mail.

Blade put his feet up on his desk and leaned back in his chair. "It's too soon to talk to the people at the market." He looked at the burglary report. "Fran's Market? Anyway, if we start asking questions, they'll all be running off at the mouth. I can just see Clarence Allen walking in and buying a six-pack of beer while the owner tells him that we have been in the store asking about the checks. So, we wait on that. It's time to go see Mary Sue Kitts' folks." Blade stood up and started walking toward the door.

9

"The toughest part of a cop's job …"

January 24, 1977
Kitts Family Home
Fresno, California

No matter how many times you have done it before, the worst part of any cop's job is having to face the parents of a murder victim. You're talking about *their* child, no matter how old the child is, and you have to tell them that their child is gone. Blade had done it so many times he had lost count. Lean could still remember his first experience. Both men knew that today they would hold that information inside them a while longer and regret that they had to make these parents wait for what they desperately needed to hear but would never be ready for.

It was almost 11:00 A.M. when Blade and Lean turned onto the street where the Kitts lived. Driving a little slower than usual, Blade acted as if he was looking for street addresses. What he was really looking for was a little more time before he had to knock on the door. Two years earlier he had been to this house to do the preliminary investigation on the missing person report that Mary Sue's parents had filed. The street was lined with compact little houses that were beginning to show their age. Trees that had once been planted out of cans from the nursery were now shade trees that dwarfed the small front yards. Sidewalks that had seen children take their first bike rides were now pushing up in places, as roots cracked the surface.

The Kitts home was a shade of pink, not bright pink or light pink, just pink that had taken the sun into its pores. White trim outlined the windows. The yard was clean and the winter-yellowed Bermuda-grass lawn was neatly trimmed.

They waited in the car, stalling for a moment, picking up papers and notepads. "This woman, Mrs. Kitts," said Blade, "I remember her. We need to take it easy, not that you wouldn't, Tommy, but it's something you ought to know." Lean didn't respond. They got out of the car and adjusted their holsters.

As they made their way up the walkway, the detectives knew this was probably where Mary Sue Kitts had grown up, where she had played as a child. It would hold a lot of memories for the parents. Mary Sue had only been nineteen—to parents putting their hopes and dreams on a nineteen year old that is just a beginning. Blade and Tommy knew that this would be all that Mary Sue's parents would have—a beginning. Unlike most parents who get the reward of seeing the fruits of their labors, Mary Sue's parents would not. Worse, if Blade and Lean didn't find the body of Mary Sue Kitts, her parents would not even have the small amount of peace that closure might bring them.

Tommy put his hand on Blade's shoulder and slowed him down. "Maybe we just tell them that we're doing the missing person report follow-up, trying to find out if they've heard anything new. There's no point in saying anything today, right?" Blade nodded. Each of them felt the nervousness that comes from doing something loaded with unpredictability, except for the certainty of its unpleasantness.

Blade had learned that Mary Sue was adopted when they took the original report, but given Mary Sue's high school picture and the pink color of the house, the detectives had already formed an image of the woman who had fixed her child's hair for that picture, and the woman who came to the door fit that mental picture. She was maybe five-foot-one, plump, but not heavy, with hair starting to go to gray. She appeared to be the kind of person who was comfortable with what age was going to bring to her body and didn't make an effort to hide it. Moving gracefully toward middle age, she was obviously a woman who had spent her life raising her child and taking care of her husband, and she looked to be a woman who had lived a life that had been, until recently, a happy one.

When you visit the home of the parents of a missing or murdered child, it feels robbed of all warmth and comfort. And when parents see officers at their door, there is fear and tension, but, most of all, there is sadness.

There are also the long periods of silence, filled by a palpable sense of loss. It's always the same. You look at faces that are etched with the lines that come from grief, lines that never disappear unless that child comes back—and you already know that child is not coming back. However, the Kitts didn't know this yet, or they hadn't accepted it. The lines on the faces of Mary Sue's parents were only going to be drawn deeper by the lack of news, but neither Lean nor Blade was ready to take away their hope, at least not yet, not until there was no choice.

Mrs. Kitts opened the door wider than she should have, but she wasn't afraid of who was out there. She lived in a safe place where one had nothing to fear. Seeing the two men standing on the porch, she asked simply, "Yes, may I help you?"

Blade reached inside his pocket and took out his badge holder with its gold star and the seal of the Fresno County sheriff's office. "Mrs. Kitts? Maybe you remember me? I'm Detective Christensen from the Fresno County sheriff's office and this is my partner, Detective Lean. Ma'am, you filled a missing persons report on your daughter, Mary Sue. We talked two years ago."

Before Blade could get anymore out, Mrs. Kitts stepped back and covered her mouth. "Do you know something? Have you found her?" Clearly, she was preparing herself for the worst.

Lean intervened quickly. "No, ma'am, I'm sorry, we haven't found her…yet. We're here to do some follow-up work, maybe see if you know anything more or have heard anything. Sometimes missing persons show up and folks forget to let us know and sometimes they hear other things that might help us. May we come in?"

They kept their badge holders out in front of them so that the sheriff's stars were clearly visible, but they didn't move until she opened the door wider and let them in without saying anything more until they were inside their living room, the room that held the memories. It was where you put the television when you could afford one and the Christmas tree, where your children made their mess, and where all the family gathering pictures were taken that now were hanging on walls or sitting framed on the mantle—the room that resonated with life.

A heavyset, middle-aged man sat in a recliner, looking at them. "This is my husband," she said. "He has a disability so he doesn't move around that much anymore."

All Mr. Kitts got out was "Hello" and "Hope you don't mind if I just stay in this chair." He had the look of a man who was bracing himself for something he didn't want to hear. He had obviously heard the conversation at the front door. Tom could feel his stomach tighten. He hated every minute of this. They couldn't be completely honest, and he didn't want to be. He didn't want to tell them what he already believed was true. Not yet.

Mary Sue's mother moved over to the couch and pushed pillows to the corners. "Please, here, sit down."

As he sat down on the side of the sofa, Blade observed the two people waiting expectantly on his every word. "I'm sorry we don't have anything new to tell you. We're checking on the report you made back in November of 1974." He looked at his notes. "November 6, to be exact. We want to check on some of the things in that report to make sure they're still correct, to see if you have anything more that you recall or any new information you may have forgotten to tell us."

Mary Sue's father started to say something and paused, waiting a moment before breaking the silence. "Have you men heard something? Is that why you're here?" He looked at his wife, who was twisting the bottom of her blouse with her hands.

Blade had known that the parents would ask. He wasn't going to lie, but he wasn't ready for the truth either. "Well, sir, we've gotten some information that she may have been in the San Diego area before you made out that report. It isn't much. I guess she may have been seen with a Roger Allen down there. We're looking into that. Did Mary Sue talk to you about going to San Diego or what she might have been doing down there. Anything about Roger Allen?"

Mrs. Kitts' hands were still twisting and pulling on the bottom of her blouse, but as she looked up, the tightness of her hands gave away more than her face did. "Like I said when we talked to you and the other detective, I'm quite sure that the last time we saw Mary Sue was in July of 1974. She was with Roger Allen. They came by the house. I didn't like him and he knew that, but Mary Sue, she wouldn't listen. Never would. We're not headstrong people, but Mary Sue was real headstrong. She was adopted, you know, but she was ours. I guess being headstrong was just part of her. But she's ours. We love her and we want to know where she is, what happened. We want her to come home."

Lean looked at the father sitting quietly in the chair; his head never moved. Blade pressed forward. "Ma'am, do you remember what kind of car they were in? Our report says that it was a security vehicle of some type."

She nodded. "Yes, it was an El Camino, you know, one of those cars that's like a truck but looks like a car. It had Allen Security printed on the side. Roger's father, he had some kind of security business; we don't know much about it."

"Do you remember anything else that might help us? Anything else about Roger Allen or anything you might have heard from your daughter? Did she have any friends that we can talk to?"

"After Mary Sue left high school, she worked at Denny's, the one downtown. Her boss called, I don't remember his name, but he said she never came in for her last check. We weren't happy about her being with Roger Allen. After we saw her last, she called us maybe three times. She said she was working for Allen Security and that she was calling from Roger's house. Of course, we didn't like that, but there wasn't much we could say. You know how it is?" Blade nodded his head; he understood, and he agreed that far too often there wasn't much that parents could do.

Mr. Kitts cleared his throat and spoke up. "Don't get the idea we didn't try to do something. I went over to Roger's house, but I didn't see Mary Sue. My wife, she went over there a couple of times trying to find out something."

Mrs. Kitts cut him off. "That's right. I went over there and kept telling Roger that we needed to know where Mary Sue was, but he was real nasty. He said, 'Why would we hire her?' I kept asking him, going back, and I kept after him. He finally admitted that she had stayed there, so I asked where she was. He said that she had run off with some guy who rode a motorcycle. But we didn't believe that. She would never have done that. We haven't heard a word since those phone calls in July. We got a notice in the mail from the Department of Motor Vehicles for a driver's license renewal, but they never said whether she renewed it or anything. We still have that. I saved most everything that came for her—so she would have it."

Tommy coughed. "Yes, ma'am, we understand. We'd like those letters if we could. It might help."

Mr. Kitts, his voice rising with emotion, moved forward in his chair. "We just want to know where she is, if she's all right. We need to know. You understand? You said you had some information that maybe Mary Sue was in the San Diego area? What kind of information?"

"Yes, sir," Lean said, skirting a direct reply. "We understand. We have kids ourselves. Look, we need a few things that might help, you never know. Do you have anything that has Mary Sue's handwriting on it? Anything she might have signed or letters that she wrote?"

"Just a minute." Mary Sue's mother got up and walked into the hallway. She returned holding a handful of papers, tenderly, as if she were afraid they'd break if they slipped from her hand. "Some of these are schoolwork and things. Here's a few cards where she wrote her name. We'd like these back if we could get them, especially the cards. It's all we have right now, you know."

Lean took the papers. "Yes, ma'am. We'll be careful with them. We can't make any promises, but maybe these will help. We're going to do some more work on this. We'll let you know. Oh, and one last thing. Where did Mary Sue do her banking? Maybe they have something?"

"We still get statements from Bank of America," Mrs. Kitts answered. "We open them and keep them. They always show the same balance, just like it was when we last saw her. I'll get you a statement so you can look at it. "

"Yes, ma'am, that would help, and could we get the name of Mary Sue's dentist?" Mr. Kitts gazed at Lean with a puzzled expression. The implication of the question was lost on the parents, and neither Tommy nor Blade wanted to be the one to help by saying that could be a help in case they found teeth.

Blade stepped in. "Sometimes people go see the same dentist even when they don't visit other people that they know, and sometimes they have their dental records sent to a new dentist. You never know; it's worth a try is all." Tommy smiled at his partner's kind lie.

"Well, he's the same dentist we use, so I'm sure he would have said something to us."

Blade smiled. "You never know. It's worth a try."

Mrs. Kitts left the room and returned with a business card. "This is our dentist and these are the bank statements and the notice about her license."

Blade took the documents and rose from his seat. "Well, thank you. We'll be in touch if we find anything, or if we don't. Hopefully, we'll turn up something. You folks have a good day."

He and Lean walked to the door, followed by Mary Sue's mother. The detectives wanted to leave without saying another word. They both felt uncomfortable not being completely truthful. But they also knew they couldn't be sure about what was completely true, not yet anyway. At least, that was how they justified their obfuscation with those two parents who had been desperately hoping for news.

Neither man said anything until Blade pulled away from the curb. Tommy spoke first. "Well, that was a shitty deal. You look at those parents. They're sitting around waiting and no good news is going to come, ever. Guess we wouldn't be any different, huh?"

Blade looked over. "Tommy, you want to hope it's all going to turn out all right. We both know that asshole Allen did this. We can't do much for those two people, but we're going to get Allen one way or the other. Let's go down to Denny's and talk to the manager. Maybe something will turn up, but I don't think so. That girl's dead. We got enough now to take to Tabler and the captain. Maybe those money orders will be in and we'll see where they take us."

Tommy broke the silence of the drive downtown. "You think the father believed us, that we didn't know anything?"

Blade shook his head. "Hell, no. But he isn't going to say anything. He'll let his wife hold on to what she has. And, he just doesn't want to face it yet himself."

10

What Happened to Mary Sue?

January 24, 1977
Fresno, California

Blade turned the yellow Ford Torino into the Denny's parking lot. Lean called their car "Old Yellow." It was just another example of some county purchasing agent who got a good deal on a car in a color nobody else would buy. Within minutes, they met with the manager on duty. They explained that they were working on the missing person's case for Mary Sue Kitts. The manager looked through his personnel files and handed them Mary's Sue's unclaimed check. "Here it is. She last worked July 18, 1974. Just never came back in. Didn't call or anything. Sometimes that happens, but they almost always pick up their check if they have one coming. Nobody leaves their check, you know?"

When they got back to the office there was a note from Tabler. An envelope had come in from the El Cajon police department. Tabler glanced up when they walked through the door. "This manila envelope came in for you two. I signed for it. You on to something down there?"

Blade sat down. "I'm guessing those would be the checks that were passed in the El Cajon area that were taken in the Fran's Market burglary. We'll get back to you pretty quick, but it looks like our dead girl is Mary Sue Kitts. She was last seen with Ray Allen's kid, Roger. It's starting to fit."

Tabler was listening intently. "All right. I'll wait until I hear from you before talking to the captain. But I don't need to tell you, so far you don't have much."

Blade reached for the envelope. "We'll have more. Give us a little time, but that asshole Allen did this. We just need a few breaks." Lean nodded, as if his agreement with Blade might help convince Tabler.

"Okay, bring it back when you have more. By the way, I haven't seen any reports. You boys still not doing reports?"

Blade shook his head. But Tabler understood; sometimes a detective has to break the rules. Both he and Blade could remember cases that they worked together when every time they turned in a report with a statement from a witness, the witness would start turning on them a few days later. Finally, they stopped turning in reports and their witnesses stopped turning up beaten or intimidated. "I don't want any of your witnesses turning up DOA either," said Tabler. "Just make sure you protect your dictation so we don't have problems later."

When they got back to their office, Blade pulled open the manila envelope. There were five Traveler's Express Money Order checks and a note from Tom's buddy in the El Cajon police department. The note indicated that the checks were passed in El Cajon by a Margaret Jackson, using a California license. The license number was written on the back of each check. The police report described Margaret Jackson as a white female, five-foot-three to five-foot-four, 100 to 110 pounds, approximately eighteen to twenty years old, with blond hair. All but one of the checks had the endorsement of Margaret Jackson on the back. The other check was endorsed by a man, Robert Wood.

Lean thumbed through the checks. "What do you want to bet that when we run that license number it isn't going to come back matching the description of the real Margaret Jackson, assuming there is a real Margaret Jackson or a real Robert Wood."

Blade picked up one of the checks and looked at the feminine signature on the back. "No bet, the physical description from El Cajon is just about an exact match for Mary Sue Kitts. I'll call down and have records run a department of motor vehicle check. DMV should be back on this pretty quick. I'll have them send along a Soundex, with a picture of the real Margaret Jackson."

It didn't take long before the DMV check came back. The license number was real, but the description of the person who had the license number didn't match the physical description of the person who passed the checks, unless she had grown at least two inches, aged twenty years, and added thirty pounds. It was a phony driver's license that had been done up with the picture of the woman passing the checks, a woman who looked exactly like Mary Sue Kitts. The DMV return also showed that Mary Sue Kitts' driver's license had expired in 1975, with no renewal.

Lean's sunny expression suddenly turned glum. "That girl is dead. What doesn't make any sense is why kill her."

Blade rocked back and forth on the chair legs. "Remember, Carrasco said she heard the girl was talking, heard it from Furrow. I'm guessing the girl said something to the wrong people about what she had done with the checks and it got back to Allen."

Tommy thought about it. "Still doesn't make any sense. They could have just threatened her and scared the crap out of her. Why kill her? Wasn't she Roger's girlfriend?"

Blade brought his chair down onto all four legs. "If we knew why people did some of the stupid things they do," he said, draining his coffee, "we wouldn't be busting our asses as detectives. We'd both be *inspectors*."

"Yeah, or maybe sergeants, but I think inspectors would be better. I'll call El Cajon P.D. and request any other checks that they have from our list."

It hadn't taken long to get Tabler to okay using a handwriting expert to do comparisons between the known handwriting of Mary Sue Kitts and the signature of Margaret Jackson. But now he wanted the district attorney's office involved. "Time to start splitting the costs on this. You two go over and talk to Bill Smith. I told him what it's about. He just wants to know some of the facts."

Bill Smith was the district attorney. He had come back into the district attorney's office after spending a number of years as a criminal defense attorney. Bill was popular with cops and he wasn't encumbered by any pretenses. He was a Louisiana boy and he never made himself to be anything more than a regular guy who got lucky. He didn't spend a lot of time asking questions. He knew who Allen was and he could sense what was going to be needed. "The best guy around with handwriting is Dean Ray over at Fresno State. That who you want?"

"Dean would be our choice, too," Blade nodded. "Tabler wants to have you help out on the cost. Our budget's not that big."

Bill laughed. "Okay, go ahead and get Dean. We'll split the costs, but I need to know what's going on, and I'll get one of our guys on the case so you have somebody to talk to if you need anything."

"Just make sure it's not some snot-nosed kid. This is going to be a tough case, no matter what."

"I have a few of our boys in mind. Don't worry. You'll get somebody who knows what he's doing."

As soon as they got back to the office, Lean made the call and Dean Ray agreed to see them the next morning. Lean sat heavily in the chair at his desk. "We still have no idea who was involved with Allen in this mess, other than Furrow. Carrasco said only that they were people that he worked with or was associated with, but that doesn't tie things down. How're we going to get that information without talking to people? When the time comes, we have to be ready to move with arrests. We have to know where these people are and it would be nice, damn it, to know *who* they are."

Blade sniffed and raised his hand up to stop the conversation. "I think we'll get all that. We can sneak around and quietly find out who was licensed to work as a security guard with Allen, but we have to ask the right person. And there are other ways. Through back channels, we can see if they can get us what we need without going through all the paperwork."

Tommy's eyes narrowed. "You mean people inside giving us—you—information without putting anything down on paper."

"You have a problem with that?"

Tommy shook his head. "I don't have a problem as long as we don't get our asses caught in a crack if we have to use it to get a search warrant or make an arrest. Otherwise, we're going to have a problem. And we're going to have to explain to Tabler or, worse, to the captain, why we're looking at certain people."

Blade threw his head back and looked at the ceiling. "We don't have to explain anything as long as we're the only ones who know. I'll get the information. People owe me. You don't need to know and you don't need to ask. They won't ask either, because I never ask when they want something. I'll handle it. Anyway, the first thing we have to do is find Furrow and we're going to need Carrasco for that."

Lean nodded his head slightly. Blade was right, better not to know. Cops understood what other cops needed. It was a network that you couldn't trace on paper. It would all work out in the end, probably over a beer and a wink. He was okay with that. Carrasco was another matter. "Well, Blade, she took a liking to you, so that's your department. We're going to have a hell of a time getting her out of that federal prison."

"That's something else you can leave to me. We did okay with the warden at Alderson. We just have to figure out who to call, and I think I know just the guy."

The next morning, the two detectives stood outside the door to Professor Dean Ray's office in the criminology department at Fresno State College.

Dean Ray was sitting behind a desk spread with paper and magnifying equipment. His extensive training in handwriting analysis had been relied on by law enforcement agencies across the San Joaquin Valley, including the F.B.I. He peered over his glasses at the two men standing in front of him. "So, Blade, this your new partner?" He stood up and extended his hand to Tom. "Dean Ray."

Tom shook his hand. "Tom Lean. I've heard a lot about you."

The professor grinned. "Hopefully not from Blade. You fellows have something you want me to look at? What kind of case have you got?"

Lean waited for Blade to say something. "Murder. At least we think murder. It's a tough one. What we need from you is to look at the handwriting of the girl we think was murdered and then at some checks that have a signature on the back. It isn't her name on the endorsement, but we think she wrote them." A puzzled expression formed on Ray's face. "What do you mean 'you think was murdered.' Don't you know?"

Lean shook his head. "We don't have a body or a crime scene. It's a long story."

"I'll bet. Okay, give me what you have and I'll look at it. How soon?"

Blade set the file down on the desk. "As soon as you can."

"Let me take a look." He opened the folder. "This the girl's name, Mary Sue Kitts?"

Lean reached over and pushed the papers around to show the different samples. "Yeah, that's her. The name on the checks is Margaret Jackson, but we know Margaret Jackson didn't sign the checks. It was a phony driver's license. What we don't know is if Kitts signed the checks."

Dean Ray pulled the samples alongside one another and moved his light and magnifying glass over them while he peered at the signatures.

"I'll get back to you with a full report and my conclusions, but it'll take several days."

Three days later, Blade got a call from the professor. "Blade, this is Dean Ray. I've been looking at the documents. You have a minute to talk?"

"Sure, what do you think?"

"Well, that's what I want to talk about. I'm not sure what you need, but I know you wanted an answer as quickly as I could come up with one." He had shuffled several different samples of the known handwriting of Mary Sue Kitts with the endorsements of Margaret Jackson on the backs of the Traveler's checks. "I *can* say this without hesitation. Whoever wrote 'Margaret Jackson' was no professional. This was just somebody who was passing bad checks and didn't have that much experience. Was this Mary Sue Kitts a young woman? The Margaret Jackson signature looks like a younger woman's signature and the Mary Sue Kitts handwriting definitely looks like a young person."

"Anyway, on two of the money orders, I'm of the opinion that the signature of Margaret Jackson was signed by Mary Sue Kitts. I've looked at the Kitts girl's known handwriting and I would be prepared to testify to that in court. As for the other checks with the Jackson signature, I would have to say that they were probably written by Kitts, but I can't be positive. Those other checks that had the Jackson signature on them were written by somebody who was definitely trying to alter their handwriting. There are some fairly distinct similarities, but just not enough to be certain. They do have a feminine quality to them, and I'd be able to say that they appear to have been written by a woman, but I would have to admit that I couldn't be sure. Does that help at all?"

Blade grimaced. It was what he expected, but he still didn't like to think of what it was going to mean for Mary Sue's parents. He thanked the professor, hung up the phone, and finished making some notations in his notebook. Ray's opinion that Kitts had endorsed the checks would place the Kitts girl in San Diego, confirming what Carrasco had said, and it would also prove that she'd had knowledge of Allen's illegal activities. However, it wouldn't prove they killed her, but Blade knew it meant that Carrasco would be able to give information that could hurt Allen and the rest of those involved. That was motive. The question was whether it was a motive strong enough for murder.

Blade thumbed through his personal list of phone numbers. He had been around for a long time; he had friends in many agencies and, through the years, they had done each other many favors. One of them would simply leave a file on the desk and walk out of the room. No questions would be asked about why he needed it and no one needed to tell him that he couldn't say where it came from. It was understood. Blade would never talk. This was an off-the-books deal, and everybody knew that meant that you covered the back of the guy you were asking for a favor. They would do the same for you.

There would be no report. Nobody needed to know how he got the information because it wouldn't make any difference. It would just tell Blade and Lean where to start looking so they would know the names when they broke the first link in the chain. That had to be the weak link— they had to get Eugene Furrow. Blade dialed the first number on his list and waited for the phone to ring in his friend's office.

Within three days, Blade's contacts began to pay off. Just as he expected, nobody asked why he needed the information and nobody busted his ass because he asked for it. They assumed he wouldn't have asked if it wasn't important. Only one female appeared on the list of names Blade had gathered. The secretary Carrasco talked about was a woman by the name of Shirley Doeckel. He ordered a Soundex of her driver's license picture. When he and Tommy looked at it, they knew she was the one. She fit the description, except she was a blond. They went through the other names on their list and ran criminal and department of motor vehicle checks on each one. When the time came to make arrests, they would have to move quickly and bring them all in. It needed to be a lightning strike so that nobody had time to run or to talk.

But there was another problem. Blade and Tommy had to figure out how to have Barbara Carrasco transferred to California. They had no idea how to move a prisoner out of federal custody to another location, but they did know someone who did, the United States attorney for the Eastern District of California, Dwayne Keyes. It was just a matter of a phone call and a confidential explanation. Keyes promised cooperation, but already they learned that there was a problem. Carrasco had fallen and broken her leg. And their problems mounted. They had no suspects in custody, and rumors were filtering in that Allen was going to make bail on the Sacramento case.

Then things got a bit worse. Dwayne Keyes called; no federal women's prison in California would take Carrasco. If wardens hadn't already heard of her penchant for troublemaking, they soon did after making calls. Carrasco's reputation was enough to close the front gate of every women's prison in the state to Barbara Carrasco.

And, just when things seemed to reached bottom for Blade and Lean, they got even worse news. Clarence Allen made bail on the Sacramento robbery, and he was out and back in Fresno.

Blade digested the news of the setback on the Carrasco transfer with his usual look of disgust. He had a hard time with bureaucrats and this wasn't making his opinion change at all. He called the warden at Alderson. Blade asked if there was anything that could be done. After the call, Blade told Tommy, "The warden at Alderson is going to furlough Barbara to us for the time we need her to help us. We have to pay to get her out here and we have to pay for her food. But she's still a federal prisoner, so we have to make sure she's monitored at all times. That means one of us has to baby-sit her."

Tommy shook his head. "She's your age."

Blade leaned back on the two legs of his chair. "Yeah, partner, but you're junior on this team." Tommy was quickly learning the disadvantages of the seniority system.

It takes perseverance to put together any criminal case, but it also takes money to put together a big case. Detectives have to be constantly aware that whatever they do that costs money requires the approval of their superiors. Blade knew the drill.

The deal turned out not to be as rough as Blade thought it would be. Captain Lauter and the sheriff, Hal McKinney, approved additional expenses for Barbara, but only after the district attorney agreed to pay half the cost. All they had to do now was get Barbara on a plane to Fresno, broken leg and all. There was at least one advantage to the broken leg: Barbara couldn't run. She would be in Fresno on March 18th, and they would put her up at the Airport Marina Hotel out by the air terminal. Tommy got to work finding a female deputy to provide security.

11

A Robbery at Kmart

March 17, 1977
Visalia, California

In the Central Valley of California, Fresno is the big city; maybe not big by the standards of people in San Francisco or Los Angeles, but certainly by the standards of the surrounding smaller counties and cities. Forty miles south of Fresno is the town of Visalia. In 1977, it was on the verge of moving past being a country town to becoming a small city. Big crimes just didn't happen in Visalia and, most of the time, the only shooting was done by people hunting doves and pheasants. It was a nice place to live. It still is. It just wasn't a nice place on the night of March 17, 1977.

The white 1975 Lincoln Continental sat across the street from the Kmart store on Mineral King Avenue in Visalia. It was almost 9:30 in the evening. The night air of March carried a chill and the Continental's windows kept fogging up, which forced the driver to leave them open so that he could see. The lone occupant of the Lincoln was watching a man waiting near a pay telephone located in front of the grocery store near the Kmart. Clarence Ray Allen, never a patient man, pushed himself back in the green leather seats of the Lincoln and waited for the events that he had set in motion to unfold. He was out on bail for the Sacramento robbery and he needed money.

The day before, Allen had met three other men, his son, Roger Allen, Ben Meyer, and Larry Green at the Holiday Inn in Visalia. He had flown Green in from Oklahoma when Green called him earlier, saying he was in trouble. Allen hadn't asked what kind of trouble because he didn't care. He simply needed Green. Allen asked his son, Roger, and Meyer to drive to Visalia and pick a place to rob. By the time Allen arrived at the hotel, Meyer and Roger had selected the Kmart. It was a good call. Only a few weeks earlier, Allen, Roger, Ben Meyer, and a fourth man had hit another Kmart in a nearby community. They had gotten away with thirteen thousand dollars. After Ray had listened to the reasons for the decision to take down the Kmart in Visalia, he looked over the situation himself. He agreed. It was a good choice.

Now it was almost closing time for the store. The plan was simple. Meyer and Green would enter the store and hide until closing time. Roger would wait at a pay phone nearby for a call from them telling him when they were ready to leave. They would call as soon as they had the manager open the safe and had the money in hand. When Roger got the call he would signal his father. Clarence Allen would pull up to the side of the store and Meyer and Green would toss everything—the money, their masks, guns, and gloves—into Allen's car, and he would leave. Meyer and Green would get into a car driven by Roger. They would meet at the Airport Marina Hotel in Fresno where they would get a room and split the money.

A half hour earlier, Clarence had gone into the store and distracted one of the employees in the hardware department while Meyer and Green slipped through a storage room door and up a short stairway to hide. Then he had walked out, gotten into his car, and driven across the street where he could see his son and wait for the signal. Each man was armed with a handgun. Meyer and Green wore clown masks and green, latex gloves. The store had one security guard and Allen didn't expect him to be a problem. After all, he had his own security business and he knew two things for sure: Those guys are only there to assist in minor problems and, most important, they aren't there to be heroes. Once they saw the guns, he didn't expect anybody inside to be a problem. One of the axioms every criminal learns early in the game is that the sight of a gun stops most people from doing anything.

It was almost 9:30. Through the store public address system, the announcement was made that the store was closing. Meyer and Green watched the movement inside the store through a one-way mirror located in the storage area where they were hiding. They were waiting for the clerks to take the money out of the cash registers to be placed in the safe. It looked like everything was ready. The two men put on their masks and green rubber gloves, pulled out their weapons, and started down the stairs.

They encountered a maintenance worker, who was walking up the stairs. The man's head drew back at the sight of a man in a clown mask and his eyes widened when Green pointed his gun at him. Just as they pushed the maintenance man down the stairs and back into the store, a female employee walked right in front of them. Now there were two people that they had to watch and they still hadn't confronted the manager. They decided that Green would take the female hostage to find the manager. Meyer would wait with the maintenance worker.

John Atteberry, another maintenance worker, was pushing a dolly to the back of the store to carry out trash bins. As he moved along the aisle, he heard another employee, Bernice Davis, call his name. He looked over and saw a man holding Bernice and pointing a blue-steel handgun at him. All Bernice said was "This is for real, John." He looked at the gun. It had to be a toy, he thought to himself. It couldn't be real. He pulled a pipe off the dolly and raised it over his head, approaching the man with the toy gun.

Larry Green looked at the large man coming at him with the pipe in his upraised hands. He didn't hesitate. All he said was, "I mean business." Big John Atteberry took another step. Larry Green fired once, hitting Atteberry squarely in the chest. The big man went down.

Meyer heard a shot coming from somewhere inside the store. Within seconds, Green came running, yelling "There's trouble!"

Meyer looked around. "What are you gonna do?"

Green's eyes were wide and he looked frantically in every direction, waving the gun back and forth as he searched for an exit. "I'm getting out."

Meyer watched Green run off in a different direction. Meyer looked for an exit door, but there were too many doors. He kept pulling on each door, trying to get out. When he discovered a locked door, Meyer fired at it, trying to destroy the lock, until the gun wouldn't fire any more. He pulled off his gloves and jacket and tore the clown mask off his face. The gun was empty. He threw the gun to the side and forced the door open slightly. Outside he could see numerous police cars. There was nowhere to go. He looked back to where the maintenance man stood cowering.

Meyer ordered the man, "Go ahead and grab me. When we go outside they won't shoot." His captive looked at him for a moment, unsure of the situation, then he grabbed Meyer and pushed him through the door.

As Meyer walked through the door with his former captive holding onto him, Meyer heard numerous voices yelling at him to lie on the ground. The maintenance worker ran toward the police. Meyer waited on the cold asphalt while an officer slowly approached him with his gun drawn. He didn't know where Ray Allen was. All Ben Meyer knew at that moment when the cuffs slipped around his wrists and he was pulled to his feet was that he was all alone. Everybody had left him.

From across the street, Allen saw the police cars rolling up outside the Kmart, red lights flashing. Meyer was nowhere to be seen and neither was Green. Roger had run for his car. Allen started the engine and drove slowly out onto Mineral King Avenue, heading back to Fresno, hoping that everybody would make it out. If they didn't, he was confident his boys wouldn't talk.

It was 3:15 in the morning by the time Detective Hartman of the Visalia police department sat down across from Ben Meyer. Hartman took a moment, sizing Meyer up.

Meyer sat in his chair, his wrists still in handcuffs. He was just able to run his fingers over the thick mustache that ran down the sides of his mouth. He was tired and he could feel that both his hair and face were oily, but it didn't make any difference. It was just a question of how much he was going to give up. He was alone. They had left him. He waited for Hartman to ask his questions. It didn't take long. First, he gave up Larry Green.

Hartman didn't give Meyer any opportunity to think about what he was doing. "Okay, you want to say who else is involved? In the robbery or the planning—the conspiracy—you best tell me now."

"That would be Clarence and Roger Allen."

Hartman leaned back in his chair. He had heard Clarence Allen's name before from detectives at the Fresno sheriff's office. He made a note to call them.

It was almost 4:30 A.M. by the time Hartman was finished with the interrogation, but there was no time to sleep. He had calls to make and the first one was to Fresno.

As soon as he came into the office in the morning, Blade saw the message to call a detective at the Visalia police department. The message didn't say very much, just that it regarded a robbery the night before in Visalia—and that Clarence Ray Allen was involved. He had heard reports of the robbery and the shooting of a store employee on the morning news. Blade knew Allen was out on bail on the Sacramento charges, but there was nothing he could do about that except mutter about lenient judges. Blade made the call and listened while the detective filled him in. He hung up the phone and stared at the notepaper on his desk. The Kmart employee was in critical condition. The two Allens were at large. This was the first he had heard of Ben Meyer, but at least Meyer had talked, immediately pointing the finger at Clarence Allen and his son. The fourth man still hadn't been positively identified. Blade kept his hand on the phone as he rested it in its cradle. How many others were out there that he didn't know about? Allen was armed and he would be a threat to any cop who came near him. Blade looked up when Tommy walked into the office. "You know about that robbery that went down last night in Visalia?" Tommy nodded. No further words were exchanged. The two detectives knew they had to move quickly.

According to the Visalia police department, Meyer said that the gang was going to meet at the Airport Marina, the same hotel where Blade and Tommy's chief witness, their *only* witness, was registered to stay that night. Even for Blade, not a man given to the appreciation of irony, the situation simply seemed like the fates were moving their hand back and forth to manipulate a drama in which he was meant to suffer.

They had to find another place to house Carrasco, and fast. That wasn't nearly as much of a problem as the chance of her being seen back in Fresno, with two detectives pushing her around in a wheelchair. What if Allen should see them? He would remember the faces of Blade and Tommy, who had arrested him on the Sacramento warrant, and it wouldn't take him long to figure out why they were talking to Carrasco.

Blade and Lean were waiting on the tarmac at the Fresno Airport when Carrasco's plane rolled up to the terminal. Carrying Barbara Carrasco was not an option. Even though she would never admit it, it was obvious that she weighed well over two hundred pounds and, with a full length plaster cast on her leg, she probably came in at over two fifty. Carrying a woman that big with a leg sticking straight out would be almost impossible, even if she were cooperative. And they suspected that cooperation was not something they could count on with Barbara.

Blade waited until the other passengers had disembarked and entered the plane. Barbara was near the front; her wheelchair was sitting folded alongside her seat. She was not in a good mood. The first words out of her mouth were, "What the fuck are you planning to do to get me off this goddamned plane?" Barbara was nothing if not expressive.

Blade glanced back at the stewardess and shrugged. "Long trip?"

The stewardess just rolled her eyes. "I've had her all the way from L.A. A federal agent put her in the seat and said there would be officers to meet her when we got here. She's all yours." Every head in the terminal snapped around when Blade pushed Carrasco through the terminal doors from the tarmac, while she screamed, "You sons of bitches are trying to get me killed."

Tommy hung back and let the people observe Blade push the red-faced woman, with the plaster-coated leg that stuck straight out, through the terminal. He followed Blade as he rolled Barbara out to their yellow Ford Torino. Tommy hadn't heard that many four letter words since he had gone through police training. Maybe people would think she was Blade's wife. Served him right.

12

Kmart Robbery Aftermath

March 19, 1977
Fresno, California

Although the Ramada Inn was only several miles from the airport, it seemed farther because Carrasco carped the entire way about the flight and about getting her off the plane. All Tommy could think about was that in a short time he wouldn't have to listen to her anymore; she would be a female deputy's problem.

The next morning, Barbara was in a better mood, but it came as no surprise to Blade and Tommy that the deputy assigned to watch her was not. She had suffered through Barbara's complaints for most of the night. Tommy was sympathetic, but then again the female officer got to go home while Tommy and Blade had to spend the rest of the day with Carrasco, who was clearly still in a talkative mood. Lean wondered if prisoners weren't allowed to talk at Alderson because it seemed like she had saved up a whole lot to say. They took her down to breakfast. The detectives had something to discuss with her and they weren't sure how she would respond.

Blade waited until after she had ordered before getting to the point. "Barbara, we've been thinking about trying something with you that's a little different."

It was the wrong line to use with Carrasco. "Honey, every man thinks about trying something different with me. What did you have in mind?"

Blade reddened. For all his experience and occasional hard demeanor, he was still a gentleman when it came to women, even women with as hard an edge as Carrasco. "Well, that's not what, ah, I meant. I meant that we'd like to have you hypnotized by a psychologist. Sometimes it helps people with their memory. Kind of relaxes 'em, I guess. It won't hurt or nothing."

Barbara laughed. "What the hell. If you think it'll help, I'll try it." Tommy could see that she was amused by Blade's embarrassment. He decided he would stay out of the line of fire for the time being.

By that afternoon, the psychologist had come to the hotel and started the hypnosis session with Carrasco. The goal here wasn't about making someone act like a monkey when the hypnotist snapped his fingers. It was about helping someone relax and intensely focus on their memory of events. The focus was on who was around Clarence Allen around the time of the murder and the El Cajon visit. It wasn't long before Barbara remembered the name of the man with the missing tooth who she had described to them in the interview at Alderson—Carl Mayfield. She remembered that Mayfield had been in the car with herself, Allen, and his girlfriend, Shirley Doeckel, and a man by the name of Chuck Jones when Allen had remarked that they had "wasted" Mary Sue Kitts. It wasn't much more than what she had already told them earlier, but it did give them a name they hadn't been sure of. Both Mayfield's and Jones' names had shown up in the list of names of employees of Allen's security business, but before they had just been names. Now they were suspects.

Later, back at the office, Blade and Tommy heard that Furrow had disappeared back into his hole. They agreed that the only way to find him was to go to El Cajon and start looking. If they wanted Allen, they needed to get Furrow. To get Furrow, they needed Carrasco.

Doing what they had to do to get Allen was one thing. Riding with Barbara Carrasco the next day from Fresno to El Cajon was something entirely different. She never stopped talking the entire six hours of the trip. Blade stuck Tommy in the front seat with her while he sat in the back and dozed. When Tommy turned the radio on to listen to something else, she turned it off so she wouldn't be interrupted. He kept turning the radio back on. Barbara kept turning it off. Finally, Tommy just gave up. Barbara never gave up and she never shut up.

It was 4:00 P.M. by the time they reached the El Cajon Police department office. Anytime law enforcement officers from one agency go into the jurisdiction of another agency, they routinely check in with the local agency. Local agencies like to know who is in their neighborhood and they want to know if something is going to go down. The last thing you want is for local cops to shoot a cop from another agency because they don't know that he or she is authorized to have a gun out or to make an arrest. Besides, the local cops know who the local players are and where the most likely place is to find them.

Blade and Tommy found and checked into a hotel that would be the kind of place Barbara would likely stay. Furrow would be suspicious if he came to see Carrasco and she were in a Hyatt or the Hilton. Barbara normally ran with dogs. A fleabag hotel was the right place. The plan was simple: Blade and Tommy would stay in an adjoining room and record the conversation between Carrasco and Furrow. They would photograph him going in and out and then make an arrest.

There was only one problem with the plan. They couldn't find Furrow. Her suggestion was for them to take her to check out places where he might be hanging out. Blade and Tommy had serious reservations; they couldn't be seen driving her around in the yellow Torino. They looked exactly like what they were, cops. They needed two things, a car that would fit the part and a driver who would fit the role with Barbara.

The car was the easy part. El Cajon P.D. arranged for them to get a Cadillac convertible. The hard part was the driver. Barbara made it clear that everybody knew she didn't like to drive so she would have a driver. He had to be Mexican and he had to look like he came from the other side of the border. With his blond hair and sunburned face, Tommy wasn't going to come close and Blade looked about as much like an illegal as any six-foot-three man with sandy blond hair could look. They were at a loss until Tommy spoke up. "Mercado. We get Henry Mercado from our department to come down here. He's been working undercover narcotics; he's got the look and he's got the lingo and the act down pat. Besides, Mercado speaks Spanish like a native and he's used to working with illegals. I say Mercado is our man if the captain will go for it."

Blade nodded agreement. "I'll call him."

It took a bit of talking and some maneuvering to get Mercado out of a trial he was involved in, but the captain finally approved it and the next day Mercado was on a plane. He would arrive in the afternoon. All they could do was wait and watch the working girls who plied their trade in and around the motel where they were staying. Some of the girls had even left business cards in their door, listing the services they provided. Barbara called the girls *pinche pollos*, which she roughly translated as "sex chickens." As she said, "Everybody's got to make a living."

Tommy was waiting inside the terminal at the airport in San Diego when Mercado's plane landed at 8:00 P.M. He looked right for the part, except for the fact that he was obviously intoxicated. It turned out that while Henry Mercado wasn't afraid to work undercover with armed drug dealers, he was terrified of flying. Tommy and Blade had planned on him driving Barbara around that night. Tommy wasn't sure he should drive in his condition, but Mercado was confident. "You want me to drive this broad around and pretend like I'm a wetback, right?" Mercado laughed. "Well, *amigo*, then I'm perfect the way I am. I can drive; I'm not worried."

Tommy was less sure. "I'm worried about the car, is all. We borrowed a Cadillac convertible. Just don't wreck it, okay?"

"Yeah, yeah, don't worry, white boy. I'll take good care of it." Mercado never lacked confidence, drunk or sober.

Tommy drove back to the hotel with Mercado following in the Cadillac. As soon as he got out of the car Mercado, shook his head and scowled. "Tommy, man, you expect me to stay here? I'm an undercover police officer, a *specialist*." Mercado pronounced "specialist" as "specialeest," with the accent he affected when he wanted to play the role of a Mexican drug dealer. He rolled his eyes. "Just because I run with bad guys, man, don't mean I live like them. This place is shit, a dump, man." Mercado looked doubtful. "I don't suppose this broad is good-looking?"

"That depends on whether you like big girls, Henry. Let's go up and meet her."

Two days of looking were unsuccessful. Furrow's arrest record had turned up an employer's name. The employer hadn't seen Furrow for several weeks. Finally, Carrasco reached Furrow's grandmother. She hung up the phone and looked at the men waiting expectantly. "He's gone to Oregon. I don't know where."

Tommy called Furrow's parole officer. Furrow was on federal parole and there was a possibility that there was a contact that he had given his parole officer for a relative in Oregon. The parole officer gave them an address in Medford, Oregon. The detectives had waited on calling the parole officer because they didn't want Furrow to know they were looking for him. Their concerns were reinforced when the parole officer told them he had learned that Furrow had heard Fresno County officers wanted to talk to him about a murder. Apparently, when he was mugged and printed in the El Cajon police department at Tommy's request, somebody had told him that he was being looked at by Fresno detectives about a murder case. Now that Furrow knew they were looking for him, he wouldn't make himself easy to find.

The drive back to Fresno seemed even longer than the drive from Fresno to El Cajon. Blade and Tommy realized there wasn't a choice in the matter. They would have to go to Oregon and they would have to take Barbara with them. Tommy was discouraged and he was not optimistic about the prospect of going in to see the captain about more money. Blade, on the other hand, seemed confident that they would get the permission and the money.

"You see, Tom, the problem that the captain and the sheriff got is no different than the problem the bank had with my father-in-law buying a new bull."

Tommy was used to Blade's farming and cowboy analogies, but this one wasn't sinking in. "I don't understand what buying a bull has to do with what we've got to deal with."

"You see, boy, that's the whole point. My father-in-law went to the bank to get money to buy some breeding cows, brood cows we call 'em. Anyway, they gave him the money and then his bull up and died. So he went back to the bank and told them he had to buy another bull. The bank said that they weren't going to give him any more credit. So my father-in-law just pointed out to the banker that you couldn't have a baby without a father and you couldn't have a calf without a bull. If the bank wanted him to pay back the money they had already lent him, then they had to give him more so he could buy a bull and get some calves so he could sell the calves and pay back the bank. See, it's the same thing with the captain."

Tommy took his eyes off the road for a moment and looked sideways at Blade. "The only thing I'm getting out of this is your bullshit. What's the point?"

"The point, boy, is that they already have so much money invested in this case that they have to give us more or they won't have nothing to show for the money they already spent. Just like the banker and the bull."

It didn't take as long as they had anticipated. The next morning, Tabler had already talked to the captain, and the trip was approved. As they left, Captain Lauter told them to be careful and have a safe trip because, but he cautioned that they needed to get moving on the case. Tommy turned as he was walking out the door. "Yeah, thanks. We got to go buy a bull."

The last thing they heard as they walked down the hall was Lieutenant Hogue asking the other supervisors what "buying a bull" had to do with anything. Tabler was laughing. Obviously, he had heard Blade's stories before.

By late morning they were back on the road. By 7:00 that night they had made it to Medford, Oregon, just across the state line from California. After working with local officials, they arrived at the hotel with the warrant needed to record any conversation. Barbara called the family that Furrow and his wife were staying with. It took only a minute to find out that Furrow had moved on to Corvallis, Oregon. That was the first piece of bad news. The second piece was that Corvallis was in a different county and they would need a new warrant.

By 9:00 P.M., they were in a new hotel with a new warrant and ready for Barbara to call the local family with whom Furrow was supposed to be staying. Barbara inquired if Eugene was there, and it was only a moment before he came to the phone. When he heard Barbara's voice, Furrow's reaction was one of anger. He told her he knew that she had to be calling about the murder, because he had heard Fresno was looking for him when he was picked up in El Cajon. He wanted to know if she was working for the police, because he didn't believe she would be calling around looking for him in Oregon just for old time's sake.

Finally Barbara was able to calm him down. She said she would send a cab to pick him up and she would pay for it. Tommy and Blade were surprised when Furrow agreed to meet with Barbara if a cab picked him up.

They waited several hours, but he never showed. Corvallis police covered the house until morning, but Furrow never appeared. By early afternoon of the next day, the family that Furrow and his wife had been staying with was contacted. They had driven Furrow and his wife, Debbie, to the Greyhound bus station. He was on a bus for San Diego. Blade and Tommy were already several hours behind him.

Assuming Furrow had taken the bus to San Diego, he would have a stop in Eugene, Oregon, and, in a matter of hours he would cross into California. They would no longer need to be concerned about Oregon law. They could arrest him as soon as he crossed the border. The question was when to arrest him, and although they were desperate to talk to him, they needed to take him in a situation where they could control the arrest. The best place, of course, would be Fresno. And, when they checked the schedule, they were pleased to discover that the bus stopped there. Blade made a call to the detective division. Maybe they would finally get a break. That break finally came while they were driving home.

It was 8:00 Thursday night, a week after the Visalia robbery. Allen and his son Roger had been lying low, but nothing untoward had happened. He was beginning to feel more confident. As long as the police didn't find out about the Visalia Holiday Inn or the Airport Marina, they wouldn't have anything to go on—as long as nobody talked. He knew that Ben Meyer wouldn't talk—*all* his boys knew better than to talk. If you worked for Allen, you didn't talk about him, because if someone even hinted at it, Allen made sure of letting him know about others who had made that mistake and the reason they were never were going to make it again.

Feeling almost cocky, Allen left his house and got into his Lincoln and backed out of his driveway. When he glanced into his rearview mirror, he saw a car blocking his way. Looking over his shoulder, he could see several other cars. And then he saw the flashing lights and men walking to both sides of his car, and he heard the man on his side yelling for him to keep his hands on the wheel. Detective Hartman of the Visalia police department walked up to the car, keeping his eyes on Allen, watching for any sudden movement. Hartman glanced through the rear side window of the Lincoln, where the muzzle of a semi-automatic rifle was clearly visible. Hartman kept his gun pointed at the driver, while other officers moved in to back him up. As long as Allen kept his hands on the wheel, Hartman wouldn't have to shoot.

Allen knew better than to move and he sat in the Lincoln with his hands gripping the wheel. In the side mirror, he could see the badge on the belt of a man holding a gun. He kept his hands on the wheel as the detective jerked the door open.

Across town, Roger Allen and his wife had been stopped while he was driving, and he was taken into custody by Fresno police officers at the same time as was his father. By the time Clarence Allen was sitting in the back of a Fresno sheriff's patrol car, his son was already at the Fresno police department. Roger's wife was also in custody on suspicion of robbery for her role as an accessory in the Visalia robbery, and Roger Allen's fourteen-month-old son was now in the custody of her parents. Roger's wife asked to go home for different clothing. The officers agreed; it was an excuse for them to get inside the house without a problem. When they followed her into the house, they spotted a .45 caliber automatic in plain view on the night stand. The search of Clarence's Lincoln had turned up a green rubber glove, like the ones that had been dropped at the scene of the Visalia robbery.

It was after midnight by the time both Clarence Allen and his son walked into the Visalia police department. They had been intentionally kept apart. Detectives moved Clarence into an interrogation room and read him his Miranda rights. He was polite and acknowledged that he understood his rights. He had nothing to say without talking first to his attorney and having him present. This didn't surprise the detectives. They hadn't expected him to say anything. Neither had Blade or Lean, who were still on the road returning from Oregon.

13

Fear Has Its Own Smell

Saturday, March 26, 1977
Fresno, California

The trip back from Oregon was exhausting. Hour after hour, throughout the night they had trailed the Greyhound bus, stopping at each stop where the bus had stopped, watching to see if Furrow had gotten off. The fact that Carrasco never shut up didn't help. They were at least three hours behind the bus when it stopped in Fresno on its way to San Diego, and the only good news was that Allen had been taken into custody. Blade called ahead to have Furrow arrested when the bus pulled into Fresno. Presumably, Furrow would get off to stretch his legs and at that moment the arrest team would take him down. The arrest shouldn't be a problem, but that was the problem—there were always problems.

It was not an easy assignment. The Greyhound bus depot was located in a marginal section of town and it was filled with crowds milling around, either waiting for a bus to take them somewhere or waiting for someone to get off the bus. Some people were just hanging around because the bus depot was a warm place. As long as Furrow got off the bus they could take him without needlessly jeopardizing people in the station. The arrest team wasn't worried about whether Furrow would resist; what worried them most was not knowing if he was armed. Blade said he didn't think so, but he knew making that kind of assumption is what got cops killed, and in this case, it was an assumption that might get civilians killed. As any cop knows, the only thing that you know for sure about an arrest situation is that you don't know anything for sure until it's over. This guy was a suspect in a murder and that meant that he was likely to be violent and that he had nothing to lose. They had to take him by surprise. The detectives kept looking at their watches and drinking coffee from thinly insulated paper cups. The coffee did nothing to help the acid roiling around in their stomachs, mingling with the adrenalin.

At 9:57, the loudspeaker barked that bus 7558 from Eugene, Oregon, was now arriving at gate 3. There were only four gates, so they weren't concerned about which door Furrow would come through. They moved to the door of gate 3. The Greyhound employee that normally would keep them inside the gate had already been informed that they were on law enforcement business.

People began to get off and walk past the two detectives. Nobody exiting the bus matched Furrow's description. Finally, the stream of people thinned down to just a woman and a small child. That was it. Nobody else got off.

The whole point was to make sure Furrow didn't have any room to move and could be controlled if he tried to reach for a weapon. The detectives boarded the bus. The first thing that hit them was the smell. The closed confines of the bus emphasized the lingering aroma of stale sweat, food, and people. The only passenger fitting Furrow's description was sitting toward the back, on the outside seat, with a woman next to him. A few others were still seated, scattered around the bus, but most people had gotten off. The first detective walked down the aisle as if he were looking for a seat.

Furrow looked up as the detective walked by. His face was impassive. Furrow wasn't interested in him, which meant Furrow wasn't expecting anyone to know he was on the bus and arrest him. The first detective walked by and turned as the second detective moved into position. He reached out, ready to grab Furrow if he moved. "Are you Eugene Furrow?"

Furrow looked up; he had a puzzled look on his face as he answered. "Yeah, I'm Lee Furrow."

A handcuff is shaped like two letter "C's" on a hinge pin. The outside "C" is the side with the ratchet that slides into the inside "C" that closes the cuff. An experienced cop can bring half the cuff down on a wrist and the ratchet side will slide with momentum around the wrist and lock. The only sound the prisoner will hear is the sound of the ratchet as it closes the circle around his wrist. An experienced cop can do it with one hand if he has to.

Furrow's puzzled expression suddenly turned to realization, but before he had could say a word or register another thought, the second detective moved the cuff over Furrow's hand in one smooth motion, snapping the cuff over one wrist as he grabbed for the other. "You are under arrest for murder."

Stunned, Furrow didn't move. There is nothing more sobering to a man than hearing the sound of cuffs snapping around his wrists. Well, there is one thing—"You are under arrest for murder." Those words get everybody's attention.

The woman sitting next to Furrow reached over, but the detective stopped her hand from touching Furrow. "You Mrs. Furrow?" She nodded, her fright at the situation evident. He kept his hand between the woman and Furrow, while the other detective pulled Furrow by the arm and guided him out into the aisle. "Your husband is under arrest, ma'am. Check with the detective division at the Fresno County sheriff's office." Almost as an afterthought the detective hesitated and said, "I'm sorry about this, ma'am." The detectives moved Furrow down the aisle and off the bus.

Blade had made it clear that Furrow was not to be taken to the jail and booked. All the booking paperwork would be handled in the detective division and Furrow would be kept in a holding cell near the offices of the detectives. Under no circumstances was a booking record to be made at the jail where another inmate might see it, and Furrow was not to be mixed in with other inmates. Furrow would sit in a holding cell by himself until Blade and Lean arrived in a few hours. No word of the arrest could be allowed to leak to Allen—at all costs. Blade and Tommy knew that word moved between jails with the speed of a jungle drum. If people inside knew that Furrow was in jail, it would only be a matter of hours before Allen knew it, too.

Three hours later, Blade and Tommy deposited Carrasco at the local Hilton hotel and met with a female sheriff's deputy who would keep an eye on her. Barbara Carrasco may have been a cooperative witness, but she still was what she was, a criminal. If she had the chance to run, there was a possibility that she would take it. They couldn't afford to take that chance, even with Carrasco in a cast.

Blade sat in his office drumming his fingers on his desk, while thirty miles away in Visalia Clarence Ray Allen and his son sat, unknowing, in their cells. Furrow was in a holding cell near the main office. Blade and Tommy decided they would leave him there for a while, let him sweat. They had sized him up based both on his record and from what Carrasco had told them. He didn't look to be a tough guy, but he may also have killed a woman by strangling her with his bare hands. The decision as to who was going to interrogate him was important, and Blade made it. He was the senior detective, but he also had a sense of Furrow; maybe Furrow would relate better to Lean. Tommy was younger and guys Furrow's age related to him a little better. Blade had his own kind of presence in the room, but he didn't fool anybody. When Blade grinned, it was like a wolf smiling. When Tommy grinned, he looked more like one of the Beach Boys. So the wolf would remain hidden in a separate room and monitor the recording equipment.

When you interrogate someone, the personality that you use is critical to establishing a rapport with the suspect. Some suspects will simply stop talking or will never start talking if you raise your voice. Other people won't respond to anything but a forceful personality. Sometimes you raise your voice and sometimes you keep your voice well modulated and friendly. It all depends on how the suspect reacts to you. The advantage you have when you are the interrogator is that you are in control of the suspect's world. You do not want him to see you simply as the enemy. You have to project an aura of concern and be sure that it's transmitted to the suspect. It may be the empathy in your voice or perhaps the subtle expression on your face. You keep him talking until you feel the suspect reaching out, no matter how slender the reed, for whatever he thinks you can offer—even if it's simply a friendly voice in a frightening world.

A good detective can shift in response to what he sees in a suspect's eyes, his face, his hands, or detects in his voice, or in the pungency of his sweat. You read the suspect and you use everything you read. You're there for one purpose only, to get a statement of some kind, a confession if you can, a lie if that's all that he offers. You take as long as you need and use every advantage you have. One advantage is your option of putting the suspect in a holding cell by himself and letting him sit. And sit some more. You want him to be scared and you want him to see you as the only way he can possibly get out of this. You are his passport to freedom, even if the only way out means that he has to confess and purge his soul.

Barbara Carrasco was right. Most people have a conscience. Blade was also right. Once you find the conscience, you stroke it, caress it, nurture it, tug at it, until they have to talk—until they *need* to talk—and then you *let* them talk. You let them talk and talk and talk as long as you can, even if they lie—and most do, at least at first. When they do, you twist the lie around them; you help them embellish it and you wait until you're sure they have spun their tale. You twist just a little more, enough so they will perhaps remember a little more and this time tell their tale a little differently. You let them remember it better, and when the time is right, you point out why you have some confusion about their version and the facts as they appear to you.

Tommy asked Blade, "How long has he been in there?"

"About three hours. Give him another ten or fifteen minutes. I told the guard to open the slide window in the door and peer in, not say anything, just peer in and then shut the window cover. He'll start squirming pretty quick, I think. You ready?"

Lean nodded his head. "Ready as I'll ever be." He sat for a moment longer at his desk, sipping what was left of the cold coffee in his cup. He had been thinking about how he was going to do this interrogation. Blade had made a major decision and although he didn't want his anxieties to be obvious to his partner, Tommy was feeling a little insecure. Everything turned on getting Furrow to break. He had written down all types of scenarios. What he would do if Furrow said this. What he would do if Furrow said that. Tommy had gone over it in his mind a hundred times, but he had questioned enough suspects to know that it never went the way you planned it. The only thing you could really count on was your instinct and your ability to read the situation.

Most people have never seen a murderer except on television. When you actually are sitting across the table from a man who has committed murder, it's different. Sometimes, you can sense that they have moved past what they've done and they're looking for a way out. Sometimes, they're still thinking about what they've done and it is pushing against their conscience. Other times they have carefully devised the story they will tell. You have to be prepared for whatever kind of man you are facing across the table. How they act in front of the news cameras or when they are arrested isn't how they necessarily will act when you are looking at them, face-to-face, inside an interrogation room. Most of the time, you won't know until you both sit down. You have to be able to size them up while they are sitting there, because you may not get a second chance, especially after they talk to some lawyer. Tommy checked his watch and nodded to Blade, who walked into the room adjoining the interrogation room. That would be his listening post.

Normally, Tommy would have another officer with him, but he felt he could handle Furrow, and he wanted to be Furrow's only human contact. Sometimes, if you approach a suspect with too many people, it gives him a sense of power, the sense that you fear him. Approach a man by yourself and you are letting him know that you are in control—that he is helpless. Tommy slid the viewing port cover back and looked into the holding cell. The metal walls were scratched with the graffiti of hundreds of other Furrows who had etched into the paint some small measure of defiance, or some meager effort to make sure the world knew they had been there. The detectives allowed the graffiti to remain. It made the others wonder what had happened to those who had come before them—and what likely was going to happen to them. Tommy could see Furrow's head snap up when he heard the slide of the door to the viewing port. They had left him handcuffed but had moved the cuffs to the front to give him some measure of comfort. There was no pad on the metal shelf that passed for a bunk. It wasn't intended to be comfortable and it wasn't. That was the whole point. Each small thing was designed to push the suspect off balance—the waiting, the silence, the bright light of the room and the persistent discomfort—all had a purpose.

Tommy jangled the keys, letting the sound echo through the steel door, and then he inserted the big brass key into the lock, throwing the bolt and turning the metal handle, pulling the door open. It was done slowly, allowing each sound to have its own distinctive peal. He stood outside the door looking in at Furrow. It was like looking at an animal caught in the headlights. He could see it in Furrow's eyes—fear, and maybe a hint of defeat. All useful. "Eugene, you want to come with me, please?" Tommy kept his voice warm and low-keyed, businesslike but not impersonal; with just a hint in his tone that he was someone who might listen, someone who might care. The man sitting on the metal bench didn't look like a cold-blooded murderer, but Tommy had seen too many murderers to be caught up in mistaking what they looked like for what they were.

Furrow rose slowly from the metal bench, his long hair falling in greasy strands around his face. Wisps of hair that made up a scraggly goatee and a mustache framed a thin-lipped mouth, the facial hair a dark smear against a sallow complexion. Furrow studied the detective standing in the steel frame of the cell door and threw his shoulders back, raising his chin in a gesture of defiance. Tommy observed Furrow's attempt at bravado, a contrived swagger. About five-foot-ten with a medium build, he had on blue jeans, a T-shirt, a black leather vest, and biker boots, the kind with the strap and buckle across the instep. Tommy had seen his kind before. He made an effort to look tough, but when it got down to it there was no hard-core there. Tommy would let him make his little show of bluster. All the air would be out of him when he sat down in the interrogation room.

They had left him in the clothes he was arrested in. They didn't want him to feel too much like an inmate. Put a man in an orange jumpsuit and he knew where he was and where he was staying. Leaving a man in his street clothes gives him a sliver of self-respect and a glimmer of life outside the cell; maybe, if he told the story right, they would let him go. It never ceased to amaze Tommy how many suspects held that slender hope hidden in their pocket when they left the holding cell and entered the interrogation room. It was probably a little like people felt during the French Revolution when they walked up the steps to the guillotine: "You never know, the blade might stick." Human nature allows us all to indulge in a little magical thinking; you just might get lucky. Tommy knew—although his suspects never did—their sliver of hope was also useful to him. If they believed that all it took was saying the right thing and then the detective would let them go, that hope might give them a reason to talk.

Tommy led Furrow into a room that was reserved for interrogations. The room was wired, but Furrow wouldn't see a microphone or a tape recorder. All he would see would be Tommy sitting across from him, measuring him and waiting.

"Eugene, or is it Lee? They call you Lee?"

"Lee, yeah, that's right. I never really liked Eugene." Furrow moved his hands up in front of his chest and rubbed his wrists, the short chain between the cuffs making a clicking sound as the links rubbed against one another.

"Have a seat right there." There were two chairs in the room. Tommy pointed to the chair with its back to the wall. He would take the one with its back to the door. Furrow looked around and sat down, pushing himself against the back of the chair and then sliding down a bit. Tommy remained standing for a moment, watching him. Body language can tell you a lot right at the beginning. If a man keeps himself erect and looks you in the eye, you know that he is waiting to see what you have, much like a man waiting for a fight. With a man like that, you have to circle for a while, trying to figure out what is the best way inside his defenses. With other men, their body sags a bit, and there isn't the tension in the back, the squaring of the body; it is a measure of resignation. With a man like that, you move inside smoothly and quickly, trying to get close. Furrow looked at Tommy and then looked down, staring at his cuffs. All of his bravado had been spent when he walked out of the holding cell.

"Cuffs bothering you?" Tommy asked, so he could make a gesture that would imply concern.

"Yeah, I'm not used to them, you know."

"Our records show you've been arrested before." It was a statement, not a question. If you do a custodial interrogation, you have to be careful not to ask a question that might call for incriminating information. You can talk to a suspect, maybe lay out what you know if it's beneficial, but you can't ask an incriminating question. If you ask an incriminating question before you read somebody their rights, you'll have a problem. Not only will you be unable to use the statement, it might also be interpreted as being responsible for any other statement that has been made during the entire interrogation. In legal jargon, incriminating questions are referred to as "fruit of the poisonous tree." It means that any evidence that is attributable to illegal conduct is not admissible. Unlike in television shows, when an officer reads people their rights as they are hooking them up with cuffs, in the real world you aren't constitutionally required to read anybody their rights until you ask a question that might be construed as calling for incriminating information.

Reading somebody their rights is a decision, and timing is everything. Read them their rights before you are ready to interrogate and you give them time to think. The law requires you to inform a suspect of his rights. The law doesn't require that you make every effort to encourage them not to talk. You talk to them for a few minutes and maybe you share with them why they are there and possibly a few of the facts that you know. Maybe you tell them that you have one side of the story but you don't know what their side is. You talk; you don't ask questions until you have a feel for the man in front of you. You read them their rights when you sense that there is a rapport, when you sense that they are ready to talk—when you are ready and they don't have a long time to think.

Lean wasn't quite ready to read Furrow his rights. "Let me take those cuffs off," he said, sympathetically. He reached over and held Furrow's wrist while he unlocked the cuff. He wasn't worried that Furrow would attack him. At this point, most suspects have already realized there is no way to escape and they also know that if they hurt a cop, there is no way that they won't end up in a bigger world of hurt than any damage they could possibly do to any cop who is waiting for them to make a move. After the cuffs were off, Furrow rubbed his wrists and laced his fingers, pulling back with his arms as his knuckles cracked.

"Thanks."

"No problem."

Furrow studied Tommy like he was trying to remember something. Finally, he spoke up. "Hey, I remember you. I know who you are. Didn't you used to play ball for Grossmont College in San Diego? You were a pitcher, right? I went to Grossmont, at least for a while. I used to come to some of the games; I saw you pitch. You were pretty good."

Tommy leaned back. It was a small world. Here was a guy who had once sat in the stands watching him play ball, and now look where they were, sitting across from one another, with no idea all those years ago during a ball game that their paths would cross like this. "That right? You watched me pitch? That was a long time ago."

"Yeah, long time ago. Guess things change, huh?"

"Yeah, that's for sure, Lee. Things change." Tommy could sense it. He could see the look in Furrow's eyes. Here was a man looking for somebody who would treat him with a little respect, a guy who desperately needed respect, wanted respect, but who couldn't earn it by himself. Most of the time, he got it from being a part of something that made other people afraid. Furrow was a follower. He needed some kind of approval. With this kind of guy, you just kept your voice low and slow. This guy was used to somebody else being the dominant wolf. Tommy's sense was that this was the role he needed to take, paternalistic but dominant.

"Look, Lee, by now, you know why you're here. You have been arrested for a 1974 murder. The girl was reported missing by her mother on November 6, 1974. Her name was Mary Sue Kitts—Mary Sue." Tommy drew out Mary Sue's name to personalize it. "She lived in Clovis. She was last seen with a man named Roger Allen. She left her parents' home in his car. That's what you've been arrested for." Tommy watched closely for any reaction.

At the sound of Mary Sue's name, Furrow lowered his head and slowly shook it from side to side in a gesture of resignation. "Yeah." He kept shaking his head from side to side, moving his hands up and down the thighs of his jeans. Tommy heard the friction of Furrow's hands against the denim, pressing hard against the fabric. Tommy saw beads of perspiration appear on the backs of Furrow's hands.

Tommy pushed forward to keep him talking, asking no incriminating questions, just building the kind of rapport that these moments required, before reading Furrow his rights. "When were you arrested?"

"This morning." Furrow's voice faded off into a mumble.

Furrow was beginning to move around uneasily in his seat. It was time to move forward, time to massage the conscience. "Okay, so before we talk further, being a suspect, I have to advise you of your constitutional rights." He never said it as if there was a choice. When you tell someone you are going to read them their rights, you say it in a way that assumes you are going to talk to the suspect and his rights are simply part of the conversation, something like telling somebody that the coffee is hot when you are offering him a cup.

"All right."

"And, all I'm interested in is the truth, okay?"

"All right." Furrow was watching Tommy, while he pushed his long hair back from his face, looking at Tommy with renewed alertness. Furrow was waiting for only one thing—what was going to happen to him. There was a strong smell coming from his body. Fear has its own smell. When you smell it enough you learn to recognize it.

"We're interested in the truth. You have the right to remain silent. Anything you say can and will be used against you in a court of law. You have the right to talk to a lawyer and have him present while you are being questioned. If you cannot afford to hire a lawyer, one will be appointed to represent you before any questioning, if you wish. You can decide at any time to exercise these rights and not answer any questions or make any statements." Tommy read from the department issued card, but he knew the rights by heart. Mostly, he was watching Furrow to see if his body tightened up as he heard his rights. When a man hears his Miranda rights being read to him, he knows that things are serious.

Tommy sensed that Furrow was ready for him to get through the ritual. "Do you understand these rights that I have just read to you?"

"Yes."

"Having these rights in mind, do you wish to talk to us now?"

"Yes," he replied, his voice barely a whisper. There it was. Now, you could ask him whatever you wanted. You just had to keep him talking. But it is a process. Sometimes, usually most times, they lie a little—or a lot. It's a mistake to think the suspect is stupid. Most suspects know that telling you the truth is not in their best interests. Even letting him lie to you is a good thing because eventually you will confront him with the lie, and then he will start to stumble. You keep them off balance, trying to get them to repeat the lie they told and trying to reconcile it as they inch closer and closer to some version of the truth that they think is most helpful to them, until you are ready to confront them with all their contradictions.

But there are those who do feel remorse. Every detective knows that for these types, talking makes them feel better. All you have to do is make one of these kind of guys want to talk. You have to make him feel that he is unburdening himself and you are just helping him. You start slowly, building up to the big question—keeping them talking as you let them know that you may be aware of more than you've let on. Without saying so, you're helping them think they will feel better if they just let it all out to you. Sometimes, you give them a few facts, just small things to get them started.

Tommy nodded at Furrow, a gesture that said this was the right thing to do. "Let me introduce you to some of the people that we know are involved, including yourself. Roger Dale Allen. Have you ever met Roger before?" Tommy would give him just enough information to let Furrow know he had some idea who was involved.

"Yeah, I know Roger."

"Okay. Clarence Ray Allen. Do you know him?"

At the mention of Clarence Allen's name, Furrow shifted his body, threw his head back, and looked up at the ceiling. "Yes."

Tommy took out a photograph from his folder. "I'm going to show you some old pictures, El Cajon pictures. This lady here. Do you know her?"

"Shirley."

"Shirley? You don't know her last name?"

"Shirley Doeckel."

"You know Barbara Carrasco?"

"Yeah."

Tommy decided it was time to push Furrow, who was fidgeting and looking around the room. "Like I said, truth is of the utmost importance; it's the best thing that you have going. Okay? That's all anybody is interested in. I'd like you to tell me what you know about this incident and the part you played in it and—like I said—all we're interested in is the truth and—and please, as you're telling me the story, tell me everything you know about what your part was, and we will go from there, okay?"

Furrow was rocking back and forth; his voice came out in a strained, high-pitch tone. "Can you help me?" His eyes were imploring Tommy; his feet were making a shuffling noise, the hard leather soles of his biker boots scraping back and forth against the linoleum. If he had looked down, he would have seen the wear pattern on the linoleum floor under his chair. Other shoes had scraped against the floor when other men had sat in the same chair, making the same plea.

Tommy paused and slowly closed the folder, resting in front of him before he looked up. He had heard this question many times before. "Can I help you?" Tommy repeated. "I'll do everything that I can possibly do to help you. I hope you don't feel angry toward me or any hostility toward me at all, because I have nothing against you. I have a job to do and I'm doing it the best way I know how. Okay?" He promised nothing specific. He shifted the subject to what was Furrow's moment of decision. He could feel the conscience throbbing in front of him. Furrow was on the edge. Tommy had merely told him that the only thing that would help him was the truth. But Tommy also knew that the truth could just as easily send Furrow straight to hell. That wasn't his problem. His job was to lead Furrow where he wanted him to go—to make him talk and talk until there was nothing more to say. He could sense the moment. Furrow would talk. The question was whether he would admit to murder. He kept his eyes on Furrow, watching to see if there was any hesitation. If he saw any sign of reluctance, Tommy knew that he had to say something, *anything*, to make sure there wasn't a gap—the silence that sometimes comes when the suspect is thinking about whether he should stop talking and ask for a lawyer. Furrow looked around and then opened his mouth.

"Okay."

Tommy kept his voice low and careful. He slid a picture of Mary Sue Kitts in front of Furrow and let it sit there while he watched Furrow stiffen up. "Do you know this girl?"

"Yeah." It was out; he would talk. The only question was how much and for how long.

"How did you know her?"

"I met her through Roger and Clarence Ray Allen."

"You remember when you met her?"

Furrow looked down at his hands. "Down in San Diego."

"Where in San Diego?"

Furrow sighed in that way that sounds like a person letting all of the air out of his body. "Chula Vista. It was a restaurant."

"Was there anybody with you at the time?"

Furrow started mumbling. Tommy backed off and went another direction. "Do you know what month that was in?"

Furrow shook his head. "No, it was around three years ago."

"Okay. She was reported missing by her mother in November of 1974. Had you met her before—maybe about a month before she disappeared?"

"It was a couple of weeks."

"So you met her down there, and Roger was present?"

Furrow shook his head. Tommy had to tell him to give an answer that would show up on tape, and then he asked who else had been present. Furrow named Clarence Ray Allen, Shirley Doeckel, Barbara Carrasco, and two other men whose names he didn't remember.

Tommy needed more specific information about the two other men. "Well, maybe you could describe them for me?"

"One guy's about six-foot-one, kind of got short brown hair. The other guy's about my height and kind of stocky. They're both white guys."

"Okay. Did they appear to work for Clarence Allen?"

"Yeah, for the security company, but I don't remember names. We were at this restaurant, and they wanted me to show them where there's some good shopping centers. So, I told them where they were at and then I went home. Later, I came back up to Fresno."

"Then what happened?"

"Then Allen took me on as a security guard. I was up there a day or so, and he hadn't put me to work yet, and that's when I learned about them ripping off that store here in Fresno."

Tommy slid the picture of Mary Sue Kitts forward so that it was directly in front of Furrow. "Do you know anything else about this girl? How did you know her? What name did you know her by?"

Furrow stared at the picture sitting on the table. His head kept bobbing up and down and he closed his eyes. His voice dropped down to a raspy sound. "I knew her as Mary. All I knew was Mary."

"Okay, so that is the picture of the girl that you remember?"

"Yeah."

"And then what happened?"

"And then we—we, ah—we were all swimming in the pool at Allen's house and he came out and said he wanted to talk."

"By Allen, you mean Clarence Ray Allen?"

"Yeah. The way I got it, this girl told the store owner's kid that Allen and another guy had ripped off the store. That's when Allen said, 'We're going to have to get rid of her.'"

Tommy leaned back in his chair. It wasn't like he hadn't heard cold-blooded decisions before, but this girl was just a kid. The tension on Furrow's face was beginning to show. Tommy couldn't give him time to stop and think about where the conversation was headed. "Was anyone else in on this conversation with you?"

"Yeah, the other two clowns."

"The other two men that you don't know their names?"

"Yeah, and then a couple of days later Barbara got put in jail and I went and collected the money and then I came back and she—that Mary girl—she was staying over at Shirley's."

"I'm going to show you some pictures of an apartment." Tommy reached into the folder while Furrow followed his hands as they removed a photograph. "Does that look like the apartment?"

"Yeah, that's the apartment."

Tommy could see that again Furrow was rubbing his hands on his jeans. Perspiration was streaming down his face and neck. The air in the room was thick with the smell of sweat. Tommy recognized the vacant expression on Furrow's face. It happens sometimes when men under interrogation stop listening and start to relive what had happened. Furrow was beginning to think back. His lips were pressed tightly together and his head pulled down against his neck, the veins on his neck and throat beginning to throb as his blood pressure increased. He needed to keep Furrow from freezing up. "Okay, and the girl was staying with Shirley at that apartment?"

"Yeah."

"And then what happened?" Furrow was looking around the room, crossing and uncrossing his arms. His face still had the vacant look. Tommy had seen it before; all of what had gone down that night was passing in front of Furrow's eyes. Tommy could only wait until he refocused.

Furrow closed his eyes and reopened them, squeezing them, pushing back the tears that were seeping out and trailing down his cheeks. He no longer saw Lean sitting across from him; he could only see images of that night passing in front of him. It was like it was happening all over again, only he was watching it inside his head.

It was getting dark and everybody was at the apartment. The girl, she was there. And Roger was there—no, Roger, he wasn't there. Where was Roger? He couldn't see Roger but Shirley was there and Clarence Ray was there. That bastard was there. And that guy that worked around the ranch, he was there, too. But it was the girl. He kept seeing the girl. And Clarence Ray, he kept seeing him in his mind. Clarence Ray wanted him to go outside. He said he wanted to talk. They went outside and Allen said that he had to kill that girl, and that when he got back, if she wasn't dead then he was going to kill them both. God, he was so scared. Just looking at Clarence made him scared. He could feel it all over again, the way he looked at him. Clarence Ray would have killed him if he didn't do it. He would have killed her, too. Didn't anybody understand that? And they just left them there, him and the girl. The two of them just sat and talked and he couldn't stop talking. He didn't know what to do. He didn't want to do it. How could he make people understand? He didn't want to hurt anybody. He wasn't a killer—but now he was. It was all that bastard Allen's fault.

Tommy let Furrow have a minute. He knew that Furrow was reliving his memory of that night. Furrow started rubbing his face, breathing heavily. Tommy tried to get his attention. "Lee, Lee. What happened next?"

Furrow was shaking. He didn't want anybody to see him cry but he couldn't help it. "They left me there, just her and me. He said he would kill me if I didn't do it. He said he would kill us both. I waited and then he called on the phone. He asked me what was going on. He said, 'I told you I want her taken care of'—either that or it was going to be me. He said if I didn't do it, he would kill me, too. I didn't know what to do. Shirley had given her some pills before they left. She told that girl we were going to party, but they were red pills, and I waited but nothing happened. Allen said he would kill me too. 'You better do it, friend,' he said. So I did it. I strangled her."

Tommy inhaled and slowly let his breath out. It was always like that when they crossed the line and admitted it. Even the tough ones—that was when they either got very calm as they began to unburden themselves or else their emotions welled to the surface and they began to cry. Sometimes they cried for what they had done. Most of the time they cried because of what they thought was going to happen to them, as they felt their life sliding down the drain. You couldn't have sympathy. You couldn't let them compose themselves. It wasn't about sympathy or compassion. It was about murder and Tommy's job was to prove it—with their own words if possible. He left the compassion for judges and juries. He had left all his compassion on the floors of too many dirty bars and blood-soaked carpets.

"You strangled her? With your hands and nothing else?"

Furrow's head dropped so low that his chin was touching his chest, his breath coming in shorter and shorter gasps. "I just strangled her." Furrow could see the girl right there in front of him.

She was in the front bedroom. She was standing at the end of the bed and he had grabbed her and started choking her. He kept choking her as she slid down to the floor. She didn't move. She kept looking at him. It was her eyes. She wouldn't close her eyes. He squeezed as hard as he could and she wouldn't close her eyes. He kept squeezing and pushing in with his hands, but she wouldn't fight. She kept looking at him, even when she was on the floor, even when he removed his hands from her throat. She was staring up at him but not moving.

"Lee, Lee." Tommy put more urgency into his voice. Furrow had drifted away again. Furrow was looking down at his hands. His voice was raspy and soft. "She looked dead. It was her eyes. She just kept staring at me. I can still see her eyes. I can't sleep nights sometimes because I still see her eyes staring at me." He was crying, wrenching sobs that shook his whole body.

For Tommy, seeing men cry in this room was not a new experience. Furrow was crying for what he had done. He had given up on himself a long time ago. He waited until Furrow tried to compose himself. "Okay, Lee, then what happened?"

Furrow was breathing more slowly, trying to gain control. He described Allen and another man putting the body in the trunk of Allen's Cadillac and driving to Allen's house while he and the other man followed. Then he described putting the body in the back of the Ranchero he was riding in and following Allen to the mountains where they dropped Mary Sue's body over the side of a bridge.

Tommy could see the guilt on Furrow's face and he could sense that Furrow was on the edge, but he needed the body. He kept his voice firm but he told Furrow he needed to help find the body. "I know it was dark. I know it was dark. Do you think about that girl's mother? You know for two and a half years now she has been sitting over in her home wondering where her daughter is. And, if we can find her and bring her back and give her a decent burial—I think it would be better for everybody, don't you?" Tommy kept his hand on the edge of Mary Sue's picture, moving it just slightly toward Furrow.

Furrow's shoulders were shaking. He had his arms wrapped across his chest. Tommy's comment about Mary Sue's mother had struck him like a board in the face. "I'm so sorry about the whole thing. I wouldn't have done it except—." He didn't finish.

Furrow was coming apart right in front of Tommy. He hadn't seen it happen so obviously as this but he had seen it before. He needed to back off. "If you want to cry, go ahead and cry. Go ahead."

Furrow looked up. His face and eyes were swollen. "What's going to happen?"

"What's going to happen to you? I don't know. I mean, I'm going to work with you, protect you, but you have to tell us all about it."

Furrow was shaking his head. "They'll kill me." Furrow stared at the ceiling. "It must be pretty nice to pray. I didn't want to do it. I was scared to death. I never met anybody that was crazy like these people." He began to mumble, once again rocking back and forth in the chair.

Tommy waited a moment before continuing. "Do you think you can help us find her?"

Furrow kept shaking his head. "All I know is there was a river or something. I couldn't see the water."

Tommy stood up. Furrow was now crying uncontrollably. Tommy started for the door, embarrassed for feeling pity for a man who had committed a grotesque murder, taking the life of a young girl who had barely lived. He knew it should not invoke pity in anyone, especially a cop. But Tommy did feel a degree of sorrow for Furrow and he could understand how frightened Furrow was. He could also see how a man like Clarence Ray Allen could terrify someone like Furrow. But Tommy also couldn't find it in himself to overlook what to him was a coward's choice. Furrow could have refused. He could have taken Mary Sue and run for it. No matter how you looked at it, Lee Furrow had killed a young woman, strangled her, to save his own life. But whatever Lee Furrow had done, it wasn't as evil as the man who made him do it, a man sitting just a few miles away in a Visalia jail, likely counting on a high-priced lawyer to get him off on a simple robbery, never giving a moment's thought to that girl and the man he coerced into killing her—yes, Allen was a man perfectly willing to kill anybody who got between him and getting away with robbery or murder.

Tommy took Furrow back to the holding cell and then stopped at the office next to the interrogation room, opened the door, and stepped inside. Blade was sitting there with his earphones on. He slipped them off. Tommy looked at him. "Did you get it?"

"Yeah, partner. We got it."

14

Like the Scales of a Snake

Sunday, March 27, 1977
Fresno, California

Blade and Tommy were in Sanger, a small rural community to the southeast of Fresno. It had its own police department, but the officers were very accommodating to the out-of-town detectives. They were used to sheriff's detectives coming in to assist on major investigations, although major investigations were actually very rare in Sanger. Blade and Tommy were tight-lipped. They asked only for an office and the use of a phone.

It was the day following the Furrow interrogation. Blade and Tommy had traveled to the country area near Allen's home in order to give the area a general look-see. It quickly became clear they weren't going to have any luck on their own finding anything remotely resembling the area where Mary Sue's body had been dumped. They hadn't really expected to find the location easily, so Blade decided to have Furrow transported to the Sanger police department. He wanted Furrow to go with them and point out the bridge. Furrow didn't arrive until early evening, but that wasn't a concern, as Furrow had seen the area in the dark and it would probably be easier for him to find it again in the dark.

Sheriff's Deputy John Hergenrader, who worked patrol in that sector, had been dispatched to the Sanger police department because of his familiarity with the area. Blade told Hergenrader that he wanted him and Detective Bill Lehman to take Furrow to look for a bridge where a body had been dumped. Hergenrader listened carefully to the description and suggested that the only place that fit all of the criteria was located a good twenty miles away near a small community called Piedra.

Furrow took a seat in the back of the unmarked car and watched from the window as Hergenrader and Lehman drove out the Kings Canyon road. It all looked the same, a lot of open space and a few low bridges over creeks and streams, but nothing like that night when he had followed Clarence Allen. *Whether the cops believed it or not, he was trying to help find her. There hadn't been a day when he hadn't thought about that night and saw himself standing on that bridge. He needed to do something to feel he had made up for it—at least as much as he could. He knew nothing was going to change his responsibility for what happened that night, but maybe it would help him feel better.* He settled into the seat, his handcuffs making a metallic sound as he moved around to look out of the window. He knew it might be a long time before he would see this much open space.

Furrow watched his breath fog the window. It was late March, but it was still cold outside, especially out in the foothill area. The road serpentined back and forth near the river and then away as it worked its way into the foothills. There was enough moonlight to catch the glistening of the river water, but nothing could be heard over the sound of the car. Branches of ancient valley oak trees extended over the road, hanging down in the dark like shadowy claws, but all you could really see was darkness. Furrow assumed that not many people lived out there, or if people did live there, they had no lights on. Furrow leaned forward again. "I think this is right. It looks the same. I remember the river was on the right and the road was really winding around. Allen was moving pretty fast, like he had been on the road before a lot of times; he didn't slow down except when the curve was real sharp. I remember that—and it was pitch black out. If you didn't know where you were going, you couldn't drive that fast."

They reached the Piedra Road turn just outside of the town, if you could call Piedra a town. Furrow sat back in the seat. "Yeah, this is it. I'm pretty sure. I don't think it's much farther up this road."

A little less than four miles after the turn, Furrow's voice came from the backseat. "The bridge, it's just ahead, I think."

Hergenrader pulled over across the oncoming lane into an access road just short of the bridge. He turned in and then backed around so his lights shined out onto the roadway. There was no traffic. No lights other than the headlights and the silvery sheen cast by the moon illuminated the area, but these caught the sweeping movement of the tall grass growing on either side of the canal, which had been dug into the low foothills.

Detective Lehman and Deputy Hergenrader got out and opened the rear door, which couldn't be opened from the inside. Furrow swung his body around and stepped out of the car with a little help. He had cuffs on and couldn't use his hands to balance himself. Furrow looked down at his cuffs and then up at Lehman. Detective Lehman nodded to Hergenrader, who took off the cuffs—there wasn't anywhere to go out here and they all knew it.

The night was silent, except for the crunch of the gravel under their feet and the low sound of rushing water far below them. The men stood quietly, waiting for someone to break the silence. Furrow walked to the edge of the roadway and looked back at the two officers. "When we got here, to the bridge, Allen blinked his lights on and off so we'd know we were here. He parked his Cadillac about right here, in this dirt area, where we are."

They looked down at the gravel-covered roadway, realizing that on another night a yellow Cadillac Eldorado had sat in the same spot, waiting like some night predator, its eyes glowing in the moonlight. Furrow walked back toward the car and looked across the canal. "Allen and Shirley waited while Chuck and me drove onto the bridge. That's where we did it; we threw her over the side."

Lehman walked across the roadway to the upstream side. From the top of the bridge to the water below looked to be at least eighty or one hundred feet. It was hard to tell, because standing at the rail and looking down would give anybody vertigo. You didn't want to look straight down. It was easier to look along the length of the canal and watch the flow of the icy water. There was nothing around for a mile at least and very little for several miles. It was not lost on Lehman that you would have to know where this place was if you wanted to do what was done there that night. Lehman stepped back from the barrier and walked silently over to the car.

Furrow was staring down the steep embankment at the water moving through the canal. The water glittered like the scales of a snake undulating in the moonlight. He could hear the sound of the grass swishing lightly against the faint movement of air—just like that night when the searing valley heat had reduced it to the brittleness of straw. The crunch of his footsteps at the edge of the bridge brought it back to him and he closed his eyes to the image, but it was there still.

He could hear the silence of his own voice, saying nothing, protesting nothing, as the other man ordered him to hurry. He heard again the slight rustle of the blanket as it rubbed for a moment against the cement wall, and then in his mind there was only the sound of rushing air as gravity drew her down into the icy arms of the rushing water, and her silent scream that had come back to him again and again in so many sleepless nights—and now it came again as he looked down once more at the glistening blackness below.

Furrow shook the image from his mind, pushing it back as far as he could. He didn't turn around when he spoke. His words were uttered into the darkness. "Chuck Jones parked the Ranchero on the bridge and I helped him lift her from the back of his car, you know, the truck bed. She was wrapped in a blanket and there was six big stepping stones wired on her body. She was way too heavy for one guy to lift over the rail. We had trouble carrying her. He got her head and I got her legs and we pushed her up on the rail and shoved her over." Furrow pointed to the rail on the upstream side of the bridge. "I didn't hear anything for a long time. I know it wasn't that long, but it seemed long, you know? It was just a long time and then I heard like a splash. That was it. I didn't stay there and look. I walked back and got into Chuck's car. Allen pulled out and we followed him and Shirley along the road for a couple of miles until we came to that other road, Kings Canyon, I guess. Then we went back to Shirley's."

Furrow wiped his hand across his face. He walked back to the car and stood at the door until Lehman came over and opened it. He was silent throughout the trip back to the jail. Nor was there any conversation between the detectives. Each man was lost in the darkness of his own thoughts, thoughts which blended with the blackness of the night, and with the image of the glittering water below the bridge.

15

The Weakest Link

Monday, March 28, 1977
Fresno, California

District Attorney Investigator Willie "Bill" Martin sat in the sheriff's detective's office, listening as Blade and Tommy filled him in on the information they had gotten from Carrasco and Furrow. Martin had been made aware of the ongoing investigation by the district attorney, Bill Smith. He had wondered how long it would be before Blade finally called him. But he had been patient. He had worked homicide too many years at the sheriff's office not to know that the detectives didn't like calling in the D.A. or his investigators until they had to, even guys they had used to work with like himself. It was more than their fear that just too many cooks would spoil the soup; it was a combination of competition and turf protection.

On scene detectives knew that when the D.A. got involved, they were going to start getting directions from one more level of Monday-morning quarterback, or worse, from some fuzz-butt young deputy D.A. who would start trying to run the investigation, because he had seen too many episodes of "Dragnet" or "Hawaii Five-O." Fortunately, Bill had been a homicide detective. For a period of time, he had been the third man working with Tabler and Blade, until he had left to join the D.A.'s office. Not only did he know what he was doing around a homicide case, he also knew his place now. They had called *him*, so he wasn't interfering. But he had no illusions why they had called—they needed the district attorney's money.

Blade finished relating the facts and background of the case. He watched Bill's expression, which had always been difficult for him to read. Martin rubbed his mustache and sighed. "So, Blade, what we've had here is a failure to communicate." Blade looked over at Tommy, who broke out laughing.

Blade's expression remained blank so Tommy explained, "It's from a movie. You know, Paul Newman, in *Cool Hand Luke*?" Blade didn't watch movies unless they had John Wayne in them. *Cool Hand Luke* wasn't registering.

Bill laughed. "Just jerking your chain, man. I been filled in on the background. Just been waiting for you to call. The D.A. says to give you any help we can, so I'm here to do that, okay?" Bill focused on Blade and he waited for Blade to accept the acknowledgment that he, Blade, was still in charge of the investigation. "Looks like we got to make some arrests, so where do we start?"

Blade, his confidence restored, settled himself more comfortably into his chair, rocking back on the rear two legs. "My thinking? We go after Allen's girlfriend, Shirley Doeckel, and then we take down Mayfield and Jones."

Bill considered the proposal. "So, do you know where they are?"

Tommy broke into the conversation. "Mayfield works here in Fresno at a plumbing outfit. Doeckel is in Visalia. We got Jones tracked down. He's in Porterville, just south. We've talked to the detectives working the Visalia 211. They suspect Doeckel let Allen and his boys use her apartment to plan the robbery down there. According to them, she's the manager of a smorgasbord restaurant. Her apartment is right across the street from the Kmart. Allen and his boy, Roger, are in custody, so at least we don't have to worry about them. The Visalia P.D. wants our help in getting Doeckel to agree to a search of her apartment. So the question is which one first, Doeckel or Mayfield?"

Sometimes making the decision as to who to interrogate first is the most important decision made in a case. If you pick the suspect you think will crack the easiest, you can use the information you get from the weak link against the others. Sometimes you can get somebody to break just because others have already talked. You use everything you have against the toughest. If they think others have already broken, they may decide not to fight all by themselves.

The detectives knew playing Furrow off against the others might not turn out to have much impact. It would be his word against theirs. You need to work your way up the food chain, find the person who is least involved and get that person to talk. Usually, any suspect is only too happy to tell you what somebody *else* did. It is said that "There's no honor among thieves." That only means that the finger pointing starts early and the finger is always pointed away from the person doing the pointing. Sooner or later, you're going to have to make deals in order to get testimony, because every suspect is usually criminally involved to some degree. How you're going to get that information and how it's going to look in court is your next decision. Juries typically aren't pleased when it appears the witness is getting a deal because he won the race to the courthouse to turn over others. The reality is that sometimes you have to let some of the little fish get away in order to get the big fish. The trick is to let as few of the guilty parties get away as possible. Mayfield, according to Furrow and Carrasco, probably had the least to do with this deal, and there wasn't much to tie him to the murder.

"I would say we pick up Mayfield first," Bill said to Blade, being careful to make sure it didn't sound like an order. "He seems the least involved, at least so far, and we can probably take him without much problem. Word won't get out that we have him and we can hold him here if we have to; that is, if we decide to hold him at all. But Doeckel is a different problem. We can't hold a woman here without putting her into the jail. So, I think we get Mayfield and squeeze him before we go after her. My guess is she's going to be tougher to break, but you guys have been following up on her, so it's your call."

Blade leaned forward, bringing his chair down squarely onto the floor. "Yeah, I agree. We take Mayfield, and then we take Doeckel and Jones." It was agreed: Mayfield was the weak link, and they would go after Mayfield first and then risk letting him go after he talked—unless, of course, he put himself in the middle of the murder. It was a strategy that had to be considered and it was a risk that had to be accepted.

Blade grinned. "Now we need somebody to supervise out at the canal, while the arrests are being made." He looked at Tommy, who just shrugged. It wasn't hard to figure out what was coming. Somebody had to make sure that evidence was properly tagged and bagged at the canal; that is, if any evidence could be found.

Bill looked over at the young detective. "I'll go out with you and take a look around." Tommy smiled his appreciation. Bill didn't have to go.

After an hour of driving from the sheriff's office, Tommy stood on the edge of the Piedra Bridge, looking down into the dark, green water that looked to be at least seventy-five to a hundred feet below. The canal cut deeply into the rising foothills. It was intimidating in the daylight, and Tommy couldn't imagine what it was like at night. The sides of the canal rose steeply to ledges along the edge where piles of rock and debris from past dredging operations were scattered. The footing was treacherous.

Watching while the sheriff's divers prepared their equipment to enter the water, Lean didn't hold out much hope. It had been several years. Maybe they would find some bones, or, if they were lucky, some debris from the blanket the girl had been wrapped in. Probably, they would find nothing. Any current would carry the body, whether it was above or below the surface. And if the current was slow and the body couldn't move as a result of the weights attached to it, over time both the blanket and the body would have dissolved, leaving nothing but the wire, the stone weights, and water-washed bones. Chances were that Mary Sue Kitts' remains had just washed away over time, the rushing water slowly carrying her downstream bit by bit, just as rushing water slowly erodes the largest stone to a grain of sand. The best Tommy could hope for was to find bones that were identifiable as human—and maybe, if he got very lucky, to find one of the weights used to sink the body.

The plan was simple. Sheriff's divers would enter the water and look for physical evidence, while Lean would supervise a recovery team that would walk along the ledge, searching for anything that looked like a bone or other piece of evidence. If they had no luck in the search, they would start going through the dredge piles, rock by rock.

Tommy couldn't help thinking about the last night of Mary Sue's life. She had made mistakes; that was for sure. But she certainly hadn't deserved this fate. He stared out at the water. The concrete sides of the canal were visible from the heights down about five or six feet to where the sides disappeared into the watery blackness. He looked at the barrier on the roadway. She had been pushed over the side of the bridge and fallen through the night air into that inky water. Tommy shuddered just looking at the drop from the edge to the rippling surface below. Mary Sue had been only nineteen and he was not even ten years older than she had been. For a nineteen-year-old girl, ten years was a lifetime. He wasn't so far removed that he couldn't remember what life had been like at nineteen, with everything ahead of him.

Now, nothing lay ahead for Mary Sue Kitts, and only her parent's grief was left behind. This was Tommy's job, to try to bring something back for them to bury. He sighed. If he could give them nothing, nothing to bury, all they would ever have would be their questions about what had happened to their little girl. Tommy could feel the hair stand up on his arms as the thought of it crossed his mind. Clarence Ray Allen had taken all happiness away from Mary Sue's family, and he had taken everything away from Mary Sue. Tommy turned from the edge of the bridge and walked over to where the diving crew had gathered.

16

"We rob and steal and those who squeal ..."

Monday, March 28, 1977
Fresno, California

M r. Ardaiz, please report to Mr. Smith's office." I had just arrived at my office in the Fresno County district attorney's office building when I heard my name being paged over the PA system.

I was almost three years out of law school—the University of California, Hastings College of the Law, to be specific. Normally, it would take at least three or more years before a deputy district attorney would get to handle major cases, but I had been lucky. I had gained a reputation as a "law guy"—a lawyer who could make strong legal arguments on difficult issues. As far as I was concerned, there was no better job in the world except to be chief of homicide, but that was way beyond any expectation I had at the moment.

When my name came across the public address system to report to the district attorney, I knew it could only be one of two things, either really good or really bad. It was similar to the feeling you get in high school when your name comes over the PA system to report to the principal, and, I must admit that the few times that had happened to me, it had never been good news. I wasn't so sure this was going to be good news, either. I also had a reputation, undeserved as far as I was concerned, for doing things "my way," regardless of whether it was the way my bosses wanted things done. So far, I had been lucky and things had always worked out, but that didn't change the fact that I knew I had stretched the tolerance point of my bosses on a number of occasions. Since I wasn't known for my warm disposition or my humility—again undeserved as far as I was concerned—I didn't have confidence that my good nature would get me by. No matter how many times I promised myself that I would do exactly as I was supposed to, the reality was that I didn't. I just couldn't help it. It didn't make any difference; I couldn't change what I had done. The problem was that this time I didn't know what I had done, so there was no opportunity to come up with a passable explanation.

Inside the D.A.'s office was the district attorney, Bill Smith, the assistant district attorney, Steve Henry, several men in plain clothes whom I didn't recognize but who were obviously cops, Bill Martin, the homicide investigator for the D.A., and two detectives I did recognize, Art Christensen, generally known as "Blade"—except to me he was Detective Christensen—and Detective Tom Lean. Everybody looked directly at me and Christensen and Lean did not look happy. Just the expression on Christensen's face and the fact that I had been summoned into the district attorney's office, with Christensen sitting there, did not give me any reassurance. Art Christensen and his former partner, Art Tabler, were legendary in the sheriff's office as homicide detectives. If I had made Christensen mad, then I had really done something bad. Mentally, I ran through my last several cases, trying to think of what I might have done wrong and who I had pissed off, when the district attorney turned to the plain-clothed detectives I didn't recognize and said, "Gentlemen, this is Jim Ardaiz; he will be working on your case." He looked at me and said, "Jim, these detectives are from the Visalia police department; they have a search warrant that Steve Henry helped prepare and it's been signed. Your assignment is to work with them and help with the search."

Aside from the obvious sigh of relief because I wasn't in trouble, I immediately moved over and shook hands, eager to find out what was going on. That was when the district attorney asked the Visalia officers if they would excuse us for a few minutes while he talked to me. I looked around the room; Christensen still had the same look on his face. He was definitely pissed.

District Attorney Bill Smith was normally what you would call "a good ol' boy." He had come up the hard way and he had rough edges, but he was what attorneys would call "a natural courtroom lawyer." Bill could charm a jury; legal arguments weren't his strong suit, reading people was. He wasn't pretentious and, if he wasn't mad, he had a warm personality. If Bill was mad, there was nothing warm about him. I had been at the receiving end of his temper on several occasions, and I didn't want to be at that receiving end again, especially in front of others. But Bill also knew his politics; sometimes, you had to take the heat in front of police and sheriffs if you screwed up. Sometimes, the heat fell on Bill and sometimes it rolled downhill. It was part of making sure the cops didn't think "the suits" got away with "screw-ups," even though they would always think that all lawyers stuck together. Since Christensen was glowering at me and I was definitely "downhill" when it came time to hand out blame, I had no reason to think I wasn't the one who was going to get the heat. I waited quietly, knowing I had no control over what was coming next.

The district attorney smiled at me, as did the assistant district attorney. That was definitely a good sign. Bill didn't smile at you before he stuck the knife in. It was a mark of character with him. If he was going to stick it to you, he did it right to your face, never in the back, and he didn't smile when he did it. "Jim, you are going to be assigned to work on a case that is just starting to turn. We have a murder case involving a man named Clarence Ray Allen, a real asshole. This is a difficult case. Get up to speed on it with Detective Christensen here and Detective Lean. Keep me informed of what's going on."

That was it. Nobody mentioned to me that they didn't have a body yet and nobody told me that Art Christensen was absolutely pissed that some "wet behind the ears kid" had been assigned to one of the biggest cases Christensen had ever handled. Of course, I wouldn't find out about what Christensen really thought until later when the assistant district attorney told me, but looking at Blade at the time, it wasn't hard to figure out that he wasn't pleased about something.

As for me, I was very pleased. Thrilled, in fact. The chief of homicide assigned the "Saturday night specials." The big cases were assigned directly by the district attorney himself. That meant this was a big case, a major homicide. I would have said it was "a serious murder case," but that is hard for people to understand. Everybody thinks all murder cases are "serious," and they are, but there is the "Saturday night" variety of homicide that gets reported in the local news section of the paper, and then there are the homicides that spill ink across the front page. This was a case that would spill ink by the gallon. I just didn't know it—yet. Looking back on it now, I had no inkling that it would intertwine with the next thirty years of my life.

I walked down the hall to my office with detectives Christensen and Lean following behind. After they sat down, eyeing the mess of paper on my desk, I leaned back in my chair and addressed the two detectives. "So, tell me about the Allen case."

Later, I learned that Blade had raised hell with the district attorney when he found out I had been assigned the case, and he even went all the way to the sheriff himself to have him intercede with the district attorney. Of course, I didn't know that at the time, and I also found out later that the sheriff, who had seen my work on other cases, told Blade to calm down and see what I could do. As I reflect now on that day, it's evident that as far as Detective Christensen was concerned, I couldn't do anything, and he had already decided that wasn't going to change with time. Lean, with his Hawaiian shirt and willingness to offer an occasional smile, was, I decided, my best bet in the friend department.

Given Blade's evident unfriendliness, I decided to ride with District Attorney Investigator Pete Major, assigned to the search team. Blade and Bill Martin left to handle arrest issues and Lean took the lead for the Fresno search team. The first place we headed was the home of Roger Allen and his wife. Both Allens were in custody on the Visalia robbery, about which I was just getting the details. It was almost 3:00 in the afternoon and nobody answered the door. The officers leading the search team rang the doorbell and knocked loudly. This is standard procedure when executing a search warrant. It is required by law except in an emergency. The whole idea is to ensure that officers don't come bursting through a door and get shot by someone who doesn't realize they are police officers. The knock and notice is only intended as a warning; it isn't intended to give the occupant time to dress and get ready for company, nor is it intended to give time to destroy evidence.

When nobody answered, we went through the rear double doors. "Went through" is an appropriate description. After they were opened, they would require a repair man to close them. If people inside don't answer when you knock, you go through prepared for any possibility. After four years of college and three years of law school, I stood back and watched the process. I had no intention of being the first person through. Besides, I hadn't been invited.

The search of Roger's house uncovered a clip and ammunition to the .45 automatic that had been seized when Roger's wife was arrested. A green rubber glove was found in the dresser. Room keys from the Holiday Inn in Visalia, as well as twelve other motel keys, were seized. We even seized the bath towels in the bathrooms—they were also from the Holiday Inn.

It was 4:20 in the afternoon and I was happy when we finally got to Clarence Allen's home. Another investigator had been waiting there, watching the place. The same knock and notice process was used. Nobody answered. The Visalia officer went to the back of the house where the stables were located while the rest of us stood near the front door.

I remember thinking that this was a really nice home. I was standing there waiting when Tommy Lean said, "Kick in the door."

With my refined legal education and acute awareness of search procedure, based on hours of text book study, I responded, "No, let's wait. This is a nice house. We don't want to smash through these doors if it isn't necessary." I remember that Tommy stared at me and shook his head in disbelief. But, we waited. We waited until we began to smell smoke. It was coming from inside.

This time Tommy said, "Kick the goddamn door!" I got out of the way. When it was safe for me to go inside, I followed the commotion and the smoke. Clarence Allen had a young wife. She was in the bathroom burning paper and trying to flush it down the toilet when the door was finally kicked open. I had delayed the entry when Tommy's instincts told him that we needed to go through immediately. I could hardly look anyone in the face. Tommy was the only one who would look at me and he didn't say anything; he just shook his head again. My first big search and I was responsible for an attempt to destroy evidence. I retreated to the living room.

Mrs. Allen requested to speak to an attorney. She was given the opportunity to make a phone call. I was given the job of talking to her lawyer. I guess they decided I couldn't screw that up. I decided it was probably not a good time for me to make any more legal observations or give any advice. They seemed to be doing fine without my input.

Officers recovered more towels from the Holiday Inn. Like father, like son. I opened the drawers of a credenza in the family room. Inside were numerous sheets of paper with writing on them, obviously penned by Clarence Allen. It seemed that Allen fancied himself a poet and he had written about what he knew best, robbing and stealing. He had also written about killing people "who squealed." I looked at one of the pages, entitled "Allen Gang":

> Ray and his sons are known as the Allen Gang.
> Sometimes you have often read

how we rob and steal and for those who squeal
are usually found dying or dead.
The road gets slimmer and slimmer
and at times it is hard to see,
but we stand like a man
robbing every place we can,
because we know we'll never be free.
Someday it will be over
and they will bury us side by side.
To some it will be grief,
but to us it's relief
knowing we finally found a safe place to hide.

I called the detectives over and they started pulling out more sheets of paper, all covered with Allen's handwriting.

Finally I got a nod from Tommy Lean. I think he decided there was hope for me yet. Thank God that Blade wasn't there. He was with Bill Martin out handling arrests of people whose names I didn't know at the time, but would become very familiar with in the near future: Mayfield, Doeckel, and Jones. That little piece of "poetry" would prove important, but I will also never forget the lesson I learned standing outside that front door.

I returned to the district attorneys office, figuring that now the case would go to a more senior attorney and I would no longer be asked for my advice. I figured that Lean and Blade and Clarence Allen were names that would fade in my bank of memories. Certainly, I wasn't going to be asked for my advice about entry into houses. I felt terrible. I had failed in the field because of lack of experience and I had interfered in what was appropriately a decision to be made by a sheriff's officer. I wasn't used to failing and I didn't like to feel embarrassed. I went home that night and decided that if given another chance, I wouldn't make either mistake again, but I didn't know if that chance would come. I will never forget that Tommy didn't find it necessary when he wrote the reports to explain my role in the delayed entry into Allen's home. As it turned out, I was right about not being asked for my advice for a while. However, time would prove me wrong about whether I would again cross paths with Clarence Ray Allen or Blade and Tom Lean.

17

"If I was guaranteed protection …"

Wednesday, March 30, 1977
Fresno, California

While I had been out giving advice to sheriff's officers about appropriate search procedures, Bill Martin, and Blade had been preparing to make the arrest of Carl Mayfield, a name that would ultimately become familiar to me but meant nothing at the moment.

Blade and Martin confirmed that Mayfield worked for a plumbing company in Fresno. They drove to the office of the plumbing company, backed by a unit from the sheriffs department, just in case. Hopefully, Mayfield wasn't expecting anybody to show up at his workplace about the Kitts murder.

Mayfield was working in the back when the two detectives arrived. Blade showed his badge to the woman working the counter and asked for Carl Mayfield. She saw the gold star in the leather badge holder and she started to ask what they wanted, but she never finished her question. She realized the men in front of her didn't look like they were there for a friendly visit and she told them where to find Mayfield in the supply yard.

When they found him, Mayfield was moving pipe. He looked just as he had been described, tall and skinny; maybe raw-boned would be more accurate. The short sleeves on his shirt were slightly rolled up, tightening the sleeve against ropy muscles. His dark blond hair was combed into a greased pompadour, with a curl falling down from the widow's peak. It was a fifty's hairstyle that had seen its day. When they approached him, he seemed surprised and then resigned when Blade showed him his badge and told him what they wanted to talk about. He nodded like he had known that someday they would come and now they were here. All he said was that he wouldn't give them any trouble. He didn't.

Blade and Martin had made a decision before picking up Mayfield. They would feel him out. If he was cooperative, they weren't going to arrest him and they weren't going to advise him of his rights. There was a risk to the strategy. If they didn't advise him of his rights and the questioning could be legally perceived as custodial in nature—that he wasn't free to go at any time—then nothing he said could be used against him. On the other hand, they couldn't link Mayfield to the crime without Furrow, and maybe Carrasco. But they needed more than Furrow and Carrasco to testify against Ray Allen. Mayfield looked like the weak link. If they could get him to cooperate, they would have an additional witness that could be used against Clarence Ray Allen and Shirley Doeckel.

It was almost 3:00 P.M. by the time Blade and Martin got back to the sheriff's office with Carl Mayfield. They hadn't cuffed him and they didn't intend to. They let him sit in the back of the car until they got to the office, and then they walked with him to the detective interrogation room. When they had initially approached him, Bill told Mayfield that they just wanted to talk, that they knew he had information involving the case, and that if what they had heard was true, it could all probably be worked out. Of course, how it could be worked out was not something Bill discussed in detail. He always approached a suspect as if he could clear everything up if the suspect would just talk to him. Most suspects believed this and, for some of them, it even turned out to be true. It was just Martin's style. Even most of the people he arrested liked him. Not all, but most. He said it was a gift.

Bill directed Mayfield to a chair and sat down across from him behind a desk. Blade sat to the side so that he could watch Mayfield but wouldn't be the focus of Mayfield's attention. It was clear that Mayfield was a good, ol' boy who had been raised in hard times around cotton fields and oil fields. Most people like that had been around black people much of their life. They didn't necessarily like black people, but they were used to them. Chances were Mayfield wouldn't view Bill as the cop, but he definitely would view Blade as the cop. It was a judgment call. Bill would do the interview and Blade would be the one who would wade in because Mayfield would probably expect the white cop to be in charge. Bill didn't care. As far as he was concerned, when you got what you wanted, you had nothing to prove to anybody.

Blade placed a tape recorder down on the desk and flipped the switch.

Bill smiled and opened his notebook. He never really took notes during an interview, but the fact that it looked like he was writing things down made people nervous, and he used the distraction to his advantage. "Would you state your name, please?"

"Carl Walter Mayfield—M-A-Y-F-I-E-L-D."

"How old are you, Mr. Mayfield?"

"I'm thirty-one."

"Can you just give me a past—a little, short history on your prior arrests?"

Mayfield sat back in the chair and sighed. It wasn't the first time he had been asked this and he knew it wouldn't be the last. He had done joint time in Florida, Texas, and California for robbery and forgery. He was still on parole in California.

Mayfield looked at Blade with a questioning expression. What he was being asked about could cause a problem with his parole. Blade narrowed his eyes. He didn't give any indication one way or the other.

Mayfield turned his face back toward Bill when Bill asked another question.

"It is our understanding from our investigation that at one time you had a job as a security officer?"

"Yeah, that's right."

"Who did you work for?"

"Ray Allen Security Patrol."

"When you went to work for Ray Allen, was he aware of your prior arrest record?"

"Yeah, I believe he was." Mayfield indicated he had worked for Allen for almost two years. Bill decided to move right to the burglary of Fran's Market. Moving abruptly to areas of lesser culpability often starts the slow slide into admitting major culpability. Bill told Mayfield that they knew about the safe and the money orders taken. He asked if Mayfield had been involved? What did he know? Bill asked in a way that implied he certainly wasn't asking the question because he didn't already know the answer.

Mayfield looked at Blade again and then back at Bill. He sat there for a moment, thinking about his options. In fact, there really weren't any. He had done the burglary and he knew about the murder but he hadn't done it, at least he hadn't done any murder to his way of thinking. He wasn't stupid. He had been questioned before and he knew if the detectives had enough to pick him up for questioning, then they had enough to know what happened. As far as he was concerned, he didn't owe Allen anything. Mayfield's thoughts were a jumble of contradictions. He didn't like to think of himself as a snitch. But this wasn't informing on someone for a two-bit burglary; this was murder and he wasn't a murderer, a thief maybe, but not a murderer. He sniffed and looked over Bill's head, avoiding his gaze. "There was a swimming pool party at Allen's home, at which time the owner's son was invited down to the house."

"Excuse me. That is the owner of Fran's Market?"

"Yeah. His son. He went into a room and changed into his swimming trunks. And it was then that someone entered the room and took the keys to the store out of his pocket. Later on, I don't remember the time, but it was getting dark, I went over by Allen's house. I believe I met him outside. We drove down to the market."

Mayfield filled in the details that Ray Allen opened the door with the key and Chuck Jones got a horse trailer to carry the safe. Jones and Allen put the safe in the trailer and drove away. He, Mayfield, got $200 and Allen took the money orders for himself.

Bill listened carefully. Mayfield was in. He had implicated himself. Now it was time for Bill to draw him in deeper with a question about San Diego. Mayfield admitted that he had helped pass the checks in San Diego, along with Ray Allen, Shirley Doeckel, Roger Allen, and a young woman whose name he couldn't remember. "I think she was a past or present girlfriend of Roger Allen."

Bill glanced at Blade. The communication between them was almost imperceptible. They would go straight to the murder. Mayfield was ready. "Did you have an occasion to be present when there was conversation between some people regarding a girl that was a problem that they needed to do something about?"

Mayfield straightened in his chair, closed his eyes, and sealed his mouth tightly, the corners of his lips turning down. He then opened his eyes and stared off to the side, wiping his nose with the back of his hand. Bill gave him a moment and waited for an answer. "Yeah." There was resignation in his voice. Bill knew that Mayfield just wanted to get it over with.

Mayfield hesitated and then shook his head, accepting that he would have to admit that he was present when the subject of what to do with Mary Sue Kitts came up. Mayfield said that he had been at Ray Allen's house. Lee Furrow and Chuck Jones were also there. "It was brought up by Ray Allen that he thought that the girl should be taken care of." Mayfield's words hung in the air for several seconds that seemed interminable, while each of the three men weighed the word in their minds.

Bill cut through the heavy silence. "Did he use those words 'taken care of'? In your own mind at that particular point, what did you think he meant by that remark?"

Mayfield's voice came out in a low rush of sound. "That the girl should be killed."

"Did you have an occasion that same day, or at a later date, to have a conversation with Eugene Furrow, the person you refer to as Lee?"

"Yeah. That he was the one that was to take care of the girl."

Bill glanced over at Blade. "Furrow told you that he was the one who was to take care of the girl?"

"That's correct. He said, well I think that he used the words, he 'had been chosen.'"

"Chosen to do what?"

"To take care of the girl." Mayfield's voice was now a dull monotone. Whatever Furrow was saying, he could still picture it in his mind.

"And did you see that girl at any time after that?"

Mayfield shook his head, looking down at the floor. "No, I didn't."

"Did you have a later occasion to talk to Furrow?"

"Yeah." He admitted that he had asked Furrow about it and he said he had killed the girl.

"Did you ever talk to Allen about what happened to Lee? Did you know whether Lee left Fresno or anything?"

"Yeah, I asked Allen if he had seen Lee, and he told me that he was no longer around and I asked him if he went back home. And he says, 'He's no longer around. I took care of him and sent him down to Tijuana.'"

"And what did you take that to mean?"

"I took it to mean that he had killed him. He said that it could be very easily done in Tijuana, either by paying an officer down there $25.00 to go out to the dump and you kill him, or paying the officer $50.00 and going to the dump and the officer would do it."

Bill looked at Blade to see if he wanted him to ask anything more. Blade shook his head. He was satisfied for the time being. Bill stared at Mayfield, and then asked him if he would testify against Clarence Ray Allen.

Mayfield stayed silent for several seconds, looking at the ceiling and at any place in the room where he was not looking into the eyes of Bill or Blade. Finally, he looked Bill squarely in the face. "I would if I was guaranteed protection."

"You have a fear that Allen would do something to harm you or contract someone out to try to harm you or your family?"

Mayfield's voice was very subdued. "Yes, I do."

After Mayfield had left the interrogation room, Bill and Blade sat in silence. Finally, Blade shook his head, a satisfied expression on his face. Bill took the tape out of the recorder and put it into an envelope. "You want to hold onto the tape or me."

Blade held out his hand. "I'll keep it with me until we're ready to make reports." Bill laughed. Blade never changed. He didn't trust anybody except his partners. They would have to wait and see what Tommy turned up.

Tommy was still out at Piedra looking for bones. Somebody had to run that part of the investigation and Tommy had drawn the short straw. Actually, Tommy was the only one who got a straw. Neither Blade nor Bill Martin had any enthusiasm about digging through piles of garbage looking for what was left of a body. Sometimes, seniority counts for something.

The divers had searched the canal bottom as carefully as they could. Fortunately, the water wasn't moving as fast as it would be at the beginning of the heavy snow melt. Anything underwater that looked like it might have value had been photographed with an underwater camera, retrieved, and sealed in plastic bags. The divers had searched a quarter of a mile upstream and downstream from the bridge. A few bone fragments had been recovered, but they had quickly been identified as animal bones. Nothing else had been found. It wasn't surprising. Late in the first day of diving, Tommy talked to a representative of the U. S. Bureau of Reclamation. In December of the year before, the canal had been allowed to dry and then scraped. Anything that had been in the canal had either been washed away or was piled in the large mounds along the ledge. Tommy was relieved to stop the diving. It was extremely dangerous in the cold water and there wasn't any point in doing any more. They had thoroughly checked the canal bottom, which would be the big question that would be asked when the time came. Nothing was there. Now, this job was going to be done rock by rock and there were a lot of rocks to be turned over. He hoped that Blade and Martin were doing better than he was.

In fact, back at the sheriff's office, the two detectives had finished putting their notes together. Blade spoke first. "So, tomorrow we take down Doeckel?"

Bill didn't look up. "You still think that's the best way to go, Doeckel first, then Jones?"

"Yeah, I think we work our way up. If we believe Mayfield's story, then Doeckel is less involved than Jones. So we squeeze her first, see what she comes up with. Then we take down Jones. I think we arrest both Doeckel and Jones. We can figure out later how to handle them. Let the D.A. make the decision. You agree?"

Bill nodded. "Yeah, I agree. So, tomorrow let's pay a little visit to Miss Doeckel in Visalia. We'll get something to eat first; I doubt if she'll serve us lunch."

18

"He is capable of anything"

Thursday, March 31, 1977
Visalia, California

The day after Mayfield's arrest and interrogation, Blade and Bill, along with a local detective working the case, were outside the restaurant where Doeckel worked. It was 11:30 in the morning. This had to be done carefully. Ray Allen was in custody in the Visalia jail and Shirley Doeckel would know that, and she would be sure to tell Allen or get word to him as soon as she could about what happened. When they entered the restaurant, they spotted her behind the counter, giving directions to a waitress. Their concern wasn't about her being armed, but they were worried about creating a fuss when customers lingering over a cup of coffee saw them take a woman into custody.

Blade walked toward the center of the counter, while Bill Martin and the Visalia backup detective moved to the ends of the counter. "Mrs. Doeckel?" Blade leaned toward her. "Are you Shirley Doeckel?"

Doeckel turned around and faced the lanky, leathery-faced detective, a questioning expression on her face. "I'm Mrs. Doeckel, the manager. Can I help you?"

"Yes, ma'am. I'm Detective Christensen of the Fresno sheriff's department. I'd appreciate it, ma'am, if you'd step around the counter. I need to talk to you."

"Now?"

"Yes, ma'am. Now."

Most people get nervous around cops who want to talk to them. Just like most people get nervous when they get stopped for a traffic ticket. It's just one of those things; cops make people uncomfortable unless they know them and are used to them. He noticed that she didn't look nervous. That said a lot about her, and none of it was good.

Doeckel went to the end of the counter and waited for Blade to say something. He leaned in toward her, keeping his voice even and low. "You're under arrest, ma'am, for murder. We want you to come with us right now. If you have a purse, you can get it. I'll come with you. There are other officers with me, so you should probably just make this easy on yourself and come with me without any trouble, okay?"

Doeckel nodded. She didn't say a word. She didn't protest or look surprised. She didn't cry. She didn't do *anything*. She just looked Blade in the eye and nodded. Blade and Bill exchanged looks; they had to be careful with this one. Blade followed her as she went back behind the counter to get her purse.

Blade had the Visalia officer transport Doeckel, while he and Bill followed him to the Visalia police station. They had already discussed who would handle the initial questioning. It wasn't a hard decision. Bill always had a way with the ladies. For some reason that Blade could never fathom, Martin could just walk up to any woman and start a conversation. He would have her laughing inside of a minute. In a personal conversation, Blade couldn't think of anything to say to a woman without taking at least a minute to stammer, unless he was reading her rights to her, or unless he was buying something at a store. Willie "Bill" Martin had a silky tongue. Blade was wise enough to use his assets, and he knew that with a woman Bill was an asset, although Blade still couldn't see what the attraction was. Martin had tried to tell him again and again that was part of Blade's problem—he couldn't see what the attraction was and it was clear to everybody else.

The answer was really simple. Bill liked women, all kinds of women—women knew that. He just liked talking to women and that made women like talking to him. It didn't hurt that he never lacked confidence. He would rub his mustache and smile, lighting up his whole coffee-colored face and that was usually all it took. Women would talk to him even after he read them their right to remain silent. Blade couldn't believe it; he would watch Bill in action as Bill just listened and listened. "And they could have just shut up," Blade would say on their countless rides back to the station. Bill would respond, "You just don't get it. Listening is my biggest asset." And, it was true. He would tell Blade that most men don't listen and women like a man who looks them in the eye and listens. The fact was it worked for him, and it was clear to everybody that hung around with him that something worked, so maybe he had a point.

Once they had Doeckel seated in an interrogation room, Bill removed her cuffs and gave her a minute to rub her wrists. "Mrs. Doeckel, I'm Bill Martin from the Fresno district attorney's office. Some people call me Willie. You can call me either one. Have a seat please. Detective Christensen, here, he's with the sheriff's office. We'd like to ask you a few questions about this homicide case we're working on. Maybe before we do that I should tell you a little bit about why you're involved. Our information is that you have a relationship with a man by the name of Clarence Ray Allen. We're looking at him for a homicide that happened a few years ago in Fresno involving a young woman, Mary Sue Kitts. Our information is that you might know something about that. To be honest with you, Shirley," Bill paused, "can I call you Shirley?" Doeckel looked at Bill and slowly nodded. "Thank you, Shirley. That makes it a little easier for both of us. I know this is uncomfortable for you. But our information is that you were involved in that homicide, along with your boyfriend, Clarence Allen." Bill paused to watch for a reaction. There wasn't one.

He kept his eyes on her and continued, "Anyway, Shirley, we have some statements from others, including a man by the name of Lee Furrow, that give us one side of the story, but they don't give us your side. So, what we want, Shirley, is to hear your side of the story, and that's real important, so we can know what happened. Now, before we talk about what you know about this—that is, if you know anything—we have to read you your rights, so listen up while I do that, okay?" Shirley nodded and kept her eyes on Bill as he went through her Miranda rights. Bill paused and looked up at Doeckel. "You understand these rights I just read to you?"

"Yes, I understand."

Bill smiled. "Thank you, Shirley. You want to tell us what you know about this, what your side is?"

"Yes, I'll talk to you, but I don't know much of anything. You said a 'homicide.' Is that the same as murder? I don't know anything about any murder and I wasn't involved."

"Okay, Shirley. Yes, a homicide is the same as a murder, at least what we're talking about here, so how about we go to Fresno and we sit down and give you an opportunity to talk to us. We can be there in about thirty or forty minutes, okay?"

"That's fine, but I didn't have anything to do with any murder, just so that's understood."

"We understand, Shirley, but we still need to talk to you, so let's head to Fresno, where we can do that and maybe help clear this up." Both men had already decided that they preferred to do this where they were in control. With Allen and his son in custody in the local jail, they didn't want to take any chance of somebody who might know Allen seeing them.

"And, if I clear it up?"

"Well, Shirley, if you can clear all this up and you aren't involved, then there shouldn't be a problem. But first we need to talk to you and get our questions answered."

By the time they got back to Fresno, a court reporter had been brought into a room at the Fresno County district attorney's office. Blade had called ahead to let them know they were bringing Doeckel in, but he hadn't counted on it being turned into what lawyers called a deposition, with a court reporter and attorneys present. I hadn't been invited. I hadn't scored any points with my reluctance to crash the door at Allen's house and, for the time being, I was still back in the trenches, out of Blade's sight. The district attorney, the assistant district attorney, and a senior deputy district attorney were all waiting for them when they led Doeckel into the room.

Blade didn't like it at all. He didn't like many people to be in a room when there was an interrogation; it was too distracting and it was intimidating. More than anything, he didn't like lawyers, even prosecutors, to be present during questioning. It wasn't just prejudice against lawyers, although Blade *was* prejudiced against lawyers. He didn't make any secret of that. As far as he was concerned, a significant reduction of the surface population of lawyers would be just fine. It was the way that lawyers approached interrogation that caused him to not want them there.

Most attorneys view interrogation like cross-examination. But it isn't the same thing at all. Interrogation is a dance, during which the interrogator controls the tempo—sometimes slow and sometimes fast.

Cross-examination is usually an exercise in setting up witnesses for contradiction, pinning them down to a position that the lawyer already has evidence to disprove. Cross-examination rarely results in a witness cracking on the stand because of the questioning. Interrogation is intended to result in the subject cracking. The rules of cross-examination are that you never ask a question without either knowing what the answer is or not caring what the answer is. In an interrogation, you frequently don't know what the answer will be, but you *always* care what it is. In interrogation, you probe the personality, looking for the signs of lying, nervousness, evasion, and you use these signs to your advantage. Unlike a witness during cross-examination, however, the subject of an interrogation can simply refuse to answer. There is no judge to make them answer. It is intimidating to have so many people present at an interrogation, and it's even more intimidating to have more than one person asking the questions. With more than one person involved, the flow of interrogation, the dance, can't be controlled. Usually, only one person asks the questions at an interrogation, unless you are running a good-cop–bad-cop routine, something that requires agreement and real communication between the interrogators.

Blade knew that even though Bill was going to conduct the interrogation, lawyers couldn't keep their mouths shut. This was too big. It was too good. They would all get into it because they couldn't stay out of it. But there was nothing he could do.

Doeckel slowly looked around the room. She only reacted when she saw the court reporter sitting in the corner. She looked at Bill, who shrugged as if it wasn't any big deal. She took a seat in the only open chair. Everyone's eyes were glued on her, and you could tell she was used to men looking at her. Shirley was what some women would call a bleach-bottle blond. Her voice had a throaty timbre with more than a hint of time spent in bars clouded with smoke. Her complexion was on the edge of going from fine lines to wrinkles, but she wasn't there yet. She had a full-bosomed figure that she either worked at or else had because she was blessed with good genes. She knew that men watched her, at least the kind of men that she was used to being around, and she knew that she could still turn most heads in the low light of a bar.

Doeckel also had an edge to her that got right in your face. She was no shrinking violet, nor did she pretend to be. This was a woman who could handle herself with rough men. She wasn't going to be somebody who would collapse in tears because she was easily intimidated. If she shed tears, it was because she had pulled them out of herself for a reason and it was *her* reason, not somebody else's. She met the gaze of every man looking at her and waited to see how the game would play out.

"Shirley, when you were arrested this morning you were advised of your Miranda rights, is that correct?"

"Yes."

The district attorney interrupted Bill and drew Shirley's attention away from him. "I think we should re-advise her in the event that there is some question in this proceeding about her rights. It will be on the record here."

Blade shook his head. *Damnit! Already, the lawyers were getting involved. He and Martin knew how to conduct an interrogation. He didn't tell lawyers how to cross examine, although he recalled plenty of times when they could have used his advice. How many times did they have to tell this woman she didn't have to talk?*

Bill didn't argue. He pulled out his Miranda card and started again.

Shirley had just a hint of a smile on her lips. She could sense Bill's irritation. She had a lot of experience reading men and his face wasn't that hard to read at the moment. "I will talk to you. I understand."

"Okay, Shirley, during the course of our investigation, we have received information that you were employed or associated with a person by the name of Clarence Allen, who owned Allen Security Business during that time."

Shirley nodded. "Allen was a neighbor of ours—it was 1970, I guess, when I first met him. I don't know what you want me to say."

"Just give us—you know—give us a synopsis of your relationship with Allen."

"In 1972, I filed for divorce and moved to Clovis, and at that time I guess I was involved with Allen, as far as a man-and-woman relationship goes, for approximately six months to a year. He was a good friend of the children. Also, his son was a good friend of my family." She explained that she worked for Allen in 1974 for three months as his secretary.

"In 1974, in the late summer of 1974, did you travel with Allen to San Diego?"

"Yes." Blade sensed a change in Shirley's posture. Her body had stiffened slightly. Bill saw that she wasn't going to be forthcoming and she wasn't going to give more than she thought he knew. "Was there also a young girl present?"

Shirley nodded a bit but she kept her voice firm. "Mary, but I don't remember the rest of her name."

Bill turned several of the pages in his file and took out a photograph of Mary Sue Kitts. "Let me show you a photograph of a white female. Is this the individual that you are referring to as Mary?"

Shirley glanced at the photograph for a second, her face expressionless. "That looks like her."

Bill returned the photograph to his file. He hadn't mentioned Lee Furrow being present with them in San Diego or Chula Vista. "Did Furrow return to Fresno with you?"

Shirley didn't express any surprise at the mention of Furrow's name. "That is what I am trying to think of—how many of us were in the car. I don't think so."

Bill glanced at the pages in his file and looked up at Shirley and then back down at the writing. There was nothing there about what he was going to ask, but she didn't know that. "Did anyone tell you that they were concerned about Mary talking too much?"

Shirley moved her head sideways and looked at Bill from the corner of her eyes. "I had heard it, yes."

"From whom?"

"Allen, I think."

"What did he say?"

"Just that she talked too much."

For a moment, Bill let Doeckel's statement hang in the air. The next question was a turning point. Whether Doeckel was going to cross that line yet was unclear, but Bill had interrogated enough people to know that sometimes the key statement had to work its way to the surface slowly, like an erupting boil. Maybe she was ready and maybe not. "Did he say anything about what he was going to do about her talking?"

Doeckel was looking straight at Bill. "No."

Bill hesitated. "Excuse me..." He thought for a moment. Bill knew he had to get to the night at her apartment. "Through our investigation, we received information that there was an occasion at your apartment in

Clovis when some people were present along with Mary, and that Lee was also present. Can you remember such an occasion?"

"Yes."

"Can you tell us about it?" All eyes in the room were on Shirley as she shifted her gaze from Bill to Blade and then looked around the room, inhaled deeply, looked down, and then back up at Bill.

"He brought Mary over with her suitcases and things, and Mary told me she wanted to stay there until her boyfriend picked her up. And my daughters—I can't remember who was with them—they all went out for ice cream. Allen took me for a ride and Lee and Mary stayed at the apartment."

"Who else remained at the apartment with Lee and Mary?"

"That's all."

"What happened next?"

Shirley looked down. "What happened next?"

"Yes."

She pulled her shoulders back and looked at Blade, quickly moving her gaze back to Bill. "I was made aware of what was going to take place. That is what the ride was all about." Her eyes were on Bill, blinking like the ticking of a metronome.

Bill kept his voice level and low. "What were you made aware of?"

"That Mary would have to be taken care of."

"What do you mean by 'taken care of?'"

Clearly, she didn't want to be more specific. Finally, she spoke rapidly— emphatically. "That they would have to do away with her."

"Okay, who told you this?"

"Clarence Ray Allen." The last name slid out of the corner of her mouth and trailed off to almost a whisper. Bill gave her a moment. She was almost there.

"Did he say how they were going to have to do away with her?"

"No. He—he just said Lee was going to take care of it."

"Did he tell you how he knew that Lee was going to take care of it?"

Shirley's mouth drew up into a frown. "Yeah." Her demeanor turned defensive. "You told me in the car on the way from Visalia that Ray has a reputation for bragging—right? For talking?"

"That's what I've heard."

"Well, he does. And you—when you hear him talk, half of it goes over your head. You don't—you think, yeah, okay. Anyway, there was supposed to have been a capsule with cyanide in it. That's what he told me."

"And what were they going to do with the capsule with cyanide in it?"

"Tell Mary it was a red—get her to take it."

"And Allen was telling you this while you were riding around in his car and at that time Mary was at your residence with Lee?"

"Yes. He told me when he brought her over there that her boyfriend was going to pick her up, but after he got me into the car alone, he tells me what they are going to do." Her voice broke and she began breathing heavily, her shoulders heaving up and down.

Bill sensed that she was about to hedge again, so he pressed her, his voice clearly carrying more of an edge. "Did you have an occasion to return to the apartment, prior to your daughters' return, and seeing Lee there?"

"Yes."

"Where was Mary?"

"I don't know. I didn't see Mary. I don't know. You know, I've tried to block this thing out of my mind for so long—believe that none of it was true—that it's hard for me to remember all these things, because Roger and I both thought it was just another case of Clarence bragging."

Bill let the statement stand. She was going to protect Roger Allen for some reason, and she wasn't going to admit to having seen the body. Bill knew she was lying, but they needed her entire statement. He would push her later. For now, she had given him Allen. She wasn't ready to give herself up—yet. "Okay. After you were at your apartment and you saw Lee outside, did you have an occasion that same night to go for another ride with Ray?"

"I rode with Ray up to the foothills."

"Were you following or was there another car following you?"

"It was Carl and Lee. Carl Mayfield and Lee Furrow."

"And what happened when you drove up into the foothills?"

"Ray and I stopped at a turnout, sat and talked, and waited for—for Carl and Lee."

"How long were they gone?"

"Just a few short minutes, and then—and then we came home."

Blade had been listening intently. Doeckel was starting to solidify her story, leaving out anything that might show she had knowledge of what was going to happen before it happened, as well as her involvement in what happened. He had to give it to her—she was cool. She was keeping up with where Bill was going and so far she was just a half step ahead. It was almost time to push back. Blade decided it was time for him to take the bad-cop role. "Did you stop off at Clarence Ray Allen's home first?" He raised his voice and took on a more aggressive tone.

Shirley's head snapped in his direction. She stared at him, her eyes narrowing. "No, not that I remember."

Blade wasn't going to give her a break. "Did you ever ask him why you were going to the foothills?"

"I—I already knew why we were going to the foothills."

Blade could see she was hesitating. He caught the nod from Bill and kept talking. "How did you know that?"

"He told me while we were out riding around."

Blade asked his next questions with a doubtful tone: "They were going up to the foothills for a particular reason? What reason?"

"Get rid of her body."

Blade nodded at Bill, who picked up the good-cop role, his voice and tone softer than Blade's. "Did he tell you how he was going to get rid of her body?"

"They were going to drop her body in the canal."

Bill stopped. Now, it was time to press her on the parts she had left out, *her* role in all of this. "During the course of our investigation we talked to several people. Our information is that you were the one that gave Mary the pill."

Doeckel straightened in her chair and threw her head back. "Me?"

"Yes. Did you give Mary any pills?"

"I did not give Mary any—I did not give Mary any pills."

Bill raised his eyebrows, his voice reflecting disbelief. "But you told us that you had knowledge from Allen of what occurred in your house and that you rode with him up into the foothills where they disposed of the body?"

Shirley Doeckel's whole body tensed with defiance. "That's right."

161

"Can you tell us step-by-step what occurred when you returned to the house with Ray?"

"No, I cannot." Doeckel's voice was getting louder. "I told you it has been a long time and I said that I almost lost my mind over this thing; it's been something I've been trying to forget. What could I do about it? You tell me."

"Go to the police," Blade interjected, lowering his voice to have maximum emphasis.

Shirley looked at him and there was no fear in her eyes. "Sure, and my kids and I would not be alive today."

"You have said that you wanted to believe that he was only kidding about killing the girl, or having her killed, yet *you* were afraid to go to the police with this because you felt he would kill you and your children?" Blade couldn't keep the sarcasm out of his voice. This woman wasn't afraid of anything.

"You know him." She said it evenly, the words snapping from her lips with the intensity of a cracking whip.

Blade's face was a mask. She did have a point—there was a difference between not being afraid and being stupid. He let her words sink in, and then he relented just a bit. "Okay. Did you feel he might kill you if you went to the police?"

"I *still* feel he will, just for me being here today."

"Did you feel at that time that he was an individual who was capable of killing?"

Shirley looked Blade directly in the eye. "He is capable of anything."

The rest of the interrogation began to push against smaller and smaller admissions from Doeckel. Her eyes never left Blade; no color reflected from them, except black. The effect wasn't caused by the light in the room, but for some reason her eyes just seemed pure black, like the irises had swallowed all color. "I did not kill anybody."

Blade lowered his head and looked out from under eyebrows, hooding his eyes. "The thing I want to know is whether you actually saw her body."

She didn't avert her gaze. You couldn't even see the whites of her eyes. She thrust her head backward in disdain. "No, I didn't. If you're going to take some scum's word against mine that I killed Mary, then—then you might as well just lock me up right now, because I did not kill Mary."

She paused to emphasize her words, spitting them out with precise articulation. "I did not." Shirley's face took on a stony expression. "You know, you're changing your whole attitude on me." Her eyes darted around the room, her lips compressing into a thin red slice across her face. "You aren't listening to me."

Bill looked over at Blade. "We're listening."

Shirley's eyes narrowed again. "Do you want to convict me; is that what you are after? Why are you here?"

Bill's expression remained unyielding. "Did you stop anywhere?"

"At a service station."

"Did Allen use the phone?"

"The phone, the service station phone—red phone booth. I'll never forget that phone booth as long as I live."

"What makes that phone booth so significant to you?"

"Because it was bright red. Because I knew after the phone calls what was going on."

"He told you after the phone call about the killing, or did he tell you before the call?" Bill could tell Shirley was beginning to lose track of what she had said. It almost always happened when suspects were trying to keep themselves out of what had happened. However, their memory and their mouth weren't always synchronized.

Agitated, Shirley sputtered. "Oh, you guys. I don't remember what he told me. I just remember that red phone booth." Then Doeckel sat there, her face a tightly drawn blank mask, and stared at them. One thing was obvious; any person who can get through an interrogation like she had been through, maintaining her presence of mind and keeping her story straight, was a person who had ice water in her veins. If she was going to come across with what she had seen and what she had done, many more hours of grilling her would be necessary. If they came at her again, they had to bring something she couldn't explain. She knew that and so did Blade and Bill. Right now, they didn't have that and she knew that, too. One other thing was obvious as Bill put the cuffs back on her: Shirley wasn't going to be nearly as friendly the next time.

19

A Gravestone for Mary Sue

March 31, 1977
Piedra Canal

While Bill and Blade were interrogating Shirley Doeckel, Tom Lean was still supervising a search crew out at the Piedra Bridge, going through the piles of dredge and searching along the edge of the canal. They had been there for three long days and still had nothing. Sometimes, late March in the Central Valley was still cool, but not this year. Spring was in full bloom and the weather was warming up. Between the dust, the pollen, and the bugs in the air, Tommy wasn't in a good mood, and neither were the others.

The first day of the search, Bill Martin had been present, but since then he and Blade brought in Mayfield and now they were going after Doeckel. Tommy would have much preferred being in on the arrests and the interviews, but he knew that somebody had to be out at the canal.

Detectives and deputies were there picking through the piles of rubble. Tommy couldn't believe they would pull that many rocks and other debris out of the canal. Not only that, there were other piles of debris every eighth of a mile. He kept wondering where it had all come from? If they didn't find anything in one pile, they would move to the next pile and then the next. He had even recruited a troop of Boy Scouts to help with the search. The growing pile of bones from deer, small critters, and a few cows now filled several boxes. Each bone was carefully tagged and photographed, and then taken to an anthropologist at a local college. And each bone that had been so meticulously collected had also been rejected, after what seemed to Tommy almost cursory examination. So far, nothing human had turned up, except for soda cans and other debris that people had discarded into the canal.

The search team sat on the pile of rubble and turned on the tape recorder. Early in the search they had decided they would record the day's work every time something of seeming significance was found. Whoever found the item would identify themselves and note the time and provide a description of what had been found. Then, the item would be put into an evidence bag and tagged with the name of the person who had found it. In a criminal case, each person who touches an item of evidence from the time it is picked up at the crime scene until the time it is introduced in court signs for that item. It is called the chain of custody. By preserving a strict chain of custody, all questions that might arise in the future could be easily dealt with. Whether evidence was tampered with or whether somebody who wasn't authorized handled the evidence became a moot point when the chain of custody had been scrupulously maintained. That didn't stop defense attorneys from questioning these matters or that innuendo wasn't implied later. It only meant that by keeping evidence under tight control there would always be a record that only those authorized to have seen the evidence were allowed anywhere near it. Everybody thought the search would be easy, but their irritation at the lack of success was beginning to show.

Tommy walked over to the pile and looked around for a comfortable place to sit. He found a relatively flat rock and sat down on it. "Anybody find anything interesting?"

Detective Harry Massucco, assigned to help with the search, picked up the tape recorder. "The time is now 1550 hours, 3-31-77, Detective Massucco. Another bone recovered and placed into evidence, one bone approximately twelve inches long, and approximately an inch and a half in diameter. One bone approximately eight inches long, and approximately three quarters of an inch in diameter. One bone approximately six to six-and-one-half inches long, and approximately three quarters of an inch in diameter. One bone fragment approximately four inches long, and approximately a half inch in diameter. One bone appearing to be possibly two vertebrae, possibly of an animal origin." Massucco looked up, shutting off the tape recorder. "Does that answer your question?" The expression on Massucco's face didn't hide his frustration.

Tommy laughed. "Exactly what does that mean, 'two vertebrae, possibly of an animal origin'? Of course, it came from an animal. People are animals. Anyway, how the hell would you know vertebrae from a finger bone?" As soon as he had said it, he knew that he had left himself open.

"This is a finger bone." Massucco held out an extended middle finger. "And this," he held up a dry-looking, brownish bone, "is a vertebrae." He looked it over more carefully. "By the way, this bone has a bite mark in it. I think I'm getting hungry."

They worked for another hour without finding anything of significance. Finally, Tommy decided to call it a day. Tired of feeling out of the loop, he was eager to learn how the interview with Doeckel had gone. He stood up and dusted his pants off, looking back over his shoulder. As he looked back, his eye was drawn to the rock he had been sitting on. There were two flat edges consistent with the rock having been cut. He looked at it more carefully. The rock was concrete and it was a fragment of a larger piece. Tommy called over to Harry. "Take a look at this rock."

Harry looked down. "Yeah?"

"Does it look like it could be part of a stepping stone?"

Harry reached down and brushed away some of the dirt and gravel around the flat rock. He looked up at Tommy. "Looks like your ass finally found a purpose besides being a place to put your head."

"Very funny." Tommy called over a photographer. He had been sitting on the remnant of a stepping stone for the last hour and a half. After it had been photographed, together the three men pulled the stone out of the pile of debris. Tommy pulled out the tape recorder. "1645 hours, Detective Tom Lean found a partially fragmented concrete stepping stone. The appearance indicates the stone's shape was a regular six-sided hexagon measuring about nine and one half inches on an edge. The stone is approximately two-and-a-quarter-inches thick and weighs approximately twenty-two to twenty-five pounds. There are several rust-colored lines across the stone, consistent with rusting wire being stretched across it."

Tommy carefully brushed off a small corner of the stone and put his initials "T.L." on the surface with a marking pen. Underneath, he wrote the case number, 77-4069. He carried it over to the evidence tech, who was keeping track of all of the bagged evidence. "Tag it and bag it. We've finally found something that isn't just an animal bone." As he handed it over, he knew in his heart that this stone was as close as they were going to come to a gravestone for Mary Sue Kitts.

20

A Lethal Vote

April 1, 1977
Fresno, California

The euphoria of the previous day's discovery was beginning to evaporate as the detectives faced the reality of the problem: identifying the stepping stone as one that was used to weigh down the body of Mary Sue Kitts. They knew it had to be one of the weights, but that didn't change the fact that neither Mayfield nor Doeckel had given them a description of the stones that was specific enough to be helpful. Maybe Furrow could, but even that was still going to be thin. And, if Jones couldn't or wouldn't identify the stone, they would have what the prosecutor would call a "foundation problem."

In the case of the stepping stone, it would remain just one more piece of debris that had been found beside a canal and wouldn't be admissible unless it could in some way be specifically tied to Allen, either by being identified as similar to ones he had used, or by their being able to locate similar stones in Allen's possession. The detectives knew that a six-sided "hexagonal" stepping stone was unusual, but it wasn't so distinctive that it stood apart from all others. The rust marks appeared to be from wire wrapped around the stone, and that would help. But they knew what a good defense attorney would do to them without more. Even if Mayfield or Furrow or, hopefully, Jones identified the stone, it only meant that it was a stone that *they* had used. It didn't prove that *Allen* had supplied it.

The detectives knew that under California law, a person who was a co-conspirator in the commission of a crime was equally guilty even if he didn't carry out the crime himself. In California, you can't convict a criminal solely on the words of other criminals who helped commit the crime. You also must have evidence that is independent of the testimony of the accomplice—something that a jury can look at besides just the word of people who are equally guilty. The concern is that some people will do anything, even lie, to get themselves a better deal. The best way to prove that Allen had something to do with the stone would be to prove that he had it in his possession before the murder, but that chance seemed remote unless Allen admitted it, and that was a non-existent possibility.

Even as Blade complimented Tom Lean on his discovery, his expression was as glum as always. "Tommy, this is one of the stones. We know that. You and the other boys keep on working out there. Bill and I will go after Jones. You found the stone. Now, it's our job to tie that rock around Allen's neck. I got a feeling things are beginning to go our way. I don't want to show it to Furrow yet. Let's see what Bill and I can get out of Jones. Before we do that, let's see if we can find some stepping stones like this. That might shake things up a bit."

Bill put his hand on Lean's shoulder. "So far, they've all talked. I got a feeling Jones will too and he was there that night. Keep digging out there, Tommy, maybe you'll find some more."

By midday, Blade and Martin were standing in front of the nail manufacturing plant in Tulare where Chuck Jones worked. They had decided that they would make an arrest. The whole plan was to soften him up on the ride back to Fresno. The detectives were accompanied by back-up officers from the Tulare police department. They recognized Jones from his photographs. He looked a lot like Mayfield, tall and lanky with sun-roughened skin, older than his real age would suggest. He had on a baseball cap, and his hair hung down in the back over his collar like a man who only got a haircut when he had extra money in his pocket.

Blade walked up behind him and placed his hand on Jones' shoulder. Jones turned around and saw the four men standing with his supervisor. It was clear from his expression that he knew they were police officers. He had learned over the years to recognize the look. Blade held his badge in front of Jones. "You Charles Jones?" Jones nodded as his co-workers stared at him. "You're under arrest for murder. Put your hands above your head." Blade ran his hands down Jones' sides and up the insides of his legs—no weapons. "Okay." He pulled Jones' hands down one at a time and cuffed him behind his back.

Blade had handcuffed more men and women than he could remember. He had grown used to feeling the tenseness in a man's body when he was arrested. He had also grown used to anticipating any body movement that might indicate resistance. Jones didn't resist. He just stood there, stunned by what was happening, but at the same time his shoulders sagged like a man who knew this day would come, but just hadn't known when.

"I didn't do no murder."

Bill nodded. "Well, we're going to talk about that."

Jones looked over at his supervisor. "My stuff?"

Blade pulled him by the arm. He didn't mince any words. "Don't worry about your stuff. Let's go." He was establishing himself as the one in charge, the tough cop. Bill would be the good guy—he would do the questioning. It had worked so far.

Blade put his hand on Jones' head to protect it when he got into the car. It was an automatic gesture learned from years of putting suspects into the backs of patrol cars. People had difficulty getting into a car when they didn't have the use of their hands. They always put their heads in first and seemed to have trouble being aware of the door opening. Blade had surmised over the years that it probably had something to do with the disorientation of being under arrest and feeling the cuffs on their wrists. Placing a hand on the top of the head served two purposes: keeping them from hitting their head and reminding them that they were no longer in control of themselves.

At first, neither Blade nor Bill said anything to Jones after they got him in the car. The silence helped keep the suspect off balance. People under arrest are uncomfortable with silence. If you wait long enough, they will almost always say something that is the key to what they are feeling. You learn to wait them out. They had done this enough times that each knew what the other was thinking. Bill slid into the backseat with Jones, and Blade got behind the wheel.

They were fifteen minutes down the road before Jones spoke. He wasn't sure what they knew, but they seemed confident, almost like they didn't care what he had to say. He could smell the sour odor of his own sweat rising up from his body. If he could smell it, then so could the detectives. He squirmed against the chaffing of the cuffs behind his back. The silence of the detectives and the sound of the tires against the roughened roadway had begun to peel away at his nerves. "I told you I didn't do no murder. What's this about?"

Bill hadn't read Jones his Miranda rights and he wasn't ready to start asking him questions. He wanted Jones to think about what he thought they had on him. This was a psychological game and it was the part he liked best, him against the mind of the suspect. He never tired of the game. He waited a bit longer, drawing out the silence and increasing Jones' anxiety. He didn't have to wait long before Jones asked again. "You guys going to tell me what this is all about, or not?"

Bill turned his head and looked at Jones. He wasn't going to ask a question, only state a fact and scratch Jones' conscience. "It's about murder, Chuck. It's about the murder of Mary Sue Kitts. You're just the tail end of arrests we've made in this case. Others have already talked, so we know what you did, at least according to them."

"Like who? Who says I did a murder?"

"Like Carl Mayfield, that's one. And there are others. Mayfield has given us a full statement and a lot of it is about you. So maybe you need to think about that for a while."

"Like I said, I didn't do no murder and if this Mayfield says I did, then he's a liar."

Blade turned his head slightly and directed his comments toward the backseat. "Maybe he is and maybe he isn't, but so far his side of the story and what the others had to say seem to be checking out. Maybe your side is different. We'll see."

During the rest of the trip, Jones kept sighing and breathing heavily, waiting for somebody to say something, but all he got was silence until it was time to get out of the car. Bill helped Jones out and walked him up to the detective division interrogation room.

As they entered the interrogation room at the sheriff's office, Bill pulled Jones' right arm a little, turning him in the direction of the stepping stones that were sitting on a table. All he wanted was for Jones to see different kinds of stepping stones, just to remind him of the weights on Mary Sue's body. Sitting on the top of the pile of stones was the fragment of the stepping stone dug up by Tommy the day before. Nobody said anything other than to direct Jones where to sit. Bill took the cuffs off and watched while Jones rubbed his wrists, looking at the stones and back at the two detectives.

Bill reached into a desk and pulled out a tape recorder, which he placed on the table separating him from Jones. As he had before, Blade sat to the side, watching and waiting. He nodded at Bill to begin. Blade could feel it—Jones was going to roll.

Bill turned on the tape recorder, fully aware that Jones' eyes were on him. He didn't make any explanation of why he was using a tape recorder, and he didn't ask for permission. "I am District Attorney Investigator William Martin. Also present is Mr. Charles Jones."

Jones leaned forward. "Charles *Allen* Jones."

Bill smiled; it was unusual for a suspect to be so specific about his name or to interrupt to make sure his name was stated correctly. "Charles *Allen* Jones." Bill stared at Jones, his dark brown eyes turning icy. For somebody who hadn't seen Bill change his expression into that of an interrogator, it was unsettling. "*Mr.* Jones has been placed under arrest today in Tulare for suspicion of murder." Bill let the word "Mr." slide out of his mouth like a bad taste. He wanted Jones to sense that he didn't need him. He wanted Jones to feel that he had to do something to make the detectives need him. Bill pulled out his Miranda card and read it to Jones, waiting at the end for the answer.

Jones nodded. These men were treating him like they didn't care what he had to say, and he knew enough to realize that what he had to say was all he had to trade for his life. He wanted to talk.

Bill glanced discretely at Blade, who gave a slight nod of his head. They had him. Now all they had to do was squeeze in just the right place. Bill had let the existence of other people's statements sit out there, to prey on Jones' mind. Experience had taught him that the mere fact that others had talked, and were still talking, would undercut Jones' confidence and break down his loyalty and bravado. Everybody talks tough about not being a snitch until they realize that there is no loyalty among thieves. The thing that eats at most people is being alone, the last man standing—the guy everybody is pointing the finger at.

It doesn't take long for self-interest to work its way to the surface. Jones wasn't hard to read. He wasn't the type to hold out by himself. Furrow was a follower. Mayfield was a follower. Allen had surrounded himself with followers. Jones was scared and off balance and they could quickly read him—Jones was a follower, too.

Fidgeting in his seat, Jones was clearly agitated. He kept his head still while his eyes moved back and forth from Bill, to Blade, and back to Bill, as he searched for what he wanted to say. "This Carl Mayfield? Is he out on bail or is he just out or...?"

Bill could hear the pleading tone in Jones' voice. He wanted to know where he stood if he talked. But Bill and Blade knew that they couldn't make any promises. They had to be careful how they answered. Bill had done this many times. He would have Jones out of his skin before he even saw the blood. "Carl Mayfield is just out. We know where he is living. We know where he's working. We have a complete statement from Mr. Mayfield, but he is out right now, primarily because he gave us a statement the other day, pretty much exonerating himself of any implication in the homicide. But he did involve himself in some other crimes, specifically a burglary of a market at Temperance and Belmont and trying to dispose of the stolen checks. He has given us a full statement. Okay? The rest of the cast of characters are in custody. As you were previously told, we are investigating a homicide, the death of a young, white female which occurred in Fresno County during the summer of 1974. Were you employed by Clarence Ray Allen in 1974?"

"Yes."

"Did you own an automobile during that time?"

"Yeah, I had two. Had a '59 El Camino and I traded it in on a '72 Ford Ranchero. They were both green."

"There was a burglary that occurred in the area of Temperance and Belmont. Our estimation is that you participated in some way in that burglary. Did you participate in that burglary?"

"Yes." Jones' voice was getting higher and more agitated. "Could I listen to this Carl Mayfield and these other tapes first or—I don't want to do it to change my story or nothing."

Jones' eyes were blinking rapidly, a sure sign that he was beginning to panic. Blade leaned over. "Let me say this. Our information is that a horse trailer was used to haul the safe away. The safe was hauled to Porterville. The kid—the son of the store's owner—was invited down to a party. He went swimming. Someone took the keys out of his pocket."

Jones nodded. He sighed and let out a long breath. "Is anybody else in my family involved or anything? You know, the safe was taken to my house."

Bill shook his head. They hadn't known where the safe had gone exactly. "It was taken to your house, we know that. If your family didn't have any knowledge?" Bill shrugged, making it clear that they didn't care about whether Jones' family knew about the safe.

Jones looked at the ceiling. "Okay." Jones' face was drawn. He was swallowing rapidly and his chin began to tremble. He rubbed his forehead, and dropped his hand down until it concealed his mouth. His body was beginning to sag. He was a man beginning to let his guard down, a man who had surrendered. "There was a lot of checks and, like, money orders and stuff like that."

Bill opened his file and removed several photographs. He spread them out in front of Jones. Bill put the photograph of Mary Sue Kitts in the center, with one of Shirley Doeckel on one side and one of Barbara Carrasco on the other side. Jones' eyes fixed on the photograph in the middle. Bill tapped his finger on the table, the sound filling the silence as Jones stared at the photographs. "Did you have occasion later to travel with Allen, Carl Mayfield, and the rest of these people down to San Diego to pass these money orders?"

"Carl Mayfield didn't go with us."

Bill tapped his finger on the middle photograph. "Now, the victim in this case, this young girl, did she go down there with you guys?"

"No."

"Do you know this girl? Have you ever seen her before?"

Jones looked at the picture and then over at Blade, who picked up the photograph of Mary Sue and held it directly in front of Jones' face, and then laid it back on the table. "You've never seen this young lady in this picture? She had blond hair at the time."

Jones looked at the photograph and hung his head. Bill slid the picture of Mary Sue directly in front of Jones, turning it so Jones couldn't escape looking at the face of the young woman in the photograph. "Once you returned to Fresno, there was a young girl that wasn't a steady friend, but sort of a girlfriend of Roger Allen, with sort of blond hair. Do you remember that girl?"

Jones turned his head to the side and looked at the wall. "They took a vote on whether they ought to get rid of her. They was talking about killing, you know. I voted no on it and this, ah, husky blond-headed kid, he wasn't going along with it all either and then Roger got to talking to him and putting him down a little bit and he said, 'Well, sure,' so he went along with it too."

Bill closed his eyes. In all his years as a homicide detective, he had never conceived of something like this, men sitting around and voting on whether to kill a young girl. He opened his eyes and shook his head slightly. "Was Lee Furrow there?"

"No. Not that I remember. I don't know."

"Then it was decided that she would be killed and disposed of?"

Jones' face had a pasty, gray pallor. He shook his head. "I never did vote for that. I never..."

Bill interrupted before Jones started to unravel completely. "What I am saying is that the majority voted. Is that what you're saying?"

"Right and ah....."

"Yes or no?" Bill's voice was edged with impatience.

"Yes." Jones said the word with the resignation of a man who realized that what he had just said described himself as being in the middle of a thing of shame. "What I wanted to do was everybody pull as much money as they could get together and send her somewhere for a while. You know, burglary is one thing, but murder's another. Anyway, what they told me was gonna happen was that they were going to cut her hands and stuff off so there wouldn't be no fingerprints and they was gonna take her out in a field somewhere and put gas on her and burn her. I told 'em I didn't want to have nothin' to do with it. I didn't want to know about it. So, I guess they got pretty scared and everything else and then they started in. Allen knows that I think the world of my youngest son. He started talking about him."

Jones looked at both men pleadingly, searching their eyes to see if they understood that he felt his family and his little boy were in danger if he didn't cooperate. He didn't see any compassion in their eyes. Bill didn't hesitate before resuming. "Okay, let's get back to that killing. On the day they discussed this and they voted to do this thing, what happened? Do you remember?"

"Well, before we left the meeting, they seen that I got so shook up that they said, well, they wouldn't do that."

"They wouldn't cut her hands off and burn her?"

"No, they wouldn't. They'd find some other way out of it. I don't know if it was a few days or if it was a week, but Allen said that he got somebody else to take my job for that night and he wanted me to go with him, that they was gonna watch a place, so we took my pick-up and drove out to a place that was near this apartment. We sat there near a phone booth and then the phone rang and Allen got out and answered it. A little while later, the phone rang again and he told me to get out and answer it. Soon as I got the phone to my ear, all I heard was this guy say, 'Well, she's dead. I killed her. Come and pick her up.'" Jones looked around the room, shaking his head. "It was crazy, you know, so I went to the car but I didn't get in. I just stood there beside the car and wanted to know what the hell, you know? So, Allen told me that it was already done and that I was into it right up to my neck, along with everybody else and he'd already talked to other people and, that if I wanted to do anything about it, just go ahead and do it but not count on seeing my family again, especially my boy. My boy, he's five now, so that would've made him three.

"I mean, one time after this, my wife goes to Allen's to pick up my check and she brung my boy. I was standing there and he picks up my boy and he smiles at me and says, 'You remember what I told you now.' He set him back down and gave him a dollar and said he could buy some candy the next time his dad stopped at a store. I got the point."

Bill nodded; he understood. "After the phone call when the guy told you that he had killed her, what happened then?"

"Allen told me all that and that he wanted me to drive over there but I said, 'No.' So he slid over behind the seat and told me to get in. So I got in, and he did some more talking going over there. Before we left, Shirley Doeckel came up in Allen's car. I don't know for a fact but I don't think she knew about it either; she was shook up and everything. Then we got over there and this Lee was there, at her apartment."

Bill sat back, his mind evaluating the possibilities. *Maybe Jones was protecting Doeckel, but there was no motive for that. Maybe she really didn't know, at least until it happened.* He decided to move the questioning to the apartment. "By Lee, you mean Furrow?"

"Yeah."

Bill moved a picture in front of Jones. "This guy?" Jones focused on the mug shot of Furrow and nodded.

"Maybe Allen was using this guy, too, but I was told that this Lee was a professional killer."

Bill nodded. "Okay, when you got to the house, what happened, when Lee was there?"

"Allen opened the trunk of his car and we went in and he told me to help him carry it out and I told him, 'No.' He pushed me back up against the wall and did some more talking to me and this Lee had already got a hold of it and was bringing her out but she was covered with a pink blanket. So anyway, I picked her up and took her feet in my arms. So we took her out and put her in his trunk and he said to follow him and told Lee to get in with me. Allen was standing out there by his Cadillac and we laid her in the trunk and shut the lid. Allen had told me before that Lee was a hard killer and not to give him a bad time or nothing. We followed him and drove into the mountains."

"Did Shirley leave with you?"

"Yes, she got in the car with Allen."

"Did you stop at any point and get any weights or anything to tie her up and weight her down?"

Jones shook his head. "They was already done up with wire and everything in the back of my pickup. I didn't even know they were there."

Bill frowned. Blade had been silently watching Jones for anything that Bill might miss. *Something was missing here. Either somebody had moved the weights into Jones' pickup while he was inside the apartment or Jones had put them there himself, which meant he knew more about what had been happening than he let on.* Blade gave a slight shake of his head. They would let it pass for the moment. "The weights were already lying in the back of your pickup? With wire attached and everything?" Bill continued.

"Yeah."

"So what happened next?"

"Well, he drove up there and stopped in the middle of the road and Allen opened the trunk and told me and Lee to put her in the back of my pickup. There was some cement blocks with wire, two or three, don't know how many, and we put wire around it and wrapped it up. Never did take the blanket off. We wrapped the wire around her and then drove back to the road. It was a few feet from the road and Allen said, 'I'm gonna go up here and stop any cars or whatever,' and he said, 'You guys throw her off into that canal.'"

Bill pursed his lips and inhaled deeply. He had looked down into that canal. The visual image of that night held him back for a moment. He looked over at the stepping stones that were sitting on the table and moved his eyes toward Blade.

Bladed walked over to the table. "See these stones over here?"

Jones looked at the table. He had seen them when he walked into the interrogation room. "I couldn't recognize 'em."

Blade put his hand on the table. "Well, did it appear to be something like that was in the back of your pickup—that was used as weights?"

Jones grimaced like he wasn't sure, and then he cocked his head to the side. He had remembered something. "Ah, about a month later Allen was sitting in his living room," Jones looked up at them, trying to explain, "where you got the fireplace and everything? And he looked up at a picture that had been taken of his ranch, from the air. And, he said, 'There's them cement blocks. We got to get rid of this picture.' The cement blocks were, you know, six-cornered."

Bill could feel the air slowly coming out of his lungs. If they could get a picture of the hexagon-shaped stepping stones in Allen's backyard before the murder, before they were presumably disposed of—that would not only help prove where they came from, it would also help prove a guilty mind because he had removed the picture and the stones. So far, nobody had given them anything to use but their word against Allen's word. They needed an independent link. They needed something that could tie Allen to the murder besides the word of other murderers. *If* the six-sided stepping stones were in the picture. The words came out quietly, measured. He was almost afraid to ask. "That's hexagon-shaped?"

"Yeah."

Bill sat quietly for a moment, the tension beginning to loosen its grip on his neck muscles. "How many were there?"

"I don't know. Like I said, I don't know how many there were."

Blade felt the knot in his stomach. This was the link. They had to get that picture. His mind raced through the possibilities. People in the valley often had photographs taken of their homes and property from the air. There were a number of services that supplied the photographs and then sold them to property owners. Chances were they had negatives. Businesses saved those in case somebody wanted another print. He just had to find the right business. He focused his attention back on the interrogation.

Bill had the same thoughts and he wanted to wrap up the questioning.

"You're saying that Allen planned this whole thing? It was his idea to get rid of her?"

"Yeah. It was his main idea. He was—he was always the brains of everything. He said, 'So you know.' That was what he told me there in her apartment and that's what he told me sitting there at the phone booth." Jones put his hand over his face, trying to make the detectives understand that Allen had involved him in disposing of the body so he couldn't talk without implicating himself. It was a way of keeping him silent.

Blade went to the table where the stones were placed. "Chuck, I want to show you something. I want to show you some stones. You can just walk over." Jones got up and walked over to the table. Blade could see his eyes moving back and forth as he stared at the stones. "Now, you mentioned that they were six-sided stones."

"I'm pretty sure."

Blade put his hand on the broken stepping stone with the rust mark across it. "All right, now this has two sides and if the rest of the broken part was here, that would make it a six-sided stone, wouldn't it?"

Jones' eyes were fixed on the stone. "Yeah, I didn't pay no attention to it in the back of my pickup, but later when he said that about the picture, that's what they were, six-cornered stepping stones." His eyes stayed on the stone, the rust mark stood out like a bloody streak across the rough surface. He knew where it had been. Everybody in the room could see the recognition, like a scar suddenly appearing on his face.

21

A Picture Is Worth a Thousand Words

April 2, 1977
Fresno, California

Blade and Martin spent the morning going over reports. Up to this point everything had been carried in a briefcase that never left Blade's side. But Allen was in custody and he wasn't going anywhere, not with bail set as high it was. They had talked to all the players, so they basically knew what had happened, but they had held off on talking to the owners of Fran's Market and their son, Bryon. The circle had been deliberately kept small, but now it was time to get confirmation for the reasons why Mary Sue had been murdered, and, hopefully, that would come from Bryon.

It was early April. The days were starting to lengthen as the sun rose higher in the sky, and the grass was still green, unburned by the heat of summer. Blade drove from the office toward Fran's Market, the place that was the beginning for all of this. The investigation had started in early December of 1976 and now it was four long months later, but they were getting close.

They drove the wide two-lane street that soon transformed into a busy country road. Bill asked, "How are we coming with the picture?" For the past five days, since Jones' interrogation, Tommy and Blade had been on the phone following one lead after another, trying to find someone who had a record of taking an aerial photograph of Allen's house. They were calling as far away as Texas, to anywhere and to anyone who had a business that took that kind of pictures.

Blade shook his head. "No luck, so far. For all we know, it could be somebody who isn't in business anymore. Anyway, there's sure as hell a lot of 'em. But if they're out there, we'll find 'em."

Bill nodded absently and watched the telephone poles pass by. He had never been to Fran's Market, but now he saw the small grocery store on the northeast corner of the road, as Blade slowed.

There were cars scattered in the front parking lot, and there was a large parking area on the west side of the store. The store was isolated, with no other businesses around it. Many rural stores like this that Bill had visited over the years had been robbed. Most of the time, these stores recognized their regular customers, but this store was on the road to Sequoia National Forest, and visitors to the area would stop for beer or chips on their way up to the mountains. There wouldn't be any comfort level for the store owner. It was the perfect setup for a robbery—or a burglary.

They got out of the unmarked car and walked through the front, double-glass doors. A vertical measuring tape was pasted next to the door that might give the height of someone leaving the store if a clerk or a camera were available, but there didn't appear to be any cameras or any other monitoring equipment. It was just a local country store run by people who dealt with most of their customers on a first-name basis. As for the others, they met them with a smile.

Ray Schletewitz was behind the meat counter when the front clerk called his attention to the two men standing at the cash register. He recognized Blade, but Bill was a new face. Ray walked out from behind the counter, wiping his hands on his butcher's apron. Ray was a medium-sized man, around five-foot-nine, with dark hair and a weathered face, and his hands had the look of a man who was used to hard work. His face had seen its share of afternoon sun. Ray extended his hand to Blade but quickly drew it back. "I've been cutting meat and my hands—well, you understand." He wiped them again on his apron.

"That's okay," Blade said. "Ray, this is Bill Martin, from the district attorney's office. Is there someplace where we can talk? And is Bryon here? We need to talk to him, too."

Ray's eyebrows lifted and his eyes opened a little wider. "Well, we can go to the office area, back in the storage room. It gets a little warm back there, but we got a fan. Bryon's not here but I can call him. We don't live far away." Ray hesitated. "You fellows still working on that burglary?" He waited for a moment for an answer that didn't come. "I'm a little surprised to see this much work. In the past when somebody's stolen something, we usually just get a report written."

"Well, Ray," Blade began slowly, "this case has taken a little different turn. It isn't really about stolen money orders anymore. Maybe we should go to your office?"

Bill looked around the small office area at the back of the storeroom. A walk-in cooler and floor-to-ceiling shelving holding boxes of canned vegetables sat next to rolls of toilet paper and cans of motor oil—all the things country people needed and wanted to be able to purchase at one place. Produce, still carrying dust from the field, was stacked in wooden boxes sitting on the cement floor. The office contained just a desk, a small chair, and on the floor against the wall a steel safe. It wasn't imposing and it was apparent that its primary function was to hold small amounts of cash and important papers and to be inconvenient to somebody who wasn't a professional thief.

Ray caught Bill eyeing the safe. "It isn't much. I don't keep much cash here, except working money. We don't get many big bills and if we can't handle it with what we have, then we just tell the folks they have to go somewhere else. At the end of the day, I take the cash and go into town to the bank or," he grinned sheepishly, "I take it to the house, just so's it isn't here. If folks want to steal it, then I guess they can. It's happened before, you know, stealing the safe and all. Guess that's what brings you fellows out here."

Bill replied, "Actually, Mr. Schletewitz, we want to discuss more than that. Do you know a man by the name of Clarence Ray Allen?"

Ray Schletewitz's smile disappeared; the words spilled out of his mouth contemptuously. "I know him. He doesn't live far from here. Heard he's in jail for that big robbery in Visalia. He and his family used to rent a place from us, and they shopped here, too. I've heard rumors about him for a long time. I never liked doing business with him, but you know how it is. You can't refuse to deal with people who come into the store just because you don't like them. You have something about Allen you want to know? Does he have something to do with the burglary here? I think Bryon heard a rumor like that."

Bill lowered his voice. "We're not sure yet whether he was involved. We'd like to talk to Bryon about a girl, Mary Sue Kitts."

"Is Bryon supposed to know this girl?" Ray waited for an answer that didn't come. "I'll call him."

They waited until Ray got off the phone before Blade asked, "By the way, do you have any other safe?"

Ray Schletewitz laughed. "No, the one you saw, that's all I have. You asking about that rumor I keep a safe in the freezer? I've heard that too, but the only safe I have is the one you saw. I don't keep that much cash here and even if I did, I wouldn't put it in the freezer."

Fifteen minutes passed before Bryon Schletewitz arrived. He was in his early twenties. His dark brown hair hung down around his face, long enough to be in style but not long enough to call attention to himself, and a young man's mustache was taking its time to fill in. Ray Schletewitz motioned his son to join them. "Bryon, this is Detective Christenson and Detective Martin. They want to ask you some questions about that burglary when our safe was stolen."

Bryon shook hands with both detectives. "Okay, what would you like to know?"

Bryon told them that he had gone to a swimming party at Clarence Ray Allen's house after receiving an invitation from Allen's son, Roger. He said he always carried the key to the store and the store's alarm key and they were in his pants when he put them on over his swimming trunks at the end of the party. He had spent most of the evening talking to Mary Sue Kitts.

Bill pulled out a picture. "Is this Mary Sue?"

Bryon took the photograph from Bill's hand. "That's her. She seemed real nice. She came around a few weeks later. Said she wanted to talk to me about the burglary. She was real nervous. I asked her about what she knew, and she acted like she wanted to say something but was afraid, you know. She said that she needed to be real careful and that's when she said she knew Ray Allen did the burglary, but she wouldn't say more than that and I never saw her again. I told my dad and I talked to Roger Allen, but we couldn't prove anything. Have you talked to her? Mary Sue?"

Bill took the photograph back. "Bryon, we think Mary Sue Kitts is dead, and we think she was murdered because she was talking about the burglary to you and to others."

Bryon stepped back and looked over at his father. "Somebody killed her because of that?"

Blade and Bill drove slowly out of the parking lot. Bill broke the silence. "That's it, the whole motive. They killed that girl because she was starting to talk about what had happened."

Blade glanced over, taking his eyes off the road for a moment. "Well, that may be what happened, but nothing she told Bryon is going to help us pin this on Allen. She's dead and we can't prove Allen took the keys except with the word of people who all have something to gain."

Bill sat quietly for a moment. "We can use it for one thing. It shows that Mary Sue Kitts was talking and that proves motive. Now, we have to prove that Allen was involved and we need something besides those assholes he ran around with."

Blade gave way to a note of optimism, which was unusual for him. "Maybe Tommy's had some luck on the picture." But a quick check with Tommy when they got back to the office wasn't encouraging. No luck so far.

The ringing phone broke his concentration, but anything was preferable to writing reports. Blade picked up the phone. It had been two weeks since the interview with Chuck Jones about the aerial photograph of Allen's home. He and Tommy had left messages with every aerial photography company they could find in the western United States, and there were a lot more than they had figured. No luck so far, until the phone rang. It was an aerial photography service he had called earlier. There was a record of an order for a large photograph of the home and ranch of Clarence Ray Allen. Finding the order wasn't the lucky part; the lucky part was the fact that they still had the negative and they could produce the exact photograph that Allen had ordered, including the frame. It was a large, color photograph and with the frame the duplication would be expensive.

When Blade and Tommy asked the D.A. to pay for the photograph, he authorized it. The D.A. didn't discuss it with me. He didn't need to. He hadn't assigned the trial of the case to me and after my performance a few weeks earlier I didn't expect it. I'd had my day in the sun. As far as Blade was concerned, I was too wet behind the ears. He still didn't trust the district attorney because he had been a defense attorney and the

D.A.'s confidence in me only reduced my credibility in his eyes. The Allen case had moved on without me. All I knew were the rumors and pieces I picked up. I expected a senior deputy was going to get it. I had gone back to felony trials, and as far as Blade was concerned, I could wait until my ears dried before I got one of his cases.

Several weeks later, the package arrived in the mail, containing a copy of the exact photograph and the exact frame that Clarence Ray Allen had ordered to show off his ranch. Bill got a call from Blade to come right over to the sheriff's department. The wrapping paper came off slowly. There was only one thing they wanted to see.

"Son of a bitch." That was all Blade had to say. Even from several hundred feet in the air, the detail of the Allen ranch stood out clearly, right down the side of the house and leading into the backyard toward the pool. And there were hexagonal stepping stones just like the fragment pulled from the Piedra Canal. Just like the ones Chuck Jones described.

Blade exclaimed, "We got him."

22

"Ready for the People"

April, 1977
Fresno, California

I heard the summons over the public address system. "Mr. Ardaiz, please report to Mr. Smith's office." The district attorney waved me into his office. He had a smile on his face. That was good. I relaxed. The senior deputy who I expected was going to handle the Allen case was just leaving the office, and the D.A. wanted to know would I take the case? Actually, he didn't ask if I would take it. He basically said I was being assigned the case and he had confidence I could handle it. *Then* he asked if I would take it. *Would I take it? Let me think.* I probably thought all of a nano-second. Then as calmly as I could, I indicated that I would be happy to handle it. I could barely contain myself. I didn't want to seem too eager, but I'm sure the D.A. couldn't miss the undisguised joy on my face. This was one of those moments when something is held out to you that has been just out of reach, and you either jump for it or you lose it. I jumped. I wasn't going to share whatever reservations I might have about my experience. Nor did I let the fact that there were few cases ever prosecuted at that time where no body had been found interfere with my excitement. Would I take it? I was out of the D.A.'s office and down the hall before he could change his mind.

I later learned that Blade was angry. But I didn't have to hear it from other people; I saw it on his face the minute I showed up in the sheriff's office and announced I had been assigned, which was about fifteen minutes after the assignment had been made. By now though, he had heard that I had tried some bigger cases and other people had assured him I was all right. But what other people told him didn't matter. It was only after Bill told him that he had watched my work that did it. He told Blade and Tom that I could do it, but Bill warned me that I better not screw it up.

On television, cases are won in the courtroom when a witness cracks under cross-examination or the prosecutor or the defense attorney has an epiphany. In real life, that rarely happens, and cases are won or lost based on the quality and thoroughness of the investigation. By the time you get to court, the investigators have done the job that allows the prosecutor to lay out the case. It is the prosecutor's job to figure out how to get the evidence in front of a jury. Blade, Tommy, and Bill had put together an incredible case, but many evidentiary difficulties remained.

Having evidence and getting it admitted are two different things. Understanding the inferences you want the jury to draw and getting them to draw those inferences are two different things. Reading what a witness had said and hearing the witness say it are two different things. A good D.A. has to talk to each witness to see how the case will unfold. Just because somebody told a cop something doesn't mean he or she will say it in court or repeat exactly what the report says. I needed to talk to every witness and decide how to present the case. I needed to decide how we were going to get Allen's gang to talk in court and what we were going to do with Lee Furrow.

It's very hard for the public to understand plea bargains, and it's even harder for them to understand making deals with some criminals in order to get other criminals to talk. Sometimes, you have to make a choice and decide who the worst player is. Then you have to decide how much you need to give up in order to get the worst guy.

The only reason for offering a deal in exchange for testimony is because you need that testimony to fill in the holes in a weak case. The reality was that legally we had a very weak case against Clarence Allen. The only way to link him to the murder was through the mouths of people who had helped commit the murder or the burglary or both.

When you offer a deal in exchange for testimony, your leverage and bargaining room depends on the strength of the case you have against the person to whom you are making the offer and how badly you need the testimony. The first thing I had to decide was what kind of a case I had against each of the witnesses and how much I needed them to fill in the holes in my case against Clarence Ray Allen.

After reading the reports, I knew we had no case on Shirley Doeckel. The only way to link her was through Furrow and Chuck Jones. Without them, she walked, and without her, the chances of Allen walking became significantly better. Like her or not, I needed Shirley Doeckel. I had to make her a deal and I had almost no bargaining room. All I could get in exchange for her testimony was immunity if she provided truthful testimony.

I had the statements of Jones and Mayfield, but without them I had no real context. I had to prove how the burglary happened and that came through them. I had to prove how the murder happened and that came through them. I had to have Jones in order to prove that Allen had destroyed the picture. The stepping stones were the link to Allen. I needed Jones to provide the foundation for the stepping stone. I needed Jones. I had no leverage in exchange for his testimony. He would get immunity and so would Mayfield.

The hard question for me was how much do you give a murderer to get a murderer? I could convict Furrow of first-degree murder, but Furrow's testimony could provide the key to the conviction of Allen. We wanted Allen. I needed Furrow. The only question was how high a price was I willing to pay to have the actual murderer help me convict the man who instigated the murder? Who was worse, the man who orchestrated the murder or the man who actually committed it?

Giving a deal to a man who closed his fingers around a young girl's neck and strangled her to death in order to get the man who ordered it presents a Hobson's choice for a prosecutor. You are damned either way. I had to talk to Furrow. I had to know how he would look on the stand. For a jury to believe Furrow, they had to feel sorry for him. They had to feel as if he, too, was a victim of Clarence Allen. If Furrow came off like a cold-blooded murderer, a jury could easily believe he was just trying to save himself and would tell us whatever we wanted to hear in order to save his own skin. And Allen would go free.

No defense attorney in his right mind is going to let a prosecutor talk to his client without some assurance, some promises, and a lot of trust. But I had one small advantage. I had Lee Furrow by the short hair and his attorney knew it. Furrow had confessed to Barbara Carrasco and he had confessed to Blade and Tom. I didn't need to connect him with the stepping stones, and I didn't need the aerial photograph to prove he murdered Mary Sue. But I did need Furrow in order to prove why he did it and to prove that Allen ordered him to do it. I needed an actual murderer to catch a worse murderer.

Furrow had only one thing to trade in order to get a break. His attorney agreed to let me talk to him in order to get a sense of what he was like. Repeating his earlier confessions to me wouldn't improve my legal position in terms of Furrow's case, and if it worked out, it could only help him. It was a simple proposition. If I was satisfied with Lee Furrow as a witness, then he got a second-degree murder offer instead of going down on a first-degree premeditated murder charge. He would have a chance to eventually get out. He would have a chance to make a new life. But he had to testify. I never considered giving him immunity or anything less than second-degree murder. I was willing to trade to get the devil, but I wasn't willing to put my own soul on the table.

I sat in a room with Furrow and Bill Martin. Furrow wasn't much to look at, not very muscular, not intimidating. There was nothing threatening about him. That was good. I didn't need a jury to look at him and see their stereotyped vision of a murderer. They needed to believe he was a victim, too. The red jumpsuit worn by inmates hung loosely on him. Even on the high-fat, high-carbohydrate jail diet, he hadn't put on weight. His lank hair hung around his face. When he sat down in front of me, there was no defiance, no arrogance. I looked straight into the face of a haunted man. I hadn't seen it very often and neither had Bill, but Lee Furrow was a man torn apart by conscience. He had dark circles under his eyes and he could barely hold up his head. I talked to him and avoided any specific details of the murder. I had his confession. What I wanted to determine was how he would look on the stand. I needed to know if he could be viewed by a jury as a sympathetic figure. I decided I would take a chance on Lee Furrow. I actually felt sorry for him and I was a lot harder to sell in the sympathy department than a juror would be. I made the agreement with his attorney: second-degree murder for Furrow in exchange for his testimony. Everyone else got immunity, or no time in custody. There was no choice. I made the decision that the one man who got no breaks was Clarence Ray Allen.

It took almost six months to get the Allen case to trial. It was late October, 1977, when the trial of the People versus Clarence Ray Allen began. A jury was empaneled after four days of the selection process. I had been over every aspect of the case with Blade, Tommy, and Bill. I knew every statement made by every witness. I knew the evidence. I knew what I was going to do. But there were two things that I didn't know. I didn't know what those twelve people sitting in the jury box were going to think, nor did I know what Allen's defense attorney was going to do.

Whenever I tried a case, I laid it all out in my case file: the expected testimony of each witness, the anticipated cross-examination, and the rebuttal, including the questions I was going to ask. Before I walked into court, I had tried the case in my mind and written it out in my book. When I put a witness on the stand, I would open to his or her page, but I only looked at it again when I got to the end, just to make sure I hadn't missed anything. I knew every word of what I was going to ask; I didn't need to read it again.

When people ask me about what it's like to try a murder case, I always give the same explanation. A trial is like a play or a musical. Jurors don't remember every word a witness says, but they remember impressions and—if you lay them out right—they remember the important points. When you walk out of a musical or hear a singer, you don't remember every word or note that was sung, but you remember how the words made you feel, how the orchestrations and notes moved you or failed to touch you at all. That is the objective with the presentation of a case. You lay it out like a play and you create the series of impressions that you need to leave with the people who will decide.

Some attorneys look at a trial as a game. I can't respect that attitude. A good attorney doesn't try to trick anybody in order to win. Winning isn't the objective. The objective for the prosecutor is to prove the case beyond a reasonable doubt, and the objective for the defense is to make the prosecutor prove his case. For a defense attorney, pointing out the weakness in a prosecution's case isn't playing a game. It is doing your job. However, hiding witnesses and putting on contrived evidence isn't acceptable, nor is it ethical. A good defense attorney who makes me prove my case wins my respect. But I never respect those who think that getting their clients off is the objective. I have often wondered how defense attorneys can live with having shaded the rules to put a criminal back on the streets. I knew that Clarence Allen's attorney was excellent. He was ethical and passionate. He would fight, but he would fight fair. He would make me prove my case, but he would do it with dignity and energy.

When the jury arrives, the defendant is usually already seated at the counsel table, so that jurors are shielded from seeing the defendant shackled. This time-honored piece of courtroom practice is designed to keep the jurors from getting the idea that the defendant is dangerous. Of course, this is a fantasy that lawyers and judges indulge themselves with. The jury knows the defendant is in custody, and they have seen enough television shows to know the defendant is handcuffed when he is brought into the courtroom. But we like to indulge the myth that jurors view the defendant as if he walked in the front door for the trial and can walk out at the end of the day just as they can. Nobody wants to disrupt the fantasy with a dose of reality, like considering the fact that every day the defendant wears the same suit or coat and he's always there when they walk in and always there until they file out.

I remember when Allen arrived in the courtroom, not simply because it was such a big case, but because of how he behaved. On the first day of trial, most defendants look nervously around the courtroom. The atmosphere is different than at their other appearances at motions or at arraignment on the charges. This is the time of judgment, when the end is near, when any perception of control over their destiny is quickly slipping away, and it always shows. I had seen Allen at many pre-trial hearings. I was used to seeing him in various venues, but on that day and at the moment when he walked through the door, he strolled nonchalantly into the courtroom like he was walking in his own front door. If he felt fear, I didn't see it. He looked at me and everyone else in the room as if he owned the ground we were standing on. He wore a plaid jacket and eye glasses, and sported gray, wavy hair that he combed backward on his head. He looked like somebody's grandfather, except he never smiled and there was no humanity behind his eyes. I knew that there were people in court who cared about him, and, in fact, he acknowledged them as he entered, but I slowly began to get a sense of a man who was a reptile wrapped in the skin of a human being, and like a reptile, he viewed the trial as his time to sun himself on a rock.

The first day of a major trial is always a day of high tension. Earlier, the twelve jurors had just been people for me to make judgments about, should they stay, should they go? Were these the people I wanted to decide the People's case? Now, however, the tables were turned. Now these twelve people were studying me; they would make their judgment and decide the outcome. I sat at the counsel table in the chair closest to the jury box, watching them watch me. It's not unlike the feeling that an actor must experience on opening night on Broadway when the curtain is raised and all the critics are sitting in the audience, waiting for you to begin the performance.

I stood, as the bailiff called court to order. "All rise. The Superior Court, for the County of Fresno, State of California, is now in session, the Honorable Robert Mardikian presiding." Judge Mardikian was a mountain of a man who wore a genial expression and presided over his courtroom like a big bear, but a big bear who was used to people. He was in control and, as long as you didn't irritate him, you would get along just fine. After he took his place on the high-backed, black-leather chair, we took our seats. He looked out over the crowded courtroom. "Are the People ready to proceed?" Judge Mardikian's initial words brought everything into a razor-sharp focus for me. The emotion of the moment began to course through me. To stand and represent both the local community and the state as their representative before the court of justice, to handle a major case that carried everything on the line, and to be the voice for a person whose voice could no longer be heard was a moment I sought and embraced. I looked at the jury. All eyes were on me. I was ready. I looked at Judge Mardikian. It was a phrase that was thrilling to me no matter how often I had said it before or how often I would say it in the future. "Ready for the People, Your Honor."

"Is the defense ready to proceed?"

"Ready for Mr. Allen, Your Honor."

And so it began. I was not quite thirty years old. On that first day of trial, I did not know that I would live on for almost the same number of years that I had been alive—thirty long years—before I would see the end of this case. I did not know, could not know, that Death would cross my path again and that Clarence Ray Allen would not let go of Death's hand. I would see more blood; I would see more pain; I would see one man take his last breath before I would see the end of it all. But at that moment, all I saw was a judge looking directly at me and twelve people waiting for me to begin the prosecution.

There is a moment for me, it never fails, just a brief flutter, when the judge says I may make my opening statement, that is always the same as it was in my very first case, a rush of emotion that butts up against the clarity of my perception of the moment. I walked to the center well of the courtroom and faced twelve strangers. Our fates and our lives were now bound together in the drama of justice. From the first time I had ever stood in front of a jury, I knew it was what I had been born to do. It never changed.

I looked at the twelve faces looking back at me, expectant, tense; it was their moment, too. But it was time for my opening statement; time for me to tell the jury what I expected the evidence to show. If a trial is like a play, an opening statement is like a narration of what the jurors are about to see and hear and about what you are going to prove. And, if you don't prove everything you say in your opening statement, you know that the defense attorney is going to remind those twelve people of your failure over and over again. The opening statement must be carefully drawn, so that you set the theme of the trial. And there is no greater theme than murder, avarice, and cowardice. I turned and I pointed my finger at the gray-haired man sitting at the defense counsel table. When this case was through, those twelve jurors would have heard things they would never forget. My job was to make them see those revelations my way.

I told the jury members that Clarence Ray Allen led a gang of thieves. He orchestrated them. He manipulated them. He intimidated them. He made them murder a young woman, and I told them that they would hear the voice of the murderer tell them how he had grasped the neck of Mary Sue Kitts and squeeze the life out of her. And why? Because he was terrified for his own life. I told them that they would hear a man admit to facing this shameful moment of decision and of his hideous cowardice when he had acted. I told them of Carl Mayfield, of Shirley Doeckel, of Chuck Jones, of Barbara Carrasco. I told them they would see the stepping stone that was the last monument to a girl whose body had been abandoned to the rushing torrent of a mountain waterway.

I told the jury members that Clarence Ray Allen had surrounded himself with weak people and now those weak people were giving him up. I wanted the jury to know that each person they would hear was a person who fed on the bottom of life, and they should focus on Clarence Ray Allen, as each of those people came to the stand, and they should remember that these were his friends, the people who followed him. I left unsaid the one other thing that I wanted them to think. For this, I merely planted that seed. The witnesses were criminals and lowlifes who were

Allen's closest followers, and so what did that make Allen? You are who you run with.

I knew the defense had no choice. They would tell the jury that you couldn't believe criminals—they would do whatever they had to in order to save their skins—but that wouldn't explain why they were his client's friends. That was the first trap for the defense and it was the way I intended to frame the jury's perception of Allen. If these people were those who he had surrounded himself with, then who was he? *What was he?* I knew that no matter how hard the defense battered the credibility of each witness, the jury would in time wonder how everybody could be lying except the leader of the pack.

However, I faced real problems of my own. I had no body. I had no crime scene. I had nothing to put in front of a jury except a picture of a young woman who had gone missing. Yet, I needed to convince a jury that this crime had occurred. For that, I needed Lee Furrow. But first, I needed everybody else: Mayfield, Doeckel, Jones, and Carrasco.

Defense attorneys give their clients notebooks to write in while the case is being tried, so that the defendant won't be pulling on their sleeve every time something happens that he doesn't agree with. Jurors watch defendants. Judges watch everybody. If you are going to try the "who me?" defense, then you shouldn't be indicating to your attorney that it didn't happen the way the witness says it did or shaking your head when forensic witnesses are describing how they think the crime occurred. Clarence Allen must have filled three notebooks. He didn't shake his head. He just stared at witnesses. Maybe staring isn't the right description. He looked at them with flat, emotionless eyes, which never wavered, but pierced the distance between himself and those who dared testify against him.

When I called Carl Mayfield as a witness, he looked the same as he did when he was arrested, totally resigned to his fate. There was no cockiness. All eyes focused on him. It would be my guess that it was the first time in his life that he had the attention of everybody in the room.

Mayfield sat back in the witness chair and sighed. He knew what was coming. It had been months since he had given his story to Blade and Martin. Now, Blade was sitting next to me as my chief investigative officer, and Bill was sitting right behind in the audience. After further pre-trial questioning by Blade and Martin and me, Mayfield's story had changed a little. That almost always happens. Suspects try to make themselves look better. They tell you just enough in an attempt to make you look at them differently, but slowly you leech it out of them, draining them of the truth and forcing them back to the ultimate reality—facing what they really are. Mayfield had been no different, and now he would have to admit something in open court, to strangers, about the reality of the shameful thing he had done. He never looked at Allen; his eyes focused only on me. I asked him about his criminal record. It wasn't the first time he had been asked this and he knew it wouldn't be the last. He admitted he had done time in prison for robbery and forgery.

Did Mayfield know the defendant, Clarence Ray Allen? Yes, he knew him. He had worked for him in June of 1974 and, yes, Allen knew his record when he hired him as a security officer. Mayfield admitted he had helped burglarize Fran's Market after the keys were taken unbeknownst to the son of the owner. He, Allen, and Jones had stolen the safe and carried it away in a horse trailer. The safe had money orders in it and Allen had taken them. For his part, he had only gotten two hundred dollars.

I showed him Mary's high school photograph. Mayfield stared at it and then lifted his eyes. "It's a photograph of Mary Sue Kitts." I let him hold it for a moment and then took it back. I asked the bailiff to hand it to the jury so they could all look at it as they passed that picture full of a stolen life's promise from hand-to-hand. I waited until they were finished. I wanted them to hold as much of Mary Sue Kitts in their hands as they could, to see that photographic memory, because that was all I had to make her become real except for her grieving parents.

Mayfield admitted that he had helped cash some of the stolen checks and then he came home; he came back to work for Clarence Ray Allen in Fresno. A week later, he had gone to Allen's home. Allen and Jones were there and so was Lee Furrow. They sat in the backyard while Roger Allen stayed in the house.

"Did you have an occasion to be present when there was some conversation between some people regarding a girl that seemed to be a problem and that they needed to do something about?"

Mayfield closed his eyes and closed his mouth tightly, the corners of his lips turning down. He opened his eyes and stared off to the side, wiping his nose with the back of his hand. "Yeah." There was resignation in his voice.

"What, if anything, did Allen say about Mary Sue Kitts?"

"That she was starting to talk about the things we had done in San Diego. He wanted a vote taken to see what should be done about her."

Mayfield's words hung in the air for mere seconds that seemed to linger on and on, while I let everyone in the courtroom weigh them in their minds. Then I cut through the heavy silence. "Did you vote?" For the first time, Mayfield was forced to publicly admit what he had really done, instead of repeating the lie he told Bill and Blade to cover his own shameful conduct.

"Yes, sir."

"What was the vote?"

"My vote?"

"Your vote."

"My vote was yes."

"Mr. Allen?"

"Yes."

"Lee Furrow?"

"Yes."

"Chuck Jones?"

"Yes."

I drew out the timing for each question and answer. I wanted the murder vote to sound like the slow ringing of a bell, and it did clang in the heavy silence of the courtroom. What the jury heard was grown men sitting around the table in a yard and voting to murder a nineteen-year-old girl. I stood behind the counsel table and slowly walked behind Allen. "Was there any discussion as to who would ultimately decide who would do it?"

"Not in my presence, no." I wanted the jurors to look at me and then to see Allen, staring at Mayfield with those dead eyes. After my next question, Carl Mayfield admitted that he was there that night Mary Sue Kitts was murdered. He had gone to a winery where Allen Security provided guards and had stolen some cyanide to put into pills to give Mary Sue, but she hadn't taken them. He had gone with Jones and Furrow over to Allen's house and lifted hexagonal stepping stones out of the side yard. I showed him the aerial photograph of Allen's home and he identified the row of stepping stones as being the same as the ones he pulled up and put into Chuck Jones' truck. Then he really went to work.

Mayfield testified he never saw Mary Sue Kitts again. A few days later. Allen said that everything went all right. Mayfield testified he never saw Lee Furrow again, either. When he asked where Lee was, Allen just said that he had been done away with, that he had had Furrow killed down in Mexico.

There was one more thing I wanted the jury to be absolutely aware of. "Did Mr. Allen ever say anything to you about people who talked about him?"

"Yes, sir. He said there were several ways that they could be taken care of."

"What did he say about 'taking care' of people?"

"He said that if he was ever locked up, and people were ready to testify against him, he had other people that would be watching his back, and they would take care of the situation."

"Did you believe that?"

"At the time it was said, no."

"At the time of the meeting when Mary Sue Kitts was discussed, did you believe it?"

"Yes."

"No further questions."

The cross-examination didn't shake Mayfield. He admitted that he was a thief, a liar, a man who had voted for this girl's murder and lied about that to Blade and Bill. But nothing could change the fact that he was an associate of the man sitting at the counsel table, staring directly at Mayfield. And the eyes of twelve people weren't looking at Mayfield, they were fixed on Clarence Ray Allen. I watched them and I could see something that you don't often see with jurors. It was a slowly growing fear of what he was, something they could not relate to: the realization that they were actually confronting evil in the body of a man staring back at the witness stand.

"The People call Shirley Doeckel to the stand." Shirley Doeckel walked to the witness stand, glancing sideways at the twelve people watching her, and then raised her hand to be sworn. The bright lights of the courtroom didn't compliment her. The stress of the last few months had deepened the fine lines, and her hair had taken on a more brassy tint. If she ever had, she no longer looked like the woman next door. She had fallen into a stereotype and she managed to meet that expectation as the eyes of everyone followed her to the stand.

I had talked to her repeatedly before trial and she was growing more and more uncooperative. She was no longer a caged prisoner looking at interrogators surrounding her. Out of custody, she had time to think. She had figured out, or so she thought, how she could avoid betraying her lover, the man watching her across the open space of the courtroom. Unlike Mayfield, she looked directly at Allen. I could sense the lack of fear or animosity on her part. She still wanted him. I hoped the jury could see it also.

She admitted she was there the night when Mary Sue and Furrow were at her apartment. Yes, she rode to the mountains with Allen. Yes, she went to San Diego with Allen, but, no, she didn't recall saying that Allen told her anything about money orders. I showed her copies of her previous statements. No, she didn't recall those statements. No, she didn't recall saying Allen was at her apartment when Mary Sue arrived. No, she didn't recall. No, she didn't recall. Once again, I showed her her previous statements. No, she didn't recall. This is the refuge of the perjurer. They don't deny making the statement; they just don't recall. They don't deny events happened; they just don't recall.

I wasn't exasperated. I had been through this before and I knew you just keep pressing. Soon, the jury realizes they are lying. Then you confront them with what they said before and the jury knows that what they said before is the truth; what they said before was what really happened. But I wasn't going to let her crawl under a rock; if she was going to be a difficult witness, I was going to make her paint herself with her own corruption.

"Were you told anything by Allen about why you were leaving the apartment?" I had to repeat the question twice because Shirley kept staring at me and wouldn't answer. Finally, with a harsh edge in my voice, as I rose from the counsel table, I repeated, "Were you told anything by Ray Allen as to why you had left the apartment?" Shirley stared at me and I could see the hate in those black eyes. It radiated across the room.

"Ray told me that Lee was going to do away with Mary." Her voice was a mumbled whisper. She looked at Judge Mardikian, but his face was expressionless, giving away nothing. There was no place in the courtroom that she could look and find mercy.

"Did he say why?"

Shirley turned to me, trying to find some refuge in the seconds that she had before answering, but my question hung there, waiting for an answer. Finally, she repeated my question as if she didn't understand it. "Why Lee was going to do away with Mary?"

"Yes." The disdain in my voice was unmistakable. I intended for my question to be uttered in a tone that would not tolerate any more evasion. When she finally spoke, she couldn't look at Allen; her eyes were lowered, focused on the floor.

"Because she talked too much."

She denied ever seeing the body. She denied ever seeing Mary Sue's body carried out of her apartment. She admitted that Lee Furrow and Chuck Jones followed her and Clarence Allen in another car, but she denied knowing what was in the back of that car. But it was the final question that left her totally by herself on the stand

"Did you question Mr. Allen about whether or not Mary Sue Kitts was actually dead, Mrs. Doeckel?"

"Yes."

As I asked the next question, I left my position near the counsel table and walked behind where Allen was seated so that the jury would see him directly in their line of sight when I spoke. "And what, if anything, did Mr. Allen say to you?"

"He said to believe it."

I had no further questions. When Shirley Doeckel walked off the witness stand, she didn't have a friend in that room. What still amazes me is that as she walked past the counsel table she looked with soft eyes at Allen, but she obviously couldn't see that she had neither a lover nor a friend staring back at her from the defendant's chair.

"The People call Charles Jones." I took Chuck Jones through the same night, and I put the stepping stone on the counsel table so that all eyes were focused on it. Everyone knew what it was. Jones stared at it and then repeated what he had told us about the stone and about that night.

He didn't look at Allen as he testified. He kept his gaze on the back of the courtroom.

Jones described his fear while sitting through the vote to kill Mary Sue Kitts, but admitted he was there. He told of how Allen had threatened his son. It was a brief moment illustrating the contradictions of human behavior. This was a man who could participate in the murder of a helpless young woman, could drop her into the oblivion of an anonymous burial ground, but who could worry about his son. I remember thinking back on something he said during his interrogation when Bill asked him if he had ever told anyone what he had just told Bill and Blade.

"Did you ever tell your wife about this?"

"No."

"Did you ever tell anybody about this?"

"No."

"You just kept it to yourself all these years?"

"Yeah. I wanted to tell my wife a bunch of times, but, you know, what's it gonna do? What's she gonna think of me?"

My eyes fixed on Jones as he sat on the witness stand. There was no question what anybody in the courtroom thought of him. There was not even any question about what he thought of himself.

The next witness came to the stand. Allan Boudreau, a forensic criminologist, testified that the rust marks on the stone were consistent with wire that had been tightly wrapped around the stone. I left the stone sitting in front of me on the counsel table the rest of the day. Whenever jurors looked at the stone, I wanted them to be reminded that it had been wired to the blanket that was the burial shroud of Mary Sue Kitts. It was all that had been found, a broken marker of a young life whose years ahead had been taken away from her and her parents.

I called Bryon Schletewitz, the young man whose acceptance of an invitation to a swimming party had begun the events that led to murder. He testified that Mary Sue had come to him and told him that Clarence Ray Allen was responsible for the burglary. He had confronted Roger Allen, who had denied it. And, with that simple act, his words had set into motion a warrant of death sealed by the vote of cowardly men and signed by the defendant who sat, staring out across the void that separated him from decent people.

Each technical and foundation witness went to the stand. But none of them were there when Mary Sue Kitts was murdered. I let the natural tension of the case build. I needed the courtroom to be electric when I called my last witness.

We provided a shirt and slacks for Furrow when he came to court. I knew he wouldn't be what a jury expected. People think a murderer looks a certain way. I sometimes think they expect a murderer to be licking his fingers, hungry for traces of blood. The reality is by the time they get to court most of them are dressed to look like your neighbor. Well, maybe not everybody's neighbor, but somebody's neighbor. They don't drool and the tattoos are covered up by long sleeves, no bandanas, nothing to frighten people. When a man or woman accused of murder walks in front of a jury, most of the time they don't look much different than the people sitting in the jury pool. That is what defense attorneys want. They want you to think that their client looks like your nephew or somebody you work with, somebody who you know wouldn't commit murder. Sometimes, it actually works.

When jurors are going to be asked to evaluate the credibility of a witness, you have to prepare them, particularly if there are going to be things about the witness they won't like. People have a tendency to be more receptive to what is said by people they like and to be less receptive to what is said by people they don't like. If you are going to put a witness on the stand who is going to repulse people, you have to let them know in advance so they can get past it and listen to what the witness is actually saying. I had told the jury that Lee Furrow had strangled a young woman to death. I had prepared the jury for him. He was a murderer. They would be looking at a man who had murdered the one witness I could not bring before them, a man who had done something they could barely conceive of. I needed them to see beyond that, to see what was beneath the blood on his hands. I needed them to feel empathy for a murderer, and for that to happen, I knew they had to feel something for the human being who had become a killer. These jurors were people who mowed their lawns on Saturday and who shuttled their children to school. For them, murder was simply beyond what they could relate to, but to create sympathy in them, I had to get them to relate on some personal level to Lee Furrow.

The jurors had heard about Furrow. They had a picture in their minds. I could see their eyes on him when he took the stand. I had the handcuffs removed just before he raised his hand to testify. This was a man who had

committed an almost inconceivable act—the deliberate strangulation of a
nineteen-year-old woman. And there he was; right in front of them. They
were looking at a murderer. Now, I had to make him into a human being.

I took him through the case very slowly, letting the moment build
when we got to the murder. I wanted to draw it out, taking the questions
in smaller and smaller steps as we came closer to the moment when his
hands came up to Mary Sue's throat, drawing out the time between questions, letting each answer hang in the air, letting Furrow begin to wind
tighter and tighter as he was forced to publicly confront what he had done
in order to save himself. The reality was that I wanted Furrow to be so
pent up by the time I asked the question that everyone was waiting for
that he would come apart right in front of the jury.

It is hard to fake emotion, but if it's sincere, it has incredible convincing
force. I hadn't asked him that question before trial, because I wanted it to
all spill out in front of the jury. I didn't want any of it to appear rehearsed.
A trial is live theater. I was taking a chance because the jury was going
to see a man confess right in front of them to first-degree murder, and
I needed them to sympathize with him, to wonder whether they would
be any different if they were as terrified as he. We like to think we would
have the courage to give our own life and do the right thing. Fortunately,
most of us can indulge that fantasy; but we never have to face the reality.

When I tried a case, I seldom stood near the witness. I raised or
lowered my voice for emphasis, but I hardly ever raised my voice in anger
or put my face into the face of the witness. That may happen on television,
but most judges won't tolerate it and, worse, it can make you look like a
bully. The other reason I didn't do it is because I'm a pacer. If I stand and
start talking, I have a tendency to start walking around and that can be
distracting. I stay put. It works for me.

With Furrow, I opened with his relationship with Carrasco and Allen. I
then began to establish the motive that Mary Sue had been talking about
the burglary. Furrow testified that Bryon Schletewitz had confronted
Roger Allen, Clarence Allen's son, with the accusation of his father's
involvement in the burglary of the market.

"Were any statements attributed to Mary Sue Kitts?"

"Yes, by Bryon Schletewitz."

I then took him through the meeting at Allen's house. "What, if anything, did Allen say as to why the people had been asked to come together at his house?"

"To do something about Mary Sue Kitts."

"What did Mr. Allen say?"

"That she—she knew too much and that she was gonna talk to the police if somethin' wasn't done."

"Was there any discussion by Mr. Allen as to what should be done?"

"For—to have her killed."

"And was there any discussion as to how that was to be done?"

"Yes, about cuttin' her up and choppin' her up and throwin' her away, buryin' her somewhere, or burnin' her up in a car."

I needed to establish the basis for the fear that Furrow had of Allen. It didn't make a difference whether what he believed was true as much as whether he believed it. Allen made an effort with everyone to portray himself as a cold-blooded killer. It was part of how he controlled his followers, convincing them of this persona of violence and willingness to murder anyone he needed to, including them. It was a newspaper article about the killing of two people that would make the point. "Mr. Furrow, prior to this meeting at Allen's home, did you have occasion to be in a car with Barbara Carrasco and Clarence Allen?"

"Yes, sir."

"Was there anybody else in the car?"

"Yes, Shirley Doeckel."

"Was there any conversation about a newspaper article?"

"Yes, Allen said that he'd chopped two people down in Nevada on a contract and an article had said he was the hit man."

"Was there a newspaper article displayed?"

"Yes, Mr. Allen took it out of his wallet. He gave it to Shirley Doeckel." This was another example of how far Allen would go to burnish his image as a ruthless killer in the eyes of those around him. Was it true? I don't know. No one will ever know.

I backed up to the meeting at Allen's home. "At this meeting at Allen's home, was there any decision made as to whether or not Mary Sue Kitts would be killed?"

"No, he said they'd talk about it later." Furrow's voice was so soft I could see the jury straining to hear him. I took him through the next few days and then over to Shirley Doeckel's apartment. Allen showed up. Mary Sue Kitts was there. "When Mr. Allen arrived, did you have a discussion with him?"

"He asked me to give Mary Sue Kitts these reds. He said it was poison."

"What, if anything, did you say in response?"

"I told him I didn't want to do it."

"Did Mr. Allen say anything to you when you told him that?"

"He told me it's just as easy to get rid of two people as it is one." Furrow's voice trailed off as he looked down. I could hardly hear him but the jury was focused as the whisper came out.

"Did you agree to do it?"

There was a long silence, until in a hoarse whisper Furrow said, "Yes."

"Can you tell me why?"

"I was afraid he'd kill me."

"What was your emotional state at that time?"

"Very upset."

I established that Allen left with Shirley Doeckel and then called the apartment to speak to Furrow. "Did Mr. Allen call again?"

"Yes. He asked me if she was dead yet, and I said, 'No.' And he said, 'Well do it.' Then he hung up."

I took Furrow through the minutes after the phone call when he and Mary Sue were sitting on the bed in Doeckel's apartment, I paused for a moment, and then I rose behind the counsel table, and slowly lowered my hands until they rested lightly on the flat surface; I leaned forward, wanting the jury to stretch for the words. "So, what did you do?"

Of all the murder cases I tried as a prosecutor and of all the cases I later would try as a judge, I never saw anything like it. Furrow began to shake. His head hung down and he started to move from side to side like someone wanting to deny what he couldn't forget, trying to force it back down, and struggling to keep the sound from seeping out. And then he began to cry. I stood at the counsel table and waited. The only sound in the courtroom was his sobbing, great racking sobs. I waited. I let the jury watch him. I didn't offer him Kleenex or ask for a momentary recess to allow him to compose himself. I just stood there and let the moment speak for itself. The words came out in anguished bursts of sound. He kept saying he killed her. But it was obvious he wasn't crying simply because of himself. What was apparent to everyone in the room was his contrition, his remorse, his sense of real guilt, and the embodiment of a tortured human being. What came out was that this was not a man who could have killed anybody *unless* he was terrified. There was only one man who could have terrified him and that man sat there, with his reptilian eyes staring at Furrow. Then I asked him how he had done it.

"I strangled her."

I moved behind the jury box so that all eyes would be focused on the weeping man on the witness stand, letting my voice come from behind them. Slowly, I made him draw his fingers around the throat of Mary Sue Kitts one more time. You could see it in his eyes. He was reliving it. You could see it in his face. He could see her eyes staring at him as he squeezed. It was the face of a man who had chosen to save himself at the price of his soul.

"Did she struggle?"

"No, sir."

"Did she have her back to you, or was she facing you?"

"She was facing me."

"Did she scratch you at all?"

"No, sir."

"Did you leave her there on the floor?"

"Yes."

"Did you make another phone call?"

"Yes, to the number of the phone booth where Ray Allen was waiting. I told him that I had killed Mary Sue Kitts. That she was dead."

I let the emotion fill the courtroom, falling into the void of silence, waiting before asking my next question. My voice carried across the room. "Why did you do that to that girl?"

Furrow was sobbing. His voice came out in chunks of sound. "'Cause he said he'd be right outside and I was afraid if I didn't he'd kill me anyway."

Everyone in the room was moved by what they were seeing. Some jurors were wiping away tears. Only one man sat like a stone at the counsel table. Everybody saw it and it was enough. No amount of cross-examination would break through the guilt and remorse we had seen. Lee

Furrow would never have killed anybody unless he thought there were hands around his own throat. You can have contempt for his weakness but still appreciate that what made him kill was pure, unadulterated fear. I am sure there were people in that courtroom who liked to think they wouldn't have made the same choice, but I also know that most of those people weren't sure.

The image that remains imprinted in my memory was Furrow's description of what happened when they got to the Piedra Bridge. Allen, accompanied by Doeckel, drove up the road to act as lookouts. Furrow described the next few moments.

"Chuck got a hold of Mary Sue and was takin' her out of the back and he—she was too heavy with all the stones and stuff, so he asked me if I'd help him and then I grabbed her feet and we took her out of the Ranchero."

"Before you did that, were stones attached to her in any way?"

"They were wired around her waist and around her shoulders."

I allowed my hand to rest lightly on the gray chunk of hard-edged stone sitting on the counsel table, slashed with a bloody streak of rust. "What kind of stones were they, Mr. Furrow?"

"Stepping stones, like patio stepping stones."

"How many stepping stones were there?"

"There was four in each stack."

"What kid of wire did you use?"

"It looked like bailing wire. It was already wrapped around the stones."

"After you'd attached the stones to Mary Sue Kitts, what did you do?"

"We picked the body up and threw it over the side of the bridge."

I will never forget the look on his face when I asked if he recalled anything specific about the height of the bridge. His eyes were closed. He was describing what he saw inside his mind and the words came out in one rush of sound. "That it took a long time for the body to hit the water."

Two days later, the jury reassembled on the banks of the canal next to the Piedra Bridge. The dry grass of autumn rustled in the slight breeze as the canal superintendent testified about the scraping of the canal. The jury members couldn't keep their eyes off the ribbon of black water shimmering down below. The feet of the jurors scraped against the dirt as they took one last look. Everybody looked down at the final resting place of Mary Sue Kitts. All that remained was the relentless flow of the water and the memory of a young girl murdered at the direction of the bespectacled, gray-haired man who stood on the edge of the canal surrounded by plain clothes deputies. There was no expression on his face. The only sound was the crackle of the last dried grass of summer and the soft rumble of rushing water scouring the concrete walls of the canal, carrying with it whatever fell into its embrace.

"The People rest, your Honor."

23

"We the jury ..."

October, 1977
Fresno, California

Waiting for a verdict is always the worst part for any lawyer—defense or prosecution. I went back to the office. I did the usual drill. I walked around. I sat. I waited. In a big case, if the verdict came in before 5:00 P.M., the receptionist would usually put out a call through the intercom system that a verdict had been reached. People would give you a minute to get your file before they followed you down to court. Everybody wants to be there when a big verdict comes in. After 5:00, the excitement subsides, and you wait by yourself or with your investigator. Everybody else in the office has gone home. Big verdict or not, people want to go home at 5:00. There isn't any sound in the office except the rustle of trash cans as the janitor moves through the hallways. You sipped cold coffee and you smoked—almost everybody smoked back then. You waited until you heard the phone ring. For some reason, I always let it ring a second time before I picked it up—superstition, I guess.

A fast verdict in a felony case is several hours. Juries usually take their time with long cases. They do their duty. They choose a foreman. They go over the evidence. They talk. People take it seriously. Even in a fairly clear case, the usual time is eight to ten hours. In a big case, it can be two or more days, unless it's a Friday. The phone rang. I waited until it rang a second time, always the second ring. I picked up.

When you enter a courtroom for a verdict, everything seems a little different. No matter how many times you've done it, it's always different than the other times you've come through the swinging gate to the counsel table. In a big case, the press is there, and this was a big case and the press *was there*. I walked down the aisle between the rows of spectator seats and through the swinging gate that separated the spectators from the counsel table. Bill and I took our seats at the counsel table. Blade and Tommy both sat in the front row, Blade's face impassive as usual, but I knew he felt this case deep inside, more than he had felt any other. Tommy's nod reflected his usual confidence. We were waiting for the defense attorney, whose office was a ten or fifteen minute walk from the courthouse. I could feel the sheen of perspiration on my face, and the heavy beats of my heart. I took a deep breath. Whatever you are feeling inside, a trial lawyer must always appear calm to the outside world.

In the movies or on television, they leave out all the paper shuffling that comes before a verdict is read, the wait for the judge to enter the courtroom, the whisper of pens sliding across paper, and the rustle of the judge's robe as he takes his seat. You wait for the clerk to take her seat. It feels like it's happening in slow motion, the movement, the sounds. Judges will sometimes wait until the jury is seated before coming in, but most of the time they are already seated, looking out on the human panorama before them, waiting for the end of the play. All you have prepared for, all you have worked for, is about to be summed up by one word or two words—guilty or not guilty—words that will signal the turning point for the defendant, the victim's family, the prosecutor and the defense, all swept into the emotion of that short burst of words.

The bailiff brought Allen in from the holding cell. He looked out at the audience and nodded to his family, but there was no expression on his face, just as there had been none during the entire trial. His eyes glittered like shiny pebbles of obsidian. They had the same amount of warmth. I never saw anything in his eyes that looked alive.

Attorneys closely observe the jury when they walk in. Murder cases are different than other cases. Jurors know they are about to make a decision that will carry heavy consequences for the defendant and the victim's family. You can sense that weight in the way they walk. Sometimes, they glance at the defendant and then quickly look away. Sometimes, they don't look at all. You hope they don't smile; at least, if you are the prosecutor, you hope they smile at you and not at the defendant. This jury didn't smile at all.

The delivery of a verdict is ritualistic. Judge Mardikian, the trial judge, was a huge man, with a deep rumbling voice. He didn't just take the bench; he filled it. He asked if the jury had reached a verdict. The foreman held up several pieces of paper and nodded. The bailiff walked over and took the papers and handed them to the judge. The judge unfolded the papers, separated the sheets, and checked to see that they were all in order. Verdict forms are normally separated by crime and by verdict. One type of form is a guilty verdict and the other is a not guilty verdict. There is no way you can tell which form the judge has in his hands until it is read, unless the expression of the judge gives something away. Most judges are impassive when they look at a verdict form. Usually they look at the various forms, gaze at the jury and the defendant, and then speak these few words. "Is this your verdict?"

Judge Mardikian handed the verdict to the clerk. "The clerk will read the verdict." He stared straight at me.

When a verdict was being read, I always placed the palms of my hands flat against the top of the counsel table. In part, it kept me from fidgeting and, in part, it kept my hands from trembling. As you wait for those words—one or two—you are near the end of the ritual. The final curtain is about to descend.

"In the case of the People of the State of California versus Clarence Ray Allen, on the charge of violation of Penal Code section 187, the murder of Mary Sue Kitts, we the jury in the above entitled action find the defendant, Clarence Ray Allen, guilty, and we set the degree as murder in the first degree.

"In the case of the People of the State of California versus Clarence Ray Allen, on the charge of violation of Penal Code section 459, burglary of Fran's Market, we the jury in the above entitled action find the defendant, Clarence Ray Allen, guilty, and we set the degree as burglary in the second degree."

When a verdict is read, the final words hang in the air. No matter which side of the verdict you are on, there is a moment of suspension, when nothing moves and there is no more sound. It is just the words. Then you return to normal and adjust to what has changed. There is a certain elation to winning and there is a cold, icy feeling when you lose. I can't say I felt much except that I was very tired. The stress that had been keeping me going was suddenly seeping out of me, and all that was left was fatigue.

There was a quiet rustling of paper and whispers while Judge Mardikian prepared to poll the jury to determine if each of them agreed with the verdict as read. The jurors each answered in the affirmative. I felt detached from the moment. My mind had already closed out all sounds. I lifted my palms from the table. The imprint of my hand remained on the table, outlined in perspiration, a noticeable puddle of water. I caught the very slight nod from Blade that signaled his approval and the familiar grin from Tommy that said he was never worried. I looked out of the corner of my eye at Allen and his attorney. There was more reaction from the attorney than there was from Allen. I looked at the jury. Several were staring at Allen. Some were looking down at their laps. No matter how much jurors may personally condemn the acts of a defendant, it is still hard to look a man in the eye and condemn him to his face. Most people can't do it and it is no reflection on the character of a juror who doesn't look at the defendant. It is a hard job being a juror and they have earned their right to get out of that room and go home. I know that is what I wanted to do.

After the judge thanked the jury, he allowed them to leave. I watched them file out of the jury box. A few looked back over their shoulders. One or two looked in my direction and nodded. I nodded back. I stayed seated. There were still matters to be taken care of: the setting of a sentencing date, referral to the probation department for a sentencing report, and the setting of a calendar date for the obligatory motions for a new trial. I waited until all of the talking was over. There was one more thing to be done. I waited.

The bailiff came over and handcuffed Allen. I watched this man who had caused so much destruction, so much misery, be led from the courtroom. He wasn't in control of anything anymore, including himself. From now on out, he would be a follower. The sentencing would be anticlimactic. The Supreme Court of California had found the death penalty unconstitutional and it had not been restored as a punishment. The penalty for first-degree murder was life in prison. There wasn't any mystery to it. When he walked through the back door of the courtroom with his handcuffs on, I wanted to watch. I wasn't the only one.

I called Mr. and Mrs. Kitts to let them know the verdict had come in, guilty on all counts. There was no triumph in the call, no joy. What could I give them except maybe some modicum of closure, and I wasn't sure of even that. What closure could there be when they had no child? What closure could there be when they did not know Mary Sue's final resting place? All I could offer was that the man responsible now stood convicted.

I called Ray and Fran Schletewitz to let them know the verdict had come in. They appreciated the call. I thanked them for their cooperation and asked them to pass my thanks on to Bryon. The case and the trial had taken a toll on all of us, but now it was over. I told them that Allen would get life in prison. They wanted to know if that meant he could ever get out. Would he serve life? I told them that in California life in prison didn't necessarily mean life in prison; it would depend. He could get parole some day, but he would do at least twenty or twenty-five years. He would be an old man if he got out at all. There was nothing for them to worry about. Allen was gone from their lives. I promised them that where he was going he couldn't hurt anybody anymore. I had assured them of that when I asked them to testify.

I hung up the phone. I looked at the mess on my desk and added the Allen file to the top of the pile. I would come in the next morning, clean up the file and my desk, and get ready for the next case.

PART III

A WHISPERING VOICE

24

"A gnawing coldness …"

Three Years Later
11:50 P.M., Friday, September 5, 1980
Fresno, California

I leaned back in the seat while Bill drove. The lights of Fran's Market receded in the distance. It had been three years since I finished the Kitts murder trial and walked out of Fran's Market for what I thought would be the last time. The details of that case had never left me, unlike so many of the murder cases I had handled where victim's faces just became blurs in my memory. Now, here I was, back in the same place, with more violent deaths. Thinking about the Kitts case and the irony of Bryon's murder wasn't going to solve the savage murders of him or the other two kids lying on the floor, an image enough to shock even jaded criminal investigators, including me. I closed the pages of the book in my mind on the murder of Mary Sue Kitts. But still there was a whispering voice in the very back of mind, speaking words that I could not quite make out, and there was a gnawing coldness in my stomach that I couldn't identify.

We left before the coroner moved the bodies. The crime scene techs would take enough pictures. I wanted to get back and try to pick up the threads of where Connie Barbo, the woman found in the bathroom covered with blood, had been and who she had been with. That was the most logical course of action, work backward on her and we would most likely get our shooter. Time was the enemy now. People who commit this type of crime don't travel in circles that cooperate with cops or district attorneys. We had to get to witnesses quickly before they began to close their mouths. Just knowing who the shooter was would scare people into remaining silent. People will swallow even their highest moral impulses when they are afraid, and among the people we were hunting for, silence *was* a virtue.

Bill and I didn't talk much on the drive back from Fran's. It was a long, twenty-minute drive back to the sheriff's office, and we kept our thoughts to ourselves. It was after midnight when we arrived at the sheriff's office detective division. Tom Lean was now a supervising detective. Blade had retired, as had Tabler. Reflexively, the first place Bill and I went was to the coffee pot. Lean sat near us, waiting for us to fill him in. Detective Kenny Badiali was back out supervising at the crime scene. The Rios boy had made it through surgery, but he would never regain full use of his arm.

Bill spoke first. "This doesn't make any sense. Those kids had nothing that anybody would want. Whoever did this had a reason to kill them but it beats the hell out of me what it could be." Bill didn't need to say any more. An experienced homicide investigator can look at a crime scene and get a general picture about what happened. When you have seen enough of them, you know what a burglary looks like, you know what a robbery looks like, and you know what a drunken quarrel looks like. This didn't look like any of those things. Generally, a robber won't shoot witnesses. It may be difficult to believe, but usually the robber is as scared as the victim, and that's usually the reason why victims in robberies get shot. The victim makes a sudden move that may not mean a thing and the shooter misinterprets it. In an instant, a simple robbery becomes a capital offense.

Bill said, "I'm guessing this guy is straight out of the joint." Tommy agreed. Looking a human being in the eye and then pulling the trigger, going from one victim to the next meant only one thing: Whoever had done this had to be a hardened criminal. Our best guess was that we needed to look for somebody who had recently been released from the joint, who had a history of using a shotgun in a robbery and had a history of violence. Unfortunately, that is a big pool of people.

We went over the information we had from Jack Abbot, the neighbor who had fired at the shooter and probably hit him in a non-vital area. It was obvious to us now that the first person Abbot saw running from the storeroom had been the Rios boy, who was trying to escape.

Detective Ross Kelly had interviewed Rios just before he had gone into surgery, so we now knew that the blood-covered woman he had helped remove from the bathroom area of the store was one of the assailants, and she was currently under guard at Valley Medical Center. She now had been positively identified as one Connie Barbo, a meth user with a minor record for prostitution and drug use, but nothing in her record indicated the level of violence we had just seen. Rios said she was armed with a pistol and came in with a white male, who was the shooter. All Rios could add at this point was that the shooter had been unshaven and wearing a bandana. He had shot the other three and then opened the door to the bathroom where Rios was hiding. The shooter fired at him from less than four feet away and left him for dead. We wouldn't be able to question him further until he came out of the recovery room, and that might not be for another twelve or more hours.

Homicides are usually brought into focus within forty-eight hours. The first twenty-four are crucial. Evidence is collected, witnesses are interviewed, and the trail is picked up. The problem in this case was there was no trail. When you look at a homicide and try to figure out who did it and why, you usually look first for motive. What was the shooter's motive? We had decided this shooting didn't make sense, so the motive had to be something that wasn't obvious to us yet. It didn't look like the motive was simply robbery, but we didn't have time to dwell on it. Fingerprints, witnesses, a known associate, we needed to find something, *anything*, that would lead us to the shooter.

In this case, the known associate was Connie Barbo. If we could learn who she was running with, we would likely find the killer. We kept discussing various theories until even the stale coffee in the pot couldn't keep us going. We went home to get a few hours sleep.

We were back on the job the next day. By mid-afternoon, we knew where Connie Barbo lived. Kelly went to her apartment. Her eleven-year-old son answered the door. He had last seen his mother at 5:00 P.M. the day before. She had been with a white male, approximately thirty-five years old, five-foot-ten to six feet tall, thin build, with shoulder-length, brownish-blond hair. The boy only knew the man as Little Blue. The two of them had left in a dirty, white car that had a sticker in the windshield. Barbo's son said Little Blue had tattoos on both arms.

Kelly was contacted by Barbo's aunt, who wanted us to know that the man identified as Little Blue was wearing a blue shirt and blue Levis. He and Connie had left in an old, dull-grey or off-white Cadillac. Barbo's aunt did not have any information on where Little Blue might be but that a "Kathy" or a "Kenny," who resided in a house north of McKinley Avenue and Fresno Street, could possibly provide further information. We had no idea who Kenny or Kathy might be.

25

"Body otherwise unremarkable ..."

Saturday, September 6, 1980
Fresno, California

After you have gone to enough autopsies, you get to the point that you can eat a sandwich and watch the process at the same time. I confess that I sat through more than one autopsy eating a hamburger and asking questions. People ask how could I do that? It wasn't because I didn't care about what was going on. It was because I was too busy to eat at another time and, simply enough, I was hungry. A homicide investigation in some ways is a lot like combat. You eat when you can, because you never know when you will get another chance. Of course, if the deceased had been out in the open for a few days and deterioration had set it, having a hamburger wasn't on your agenda. But there are some days when the person lying in front of you and the circumstances can overwhelm even the most experienced investigator. This was one of those days, and this was one of those cases.

The morgue at Valley Medical Center was down a long hallway, behind painted, swinging doors. When it was in use for autopsies, it was brightly lit by the white fluorescent light. There is no need to try to make people look better in soft light or to set a mood. It is all business and it's a sad business. The first thing that strikes you is how cold it is in the room. The second thing is the antiseptic smell. The third thing is the visual effect.

All three of the victims of the murders at Fran's Market were lying on stainless steel tables. There were no sheets over them. They were unclothed and washed clean, all clothing and relevant debris on them having been meticulously removed. Most of their blood had been drained and, in the bright fluorescent light, their bodies had a strange, whitish pallor, almost like a sheet of paper, which stood in sharp contrast to the purplish stain of *livor mortis* that still lingered where whatever blood was left had settled. Blood that had poured from wounds and congealed on their skin had been washed away, leaving antiseptically clean holes at the point of wound entry. They looked so cold lying there on glinting stainless steel tables. You know they could no longer feel anything, but you can't help thinking of them in terms you can relate, too. Yet if you think of them in personal terms, it becomes too emotional, so you have to detach.

The first time you see a forensic autopsy, it is an unnerving process. After a general examination, which is described into a recording device, the wound is carefully examined for powder marks, what is commonly referred to as a "powder tattoo," the stippling in the skin that results from flesh being hit by burning particles of gun powder. If there is clothing over the area of the wound, most of the stippling of the flesh will not occur because the burning particles will hit cloth.

The second thing the pathologist looks at is the size of the entry wound—bigger bullets, bigger holes. A shotgun fired from close range spreads numerous small pellets into the victim, coupled with the force of the explosive blast and wadding from the shell. At close range, the pellets are tightly grouped but they spread out rapidly. From close range, the combination of the pellets, the blast and the wadding create an open, tearing-type wound instead of the smooth edges left by a bullet. The wounds in this case were over an inch wide and jagged. A shotgun blast hits with tremendous force and it leaves an unmistakable mark on a human body. There was no doubt that these were shotgun wounds.

Probes are inserted into wounds to determine the angle from which a shot was fired and to assist in determining the position of the victim when they were shot. As probes are inserted, photos are taken, and the investigators and the pathologist discuss various possible scenarios. Throughout the process, what is left of a human being lies on a steel bed, waiting to be treated with the reverence we give to our loved ones. However, that final reverence does not come for hours. It doesn't mean that a body isn't treated with respect; it simply means that the process requires that from the first minutes of the investigation, the focus must be on making sure the killer is found.

Dr. Thomas Clint Nelson was the primary pathologist. He was generally referred to by all of us as "T.C." and he had been doing post mortem examinations—"posts" we called them—for as long as I had been involved in investigations and prosecutions. An autopsy doesn't require the skill of a surgeon. It always reminded me of butcher's work, but I know that's not fair because I never saw T.C. do anything that was not respectful in the context in which he worked. It was not as antiseptic as watching a surgeon work in the exposed area of a carefully draped body and it wasn't performed with the precision of a strategically placed scalpel. It is a process that allows you to see the complex parts that once made a human function and now will be probed for the ripping tears created by the hand of man.

T.C. did a visual examination of the young woman lying on the table closest to him and examined his notes. "Rocha, Josephine Linda, white female, age seventeen years, approximately five foot, five inches, approximately 110 pounds, brown hair, blue eyes, DOB 1-18-63. Examination of the body shows numerous shotgun pellet wounds in the left chest. Examination of the heart reveals numerous pellet marks in the pericardium and multiple entry marks through the surface of the heart." T. C. examined the lungs and found numerous pellets in the left pulmonary tissue. He looked around the room at the forensic investigators and shook his head. "Cause of death, shotgun wound to the heart. Body otherwise unremarkable."

He moved over to the young man lying on the next nearest table. "White, Douglas Scott, white male, age eighteen, approximately six feet, four inches, approximately two hundred pounds, brown eyes, brown hair, DOB 3-27-62." The hole in the lower area of the neck folded out like the petals of a red flower. T.C. traced the wound track which ran into the upper chest. It ran at a thirty degree, downward angle. It was obvious to everyone that Douglas White had been on his knees when he was shot at close range by someone standing over him. Wadding and the cardboard structure of the shotgun shell were still in his chest. "Cause of death, shock and hemorrhage due to shotgun wound to neck and chest area. Body otherwise unremarkable."

Nelson moved to the last table. He shook his head at the massive wound. "Schletewitz, Bryon, white male, approximately twenty-two years of age, five feet, eight inches, approximately 160 pounds, brown hair, brown eyes." The entry wound was between the eyebrows, and the back of his head was gone. The cranial cavity was empty. The shooter had fired upwards from the hip. T.C. picked up the brain, which had been placed next to Bryon's body. It was riddled with small lead pellets. He looked up and stated the obvious. "Cause of death, shotgun wound of the head. Body otherwise unremarkable."

Those words, "otherwise unremarkable," always had an effect on me. In medical terms, they simply meant nothing else of importance had been visually observed. In human terms, well, you can't allow yourself to think in human terms when an autopsy is being done; otherwise you can't do your job. T.C. looked around the room at the detectives. Each examination had taken about forty-five minutes under Nelson's practiced hand. He had worked quickly, holding organs up and inserting stainless steel probes so that the camera could capture what he was seeing. As he finished with each of the victims, he had carefully replaced the major organs, taking tissue samples as necessary. There was very little talking in the room while he worked. The sheer magnitude of seeing the bodies of three young people, whose lives had ended so violently, did not allow for the usual banter.

There were no surprises here. All three had been killed by a blast from a shotgun loaded with number-4 shot, about the size of a BB. The shots had been fired at close range. If we found the gun and could recover ammunition, we could show it was consistent with the pellets taken from the victims. Unlike a bullet fired from a handgun or rifle, there would be no grooves or striations on the shotgun pellets that could show from what gun they were fired. All we could hope to show was consistency.

It was clear that Josephine and Douglas had been facing forward and had turned slightly as the gun was fired. They knew what was going to happen. Their last minutes and seconds had to have been filled with terror, as they faced an executioner methodically taking their lives.

Bryon Schletewitz was the most grievously wounded. The top of his head was gone and the blood-spatter pattern at the store made it clear that the weapon was fired from a low position, pointing upward. Indiscriminate and callous, the killer had simply held the gun in an upward position and fired. He didn't care where he hit Bryon. What was obvious was that whoever fired these shots clearly intended each shot to kill. He didn't need to aim in order to hit these young people, but he did have to reload each time, breaking the shotgun open, pulling out the casing of the expended round and putting it in his pocket, reloading, closing the breech of the shotgun, and pulling the trigger, a complex process of manipulation, all the time keeping his eyes on his helpless prey.

What was evident was that two of those kids had knelt there, knowing what was coming, their eyes fixed on the man who was going to take everything from them. It was that thought that each detective carried away from the autopsies of Josephine, Douglas, and Bryon. When you leave an autopsy, that is as close as you will get to know the human being who was walking the earth hours before and, for a homicide investigator, that is the image that you take with you as you hunt down that person's killer.

Sometimes, that image will haunt you for years after the case file is closed. I know. I can close my eyes these thirty years later and still see those kids lying on that cold steel slab. No matter how many times you have witnessed a postmortem, nobody leaves an autopsy without a strong sense of commitment.

26

"The second son ..."

Sunday, September 7, 1980
Fresno, California

It was eight o'clock at night of the second day after the murders. All we knew was that the victims died from shotgun blasts fired at close range, most likely fired by a white, male adult approximately five-ten to six feet tall, 180 pounds, with tattoos on his arms and light brown hair, and who went by the name of Little Blue. We also knew he was possibly driving a dirty, white Cadillac with a sticker in the window. And we knew that Connie Barbo, the woman found crying hysterically in the bathroom, had been with him. This may sound like a lot of leads, but, in fact, it wasn't. Without a year on the Cadillac, it was simply one of thousands, and even if we could track it by color, which we couldn't, given its age and described condition, it was probably not the original color. The description of the shooter fit half the people released from prison in the last year alone. Barbo and her contacts remained our only solid direction. She wasn't talking. So, we would have to backtrack on who she had been with if we were to find anybody who knew Little Blue. We were working from our first suspicion that Little Blue, if he was the shooter, was fresh out of the joint.

We were checking on moniker files in the Department of Corrections. Prisons keep files on the monikers, or nicknames, of inmates. Little Blue had to be a moniker, but this was 1980 and there was no computerized filing system, no central data bank. We would have to go prison by prison. We started with high security prisons. This guy had to be among the worst, so our best estimate was that he came out of a maximum security prison because that is where the worst go, unless they are still working their way up. Maybe he had already reported to a parole officer, but that would only help if he was local. If he wasn't, it would be like looking for a specific piece of straw in a very large bale of hay.

Detective Kelly had reported that Barbo was using methamphetamine heavily, and she was an associate of either a "Kathy" or a "Kenny," but who was she or he? Maybe whoever it turned out to be would have some information, or maybe they'd have nothing. But until we found out who he or she was, *we* had nothing.

It was at that moment that Connie Barbo's mother called. Ross Kelly went to see Barbo's mother. She told him that two days before, Connie had been at her home with a white male known to her as Little Blue or Blue Boy. She said that Little Blue left Connie at the house and said he would come back later, at around 5:00 P.M. Then they were going to pick up a horse trailer and take a horse to Los Angeles. Little Blue never returned, but around 6:00 P.M. a man she knew as Ken came to the house and said that Little Blue had sent him to pick Connie up and take her to meet him. Ken told Connie to bring a change of clothes. Barbo's mother said that Connie left with Ken, but before she left, she had told her not to let the kids out of the house, and if she didn't make it back, to "take care of them."

Barbo's mother confirmed the description of Little Blue as late twenties, six feet tall, approximately 180 pounds, with medium-length, brown hair. She also described Ken as approximately 30 years old, six feet tall, about 200 pounds, with shoulder-length, dark hair. According to Barbo's mother, Ken and his wife Kathy were her daughter's crank connection, a slang term for methamphetamine dealer, and that Connie had visited their house a number of times. She didn't know Ken or Kathy's last names, only that when Mrs. Barbo had left the house for a while yesterday morning and returned later, a neighbor told her to get in touch with Kathy about Connie. She also said that early that afternoon a man came looking for Connie and wanted her to make a connection for him with Ken and Kathy. To make a connection meant he wanted to score or buy methamphetamine. Mrs. Barbo told the man that she wanted to talk to Kathy about her daughter Connie, and she said that the man drove her to Kathy's house. She went inside Kathy's house and Kathy and Ken were there and both seemed very nervous. Barbo's mother said she bought $20 worth of crank from Ken. Kathy said that some guy had called Ken and said that he had a fight with Connie and she took off. Kathy added, "If you want to know about Connie, call the sheriff."

That night, two days after the murders at Fran's Market, Ross Kelly, together with another officer and a deputy district attorney, drove by the house identified as belonging to Ken and Kathy, based on the information from Connie Barbo's mother. Several cars were parked in front of the house. The first vehicle came back registered to a Kathy Allen. Ross Kelly cross-checked the other vehicles and returned to the office immediately with the information—Kathy Allen was married to Kenny Allen. They were also confirmed to be the owners of an older-model Cadillac that was not currently licensed. Bill and I sat in stunned silence. We had been here before. We looked at one another, and each of us had the same cold chill. All the memories of the murder of Mary Sue Kitts came erupting back to the surface, along with all the old names that we had shuffled through in our minds as we left Fran's Market two days before. Kenny Allen was the second son of Clarence Ray Allen.

27

Murder Doesn't Always Make Sense

Monday, September 8, 1980
Fresno, California

Three days after the murders at Fran's Market, we still had nothing on Little Blue. But we had time to think about the possibilities. It kept coming back to the same thing. The only logical reason to hit a place like Fran's Market was for a quick robbery and out the door. But the crime scene made no sense for just a robbery. These kids were murdered for a reason, but the only logical reason was either to eliminate witnesses to the robbery itself or to use a robbery to cover up an intentional killing of one of the kids, or to do both a robbery and an intentional killing. It is true that the simplest explanation in any criminal investigation is most likely true. But in this case the simplest explanation didn't make sense. Still, there is a second rule: Murder doesn't always make sense.

When a person is killed in a robbery, usually the killing is a spontaneous decision. Most robbers don't set out to kill anybody; it just happens. The only reason to stand people in a room and methodically kill them one by one is to eliminate witnesses, but why do that unless the shooter had killed one, probably the Schletewitz boy, and then decided to kill the others because they were witnesses. That was possible, but even that scenario had a lot of variables. Usually, when a killer shoots someone, he panics. He doesn't think clearly. Time after time, I've seen this. They make mistakes. They run. This guy didn't panic or run after the first killing. He made sure to recover his expended shotgun shells.

Bill and I came to the same conclusion: This guy came in either prepared to kill witnesses if he had to or intending to kill witnesses. But why pick a rural grocery store to commit this kind of heinous crime unless you expected to find a lot of money? A person that kills like this may be cold-blooded, but generally he doesn't kill someone intentionally unless he has a good reason, or unless he is just plain crazy. All of us had seen killings committed by crazy people. This didn't look like a killing by a crazy person. The shooter's obvious search of the store and entering the walk-in freezer indicated very clearly that this person was looking for something and had reason to believe that whatever he was looking for was there. The rumor that Ray Schletewitz kept a lot of money in a safe in his freezer was something that had come up in the Clarence Ray Allen murder trial for killing Mary Sue Kitts. That rumor may now have spread all over the criminal community, but with our new connection to another member of the Allen family, Kenny, Clarence Allen's son, that rumor took on greater significance. It could be that the shooter had bought into the rumor about money in the freezer and it was increasingly possible that he had gotten that rumor from Kenny Allen.

It was possible that the shooter had a relationship with Kenny Allen or Allen had met the shooter, and maybe even was involved in the decision to rob the store. We needed to bring in Kenny Allen and squeeze him for information. For that, we needed leverage. We needed something to hold over him to make him willing to give up information. It only took us a few minutes before we realized we had it.

A search warrant is required to search a house except under exceptional circumstances. Neither the sheriff's investigators, nor Bill and I, could cite exceptional circumstances, but we did have probable cause to believe that Kenny and Kathy Allen had committed a crime in the sale of methamphetamine in their home and that they were dealers, and dealers were likely to have drugs in the place where they made sales. The information about the meth sale to Connie Barbo's mother would get us a search warrant to get inside Kenny and Kathy Allen's home. Once inside, we were most likely going to find methamphetamine and we would arrest them both for sale of meth. Just the fact that we'd have them both gave us an edge. We didn't really care about a nickel-and-dime meth sale to some crankhead. We only cared about what information the fear of going to jail for sale of drugs might get us regarding the shooter. Kenny might be willing to give up something to save his wife. She might be willing to give up something to save her husband, or to keep herself out of prison. You get a true sense of family commitment when you turn a husband and a wife; it gives you the warm fuzzies. We didn't expect to find Beaver Cleaver's mother and father.

Getting the warrant took all day. Even if we didn't find any meth, we could arrest them for the sale, and while we were looking for drugs, if we found anything else, it would be a plus. It isn't illegal to use a legal search for drugs to provide access to search for something else, as long as you have a right to search for drugs and to look only in the same place where you initially expected to find drugs.

The investigators assigned and Bill and I decided we would hit the Allen home early the next morning, before they had time to be up and about. When you go into a house on a warrant, you prefer that the people don't expect you, and these were the kind of people who probably weren't going to be moving around early in the morning. These were night crawlers. It was better that they be sleepy rather than alert and holding a gun. The decision was made. Detective Kelly would lead the search team. I usually went out on searches in a homicide case, but not this time. Kenny and Kathy Allen knew who I was. They had watched me prosecute Kenny's father. Bill and I wanted them to suspect only a drug search. If either Bill or I were present, they would likely guess the search was about more—more, in this case, being the murder. We wanted them to talk and we didn't need their lawyers coming in before we had talked to them. We would start with the drugs and move our way up from there.

The house was several blocks off a main street. It probably got as much maintenance as any other street in the community, but for some reason it just looked like it needed more. Railroad tracks ran down the middle of the road. Perhaps the rumbling of trains had taken their own toll. It was an older neighborhood, and the houses had seen their better days before World War II. There were cars parked on the grass and in front of the house. The yard wasn't neatly kept and neither was the house, which was a dirty white color, with stucco and paint peeling from wooden sashes. The asphalt shingle roof had been bled dry by the sun, curling the thin sheets of tarred paper. The search team fanned out around the house, while Kelly stepped onto the porch, knocked on the door, and yelled, "Sheriff's office, search warrant." He gave them just enough time to hear a little movement, as other sheriff's officers stood ready.

Kathy Allen opened the door and directed a blank look at the search team; there was no shock or surprise on her face. Obviously, cops had been visitors to her home before. "What do you want?"

She wasn't the kind of girl that would warm your mother's heart, although, of course, that would depend on your mother, I suppose. She had long, straight, dark hair, a white, pasty complexion, and a thin build. Chances were, if she sold meth, she also used it. Meth takes a toll on people and usually you can see it on their face and in their build. You don't see many overweight meth users. Her hair hung in strings around an angular, gaunt face. She was still fairly young, but you could tell it wouldn't be long before she looked much older than her age, if she didn't already. You could also tell that she had a rough edge. Kenny came out from the back of the house to see what was going on. His hair hung in flaccid, greasy strings. He was missing quite a few teeth. I should mention that meth also takes a toll on your teeth. He had a slight gut on him but there was no muscle there. All the weight he carried didn't go into intimidation.

Kelly directed the officers through the search. The inside of the house didn't surprise anyone, after seeing the outside. Searches are messy, so it helps if you don't feel like you are disrupting an orderly home. It wasn't long before they found a small stash of meth, but it was the single-shot, break-open, twelve gauge shotgun that caught everyone's attention. Number-four shotgun shells were also found, and it had been number-four shot that had killed the three kids. However, we hadn't thought the shooter carried a long-barreled shotgun. A sawed-off was the most likely guess because it would have been more easily concealed. This was a "Long Tom" and had a standard barrel. Maybe it had been used in the murders, maybe not. We didn't have the expended shells that were actually used, so we wouldn't be able to compare firing pin impressions. Still, the fact that number-four shot was found in Kenny's house meant something. We would see. There were also some letters from Clarence Ray Allen to his son. Kathy and Kenny were placed under arrest, cuffed behind their backs, and transported to the sheriff's office, where they were put into separate cells. The social services office was called to take custody of the children.

The cuffs behind the back are designed for officer safety, but they also help make for an uncomfortable ride. They also remind prisoners of the reality of their situation, turning up the screws, so to speak. Every little bit helps. We had already decided we would interrogate Kathy Allen first and then interrogate Kenny. Eventually, one of them would contradict the other and that would give us an opening. No matter how much people talk to one another, trying to get their stories straight, they always overlook a detail. Find that detail, and they will start to generalize, and then lie about more details.

You just let them talk and you let them tell lies. Then, you trade off, getting the other one to do the same thing. Next, you confront them with the gaps in their stories, detail by detail, until you slowly get more and more of the truth, something like squeezing a tube of toothpaste from the bottom until you roll up the empty tube until the last dollop comes out. Like a toothpaste tube, however, it is always the last dollop that is the hardest to squeeze out. You have to work at it.

It was clear Kathy had become increasingly nervous. We decided to begin with her, but first she would sit for awhile and get used to the hard bench in the holding cell. The cold metal surface has a way of getting your attention. So does the smell. Maybe she would spend the time rubbing her wrists where the handcuffs had been. Like I said, every little bit helps.

28

No Promises

Tuesday, September 9, 1980
Fresno, California

B ill Martin sat in the detective office, waiting for Detective Badiali to bring Kenny and Kathy Allen downtown. He looked at his watch. It was near the end of the day, but Bill knew it was going to be a long night. It didn't make any difference. He was glad to be back in the game, in the middle of an active investigation, instead of doing the trial investigation after arrests had already been made. He liked the D.A.'s office, but it wasn't anything like the old days with Blade and Tabler.

Bill and I had decided that I was going to wait in another office. The idea was that when I walked through the door, both Kathy and her husband would realize that the stakes had risen. We wanted them to think I was holding all the cards. Even though it had been three years since the trial of Kenny Allen's father, Kenny wouldn't have forgotten me and neither would she. They also would know that I didn't handle narcotics cases. I was now the Chief of Homicide. If I was there it was about murder. I didn't expect they would remember me any more fondly than I remembered Kenny's father. Bill, on the other hand, wouldn't face the animosity that I would or generate the fear that I would. Had they known more about Bill, they would have been very afraid.

Kathy Allen was wearing a red-and-white-striped top and black pants. The top hung loosely but the pants were tightly fitted. She rubbed her thin wrists as she entered and her eyes wandered the room until she spotted Bill. It was apparent from her expression that she remembered him.

He motioned for her to sit down. Detective Fernando Reyna sat in. He was a younger detective, tall, with curly hair and a mustache. Fernando didn't talk much. He was still learning and part of learning was watching another detective handle an interrogation.

An elementary rule of investigation is that you never interrogate a woman without someone else present. If you do it by yourself, you are asking for trouble. A recorder sat on the desk. Bill gave the date and time, but he kept his eyes on Kathy Allen the entire time, looking for some small movement or look of fear. He didn't see any. Bill didn't read Kathy her rights, as we had decided we were going to treat her as a witness, and if she gave us what we wanted, we would let her go home—eventually. We could always get to her later, but now we needed her to cooperate, and now she had a good reason to do so; she was in jail. Her children were with strangers from social services and her husband was sitting in another holding cell. If she wanted out, she had plenty of reasons to continue the discussion and, if we had to, we would remind her of them every chance we had.

Bill rubbed his mustache. His face gave away nothing. He leaned forward and began talking in a quiet, soothing voice. He smiled slightly. "Kathy, let me tell you why you're here. I want you to listen to me for a few minutes and if you have questions, I'll answer them. There was a triple homicide the other night at a place called Fran's Market." He paused for effect, waiting for the glimmer of a reaction, but there was none. "Three kids were killed, shot-gunned to death. One of the people we have arrested for that murder is Connie Barbo. We are aware that you and Connie Barbo know one another, and we also know that you and your husband are her crank connection. We know that the shooter at Fran's Market came to your house with Connie Barbo. As you can see, we know a lot already about what happened, but you can help us with the details. I'm going to tell you right now that we want more information about this case, and if you help us out, then you can go home. I'm not making any promises about your case because I can't, but just let me say that the murder case is far more important than you and Kenny selling meth to some junkie. Do you understand what I'm saying to you?"

Kathy slumped in the hard-backed chair and stared at Bill, her face a brittle mask. Bill knew she wouldn't make a decision from fear, but only from self-interest. She nodded. "If I tell you what I know, then I can go home." It was a statement, not a question.

Bill nodded. "That's right, but I can't make any other promises. We will get the shooter, Kathy, sooner or later. You can help us get him sooner. He shot kids. You have kids?" Bill waited for her to react. He knew she had kids. He just wanted to remind her that she was in custody and her children were in the county's custody.

"I got three kids." She hesitated for a moment, making some sort of inner decision before she gave any more information. "I guess you're looking for Bobby—Bobby Burnett. That's all I know. I don't know if he was the shooter, but he was the one with Connie. He's my husband's cousin."

Bill nodded. His face betrayed nothing at hearing Bobby Burnett's name. He would not want her to know that it was new to him. It was better to keep her off balance and not to know or to guess at what he knew or didn't know. "Okay, so you'll talk to us about this and we'll treat you like a witness, nothing else, for purposes of our conversation. Okay?"

"I didn't do anything. I just heard on the news, you know?"

Bill leaned back. "Right. But for now I need to get an idea of what you know. I need you to tell us the truth. We're only interested in the truth. How old are you, Kathy?"

"Twenty-eight." In the harsh, fluorescent light of the detective's office, she didn't look twenty-eight, with her skin drawn tight and thin against her face. Bill guessed she hadn't looked twenty-eight since she was seventeen.

"Now, we have gone over some things about who came over to your house last week. I want you to tell us about him."

"I don't know approximately what day, maybe Tuesday."

"That would be September the second?"

"Yeah, Bobby Burnett, who is my husband's cousin on his father's side. He came to stay with us."

Bill held up his hand. "Did you notice anything about Bobby, any tattoos, or anything else about him?"

"Yeah, on his," Kathy patted her left shoulder, "on his left arm, he had a tattoo in big capital letters, about that big." She held her fingers apart to indicate.

"About four inches?"

"With the name BILLY in capital letters on his arm and the 'I' was crossed. It didn't have a dot on it, you know. I thought it was strange, him being named Bobby and havin' BILLY tattooed on his arm."

Bill's face was impassive. He didn't want to ask the obvious question about why she would think a guy actually named Bobby would have BILLY tattooed on his arm in four-inch letters. She was already lying or she was incredibly stupid. But he knew she wasn't stupid. He had seen her kind before, not sophisticated but possessing animal cunning. He didn't want to confront her. We needed her to talk. But now we knew the shooter was most likely named Billy. "Okay. While he was at your home, did Connie Barbo come over?"

She nodded her head vigorously. "Yeah, several times."

"Did she meet him?"

"Yeah, on Wednesday."

"Did she strike up a relationship with him?"

"Yeah, they hit it off pretty good together."

"Would you describe Burnett for us?"

"I think he's about six-foot-one, 190 pounds, light or medium-colored brown hair, and it's thinning, the hair, you know, in front of his head. It's not...he's not bald, but you know you can see through the hairline. He's got a complexion; he's not beet red, but he's got a reddish tint to his color. I wouldn't know what color to say, kinda sunburnt, but he's not sunburnt. That's his color. And he's muscular, very muscular."

"Big arms?"

"I'd say nineteen-inch, twenty-inch arms. And, he's tapered at the waist. He's well built. I was under the impression that he worked around horses. I do know that Kenny, when he picked up Connie, did drop her off at the county fair one time."

"Did you hear some talk about Burnett going down to L.A. to get some horses?"

"I heard something about it, but I didn't get the facts on it. I got three kids, so my day's pretty busy."

"On Friday, September fifth, was Burnett at your house?" Bill could see Kathy tighten her jaw and visibly tense.

"Yes."

"Okay, did Connie come over?"

"Yeah, she came over about 6:30 or 7:00 o'clock Friday morning."

"Did they borrow your car?"

"Not until after I got up around 11:30 and then they asked to borrow it. I told them they could but I needed it back by 1:30 to go get school clothes. They brought it back at 2:00, out of gas. He took her home later and then he just kind of, you know, kicked around, showered and stuff. That was the last time I saw 'em, until Bobby called at midnight and asked if I had seen Connie. And then he told me they had gotten into a fight and she went hysterical on him and stuff and took off walkin'. He asked me if I would go over to her house and see if she made it home all right. I said I would and hung up and told Kenny what happened and Kenny started yelling at me. He didn't want me out that late. My car might break down and stuff. I tried to contact some of Connie's relatives, but I couldn't get a hold of 'em."

"Have you had any other contact with Bobby?"

"Um, let me think. He called Saturday. I can't tell you what time it was because I slept half the morning away Saturday and in the afternoon I had someplace to go. Anyway, he called and I answered and that's when things started kind of clicking. 'Cause by that time Connie's name was on the news and she was arrested. Anyway, he calls and says—he said it was all on him. In other words, Connie didn't know what she was up against."

"Did he want Kenny or anybody to help him get out of town or give him any money?"

"He never asked for Kenny. He just talked to me. And, now I remember. It was between 2:00 and 4:00 in the afternoon on Saturday."

Bill paused and looked at her, letting her sit for a moment. "You realize we are looking for someone and you heard the description of the suspect?"

"Just that he was about six-foot-one and he was white and muscular and tattooed."

"From that, did you draw any conclusions?"

"Yeah, pretty much. I figured it was him—Bobby Burnett."

Bill leaned back and shook his head. "Kathy, now you need to be straight with me. You need to think real hard if this is the way you want it to be because I think you know more than you're saying." Kathy straightened up, and her mouth opened as she prepared to speak. Bill held up his hand. "Before you say anything else, I want a name, and you and I both know it isn't Bobby Burnett. You heard the name Little Blue or Blue Boy?"

Bill never raised his voice, the tone said everything. She was lying. He knew it and she knew he knew it, but she wasn't going to admit it. At least, not now. She would give up a little more, but it would be in bits and pieces. She was going to trade only as much as she had to. Bill understood. He would be patient—for now.

"I told you all I know. I don't know what his name is. Maybe it's Billy. I don't know. I don't know Little Blue or Blue Boy." She hesitated. Then she looked him in the eye before making her next statement. "But I have a picture of him, if that's what you want."

Bill leaned forward. "You have a picture?"

"Kenny had a picture of him. I put it away after all this happened. I'll give it to you if you take me home."

Bill paused before speaking. He needed to appear to be in control. You never want to let them think you don't know more than they have told you. "Where did Kenny get the picture?"

"I don't know. He just had it. I'll give it to you."

Bill stood up. Kathy was making her trade, the picture for her ticket out the door. "All right, Kathy. I'll have the detectives take you back to your home in a little while, and you give them that picture. We'll have you wait in a separate room until we're ready. Then we're going to let you go home, for now. Thanks for your help, but I'm not making any promises."

Kathy stood up. "What about Kenny?"

Bill's voice was firm. "No promises. Kenny is on his own. We'll be talking to you. When we're ready, one of our detectives will take you home and you give him that picture."

29

Puppet Master

Tuesday, September 9, 1980
Fresno, California

When the young sheriff's deputy walked Kenny Allen into the room, Bill didn't stand; he merely tilted his head slightly to one side, his face a mask of studied indifference. He indicated the chair where Kathy Allen had sat. He waited, watching Kenny Allen's face, reading the man. Kenny sat down heavily, slouching in the metal-backed chair, resting his head against the wall, his eyes flicking around the institutional beige walls, the short chain of the cuffs making a rattling sound. Others had leaned their heads against the same wall, trying to disappear into the hard surface that held them cornered by the men confronting them. Detectives Lean and Badiali were on the other side of the room. Bill was going to handle the interrogation. The other detectives would wait their turn. I had gone back to my office, impatiently waiting for the results of the interrogation.

In an interrogation, often detectives will automatically assume different roles, depending on the pace and tone of the interrogation. Tom Lean and Ken Badiali would watch and allow Bill to control the pace; later, they would assume whatever role seemed appropriate. Usually, the detective who remains silent while his partner asks questions plays the part opposite of the primary interrogator. If the first detective doing the talking decides he should be a nice guy, he will attempt to create a persona of trying to be helpful, compassionate, and empathetic. When the subject of the interrogation begins to lie or get difficult, the other detective will come in as the tough cop, the guy who has no sympathy. Usually, the subject will turn toward the empathetic cop. Or, in other situations, you start out with the tough cop and the empathetic cop steps in. Regardless of the order, the idea is to create a rapport with the good cop and to give the subject a reason to talk to him. The decision as to who is the good cop or the bad cop depends on the flow of the interrogation. Bill was a master at interrogation. He would decide whether he was the good cop when he got a sense of Kenny Allen's attitude.

The pungent odor of stale sweat slowly filled the room. The cold, fluorescent lights gave Allen's doughy face, framed by the black hair that fell to the sides of it, an eerie pallor. Allen was unshaven, and his darting tongue licked at lips that were thin and dry. From the first moment, it was clear to Bill that Kenny was not the man his father was. Of course, it wouldn't have been any kind of compliment to say he was like his father, but it was obvious he didn't have the spine the old man had. He also didn't have the cold eyes and the look of disdain that marked Clarence Allen's face when confronted by police. Kenny Allen couldn't hide what he had in his eyes. Fear. He looked at Lean and Badiali, but his eyes focused on Bill, and Bill's eyes gave away nothing as he stared back at Allen.

Bill looked over at the deputy who had brought Kenny from the holding cell and pointed to the handcuffs, giving a flicking motion. The metallic clicking noise of the cuffs being removed broke the silence in the room. The deputy left, and Bill continued staring at Allen, waiting for him to look away. You can tell a lot about a man by the way he looks at you when he knows you are about to interrogate him. Some men will look you in the eye and you detect the spark of defiance. You can tell they aren't going to talk, or, at least, they don't intend to talk. Some men will look you in the eye and you can tell they are measuring you for how much of a lie they can try to get away with. Others will look you in the eye and quickly look away. They are going to talk; it's just a matter of time. First, you decide what kind of man you're dealing with and then you decide how to handle him. It only took a moment before Allen lowered his head, breaking away from Martin's stare. It was a sign of submission, but it was only submission on the part of someone you would not turn your back on. This man would break—but first he would lie. It was going to be a long night.

Bill began slowly, his voice measured and low, but with just enough edge to it for Kenny to know he meant business. "Kenny, you need to stop and think for a minute. I want some information about a man who came to visit you. We know that he was at your home, and we know he was involved in the murder of three kids at Fran's Market. That's what I want to talk about."

Kenny slid back in his chair. "I thought you wanted to talk to me about the stuff at the house, the crank?" He kept his eyes deflected away from Bill or the other detectives.

Bill leaned forward, his own eyes directly staring into Kenny's face. His voice dropped to a hard-edged whisper. "You know who I am and you know I am not going to put up with any bullshit. So, let's get that straight between us right now. There's a prosecutor sitting over in his office right now who sent your old man to prison and he would like nothing better than a piece of your ass. You know who he is. You know that what I'm saying is true. Right now, I'm all you got. And I am all that stands between you and that prosecutor. So, I'm going to say it again. I want to know about the man who came to your house. I am not making any promises. I'm not interested in some crank or other shit they found in your house. I want information. This is a murder investigation. Now, I'm going to read you your rights and you need to listen. Do you understand?"

Allen slowly nodded his head. Bill could smell the sour odor coming from him. That was always a good sign. He read Kenny his rights and waited until he said that he understood and that he would talk.

"You know who I am talking about, don't you?"

"My cousin, I think, but I don't know what you want."

"I have information that someone came to visit you this last week. Did you have a visitor?"

"My cousin, Bobby."

"Bobby who?"

"Bobby Burnett. I only met him exactly twice in my entire life. He's from Oregon. He was just passing through California."

"He lives in Oregon? With whom?"

"He has a wife and family. They're up in Portland. I got an uncle lives there. Clarence."

Bill forced back his growing impatience. Kenny was screwing with him. He and Kathy had put together a story, probably in the short time they had together in a holding cell before they were separated, or possibly they had put it together after the murders were flashed all over the news. Bill knew that when that happened you needed to give them just a little bit of rope before you pulled back. "You have an uncle named Clarence?"

"Yes, sir. He's my Aunt Hazel's husband."

Bill watched Kenny's eyes darting to the corners of the room as he searched for a way to distance himself. Bill would let him talk; he would let him layer his lies with detail; he would allow Kenny to indulge his sense of cleverness. A man's inflated ego, his misperception of his own ability, is often his worst enemy. Bill was a slow dancer. He could wait. The more he let Kenny lie, the more he could confront Kenny with later on. "What day did he come over?"

"I believe it was around the second or the third, and then he left. He just stopped by to say hello, and then he went on. Only spent one night."

"Describe him for me."

"Maybe five foot, eleven inches. He's slender. That's about it. Very easy going person."

"Any tattoos?"

"No, sir."

"His eyes? What do they look like?"

"He basically looks like me, except he's olive-complexioned and he has all his teeth."

Bill leaned back and stared at Kenny, watching Allen's eyes move to any place but where Martin's face was. Either Kenny or Kathy had not thought about matching the description up, or one of them wasn't smart enough to remember it. Bill guessed that it wasn't Kathy. Kenny had obviously practiced his first response in his rodent-like mind, but now it was time to mix it up a little. If Martin pitched the questions faster and out of order, Kenny wouldn't be able to remember what he had said earlier. "Do you know Connie Barbo?"

"Yes, sir. I do."

"How well?"

"We're good acquaintances."

"Do you know whether Connie Barbo met your cousin?"

Allen paused, as if trying to remember. "I believe she did. I believe she spent the evening with him one night during the time he was down."

"Does Bobby go by any other name?"

"No, sir, no nicknames or anything as far as I know."

"And, he is how old?"

"He's about thirty-one or thirty-two."

"And how is he built again?"

"He's just a thin, narrow guy, no massive amount of muscles or beard or anything—just well dressed and like clean-cut."

"Did you see him on Thursday?"

"No, sir."

"Friday?"

"No, sir."

"On Friday, did you get a call from Connie Barbo?"

"I believe so, yeah. She wanted my wife to pick her up, but I did it around 7:00 in the evening."

"To take her where?"

"Over to the fairgrounds."

"Did she say she was going to meet anybody?"

"Yeah, Blue Boy. That's it. She said she was meeting Blue Boy."

"And who does she call Blue Boy?"

"I have no idea."

"Did you ever hear her call your cousin Blue Boy?"

"No, my cousin doesn't go by any names like that. All Connie said was she was going to meet this Blue Boy guy at the fairgrounds, and they were going to Los Angles to pick up a horse."

"Anything else?"

"That was about it, because I was upset that she wanted me to pick her up and drive her a couple of blocks when she could have walked. I just drove home."

"Since Friday, you have seen on the news or in the newspapers reports of a robbery, right?"

"Yes, sir."

"And you've also seen that Connie Barbo was arrested?"

"I didn't know that."

"Do you know she is arrested now?"

"Yes."

"Do you know she is charged with murder?"

"Yes."

"For your information, she was arrested at the murder scene, inside the store. When was the last time you were out on Belmont?"

"Maybe three months since I been in that store area."

"You haven't been out there at any time during this last week?"

"No, sir, I had no reason to be out there."

Bill decided to close things in around Kenny, to indirectly let him know that he could easily be the focus. It was obvious that Kenny would sell his mother out if he thought it would save him, but it would be a slow process. He had to believe that he was the one being looked at. Bill moved his body closer, filling the space in front of Allen, his face only inches away. "So, if somebody saw a car out there that looked like yours and got the license number that is registered to you, then they would be wrong?" Bill's voice had an almost silky texture, the softened edge drawing Kenny toward him.

Kenny tilted his head back before answering. "My car had no reason to be out there, whatsoever."

Bill sighed heavily and shook his head. "I told you we were investigating a homicide and that it is important that you be truthful to us."

Kenny's face took on a pained expression. "I am being truthful."

Bill's voice became very firm, regaining its menacing edge. "Mr. Allen, what if I were to tell you that less than thirty minutes ago I spoke with your wife and taped her statement, and your wife told me that your cousin was not at your house for just one night, but that he was there off and on for several days. What if I were to tell you that he was there up until and including Friday afternoon?"

Allen started moving around in his chair. His eyes darted around the room and then at the floor. He started to mumble. "She could have been right. I had the days mixed up because I—well, to be honest with you, after six o'clock I start drinking."

"Uh huh. Mr. Allen where was your cousin on Friday afternoon?"

"If she said he could have been there, he was there. I just got the days confused. That's all. Because I've been taking the medication for my teeth and everything."

"I have information your cousin called your house Friday night about midnight, looking for Connie."

"That could be true."

"Did anyone tell you that he called?"

"My wife could have mentioned it and I could have never paid any attention to it. That's the truth. My days were confused. My wife is correct. You can go by what she says."

"And, you just didn't pay any attention?"

"I don't pay attention to nothing."

Bill leaned back in his chair, staring at Kenny. He rubbed his mustache. "Mr. Allen, you know we're looking for your cousin for murder, don't you." It was a statement. It wasn't a question.

"No, sir. I didn't know that at all."

"You do know we're looking for the man that was with Connie Barbo?"

"Not until now. No, sir."

For the second time during the interrogation, a slight smile drifted across Bill's face. Kenny wanted to play the game, and now he would find out how it was done. Bill's voice was toneless. "We believe the man who was with Connie Barbo at the time of the murders is your cousin." Bill's face took on a hardened expression, his eyes emotionless. This was the moment when things would either turn or they wouldn't. He couldn't let Kenny sense any uncertainty. He let silence fill the air, waiting for Kenny to make the overture, the turn that would draw him into his own lies.

Kenny sighed. "That could be. Like I said, I could have had my days mixed up."

Bill knew that Kenny was starting to break, but he knew it would be a drawn-out process. There was no mistaking the tone of Bill's voice. "Are you being straight now?"

"Yes, sir. I'll tell you the truth."

Bill knew that the truth would have to be squeezed out and that every statement would have as thin a veneer of truth as Kenny could use to wrap around a lie. "If your wife said they were there, they were there?"

"That's right, they were there."

"Your wife describes the man as being about my height, maybe six feet tall, with a husky upper body, nice big arms—that's the truth—not what you just said, that he was a skinny, thin fellow."

"Well, to me, slender is well-built. I'm fat."

"Which is it?"

"I'm fat."

Bill let Kenny's evasive comment sit by itself. His patience was running out. He took a deep breath. Now was not the time to drop the hammer. "Okay, what is his physique? Is he skinny or was he well-built? Big arms, or what? Joint muscles—big arms?"

"Not my cousin, not Bob Burnett. Bob's slender, thin. Maybe six-foot-one at the most, with short, brown hair, and he has no tattoos."

Bill reached over and picked up a cassette recording tape, tapping it lightly on the desk next to him, watching Kenny's eyes focus on the tape. "Mr. Allen, your wife gave us a description of your cousin, Bob, or Robert, or Bobby Burnett. She described him with tattoos. Now which is it, does he have tattoos, or doesn't he?" Bill turned his face slightly, opening his eyes in a look of mock surprise. "Are you lying to us?"

"No, sir. Okay, I believe that the gentleman that I told my wife was my cousin isn't my cousin."

Bill tilted his head to the side, his voice taking on a tone of measured incredulity. "Now, why would you do such a thing as that?"

"Because the gentleman that we are talking about is, well, I didn't want the kids to know that he is fresh out of prison. All I know is that his name is Billy. I don't know his last name."

"Why don't you know his last name?"

"I had no reason to know his last name. He was coming into town and he needed a place to stay and then he would be on his way." Bill let the answer hang for just a moment. So there was a joint connection. *The shooter was just out of prison, but if that was so, then why would Kenny let him stay at his home if he didn't know his full name?* He filed away the observation that Kenny had to have a good reason to let a stranger stay at his house when he was fresh out of prison. Somebody had to have arranged it, unless this was just one more lie from Kenny.

"Do you remember now seeing him on Friday?"

"I think so. I'm not sure."

"Why don't you describe him for me?"

"He's about six-foot-four, has tattoos on this arm." Kenny tapped his left arm. "It was like a Viking tattoo."

"Why didn't you tell us this when we first started the interview?"

"I believed that was what my wife was going to say, sir. That's what I said when we was first brought in. She asked me about my cousin, and I said I had only seen him twice. We weren't picked up on a homicide. We were picked up for narcotics. That's where my whole train of thought has been, on narcotics."

Bill couldn't help letting a burst of air slide between his lips. "I explained to you when we started that we weren't interested in narcotics. We are interested in this triple homicide that we are working. Now you tell me that your cousin, Bobby Burnett, was not even there. That this man Billy is the one that was there."

"Right."

Bill sat for a moment, his finger slowly stroking his upper lip. *Kenny knew this Billy was just out of prison and, according to his wife, he had a picture of him. He had to have expected him, and there had to be a prison connection and, more importantly, if Kenny didn't know him, then he got the picture from somebody else.* "When did Billy get out of the joint?"

"I have no idea. Like I said, I just got a phone call that he needed a place to stay and he was on his way."

Bill pushed his lips into a tight line. If Kenny got a phone call that Billy was coming, who called him? He began to feel all his senses tingling. There was one person in prison that Kenny definitely knew, but now wasn't quite the right time to confront Kenny with that possibility. "What else do you know about Billy?"

"All I know is he's gone home, wherever that is. I don't even know where in the hell he lives. But if my father asks me to be nice to a gentleman, I will be nice to him."

Bill felt a cold knot tighten in his stomach. He hoped his face hadn't given anything away. If Clarence Ray Allen had told his son that this Billy was coming, then this was a direct connection of Clarence to the murders at Fran's Market, and the reason why the shooter went through the walk-in freezers. It also meant that the reason that those kids were killed could be more than just a simple robbery. Bill was eager to pick up the phone and call me, but he didn't dare break the rhythm of the interrogation. He took a deep breath. "In other words, your dad sent down a letter for you to be nice to Billy?"

Kenny shook his head. "No, no, my dad did not send down a letter. The last time that I was up there at Folsom talking to him is when he said it."

"Okay, so Billy was in prison then?"

"I don't know if he was in prison or not. My dad just said that one of his dogs—whatever that means in prison—that one of his dogs might needed a place to stay. All I knew was Billy. That's all I know—Billy. And, the guy does have 'Billy' tattooed across his left arm."

"What did Billy say when he called you? That he just got out of prison and he was coming to town?"

"No, he didn't say anything other than where did I live. And I was just supposed to be nice to him and let him spend the evening and he was gone. He said his name was Billy. He knew my dad and he needed a place to stay. I didn't know him a bit. I never seen him from Adam. That was the first and last time I met him. I picked him up at the Greyhound bus depot. If Kathy was in here, I could tell you to the exact detail what day I picked him up."

Bill shook his head, the words almost dripping out of his mouth. "Okay, Mr. Allen, let me tell you one thing. Number one, for a long period of time, your father has known those people out there at Fran's Market. In 1974, your father masterminded a burglary out there." Kenny opened his mouth to say something. Bill held up his hand for Kenny to keep quiet. "Now, you listen to this carefully. In 1974, your father masterminded a burglary out there and several other burglaries around this county. Your father was convicted of murder as a result of that burglary."

Allen kept shaking his head. "But on hearsay evidence."

Bill raised his voice. "I don't care what kind of evidence. You listen carefully now. You're talking about a couple two or three years later and your father is up there in Folsom and you go up to visit him and he tells you about a guy named Billy who is coming to Fresno and you need to give him a place to stay. He's one of his cronies, a man coming to Fresno, and the first place he goes is back out there and pulls a robbery and kills three people. You know what that implies? It implies that you might be implicated in a murder."

"No, sir. I'm telling you the truth. Billy is all I know him by."

"Well, where is Billy now?"

"Billy is gone as far as I am concerned. He caught the bus and split."

"Who took him to the bus stop?"

"I did."

"What did he tell you about what happened at Fran's Market? What did he tell you?"

"He didn't tell me nothin' 'cause I know nothin'. If I knew anything, you'd know it in a second. I'd tell you in a second."

"What time did you take him to the bus on Friday?"

"I took him early that morning; it was Friday at around 8:00 A.M."

"Are you sure it was Friday?"

"9:00 A.M., yes, sir."

"Not Saturday morning?"

"No, sir."

Bill rested his chin on his hand, his elbow on the desk, his other hand tapping the cassette tape on his knee. "Somebody's lying to me—either you or your wife."

"If she said it was true, it's true. We could just take out what she said and put Billy's name instead of my cousin's and you got it."

"So Billy told her, 'Hey I did it,' then that's true?"

"If she said so, yes, sir, that's what happened."

"What car was Billy driving Friday night?"

"Billy wasn't in town Friday night. I took him to the bus depot, sir. If he was in town, then he came back on his own, and that's the truth, the God's truth."

"Did he have any money?"

"I gave him sixty bucks to leave town. I didn't take him inside the station. I just dropped him off outside the station, the same way I picked him up. As far as I know, he may not have even caught the bus. Could have got in a taxi and come right back downtown."

Bill rubbed his face and tilted his head back. "What else did your father say about Billy?"

"He was a nice guy. That was it. There was no reason to talk any further. My father doesn't have to explain things to me."

"Now, when were you up at Folsom to see you dad?"

"That would be August the sixteenth or the seventeenth of this year."

"And, at that time, your dad told you that Billy would be getting out, and he might need a place to stay, right?"

"Right."

"Would you identify him for us?"

"If you've got some mug shots of anybody that's been released from Folsom, I probably could hit it right on the head."

Bill allowed himself a slight smile. Kenny had no idea the first picture had been handed over by his wife. "Well, we will have some pretty soon." Bill turned to Tom Lean and Ken Badiali, both of whom had remained quiet during the interview, observing Allen carefully. "Go ahead, Tom, Ken."

Tom Lean slid his chair over and sat directly in front of Allen. The last few years of working homicide had aged him. The youthful surfer image had given way to that of the experienced, mature detective. During the interrogation, Tom had been listening and chomping at the bit. He still had clear memories of Mary Sue Kitts. So far, Bill had been the good guy. Now, it was his turn to be the heavy, and in this case it was easy. His voice was harsh. "You never did take Billy to the bus station, did you." It wasn't a question.

The uncompromising tone in Tom's voice pushed Allen's body back against the wall. "Yes, sir, I did. I picked him up and I took him back there."

Tom raised his voice. He spit out words. "I don't believe you. I don't believe you took him to the bus station Friday night or Friday morning. I think the evidence proves that he wasn't at the bus station on Friday." Lean glared at Allen.

Kenny Allen squirmed in his seat. Lean's face directly in front of him. Allen looked around Lean, trying to find somebody else's face. "If my wife was here we could...we could...." Kenny struggled for an explanation, and time to come up with one.

Tom kept his body in front of Allen. His words came like machine-gun bursts of sound. "Your wife told me that guy you said is your cousin was at your house up until either 4:30 or 5:00 o'clock Friday afternoon. He left and went to the fair. Connie calls you and you go and pick Connie up and take her over to the fair. You said that yourself, that you took her to the fair. At twelve o'clock at night, your wife gets a call from Billy. He's not on a bus down to L.A. He's still here in town Saturday. Now you sit there and you tell us 'I swear I took Billy to the bus station.'" Tom tilted his face away from Kenny and let the silence fill the short distance between them.

Allen turned his face away and stared at the floor. "That could be. Now, like I said, if my wife was here...I didn't swear. I said I *believe* I took him to the bus station in the morning...."

Tom never gave Allen a chance to finish his sentence. Sarcasm filled his voice. "You told us that was the truth. You took him to the bus station at 8:00 o'clock Friday morning and you know that's not right. You know it's not true. Mr. Allen, why don't you just give us the whole spill?"

Kenny's face flushed with confusion. "Like I said, if my wife was here, we could get everything down pat. But I'll be glad to level with you on anything. If Kathy says it's true, it's true."

Bill leaned over. "Okay, if you need to talk to your wife, we're going to let you do it. We'll give you a few minutes."

Ken Badiali left the room and returned with Kathy Allen, who had been waiting in a holding cell. Everyone left the room while Allen and his wife talked, although they were only given a few minutes to do so. Bill called me in my office and told me that Kenny had made the connection to Clarence Allen. It took me a moment to digest the reality of what Bill was saying. There was a connection between the shooter and Clarence Ray Allen. Maybe it was as simple as a robbery based on a jailhouse conversation. But maybe it was more than that. I rushed over to the sheriff's office and got more details about what had transpired. This time, I was going to follow Bill back in just so Kenny and Kathy could see my face and would know that I was the one they had to deal with.

Bill walked back into the interrogation room where Kenny and Kathy had been left to talk. I followed Bill and I saw the two of them seated next to one another. Bill glanced in my direction and then looked at Kenny. He wanted them to see me standing there, to know that I was going to be making decisions regarding their lives. I could see the recognition and the defiance in her eyes when Kathy saw me, but I could also see something else. It wasn't fear. It was the realization that I had a measure of control over her. I could tell she accepted that fact, and it was only going to be that measure of control that was going to allow me to make headway with her.

I looked at Kenny. His whole face was transformed as he looked at me. I suppose there is a mental picture that people build around a person.

Kenny knew who I was. He believed that I would do whatever I had to in order to get to the end of this case. There was more than fear in his eyes; it was more like a recognition that had flickered across his soul. He now believed he was looking at a man who could take away all that he had. Not only could, but now he believed that I *would*. Resignation and acceptance of defeat is the cracking point for most people. In his eyes, his father had been invincible, strong and powerful, and in his perception I had taken his father down. I looked at Kenny and Kathy, my face expressionless. I waited a moment, and removing my eyes from them, I nodded at Bill. I never said a word. Bill's voice showed he was out of patience. "You ready to give us the truth?"

Kenny looked up. "Can it go bad on my dad in prison?" Nobody answered him, letting the words hang in the close air of the interrogation room. Everyone was waiting for what was to come next. And, what came next was a name. "Billy—Billy Ray Hamilton."

Bill stood directly in front of the two of them. "So, it's Billy Ray Hamilton?"

"Yes, sir."

"And that's the one who was with Connie?"

"I don't know nothing about that, just that he's supposed to be on his way to San Jose."

Bill looked over at Detective Ken Badiali. "Ken, would you take Mr. Allen back to the holding cell?" Kenny Allen stood up and looked over at his wife. Neither of them said anything as Badiali led him out of the room. Bill turned to Kathy Allen. "Now, we're going to take you over to your house and you're going to get us that photograph of Billy Ray Hamilton, right?" He waited until she nodded, trading glances between Bill and me. Bill finished the conversation. "We'll talk to you later. Good night, Mrs. Allen." We walked out of the interrogation room, leaving Kathy Allen with Tom Lean.

Bill and I walked straight down the hall into the next room. Both of us were caught in the moment, where the rush of suspicion can cloud the judgment of reality. We had a connection to Clarence Ray Allen. And we had the name of the shooter, Billy Ray Hamilton, fresh out of Folsom prison. He apparently had done his time with Allen. We still had to discover what their relationship was in prison, but we knew it would be a close one.

Bill watched me as I sat, quietly assessing where we were at in the case. Perhaps some people would expect that there would be a feeling of euphoria. I suppose people think that you get this emotion of triumph or elation when you think you're close. Maybe some do. I always seem to move right past that heady moment to the next thing. My moment of elation always comes at the end and, in that quiet moment sitting in the empty detective's office, I knew this wasn't the end. We were back where we had been before, three years ago. The only evidence that pointed at Clarence Ray Allen had come from the mouths of those who had been manipulated. We had no direct evidence, only suspicion. And suspicion of what? Maybe his father had shot off his mouth in prison about Fran's Market and the safe that was supposedly located in the freezer, and then had helped Hamilton try to make a quick score. Maybe his father was supposed to get a piece of the score. Maybe there was something more. I could hardly conceive of what that more might be. What Kenny had given us was nothing at all unless he would testify against his father. And even that would simply be the word of one more weak man. Perhaps we had a picture, but we still did not have the killer and there was no way I would give up a brutal triple murderer to get Allen.

Immediately, calls were made to Folsom to find out as much information as we could about the relationship between Billy Ray Hamilton and Clarence Allen. We waited for Badiali to return with the picture of Hamilton. If Kenny Allen had a picture, most likely he got it from his father, but we couldn't prove that without Kenny. And, if Kenny had gotten the picture from Clarence Ray Allen, it would provide some evidence that supported the growing feeling that neither Bill nor I was fully ready to accept, even though our intuition and all our senses knew what lay behind the darkening shadow of suspicion. It wasn't foreboding that began to pour into me; it was commitment, and it went well beyond the hunt to find a killer—it went to one man. As I sat there at my desk, I could feel the change in me as the case became something I tried never to allow the hunt to become—it was now personal.

I remember standing at the crime scene inside of Fran's Market and thinking that nothing made any sense: killing those kids, sticking up a country store like that. But now, with the specter of Clarence Ray Allen hanging over the last four days, the scenario was becoming painfully clear. Those kids were killed because Clarence Ray Allen wanted them killed. I still couldn't wrap my mind around the why. When I look back now, even though I know the answer, I still struggle with the reality. I suppose sometimes answers don't have to make sense, you just have to accept them as answers.

Bill and I looked at one another. Four days earlier, we had stood in a small room awash with blood. It was a place we had been three years before when we thought we were bringing an end to a manipulator of people, a man who had caused a horrible murder. Now, we knew he was back, but we didn't know why. There was no euphoria. What I realized in those few moments was that Clarence Ray Allen was like a puppet master, holding the strings of dancing marionettes, marionettes whose characters were made of paper mache.

We were only as close as the strings hanging from the wooden frame held by an evil man. We had nothing—nothing but dangling strings.

30

We Had to Get the Shooter

Tuesday, September 9, 1980
Fresno, California

We sat in the empty detective's office, staring at the walls, each of us lost in our own thoughts about where we had been three years earlier and where we were at this moment. I don't know how I looked; I could not see myself, but I could see him. Bill's dark skin had taken on a slightly gray tinge. He looked tired, very tired. Just the faintest whisper of salt and pepper stubble flecked his face, but his mustache was all black. I remember thinking it was an odd contrast. He ran his hand through his short bristle of hair. Now I could see here and there a gray hair I had never noticed before. I suppose we had known each other long enough that we no longer really *saw* one another when we were together. He had his hand around a paper cup of coffee that had obviously been refilled several times; the paper was beginning to show the stain of its contents as it finally soaked through the heavily waxed paper. Even wax paper cups won't hold coffee forever.

Bill stared at me for a moment, measuring his words. "Clarence Allen arranged for one of his prison boys to come here. Kenny isn't ready to give up the whole thing, but we know the shooter is an asshole named Billy Ray Hamilton. Kenny called him one of his old man's dogs, whatever that means. I've sent for a picture and we're running a rap sheet. Boss, this is looking more and more like a setup to kill somebody in that store, maybe Ray Schletewitz, maybe Bryon. I don't know. Those other two kids were just in the wrong place at the wrong time. It's the only thing that makes sense—but for what, I can't figure out. Clarence wanted Ray or Bryon killed for revenge? Revenge for what? There are a whole lot of other people who are responsible for putting him in the joint—you, me, all those gutless wonders he ran with." Bill looked down and shook his head. Experience whispered to both of us but we couldn't make out the words. Still, where there was a whisper, experience told us there was something behind it.

It might seem in retrospect that we were slow to realize the ramifications of it all. I can only say now that sometimes you can't relate to depravity. We understand what we know and what seems logical or reasonable to us. Sherlock Holmes said, "When you eliminate the impossible, whatever remains, however improbable, must be the truth." Maybe that's true; I don't know, but I do know that to eliminate the impossible, you have to conceive of it first. What we were confronting was simply beyond anything we had ever seen. Life is not a movie. Life is about what is possible and sometimes the brain just doesn't wrap around what does not seem possible. We had not tried to eliminate the inconceivable because it simply did not seem possible.

I sat heavily in a chair on the other side of the desk, everything bearing down on me. We had to move forward, but there wasn't any place to move toward until we got new information and, most of all, until we got the shooter in custody, *if* we got the shooter in custody. Everything pointed squarely at what we had thought when we stood in the parking lot of Fran's Market a few days before. The shooter had to be right out of the joint. The best guess was he had a rap sheet with a history of violence, and that we would soon know when we got the rap sheet. I stared at the floor. "Well, we've got the name of the shooter. We bag the shooter, we find the reason, I'm thinking. The point is that if Clarence Allen is behind this, it's going to be a bitch to prove. You know it and I know it. Even to get the old man, we're not going to give a deal to a guy who killed three kids. What we need is for somebody else to roll. We need Kenny to give up his old man and a hell of a lot more than he has given us so far, or we need Kathy Allen, if she knows anything. And we're going to need more than that, because Kenny is probably an accomplice; so, we need something or someone besides Kenny that links the old man. You think Kenny will give up his father?"

Bill nodded slowly. "Kenny Allen isn't the same man his father is. He's a lying sack of shit and he'll give us what we want if we squeeze him the right way."

I sat quietly, thinking of the dynamics of a trial. It is one thing to arrest somebody. It's another to have enough evidence to convict. We had to get the shooter. Then we would slowly twist Kenny. If I had to make a deal with anybody, it would be Barbo, but it was too soon for that and she couldn't help me with Clarence Allen. First, I would see what we had when we got to the end, but we certainly weren't at the end. "What else?"

"Badiali is taking Kathy Allen home. She has a picture of this Hamilton. I'm guessing that Clarence gave his son the picture when he visited him at Folsom, or he mailed it to him."

My head snapped up. "If we could show that Kenny got that picture from his father, even better if it was a joint picture, we might have a small link. It isn't much. But it might be just enough to link the old man. And, even though it's a slender thread, if we could link it to the old man, we might be able to hang him with it."

Bill rolled his head back, staring at the ceiling. "Well, you just know he got it from the old man."

"Knowing it isn't the same as proving it. Even if Kenny says his father gave him the picture, it doesn't make it so. There has to be something else, something that we can put in Clarence Allen's hand. Let me listen to the tape again, and then I'm thinking the next time we let Kenny Allen see me from the beginning. He needs to be afraid of me."

Bill grinned. "Don't worry, Boss. When you walk through the door, Kenny will be puckering." We'd come a long way from when I first met Bill and he was looking at a fresh young prosecutor. Now he trusted me, or at least he trusted me as much as he trusted any lawyer.

"Come on, Bill. Let's go get something to eat and wait for Badiali." There was no point in sitting around. We needed to get something into our stomachs beside coffee.

It was eight o'clock by the time Ken Badiali and Detective Linda Wilson reached Kathy Allen's home. Ken Badiali had done this too many times not to know that he had to have a witness with him at all times when he dealt with somebody like Kathy Allen. Following behind them were two officers from the crime lab.

Kathy stood in the living room of her home, a single lamp illuminating the room. "The stuff you want is upstairs." Badiali and Wilson followed her up the stairs and into a bedroom. Kathy pushed a dresser away from the wall, revealing a small compartment. She pulled out a map of the city of San Jose, along with a stack of Polaroid photographs. Even from a cursory glance, Badiali could tell the men in the photographs were in prison clothes.

Kathy Allen flipped through the pictures and slipped one out of the stack. Her finger touched the glossy Polaroid, tapping over the image of one man in the group. "This one. This is the one Kenny said was his cousin, Bobby Burnett." Badiali looked at the photograph of a white male with a heavy mustache and receding dirty blond hair, his arms heavily muscled. Badiali took the map and stack of pictures from Kathy and handed them to the identification bureau officer. He held on to the picture of Hamilton. "All right, Mrs. Allen, any other photographs?" She shook her head, no. "You come on back downtown with us. We may have a few more questions."

Kathy Allen looked startled. "I thought if I showed you the pictures that I would be released?"

Badiali's face remained impassive. He wasn't going to let her go through the house and destroy any evidence. He would take her downtown and if Bill and Lean wanted to let her go home, they would do it when they were through with her. "Well, Mrs. Allen, we may have a few more questions to ask. When those are answered, then whatever Investigator Martin or the district attorney says is what we'll do." He nodded toward Detective Wilson, who took Kathy by the arm. They were going back downtown.

31

The Folsom Connection

Wednesday, September 10, 1980
Fresno, California

We were still waiting on intelligence information out of Folsom, but by 10:00 A.M. the next morning we had a prison identification photograph of inmate B89126, Billy Ray Hamilton, released on parole from Folsom Prison August 29, 1980—six days prior to the murder of the three kids in Fran's Market and three days before he arrived in Fresno.

After you have looked at enough mug shots, you realize that most of them are taken by retired Department of Motor Vehicle photographers who can make the best-looking celebrities look bad. Figuring anything out about a person by looking at a mug shot is not much different than looking at a person you pass on the street and making judgments about that stranger. There are some things you can glean from the front and side profile, however most of your reaction about a man from his photograph is speculation until you have the opportunity to talk to him. But sometimes, just sometimes, you can look at the photograph of a man and see in the flat one-dimensional image everything you need to know.

When I looked at the photograph of Billy Ray Hamilton, I saw the face of a man that would strike fear in you if you saw him on a sunlit street. Even on a brightly illuminated street you'd want to avoid this guy. A cop seeing that face would fondle the safety strap on his gun. Hamilton had a heavy, blondish-brown mustache that drooped down around a full-lipped mouth. You could imagine that not even a close shave would ever take away the coarse, heavy stubble that darkened his face. His hair was receding, giving him a high forehead that was punctuated by the slash of thick, dark eyebrows over a thrusting brow. The cheekbones were prominent, which gave his cheeks a sunken appearance and emphasized a heavy jaw line. But it was his eyes that gave him the look of some lone and dangerous animal. If a man's eyes could look like those of a predator then those were the eyes of Billy Ray Hamilton, glaring out from the flat, shiny paper with Folsom prison number B89126 at the bottom, eyes dark-brown, almost black, absorbing light like bottomless pits. Hamilton's eyes were frightening, filled with intimidation. There was no question that among wolves he would be an alpha male.

If Hamilton was one of Allen's "dogs," then what did that make Clarence Ray Allen? I laid the mug shot on the desk, unconsciously wiping my hands. I said to Bill, "Talk to the Rios boy. See what he has to say. I don't need to tell you to take it easy. He's been through a lot." Bill looked up at me and I could just catch the slight lift of his right eyebrow. Everything he wanted to say was in that subtle gesture: If I didn't need to tell him, then why had I? I gave him a little grin and a shrug. Even cops with years of experience sometimes need a little reminder. He had never hesitated to let me know that so did young D.A.s.

Valley Medical Center was located across from the Fresno County Fairgrounds. During the fair that made it more convenient for access to the emergency room to handle the usual altercations that always seemed to happen at county fairs. I always seemed to be talking to someone in the medical center or visiting it in the middle of the night after walking through a crowded waiting room heavy with the smell of anxious, tired people. I could never get used to the scent of that emergency room, people and fear, misery and blood. The smell of anguish filled it and I was always glad to escape to some quiet place, even if it was the autopsy room.

Joe Rios' room was on the fifth floor. Bill Martin, along with Ken Badiali and Detective Fernando Reyna, Kenny's partner, took the elevator up to the fifth floor. The detectives had been to the medical center plenty of times before, sometimes on the upper floors to take statements from victims and sometimes in the back of the main floor to watch the autopsies of those who couldn't give a statement. Rios was lying in bed, his left arm heavily bandaged across the chest and down the arm. The doctors had already said he would never recover full use of his arm, but Bill and the other detectives weren't sure if Rios had been told yet.

Joe Rios was a young, black-haired man, twenty-three years old. Lying there on the white sheets of the slightly raised hospital bed, he looked tired and older than he was. No matter what happened, Bill knew that Rios had left his youth on the blood-smeared walls of the bathroom in Fran's Market. Probably, Rios hadn't realized it yet but his days of peaceful daydreaming were over, taken away in a flash of light and a blast of pellets that had left a memory that he would relive every time he closed his eyes to rest—or every time he lifted his left arm. Rios turned his head at the sound of Bill knocking on the door, his black eyes following the gold star in the badge holder when Bill held it up. Bill asked if they could talk to him for a moment. He nodded, and the trio of detectives walked toward the silver-framed hospital bed and identified themselves.

Badiali pulled out a series of photographs and began to place them on the wheeled table for Joe to look at. Badiali's sensitivity level was about the same as a rubber mallet, so he always moved quickly beyond the obligatory pleasantries like "hello" and got right to the point. He couldn't help himself, his intensity seeped from his pores, just like the smell of soap that followed him everywhere.

In any photographic lineup the standard procedure either before or while you lay out a series of individual photographs is to tell the witness that they may or may not recognize anybody in the photo spread and to look at each photo carefully before answering. They are told that if they are not sure, they should say so. A photograph often looks different than the way an individual looks in person. There is simply a difference in the depth of features that characterize a person, the movement of eyebrows, the squint of eyes, the up-turned corner of the mouth. You try and pick five or six mug shots that resemble the picture of the person you think is the suspect. That means you don't put five white guys in the photo spread with the one black guy you think is the suspect, or vice versa.

Badiali laid them down like he was spreading a solitaire hand. "Joe, we're going to show you a series of photographs and ask if you recognize anybody."

Bill listened quietly and he watched as Rios stared at the photographs. People usually remembered the eyes or the gun, but the details are just a blur. This young man had been through a lot and they needed to move slowly, patiently, to make sure that Rios could make an identification and that he didn't hesitate. He needed to be brought through the process carefully. Before Rios said anything, Bill interjected, "Joe, I'm Bill Martin from the district attorney's office. I want you to tell us about Friday night. Just talk to us. Close your eyes and take your time. I know this isn't easy. Try to remember everything you can. Move slowly and think about each thing as it happened. All right?"

Rios looked at them and then down at his heavily bandaged arm resting in a sling. He was already tired. He could feel it. The pain medication and the loss of blood seemed to wear him down. He closed his eyes and began to see it all again, just as he had time and time again after the surgery, while he lay in his hospital bed, staring at what was left of his arm. The words came out of his mouth in a rushing torrent, as the flashing images struck him again and again.

He had big arms—a tattoo on one of his arms—there was a tattoo. Both of them were wearing bandannas. They wanted meat—the storeroom— Doug White was in the storeroom. He knew the man had been to prison. He told Doug. That man came in holding a sawed-off shotgun and yelling for them to hit the floor—calling them mother fuckers, screaming at them and the woman kept waving that little gun. The man pointed the shotgun at Doug and told him to go with him into the freezer. He could still hear the low growl in the voice, like some kind of animal. He kept talking about a safe but Doug told him there was no safe in the freezer—there was no safe. He called Doug "Bryon" and that was when Bryon told him that "he was Bryon." He took Bryon to the back of the storeroom where the safe and a lock box was. He kept yelling at Bryon, demanding to know where the other safe was, yelling that he knew there was another safe, a bigger safe. He could hear Bryon's voice—pleading that he would open the safe. The sound—even now he could hear it filling the room. He could smell the burning powder— and then he saw the man and the smoke coming out of the barrel as he walked toward them—the snapping sound as he reloaded—the blackness of his eyes. He could see it on the man's face—they were all going to die.

Rios looked at the spread of six photographs. He picked up the second one, his hand trembling noticeably. "This is the one that shot Bryon and me and the others." Rios laid the photograph of Billy Ray Hamilton back down and looked up at the detectives. "How can you forget those eyes? I'll never forget those eyes as long as I live."

Rios looked up at Bill. "Bryon told him, 'These are the only two.' He goes, 'I'm going to open them. I'll open them.' Then after that, I just heard 'Bang.'"

Bill waited for a moment. "You heard one shot?"

"Yeah, and then he came back toward us."

"What kind of gun did he have?"

"It was a short rifle. I'm sure it was sawed-off and it had a short handle on it. And he goes to Doug, 'All right, big boy,' and he goes, 'where's that safe at?' And Doug goes, 'Honest,' he goes, 'There's no other safe, those are the only two.' And the guy just fired at him—shot him and then after he did that, I go *shit*—I mean, my turn's next. That's when I jumped up and I ran to the bathroom real fast, and I locked that door and there was another door, and I closed it behind me, and then I heard a 'bang' and that's when he shot Josephine and then after that he either kicked or, I don't know how he opened that door, but it flew open and he opened the other door and he lowered that gun right in front of me. I was between the bathroom and this wall and he pointed the gun at me and then he loaded it and he fired. I don't know how I did it, but I just turned real fast and that's when he caught me. When he seen blood and everything, he thought he got me real good. And after that he goes, 'All right, Baby, let's go.' And then he took off through the shop."

Bill waited for a moment before asking his next question. He could see the anguish on Rios' face. The young man had been through hell. "After he shot you—that's when he was talking to the girl? What did he say to her?"

"He goes, 'Let's go, Babe,' and they went to the swinging door. I waited for a while—about a minute, and then I came out and I looked at Josephine and Doug. They were dead. Then I went by Bryon. I—I don't know. I think the guy shot Bryon in the eye. I think, *well shit*. I opened the swinging doors real quiet and I looked inside and I seen 'em in there."

"Did he see you?"

"No, but I seen them in front by the door—they didn't know which key it was." Rios' voice trailed off for a moment. "I—I looked through there and I thought, 'I'm getting out of here.' So I ran to the back door and I threw that bar off and pushed the door open and started running. Then I heard, 'Hey,' like that. I didn't stop. I just kept on running and I heard a shot fired and then around fifteen seconds later, I heard another shot. I kept on running. There's a ditch there and I fell in but I didn't pay attention. I just got up and kept on running."

"When you ran into the bathroom—when the shooting started, did you hear this subject questioning Josephine, or did you hear her talking at all?"

"No, I just heard 'Boom.'"

Rios paused, his voice catching. Bill changed the discussion to the physical description of the shooter and then to the woman. A spread of mug shots of women, including Barbo, was placed in front of Rios. He looked at them carefully and then picked a photo—it was a mug shot of Connie Barbo.

Joe Rios turned his head away from them. "I don't know why the guy went into the freezer. There's never been a safe in the freezer."

Bill paused as an attendant brought in a tray of food. "One more question. Did he call anybody by name?"

"What do you mean?"

"When he came in, did he call you by your first name? Did he call Bryon by his first name?"

"No, he goes, 'I thought you guys closed at 9:00.' I go, 'No we close at 8:00,' and then he goes, 'I'm sorry to keep you guys after,' and then Bryon goes, 'We've got to make a livin' too.'"

Bill had no more questions. He had taken a lot out of the young man, and he knew it. Rios had seen his friends murdered before his eyes. He had stared at the face of Death, and his ears had filled with the sound of a blast that had been intended to end his young life. He had survived, but he would never be the same.

Rios turned his face toward the wall. He knew that, too.

By the time Bill and the others got back downtown, Folsom Prison officials had sent us the answer to our questions from their files. Billy Ray Hamilton and Clarence Ray Allen had been celled in the same section and were known associates. It was as Kenny Allen had described it. Billy Ray Hamilton was one of Clarence Ray Allen's dogs. And if we had ever doubted, now we knew who the real alpha male was in that pack.

32

Blood Turns to Ice

Wednesday, September 10, 1980
Modesto, California

Modesto is approximately ninety miles north of Fresno. In 1980, it was just beginning to make the transition from being a city to becoming a metropolitan area. Like all small towns and large cities, it had its share of liquor stores, and wherever there are liquor stores, there are always people who see an opportunity for easy cash. The night of September 10 was no exception.

Needham Liquors was quiet. It was almost 11:30 P.M. and business was slow. It was almost closing time, but a woman customer was still finishing the purchase of a few small items. The night clerk was working alone when a man entered and headed toward the beer cooler. The clerk had seen him in the store earlier, at around 8:00 or 8:30, to purchase cigarettes. The man had a slight limp, which the clerk hadn't noticed on his earlier visit, as he walked toward the counter with a six-pack of Budweiser beer, his stocking cap pulled over light-brown hair that stuck out on the sides from under the cap. The heavy stubble on his face gave him a rough, menacing look, but didn't disguise the fact that he also looked tired.

The clerk was used to blue-collar working men coming in late, and many of them looked like people you wouldn't want to cross. But most of them were just people grabbing a few beers to take home and relax over, spending a few hours with their family before they fell into bed and in a few hours begin a replica of the day that had just passed. The clerk kept an eye on the customer, but he didn't allow himself to be overly concerned.

The man walked up to the counter and set down the six-pack. He asked for a pint of Jack Daniels whiskey as he turned to watch the woman customer left the store. When she was gone, he pulled a butcher knife from under his shirt and pointed it toward the clerk. "GIVE ME ALL YOUR MONEY, YOU MOTHERFUCKER."

The clerk wasn't going to trade his life for the cash in the register. He backed up slightly, telling the man to stay calm; he would give him all the money he had. He began pulling the tens, fives, and ones from the register, stuffing them into the paper sack where he had placed the bottle of Jack Daniels. He could feel his hands shaking. Money dropped onto the counter as he tried to put the bills into the paper bag as quickly as possible, all the while keeping his eyes fixed on the butcher knife.

The robber scraped the spilled money off the counter and pushed it inside the sack. Then he ran toward the front door, leaving the beer on the counter, just as another man walked through the door. The clerk yelled at the customer to look out, that the man had a knife, just as the robber swung the blade toward the startled man. The robber made his way out the door as the clerk reached for the phone to call the police.

The robber ran into a backyard near the liquor store and pulled the pint bottle of Jack Daniels from the bag. He dropped it on the ground and shoved the bag into his rear pocket. As he looked around, Billy Ray Hamilton pulled off his blue knit hat, threw the butcher knife into a vacant lot, and walked quickly down the street, looking for a place to hide, while keeping his eyes out for the police, who could be anywhere.

Officer Beffa of the Modesto police department was sitting in his patrol car when a call came over his radio that a robbery had just occurred at Needham Liquor. The suspect was described as a six foot, two inch male with a mustache, wearing a stocking cap, blue jeans, and a dark-blue T-shirt. Beffa replied that he was less than three blocks away and would respond immediately.

Beffa drove into an alley and saw someone walking down the alley. There was enough light that he could see that the man generally matched the description of the suspect. Beffa jumped out of his patrol car and yelled at the man to stop. The suspect began to run and Beffa gave chase. Another officer, who had also responded to the call, appeared and joined him in the chase. The suspect turned into a blind alley, where the two officers cornered him and forced him to kneel and then cuffed him and placed him in the backseat of Beffa's patrol car. Just before putting the man into the car, Beffa removed a brown paper sack containing currency from the man's left rear pocket, a brown wallet, and a few pieces of paper he found stuffed in the man's pants.

Another officer pulled up, accompanied by the clerk and the customer from Needham's Liquor. After checking out the suspect in the back seat, the clerk identified him as the robber and the customer confirmed that he was the man who had waved the butcher knife in his direction.

Beffa inspected the wallet and said to the other officer, "Says here the guy's name is Billy Ray Hamilton. He's been mumbling that he's sick and he's on heroin." Beffa radioed in the identification and description of the man and then drove to the station to book the suspect. Then he took him to Scenic General Hospital to test his blood for heroin.

Detectives from the Modesto police department were waiting at the hospital when Beffa brought the suspect in. Detective Grogan, the night detective on call, noticed the suspect was limping and examined his left ankle. He could see what looked like healing bullet or pellet wounds. While the officers were at the hospital, the call came in from booking. After a warrant check, the wire had lit up. Billy Ray Hamilton was wanted out of Fresno for three counts of murder. Grogan told dispatch to call the Fresno sheriff's office while he brought Hamilton back to the jail. A whole new situation was presenting itself; a robbery was handled one way, but a capital murder was something entirely different. Back at the station, Grogan found the want sheet on Billy Ray Hamilton for three counts of murder out of Fresno. He looked carefully at the picture. These murders had been all over the news, and Grogan realized who the man was that he had in custody. It was going to be a long night.

It was almost midnight when Detective Badiali got the call at home that the Modesto police department had arrested a suspect in an armed robbery. The suspect's name was Billy Ray Hamilton, and he had a tattoo with the letters "BILLY" inscribed on his upper left arm. Badiali hung up the phone and called Detective Reyna and Bill Martin. It was usually an hour-and-a-half drive to Modesto, but Badiali knew he could do it in an hour as soon as he had picked up the others.

Bill called me to tell me that Modesto had Hamilton in custody and that they were on their way there. I hung up the phone and lay back down on the bed. They didn't need me. If anybody was going to get anything out of Hamilton, it would be Bill and Badiali; besides, picking me up would just delay them. I had a feeling they weren't going to get much. Hamilton had been around. He had priors for aggravated assault and robbery.

It was 3:00 in the morning when Bill, Badiali, and Reyna walked into the Modesto police department and met with Grogan. They got the background on the robbery and the condition of the man who said he was Hamilton. Someone called over to the Stanislaus County jail, where Hamilton was now being held, and asked to have him moved to a holding cell. It was also 3:30 in the morning when all four officers walked into the jail.

People wonder what murderers look like when they are confronted by their crime. Imagining the situation, most people project their own fears onto others. They think that someone accused of the worst crimes would react the way they think they themselves would react, with fear, remorse, and presence of mind. The reality is that when you bring a man in and sit him down in an interrogation room or a cell, they are all different. You can tell almost immediately what you are going to get by how they look at you and how they walk. For some, the fear is overwhelming, and for others, there is weeping or confusion, and at times, there is hope that if they say *just* the right thing you will understand and, maybe, just maybe, you will let them go. There are men not used to chains, not used to restraint, not used to being without any semblance of control. And there is another species—the ones who have been around the system, in and out for years. They are not intimidated by chains. They are players within the system—they've worn chains before. They know you aren't going to hit them. They know that there is nothing you can do to them that will match what they could do to you and would if they had a chance.

Yet, it always surprised me how many of them would still talk. Maybe, it was a vestige of conscience that lingered somewhere deep within that got to some of them. Or, maybe, it was arrogance that they could spar with you and win. Sometimes, they just didn't care what you thought of them and they would just like to get it over with. For some, it was a game, a form of entertainment to see if they could play with your mind, while you tried to play with theirs. Sometimes, their only method of control was the defiance of silence. They had what you wanted and they weren't going to give it to you, because silence was their last vestige of control.

As he waited for Hamilton to be brought into the interrogation room, Bill tensed like a man waiting for a fight. His mind raced through the categories and he wondered what kind of a man Hamilton would be. As Hamilton was led in handcuffs into the interrogation room, Bill stood still and studied him for a moment. Bill had been through this moment so many times he couldn't remember all of them. He had glared so many times at the prison photo that Hamilton's face had become imprinted in his mind, just like the faces of those three kids lying on that cement floor where their killer, the man sitting in front of him, had left them.

Most of the time, you aren't emotionally involved in a case when you make an arrest. You feel an adrenaline rush that comes with getting the person you are after, but you don't have the personal investment that a victim or relative does. That is a good thing. You are a law enforcement officer, not a vigilante. You have to stay objective. If you aren't objective, you can miss things. But sometimes it *is* personal. You can't help it, no matter how thick the emotional shell is that you build around yourself. No matter how many times you have rustled through the pockets of somebody lying dead on the floor, sometimes it just gets to you. Bill didn't often give in to his emotions, but there was no question this one had become personal for him, and he knew it was personal for me.

Hamilton's mustache hung around the edges of his mouth, framing lips that were tightly closed. The coarse, thick stubble on his face gave him a brutish appearance; his black eyes were shrouded by slightly closed lids, veiling the eyes, the windows that Bill wanted to see into for a hint of what lay hidden inside the man. Hamilton's heavy chin protruded from his face, and his dirty blond hair was matted down from not being washed and from the compression of the knit cap he had worn. Bill's eyes connected with the man he had been hunting for five days. Finally, both men's eyes locked for just a moment. Bill had seen it before, not very often, but he had seen it before—eyes that held nothing behind them. There was no fear in them. There was no flicker of anxiety or wariness. This man didn't care about anything. His eyes reflected complete emptiness. This man was a killer, and Bill knew he wouldn't think twice about killing any man present if it was to his advantage and possibly even if it wasn't to his advantage. He just wouldn't think about it. The most dangerous kind of man, predictable only in his unpredictability.

Hamilton shifted in his seat, the chains between his handcuffs making a metallic, clinking sound, but his hands didn't struggle, a subtle signal that he was used to cuffs. Bill hesitated for a moment, trying to assess whether he had an edge, something that might make Hamilton talk. But he had seen it too many times before: This one wouldn't talk. Bill waited while Badiali informed Hamilton he was under arrest for three counts of murder. No hint of concern showed on Hamilton's face. He just sat there, waiting for the rest of what he knew was coming.

Bill read Hamilton his Miranda rights, silently seething to himself about having to politely remind Hamilton about his constitutional right to remain silent. He hated Miranda cards and all they implied. I always had to be careful with Bill, because he could sometimes hedge when he didn't think I would know about it. He would look at me and tell me he would take care of it. Bill didn't engage in rationalizations about the purity or the loftiness of the law like lawyers and judges tend to do. Bill was a realist. Like most cops, he lived in two different worlds: the pleasant world of friends and family and baseball games, and the ugly world of predators and victims. Like most cops, he tried hard to keep them separate because in order to function each world requires a different persona. That's why if you go to a party where there are several cops, almost always they will be together, sharing with the only people who they think understand. Bill looked at people like Hamilton as predatory scavengers. And he looked on the people who wrote the Miranda decision as a bunch of judges who had never been to a crime scene or had to wade through blood and misery before deciding that those who caused that misery should be given an edge that cops didn't get.

Bill's mouth moved through the familiar litany. He barely heard his own words, as he watched the face of the man who stared back at him. Bill knew he would get nothing. Hamilton waited until Bill was finished. He understood his rights. He had nothing to say.

Bill slipped his Miranda card back inside his wallet and looked at the others. None of them were surprised. Badiali told Hamilton to get up. They moved him out to the car to take him back to the hospital. They wanted x-rays of the ankle.

After the examining physician at the hospital looked at the x-rays, he told the waiting officers, "It looks like he has four objects lodged in his left ankle. My guess is shotgun pellets, maybe twenty-four hours old."

Bill, Badiali, and Fernando moved Hamilton back into their squad car. First, they would take him to Valley Medical Center in Fresno for more x-rays. They rode in silence. Like other suspects, Hamilton rested his head against the backseat, while he thought about what could happen next. The cops guarding him didn't rest their heads; they too were thinking about what could happen next.

At Fresno's Valley Medical Center, Bill watched the doctor examine Hamilton's left ankle and foot. There were perforations in the skin. Metal pellets were still in the foot. More importantly, the shoe had holes in it that approximated some, but not all, of the pellet holes in the foot. The left shoe also was x-rayed, revealing three more pellets. The shoe pellets were removed, but Bill wasn't optimistic that they would be able to remove the pellets from Hamilton's foot. The pellets from the shoe were number-six, shotgun pellets, the same size shot that Jack Abbot had fired when the assailant had fled the market. Bill watched the forensic tech bag the pellets. His only thought was that it was too bad Jack Abbot hadn't aimed a little higher.

I stayed awake most of the night, falling into a fitful sleep only shortly before I got up, dressed, and went into the office. I was right. They didn't need me to be present. There wasn't anything I could have done to help the situation. News that Hamilton was wanted for the Fran's Market murders had even reached Modesto. As soon as he was identified and in custody, somehow the Stanislaus County public defenders office was contacted by the Fresno County public defender. Before Hamilton left the Stanislaus County jail, he had been instructed that he was not to make any statements. It didn't make any difference. He wouldn't have talked anyway.

The Modesto P.D. had taken a 1967 Cadillac into custody. After the robbery of the liquor store, witnesses had contacted officers in the field and pointed out the car. According to two men who had been near Needham Liquor, they had been approached by a man who fit the description of Hamilton. He told them he had just been released from prison and needed money. He looked desperate, and he had tried to sell them the Cadillac for one hundred fifty dollars. They refused, but after they heard about the robbery of the liquor store, they called the police.

Bill and Badiali went out with a forensic tech from Fresno to do a preliminary examination of the Cadillac. There was blood on the rearview mirror and a blood stain on the floor mat. Blood stains were also found on the steering wheel. A quick check with the Fresno County Department of Motor Vehicles established that Kenny Allen was the car's owner.

Bill and Badiali picked up Hamilton's personal effects from the Stanislaus jail, but they had given them only a cursory examination. After they finished at Valley Medical Center, they booked Hamilton into the Fresno jail. Both men were feeling the effects of being up all night, running on adrenalin and coffee. They needed sleep, but there were reports to write. Badiali walked back to his office and picked up the manila envelope that contained Hamilton's personal effects taken at the time of booking. Bill watched him lay all the items out onto his desk. There was an address book with Billy Ray Hamilton's name on it and his prison number. Badiali thumbed through the small book, flipping through the pages until he pulled out a loose sheet with penciled writing on it. As Badiali looked over the sheet, Bill could see the change in the expression on his face.

"What is it?" Badiali held the sheet of paper between his thumb and forefinger. Bill took it by the edge and stared at it. He felt his blood turn to ice.

33

"One of my dogs will do it …"

Thursday, September 11, 1980
Fresno, California

It was six days after the murders at Fran's Market. Bill barged into my office as soon as I arrived. It was all over the news that we had Billy Ray Hamilton in custody. Bill hadn't slept all night. I hadn't gotten much sleep either, waiting and wondering. Bill laid a plastic bag on my desk. Inside was a small sheet of notebook paper from what looked like a flip-memo pad. As I looked at it, my mind slowly began to comprehend what it was. Bill's voice was hoarse and gravelly; the hours without sleep had drained him, but what was on the piece of paper had drawn out whatever was left. "This was in Hamilton's address book, lying loose. We went through everything."

The penciled words on the paper were the names of the witnesses in the Mary Sue Kitts' murder case. Each name was hand-printed. Bryon Schletewitz's name was located toward the top of the list. Next to it was a black spot, made in pencil. Ray Schletewitz, Lee Furrow, and Shirley Doeckel were also on the list—all the main witnesses against Allen. But there were two more names who weren't witnesses. I looked up at Bill.

What I was looking at was an assassination list. The names of people who were marked for death. Bryon Schletewitz had only been the first name on the list. I put the plastic bag down. It was like I was holding blood in my hand. How had it come to this? The only person who had the motive to kill these people was Clarence Ray Allen, but for what? This changed *everything*. No longer were these murders just about some money that might have been stashed in the rumored, but non-existent, safe at Fran's Market, or about something that Allen had set into motion for another robbery. No longer could they be considered senseless murders of three young people, performed in order to cover the identification of the killer. This had been an execution—performed by one killer from a list prepared by another killer, a master manipulator, Clarence Allen, a man inside prison walls. Billy Ray Hamilton had become Allen's hand holding the gun, pulling the trigger. The list was like the stepping stone lifted from the shores of the Piedra Canal years before during the Mary Sue Kitts murder investigation. The list had to have come from Allen. He was the only one with any motive to extend the death list beyond those in the store. And the only motive had to be vengeance. The inconceivable had become reality.

The letters from Clarence Ray Allen to his son, which we had seized during the search of Kenny Allen's house, now began to make sense. Before, the scrawled letters hadn't really seemed like anything more than idle chatter, with a few angry comments mixed in. Now, however, they took on the context of a code. Allen had written something about a "country" music show coming to town around September third and then another saying for them to "remember around September third, have everything ready so you all can go to that 'country' music show. I know ya all really will 'enjoy yourselves.'" Then, Allen had written that Kenny should "give his best" to Carl Mayfield: "Tell him I am thinking of him and I hope to see him one day, but I am sure he knows that already." Allen also referred to Shirley Doeckel as a "snitch bitch," and wished her "many, many more" problems. He also talked about "his dog," who wanted to meet "Mr. Jones and Mr. Mayfield, and a few other good friends."

As I recalled the words in those letters, I'm sure my face must have drained of all color. I could certainly feel the chill spreading over me. All of these people had been involved in the Mary Sue Kitts murder case. The thought of it, the magnitude of the evil, was almost incomprehensible, but the one thought that kept screaming inside my head was the promise I had made. I had told each of these people that they would be safe. I had told them they had nothing to worry about; I had given them my confident assurance that prosecutors make every day to their witnesses: You will be safe. I had not seen it coming. No one had. Now, all I could see were those three kids on the floor of Fran's market, lifeless islands in a sea of blood.

Bill knew what I was thinking. I'm sure he was thinking about it, too. His voice was soft, almost a whisper. "Nobody could have known. We couldn't have stopped this. You know that."

I knew that. But it didn't make any difference.

We sat for a few minutes, gathering our thoughts. No matter how shaken we were, we had a job to do. We both had always known Kenny Allen was lying. The only question was how much. I told Bill, "Get Kenny Allen. That son of a bitch is going to give us his father. Now that we have Hamilton, Kenny needs to know that whatever he has to give better come quick." Bill picked up the plastic bag and left without saying a word. He knew what to do; I didn't need to tell him. He headed over to the sheriff's office. We weren't going to be nice anymore.

Two hours later, as I waited outside the interrogation room, I could hear the voice inside. Bill was talking and so was Tom. The voice of Kenny Allen began grating on my nerves. The whining and the squirming reminded me of some kind of slug slipping around between rocks. He knew we had Hamilton. Nothing is secret inside a jail. Besides, we wanted him to know.

I heard Bill raise his voice, and there was no velvet in it. "You know who's outside that door? Do you know? The man who sent your father to prison is outside there, and he's coming in. I am telling you right now he doesn't give a shit about you or your wife. He doesn't give a shit what happens to you and he isn't in the mood to be nice. So you better think real hard and real fast about what you are going to say, and this time I want the truth. That is all you got to sell, boy, and he isn't going to listen to any more bullshit. You got one person to convince that you're telling the truth and that is me because I'm the only man he's going to listen to. You understand me? I am all you got."

I waited until there was a brief lull, the silence that builds anticipation and squeezes the person waiting. I wanted Kenny Allen to be afraid of me. I wanted him to be sweating. I wanted to smell the fear when he saw me. I wanted him to know that the only man who could do anything for him was me and I wanted him to be afraid.

I walked in without knocking. Tom was sitting in a chair behind a desk. He looked straight at me, his face expressionless. I caught an almost imperceptible nod. He was letting me know that Kenny was ready. Bill looked over. "What do you want to do, boss?" I didn't look directly at Kenny Allen, who was sitting against the wall; I focused only on Bill, but I could see the expression on Allen's face out of the corner of my eye. He was trying to look cocky but it wasn't in him. Clarence Allen would only respect power and ruthlessness—none of that was in the man crumpled in the chair, not then, not ever. I kept my eyes off of Kenny Allen as I glanced at Bill and Tom. "Take him back to the jail. He hasn't got anything I want to hear. I don't need him. Just book his ass and his wife, too."

I stared at Allen, mustering as much contempt on my face as I could. It only took a second. You watch a man begin to wilt before you and once it starts he sinks into himself. Kenny Allen was ready to give up his soul and I was the only man who could save him. I turned my back on Kenny. "The hell with him."

I closed my eyes when I heard the anguish in the words. "Can I talk to Mr. Martin—alone? Please?"

I didn't ask why. I stood there with my back to Allen, reaching for the handle of the door. I let the pleading sound in Kenny's words slowly sink into silence. Then I turned slightly and nodded. "You want to talk to him, go ahead." I hoped my voice sounded like I didn't care. I walked out of the room. My stomach was churning. I needed Kenny to talk, but I didn't want him to know it. Bill and I had taken the risk to push him to the brink. He would either refuse to talk or he would slowly let loose. Kenny Allen was a weak man. He was afraid. My guess is that he had been afraid for most of his life. He was terrified of his father and he was terrified of us. But this day his father wasn't there and we were. We needed to reach inside and squeeze that fear until he thought he needed us more than we needed him. I had squeezed as hard as I could. I closed the door behind me and went to another office to wait. It was all on Bill now.

Bill came into the office where I was waiting. "I took him back to the jail. I told him that if he wanted to talk he needed to let me know and I would try to work it out with you." Bill smiled. "When you turned your back on him, I thought he was going to piss in his pants." It was as close to a compliment as Bill ever came with me. "He'll talk. He wanted to talk when you left but I think we need to let him sit for awhile. He's going to lie, play down what he did." Bill waited to hear my thoughts.

I was pragmatic. It has been my experience that people expect of others what they expect of themselves. If you are a lying, sniveling crook then you expect the same level of morality in others. Nobody wants to think that others might be better, otherwise what would that say about their perceptions of themselves? I smiled at Bill, "Kenny will expect no more loyalty than he would give and he has none. So he knows that we have Hamilton, but what he doesn't know is how much Hamilton has told us. What he's going to do is assume Hamilton will drag him into the deal and he's going to minimize his role. For now, we let him do it. We just squeeze slowly until he gives it all up. Right now, I want his old man."

Bill shook his head in agreement. "He'll give up the old man. We just have to wait." I had to admire Bill's patience in letting the pressure build up in Kenny Allen until it reached the bursting point. I am not sure I would have been able to sit there and send Kenny back to the jail without asking the question.

It wasn't long. By mid-afternoon Bill was back in my office. "Kenny sent word that he wants to see me."

"All right. You go talk to him and let him know that no deals can be made without my approval. I'll wait until you call me."

This is always the hard part, waiting until a critical witness is ready to talk and measuring what you have to do. I didn't know exactly what Kenny was going to say. I suspected he had helped Hamilton do the job in some way, or, at least, he had known about it from the beginning, but he hadn't said so. Not yet. I had also been thinking about the fact that if we had to make a deal, then Allen would need an attorney. The public defender's office had already asserted itself with Hamilton. They hadn't even been appointed by the court but they knew they would probably have to defend Hamilton, and they wanted to make sure he kept his mouth shut. They wanted our case to be as weak as possible. Even though it made me mad as hell to have them interfere in the investigation, it wasn't unethical. I knew that if I had to defend Hamilton, I wouldn't have given any breaks to the D.A. either. But they still didn't know about Kenny's role in all this and I certainly wasn't going to tell them.

I talked to one of the other senior D.A.s, Dennis Beck, about who might be somebody we could deal with. I wasn't looking to somebody who would roll over, but I wanted somebody who would recognize the gravity of the situation and would realize that a deal had to be made. I could talk to Kenny without a lawyer, but it was the deal that counted. It was a matter of "What I would give" that would involve some degree of legal advice for Kenny. Sooner or later, Kenny was going to have a lawyer anyway. Better to get to it now. We talked about several names and decided to bring in a defense attorney that we knew. He was a former D.A. He would understand the situation and he was a pragmatist. He would ask for as much as he could get, but he would also know what we expected and would demand. We would arrange for him to talk to Kenny, but before any deals were made, we would make sure that we had an idea of what Kenny could give us. I was willing to trade, but I wasn't willing to buy a pig in a poke.

It was late afternoon. We had been talking to Kenny Allen, working around the outside of the case, telling him just enough so that he'd be aware of the fact that we knew more than he thought, but keeping it general enough so he didn't know how much or how little we did know. He was meeting with his new lawyer now. We would have to wait. I told his attorney that I wouldn't agree to immunity nor would I agree to drop the drug charges. Kenny wanted a release without bail. I wouldn't do that either, but I would agree to reasonable bail and an honor release if he testified. Any other deals would depend on what Kenny had and whether I needed it.

His attorney had been around. He knew that depending on what information his client had, we would need him if we wanted to get Clarence Ray Allen. Even if his client talked and implicated himself, we couldn't use that against the father unless Kenny testified, and we couldn't make him testify because of his Fifth Amendment right not to incriminate himself. Even if Kenny implicated himself as a principal in the murders, he could still trade for more if we wanted him to take the stand. Right now, we were going to have to do the slow dance.

Everybody was there when I got into the interrogation room, Bill, Badiali, and Tom Lean. Kenny was sitting in his chair, leaning against the wall. His attorney was sitting nearby, watching. Kenny looked at me and then hung his head. He realized by now that I was the one who would decide. Senior Deputy D.A. Dennis Beck sat next to Tom and Bill. I took a chair in front of Kenny and waited until he raised his eyes to face me. His lawyer nodded that we could go ahead. He had already told us that Kenny was ready to cooperate if we kept our end of the deal, but he didn't tell us what he was going to say. The tape recorder was on.

I reminded Kenny that he asked to speak to Bill Martin. We didn't ask to speak to him. I would not agree to release without bail unless and until he testified and I told him that there were no deals on the drug charges or the murders as a condition of his statement to us. If he went to prison, we would make arrangements for that to be done in another state or in a facility where he would be protected.

I got right to the point. "All right, I want you to understand. You were told that you will not be given immunity from prosecution for anything that you say. You understand that?"

"Yes."

It was that last statement that was critical. Kenny Allen was essentially being told that we would need his testimony in order to prosecute the murders and that if he refused to testify, we could use his confession to convict him with his own words. We needed him but he needed to cooperate. He was betting that we would need him so badly that even if he implicated himself in the murder, we would still have to give him immunity in order to get him on the stand. In retrospect, it was probably a safe bet to make, so long as he cooperated. I pulled out my Miranda card and read him his rights, carefully enunciating for the tape recorder. I didn't want any questions about this, and I had waited until he consented through his lawyer to talk. I asked the others if I had left anything out or if any promises of leniency had been made. I was satisfied. "Now at this time Mr. Martin and Detective Lean will be conducting the interview." Bill and I had talked about this. I wanted Kenny to know I was watching. I didn't want him to think that he had any relationship or special link to me. I wanted him to think that the only person holding his lifeline was Bill, but he always had to believe that any time I wanted, I could cut the rope.

Kenny leaned back in his chair. It was his show for now. He had received two letters from Clarence Allen. We had picked them up in the search, but at the time they seemed to be innocuous ramblings. Kenny Allen started to talk about his father. Clarence Allen had let him know in the letter that he would be hearing "a country show." He said he had interpreted that as meaning he would hear from somebody named "Country." The man he had told us was Bobby was actually Bill Ray Hamilton. He was shifting in his seat, letting the words come out in dribbles as if, in some way, that made it seem more reluctant on his part. "Billy didn't go into any details with me at all about the store robbery. He got connected with this girl, Connie Barbo, and they set up their own plans, which I knew little or nothing about....I just knew he'd come to town to do a robbery."

Bill remained silent, sitting there, rubbing his mustache and thinking the same thing I was thinking: This was going to be slow work. Kenny was already lying. It wasn't even subtle. But now wasn't the time to confront Kenny. We needed to let him fill in details before we started to press him. Bill interjected, "Did you talk about this robbery with Hamilton?"

"Not at all. He didn't discuss it with me at all."

"And do you know where he was going to do the robbery?"

"I had assumed that it would be at Fran's Market. And that's where it wound up—Fran's Market. He and Connie spent a lot of time together. He was just using my place as a place to stay. This was on and around September third. Then, as you guys pointed out, our car was seen at the location several times, that one day before the robbery took place."

Bill's voice took on a slightly sharper tone. "Do you know who was driving your car?"

He immediately lied. He said he had no idea how Hamilton had gotten the car. He said on that Friday afternoon he dropped Hamilton off at the bus depot and gave him sixty dollars, but evidently Hamilton hadn't left town because he called Allen's wife, Kathy, later that night to say that he and Connie had had "a falling out."

Bill pulled out the letters we had taken from Kenny's house, written to him by his father, and held them out in front of him, waving them slowly back and forth before handing them to him.

Kenny clasped the letters tightly in his hand, staring at them before saying what he knew we were waiting for. "We got these letters back-to-back and dad's telling us, 'Remember around September third to have everything ready so you all can go to the country music show. I know you all will really enjoy yourselves. I know you kids never liked country music before.'" Kenny looked around the room. "That was my objection to the robbery."

Bill stared at him. "Uh huh." The sarcasm seeped through the grunting sound of his voice. Bill could be subtle when he wanted to be, but now he wasn't even making an effort.

Kenny's eyes searched the room, trying to find an understanding face. "I felt it should never have taken place. I told Dad that I didn't even want to involve ourselves with it, but it was too late. The gentleman was in town, and there was nothing I could do about it."

"And you were just reading from that letter?"

"Right, I was just reading from the letter."

"And did he say anything else about the robbery in that letter?"

Kenny read slowly from the letter. "'At least once a week, ha ha. Anyway, forget about rock and roll. At least, in country everything is fine. A dude bought the farm yesterday, but I'm just fine....'" Kenny thought he needed to translate. "In other words, some guy had got hit in Folsom; that's what that means. And, ah, he just reminded me about Country again and he's just getting that name in my head. Country turned out to be Hamilton." A pleading look crossed Kenny's face, and he watched for some sign that we had some sympathy. He didn't find any.

Bill's voice took on a soothing tone. "Okay, we've gone over this before, and at that time you mentioned a specific date that you were up there, and you talked to your father and you were talking about this robbery of Fran's Market. Is that correct? What dates were those? Do you recall?"

"I believe it was the seventeenth."

"Saturday, the seventeenth of August, 1980?"

"Yeah, he didn't go into great detail because I was against it, but I knew it was going to take place. He said some gentlemen by the name—'one of my dogs'—that's what he called Country."

"What did you interpret 'dog' to mean?"

"One of his running mates, one of the guys he says 'fetch,' and the guy goes and gets it. He just said, 'One of my dogs will be in touch with you to let you know, to get some things done for me.'"

"But you were objecting to it, and you knew it was a robbery?"

"Yes, I knew it was a robbery. My father had told me that one of his friends was going to come down and do a strong-arm. I assumed it was Ray and Fran's Market."

"Why?"

"'Cause that was one of the only out-of-town markets you could hit. I didn't believe he was going to go to Kmart and wipe them out again. Fran's seemed to be the easiest one to hit."

Nobody in that room believed that Kenny didn't know from the beginning that Fran's was the target. Bill's voice lost all patience. "All right, Mr. Allen. What did you tell Hamilton and Barbo about Fran's Market?"

"Nothing."

"Did you tell him who worked there?"

"Oh, *he* knew who worked there."

I saw the look from the corner of Bill's eye. Kenny couldn't keep his lies straight. If he didn't know Fran's Market was going to be hit, then how could he know that Hamilton already knew who worked there? "All right, tell me about that. What did he know?"

"He knew who worked there. He knew what time they'd be getting off, what time the place closed, and everything."

The words came out of my mouth in a sharp staccato burst as I broke into the interrogation. "How do you know this?"

Kenny's head snapped in my direction. He knew he had made a mistake. "Okay, I knew it just from the general observation of the way the gentleman was working." Kenny waited to see if anybody was buying his line. He shrugged. "Okay, he knew what he was going to do. He knew how to do it, and I had not talked to him about it. I just picked him up at the bus depot. So, it had been, well, discussed prior to him getting to where I was at." Kenny looked at me, waiting to see if I accepted his explanation.

I didn't. "Well, how did you know it? Did he tell you something?"

"He said Dad had gone over everything with him."

I pushed again. "What did he say that your father, Clarence Allen, had gone over with him?" My voice was getting louder. "What did he say?"

Kenny looked around. It was obvious that he was thinking about his current situation and he was panicking. He couldn't figure out how to reconcile what he had said before with what he was saying now. "Well, I, I, I—I knew that there was going to be a robbery at the market from my father telling me out there at Folsom, like I said earlier. Okay, but I didn't know there was going to be no wasted people that took place."

My voice raised. "WHAT DID MR. HAMILTON TELL YOU?" I didn't usually raise my voice during an interrogation, but I had had enough of his weaseling.

Kenny recoiled at the impatient tone of my voice and I saw him shrink back into his chair.

"Okay, I said, 'Is there anything you need to know?' He said, 'no, your father,'" Kenny looked up at me, "'Clarence Ray Allen, has gone over everything with me.'"

"Did he say, 'your father, Clarence Ray Allen,' or just 'your father?'"

"Well, I said 'my father.' You guys told me that whenever I said 'my father,' use his full name." Kenny was squirming in his chair. He was sweating. He clearly was on the edge.

Bill interjected. "We know. Just relax." Bill gave me a little sideways look, telling me to back off a notch.

I took a deep breath and lowered my voice. "Okay, you say that he told you that your father...."

Kenny finished the sentence. "...had discussed everything with him. He told him everything—the whole nine yards."

"Did Hamilton mention any names; did he give you any names of people that worked in Fran's Market? Did you ever hear him mention any names?"

"Oh, I mentioned one to him. I said, 'Bryon.' He said, 'Oh, you mean Ray's son. That's Schletewitz.'"

I looked at Kenny. "He said 'Ray's son'? Did he say anything more about that?"

"Well, once he told me who the owner of the store was, there was no sense in me going any further. He knew everything from the gate."

I looked down at my notes. "You mean from the start?"

"Yeah, from the start. He knew what he was going to do and how he was going to do it. He just lied to me on what was being done. He told me that—I didn't have to tell him anything; he knew how to do it. He had already been talked to about it."

I stared at Kenny. I was out of patience. Bill could see it but he wasn't going to stop me. This was now a good-guy–bad-guy interrogation and I was the bad guy. Allen had to believe I held his balls in my fist. My voice took on a much harder edge. "All right, now, I want to get something straight here. Before what you just said concerning Fran's Market, you told us that you just thought he was going to go hit some market and you just assumed it was Fran's Market. Now, there's a difference between that and what you've just told us...."

"Well, my dad told...."

I didn't let him finish. "I want you to level with us."

Kenny's face showed his uncertainty. "No, I'm leveling. I said my father talked to me about a robbery that could take place, and I knew that it was going to be Fran's Market, 'cause he's told me so."

My voice was rising again. "Who told you so?"

"My father told me so—Clarence Ray Allen."

"He told you Fran's Market?"

"Right."

"So, would I be correct that whenever you talked to Hamilton that you were assuming that it would be Fran's Market? Is that correct?"

"Correct."

I let my voice drop; the pace of questioning and tone is critical to keeping a person off balance. "Did Hamilton ever tell you that he was going to hit Fran's Market?"

"Yeah, I asked him; I said, 'Is it Fran's Market?' He said, 'Yes, the Belmont store,' 'cause they knew where everything was. That he'd gone over everything with my father in prison. He knew everything my father knew. He knew stuff that I didn't even know."

"Like what?"

"He said, 'Yes, there are two safes.' He said 'safes.' So, I knew then that he had greater knowledge of the store than I had."

The next question was critical and so was the answer. "Was there any discussion on where the safes were located?"

"No, other than the one in the freezer."

"Tell me about that."

"Okay, he said that he knows there's one in the freezer that they usually keep the money in, and I said, 'Oh, I didn't know that.'"

I didn't believe him. None of us did. But keeping him going, even if he was lying, was important. Later, when we knew a little more and could twist him harder, we would use his lies against him. Patience is important in an interrogation and sometimes it takes hours or even days to wring out the one sentence that spills out in a second and turns the whole case. "How many times have you visited your father at Folsom since that time?"

Kenny tried to look at me, but no matter how hard he tried, he couldn't face me or anyone in the room with a level gaze. He averted his eyes as he answered. "None, we were busted."

I nodded, signaling with note of resignation that we had exhausted the subject. "Now, I'm going to ask you one other question. It won't be the only other question, but I'll ask you a question. Where did Hamilton get the car that was driven to Fran's market? Think carefully about that. Don't lie to me."

"I'm not going to lie to you. I haven't lied to you so far, so why start now?" Kenny could see the disbelief on our faces and shrugged. "Okay, I do know that they borrowed my wife's car to take Connie home. I found out later that they had used it to run out to Ray and Fran's Market to check out the situation. They used it on two separate occasions...."

Kenny had already forgotten that he had told us that he had no idea where the car came from, but now wasn't the time to remind him of that.

Tom Lean's voice came from the corner. Kenny's head turned as Tom snapped out a question. "What kind of car did you loan him to go out there?"

Kenny looked around. We knew he was beginning to feel surrounded. You have to be careful when a number of people are doing the questioning, because they can sometimes make the suspect feel defensive and overwhelmed, and then the suspect will stop talking. Tom tried to keep his body language unthreatening as Kenny stared back at him, trying to remember what he had said or hadn't said. "We didn't loan him a car to go out there. We loaned him a car to take Connie home, a '65 Ford Fairlane or Galaxy."

He was lying. There was another car. We knew that. We just didn't know where it was.

Tommy began to press. "Do you know of any other car that Hamilton used while he was here?"

"No."

"After the robbery, did you ever, when you talked to him on the phone...."

Kenny shook his head. "She talked to him, my wife. He called back and said him and Connie had gotten into it, and he wanted to know if she had gotten back home."

Tommy leaned back. "Okay, and when was this? When was this conversation?"

"This was, ah, midnight, Friday the fifth."

"Did you see Hamilton after that?"

"No, I did not. I didn't see him until when I took him to the bus depot."

"Did you and Hamilton ever go over to a house after this robbery to recover a car?"

"We went to pick up a Cadillac at one time, but that was back in August. Nobody got it because we couldn't get it started. The front wheel's about ready to fall off of it. It's at my brother-in-law's." He was lying again. Hamilton got out of town somehow and it wasn't by bus and we had already picked up the Cadillac in Modesto. Kenny just didn't know that. But we also knew from the description that the car used at the robbery wasn't a Cadillac.

Dennis Beck interjected, "Where's that Cadillac now?"

"I thought it was still in Clovis, but Kathy tells me it's gone."

Bill pushed himself back, rubbing his face. "I'm sitting here and I'm listening. I thought you were just going to lay it all out to us. I'm talking about the killing." The tone of his voice left not doubt that he was out of patience.

Kenny felt the mood shift in the room, as all of us began moving our feet, the sound of people getting ready to get up and walk out. He looked around the room. "Now, wait a minute...." There was panic in his voice. He was feeling more and more cornered, and he was trying to buy time and figure out what he had said and how to minimize his own responsibility.

"But—but, I knew from day one when I talked to my dad that there was going to be a robbery at Ray and Fran's Market. His man Country, which turned out to be Mr. Hamilton, was going to do the job, and I know that I did pick him up on the third and bring him to my house, and he met Connie Barbo, and from there everything took shape and form."

We stared at Kenny, watching the sweat bead on his face. He was lying about himself and he was forgetting his lies. Bill bored in. "Did he have a gun when you picked him up?"

"I have no idea if he had a gun or not."

"Could he have had a shotgun without you seeing it?"

"He could have. It all depends on how big a shotgun you want it."

"He went to your house and he stayed there?"

"Yes, and I never saw any weapons whatsoever on him."

"Well, you knew he was going to do a robbery, right? Didn't you figure he'd have a weapon?"

"Well, I assumed there was going to be a weapon used, but I didn't know what type."

Tommy stuck his finger just inches from Kenny's face. "On Friday, you took Hamilton down to the bus depot and you knew when you had to loan him the car that he didn't have one? Now, when he went to get on the bus, did you wonder what was going to go on at the robbery?"

"To me, I was always left in doubt. Then, I didn't know whether it was going to come off or not. I had no idea, 'cause we hadn't discussed it in great detail and I didn't know when it was going to go down."

Bill's voice had begun to take on more menace. "What was your part?"

"My part was just to let him stay at my place."

"But what were you going to get out of the robbery?"

"Nothing. I didn't want nothing. I didn't even want the robbery to take place. Evidently, it was just a stake for Billy to get things started. What things, I don't know."

I couldn't stay silent any longer. We had been over and over this and we weren't making progress. There comes a point in some interrogations where getting information out of a suspect is like watching a slow drip from a faucet that you have put a washer in. You keep tightening and waiting but then another little drip begins to form. You know it isn't going to stop until you squeeze it down the last little bit, and the slowness of it is antagonizing. "Mr. Allen, I don't want to interrupt Mr. Martin, but I want you to understand something, okay? We've been over this, and each time we go over it a little bit more."

Kenny stared at me. "I remember a little bit more. Your questions get more explicit and I don't know what you want me to say other than, yes, my father did set it up, yes."

I shook my head. "We want the truth. Did you father set it up for the man to shoot the people out there?"

"Okay, I believe my father did set them up."

Bill pushed his lips tightly together. "What did he say?"

"My father said—I guess the robbery was just…" Kenny seemed to deflate right in front of us. He couldn't hold on to all the lies he had told. He was ready to give up, but it would be like watching air slowly leak out of a tire. "Okay, the robbery was simply something to do, but Ray and Bryon were to be the primary targets."

The words snapped out of my mouth. "TO BE WHAT?"

"Executed."

The word hung in the room, piercing the silence. It was what we thought, but it was still unthinkable. It isn't often that any flicker of shock shows on a detective's face during an interrogation, but I could see it on the faces of the men around me. I don't know how I looked. Bill said, "Okay, that's what we've been asking you for."

Kenny smirked. "Yeah, but you haven't come out and asked me the question."

I'm sure the exasperation showed in my voice. I hated this kind of little word game and the smirk on his face. I am sure my voice was raised, but I wasn't listening to myself as I pushed. "Do we have to go through that? I told you we don't play word games with you and I don't expect you to play word games with us."

"Well, that's the reason I wanted you to give me the question—I'd have given the answer."

The tone of my voice took the smirk off his face. "You know what we're asking about. Now let's get down to it."

"Okay, my dad said, 'There's going to be a robbery and if Ray and Bryon get in the way, it'll just be a bonus for me.' The bonus for him would be that they'd be dead."

I stood up and walked toward Kenny. There was no mistaking the anger in my voice or in the fact that he had pushed me all I was going to be pushed. "Mr. Allen, we're asking you to tell the truth. Now, you ought to be able to figure from what Mr. Martin and Mr. Lean are telling you that they know what they're talking about. There's no point in our sitting here and bullshitting each other. I want to know what happened."

Tommy's voice was softer and more conciliatory. "Honestly and truthfully, you didn't know it was going to take place Friday night?"

Kenny was cowering in his chair. "No, I didn't know it was going to take place, but when I dropped him off he said, 'I'll see you later.'" Kenny looked around the room, still searching for some glimmer of understanding. There wasn't one. He waited for another moment, a long sigh escaping from his entire body. "Okay, from the time I left dad at Folsom Penitentiary, I knew there was going to be a robbery and, quite possibly, two slayings. To the best of my knowledge, Bryon and Ray were going to be killed, but I didn't know how they were going to do it."

Tommy's arms were crossed. "Did your dad tell you that?"

"Yes, my dad told me all of this."

Kenny paused, sighed again, and began slowly, "Okay, there was going to be a robbery and Ray and Bryon were going to be shot or killed. I picked Billy up that morning. We discussed how he was going to do it. He said he needed a car. That brings us to the Mercury Comet. Okay, that car was used by Billy at the store to do the robbery. Then later, he called on the phone and said that he had lost his 'kitten,' in reference to Connie. Okay, he called me from Clovis."

Bill broke in. "After the robbery?"

"After the robbery. Okay, and he said he had lost his kitten and he needed a way out of there. So I said, 'Well, go ahead and take the Cadillac,' and I went out there and picked up the Comet, and he had the Cadillac, and he split right up straight to Herndon Avenue and left town in the Cadillac. He was going to San Jose. The Comet was right where the Cadillac had been parked at a friend's house."

A gap of silence filled the room. Finally, we had begun to break through, but we knew he was still lying. Hamilton had to get the gun from someone. Kenny had to know where the gun came from. My guess was that Kenny had supplied the weapon and had probably stashed it or else Hamilton had taken it with him when he left Fresno. But parts were beginning to fall into place. We weren't going to get it all in one sitting. I knew that. We would have to pin him down and wait for the next round, but first we had to pin him down. I let the silence hang for a moment while we waited for him to fully digest the looks on our faces, waiting for him to see that the men in the room weren't ready to end this. I softened my tone. "All right, now, let's go back to the beginning. We'll go slowly and we'll be asking you questions. When did you visit your father at Folsom Prison?"

"The seventeenth of August, I believe." Kenny shuffled his feat on the linoleum floor; the sandy grating scuffed the already-worn patch of linoleum. "Okay, my dad and I were sitting there at the table. He said, 'One of my dogs is going to come down there and do an armed robbery and if Ray and Bryon are there, it's going to be a feather in my cap for them to be missing when I get my appeal.' I said, 'What do you mean?' He said,

'Well, they're going to be killed,' by that 'dog' that he was sending down, which turned out to be Mr. Hamilton."

I waited, thinking about the direction I needed to push. "Did he say what this dog's name was?"

"He said Billy. He called him Country."

"Did you ever hear the full name or any portion of the actual name of Country?"

"No, it just, well, my father gave me a picture of what had B. R. Hamilton on it that he had swiped from the files and said, 'Look for this guy.'"

"Is that the picture we took out of your house?"

Kenny shook his head. "No, sir. It is not. We burnt that picture. We were told to burn that picture and we did."

"Who told you?"

"My father told us on the phone. He said he would shoot us another letter down or that he'd get us another picture, but to burn that one and I did. I looked at the picture and said, 'Okay,' and we had the kid's diaper bag, and that's what I put it in. I put it in the kid's diaper bag, 'cause the lady matron walked us down to the gate with the diaper bag. They just ran a metal detector across it to see if any metal was in it. There was no metal in it. I put the picture inside the diaper bag while she and the other kids were inside that little snack bar area. Then I showed Kathy when we got out to the car and told her that we'd be looking for this gentleman."

I glanced sideways at Bill. That made more sense than Kathy's story that she thought this was Kenny's cousin. She knew when Kenny brought this man home who he was and, I was betting, she knew why he was there. It was like watching snakes curl together for comfort. "Your father mentioned the robbery? Did he tell you why?"

"No, he did not tell me exactly why. I just knew that it was going to be like a grubstake, or giving Billy a chance to make some easy money. And Ray and Fran's market is considered an easy hit."

"Your father previously burglarized Fran's Market, didn't he?"

Kenny confirmed what the witnesses had said in the first trial. Not that I had any doubt, but this was as close as I was ever going to get to hearing it out of the old man's mouth.

"Your father told you that Ray and Fran's store was going to be robbed by Country?"

"By Country, and I had the picture that had B.R. Hamilton. I already had that picture. Okay, my dad told me, he said, 'The guy is great at getting his own rides. You won't have to worry about nothing.' Okay, Billy had called earlier, I think Tuesday, and he said he needed some money and I sent him one hundred dollars by Western Union to get to Fresno. They should have record of it down at Western Union. I think it was Tuesday, because I felt he came in on Wednesday. I thought I picked him up on the third."

I waited a moment. "What name did you use when you got the Western Union check?"

"I sent him one with my name and straight to his 'B' number—the Western Union in San Jose. My name's on the receipt. I took it down and shot it off."

Now, the story was subtly changing about Kathy's involvement. Kathy knew this man, Country, was coming, and if she saw the "B" number, his prison ID number, she would know it was someone coming straight out of the joint. She was the one we had to deal carefully with. Kenny wasn't sophisticated enough to keep it all together, but she was. I filed that away for the future. We would get back to her later. "So he showed up at your house—you picked him up?"

"Right, and I brought him back to the house, and Connie was there."

"What happened when he got to your house?"

"Well, we sat up for a little while, and then he went to bed, and I went to bed." I thought about that for a moment. Connie Barbo was at the house when Billy got there sometime after midnight. My immediate reaction was that Kenny and Kathy had set it up for her to be there for him to meet. Obviously they had hit it off. Nothing like a quick dating cycle.

"Was there any conversation about the robbery during this time when you sat around?" Tommy asked.

"Yeah, I said, 'Okay, you're going to do the robbery at Ray and Fran's?' And he said, 'Yes, and that other thing is going to be a bonus for your father.'"

"Did he say what the other thing was?"

"I knew what the other thing was—Ray and Bryon would be shot."

It was almost over. After the robbery he had met up with Hamilton and traded the Comet for the Cadillac. I wanted to know what might be in it.

"You wanted to dump the car because you knew it was used in the robbery?"

There was resignation in his voice. "Right."

My voice had lost any conciliatory tone. "Did you clean it out?" Kenny shook his head. I kept pushing. "Was there anything in that car?"

"There was a red sweater that was Connie's and, ah, a few other things."

It was how he said "a few other things" that heightened your senses. We let his answer sit there suspended in air. He would tell us. And he did. "Well, there's blood on the steering wheel from his hand, and blood inside the car. He had got blood everywhere."

So, now, it was find the car and we find the blood of the shooter. We had the blood of the shooter on the floor of the store and if we had the blood inside the car, we could match it. By matching it, we could establish that the car was used by the shooter and we could establish that it was Kenny's car. We could corroborate Kenny's story and we could squeeze Kenny. But, we had to find the Comet.

Kenny gave up the car's location without a fight. So we had the car, but now I wanted the gun. Billy Hamilton didn't come to town on the Greyhound bus carrying a sawed-off shotgun. He got the gun after he arrived in Fresno, and there was no question in our minds but that he had gotten it from Kenny. "All right, what about the gun?"

Kenny's eyes narrowed. He had given us the name. He had given us the car. He was quick enough to realize that if he gave us the gun, he was no longer just a bystander or, at least, what he thought of as a bystander. It always amazed me how many times I would hear somebody say they only gave the shooter the gun, but they didn't do anything—they didn't kill anyone. I suppose relative morality depends on the circles you run in.

We all shared the same idea about the gun: We would wait—let Kenny think we were satisfied. He was skirting the edge of direct participation in three first-degree murders and if we weren't careful, he would stop talking. We needed to flesh out the rest of it.

Tommy asked the next question. "After the robbery, when you gave him the Cadillac and took the Comet, did Hamilton tell you what he did?"

"Well, he told me that he started shooting the people and this one guy wouldn't give him the way to the safe."

"Did he say who that was?"

"Bryon. And he said that he then proceeded to shoot some other people."

"Did he say why he shot those other people?"

"They were in the store. They were witnesses."

"Did he say how he got shot?"

"He got shot by the neighbor that was coming over the fence that heard the shots. He pointed to his foot and said, 'I got shot.' I didn't see no blood on his foot, but I saw that he got cut."

So we were right. The shooter cut himself and left his blood drops on the floor of the store as he searched for the safe. Kenny had somehow exchanged cars with Hamilton or had met Hamilton and taken the Comet.

Tommy closed the gap. "You exchanged the Cadillac for the Comet." It was a statement and not a question.

"Right."

I had given up any pretense of being a good-guy. That was Tommy's role now. "What time?"

"Late Friday night, around 9:30 or 10:00. He told me where he was. He called and said, 'I lost my kitten and some dogs got in the way.'"

Tommy shook his head, like it wasn't clear. "'Dogs,' referring to people?"

"I believe so."

I broke back in. "Okay, now, when you got out there and you exchanged cars, what did he take out of that Comet?"

"He took a bundle of clothing and stuck it in the Cadillac. I saw a white T-shirt and some Playtex gloves and I saw another type of coat that had; you could tell there were shells in the one coat he had."

"How could you tell that?"

"They rattled and you could tell that they were in the stack of clothes. Well, I noticed from the way he picked up the bundle that there was an impression of about," he extended his hands apart, "this long, and it stuck out. It looked very irregular."

Tommy held his hands apart. "Okay, you're indicating approximately two feet—a foot and a half?"

"Two feet. It was sticking out towards the back. That's where the noise was being made. I was under the impression that it was a gun, a shotgun, a sawed-off shotgun."

Tommy's mouth curled at the corner. "It was just your first-off impression—a sawed-off shotgun?"

"That was it."

"He never got a shotgun from you?"

"No, not at any time. That's why I figured that Connie got him the gun. Then he said, 'Which is my quickest way out of here?' And I told him the best way to the freeway."

"Did you ever see him again?"

"No."

I had to think for a moment. Nobody said anything. I decided to go back to when Billy Hamilton came to the house. "Let me back up for a moment. When he first came to your house, you say that you talked a little bit about the robbery? What did you say to one another?"

"Okay, I said, 'Are you sure everything's going to be okay?' I mean nobody else, you know, nobody's going to get, you know, really—I was concerned about other people being in the store."

Tommy's voice came from my right, snapping Kenny's head around at the sound of it. "You knew two people were going to get shot."

"I knew two people were going to be shot, Ray and Bryon."

"But you didn't want anybody else to get shot?"

"Right, it's bad enough."

It was one of those moments when you realize the thin line of fortuity between life and death. That night Ray wasn't at the store and his son was. It was just not Ray Schletewitz's time, but I was sure that he would have traded places with his son without a moment's hesitation. We all knew Kenny was lying, but like I said before, you keep them talking and if nothing else, you let them lie. I resumed the questioning. "You said before that he said something about safes. Safes plural."

"Yes, uh huh, but then he cut it off, 'cause him and Connie were involved, and every time that they'd get together after that, they'd go upstairs and evidently he drew out everything for Connie."

Tommy cut in. 'You say you never heard from him after that, after the robbery?"

293

"No, that night when we switched cars, he took the Cadillac and went straight up the freeway. That's the last time I saw him. I got in the Comet and drove home. I felt blood all over the steering wheel. At first, he wasn't going to let me take the Comet. He said, 'I can't let you use the car.' I said, 'I got to use the car to get back.' So I got in the Comet and drove back."

I jumped in. "Where was the blood inside the Comet?"

"On the steering wheel. Must have come from the cut on his hand. He said one of the guys attacked him."

Lean switched gears. "So you have no idea where he got this gun, the shotgun?"

Kenny looked around at each of us, trying to look us in the eyes. "No, I sure don't. I'm being truthful and honest. I have no idea where he got the shotgun."

The next question came from Tommy so quickly that Kenny was able to look away from the rest of us. "Did you supply him with any shells or his shotgun?"

You could almost see Kenny's mind work. How much did we know? How much should he say? He reverted to giving a half truth. "I did. He did take some 12-gauge shotgun shells from me on Friday."

"How many?"

"Thirteen. Red cases."

"What load?"

"Number-four." Nobody looked at anybody else. Number-fours had been used in the murders. Kenny had given Hamilton the shells. We knew he had given him the shotgun, but he wasn't going to admit that.

"How do you know it was thirteen?"

"I counted out thirteen shotgun shells."

I stared at him. "But you still didn't see a gun?"

"No."

"Can you tell me when you met him out there afterwards, did he tell you what he got out of the robbery?"

Kenny shook his head. "I gave him sixty bucks. He asked for money."

"So, on Friday night, you did not take him to the bus stop to get rid of him? That was just a story you made up?"

"Right. Keep me from not being implicated." If it had not sounded so pathetic, I would have laughed.

"Okay, tell me about the dry run on Thursday night."

"They went out to the store. They were closing up the store and then they asked them if they couldn't get some food because they had been out cutting grapes."

"Is this the time that they got the shotgun shells from you?"

"Right. That's correct."

"You knew they were going to go pull the robbery, so they had to have the shotgun shells?"

"Correct. He got seven shotgun shells on Thursday for the dry run. They were going to do it Thursday."

"Did he say why they aborted?"

Kenny shrugged. "There was a little boy in the store and they didn't want to shoot the little boy. Connie wouldn't let the little boy get shot."

I thought about what Kenny had just said. The clear implication was that Hamilton and Connie intended to shoot everybody in the store and the only thing that stopped them was the fact there was a child present. Even killers have some standards, I suppose. In fact, in prison, child molesters and rapists are at the bottom of the barrel, only because other prisoners have kids and they have wives. You don't kill kids. Wives are a separate issue.

He continued talking. "And he brought back all seven shells and gave them to me. So on Friday he wanted more shells than that. He wanted seven, eleven, or thirteen, and he'd already gotten seven. He wanted eleven, so I went ahead and gave him thirteen, 'cause those were his lucky numbers and so I gave him the thirteen." Kenny sniffed and rubbed his face. He looked around like he was checking to see that what he had said made sense. Maybe it did to him. What he didn't seem to grasp was that even with his grudging admissions, he had just confessed to aiding and abetting a first-degree murder. In the species of people to which he belonged, the other creatures like him would draw a similar distinction in their minds. They would think that because they weren't there or didn't pull the trigger, that they weren't responsible. Maybe in the eyes of the people Kenny ran with, he hadn't done anything, but in the eyes of every man in the room listening to him, he was guilty of murder and he had admitted enough to put him in the gas chamber next to Billy Ray Hamilton and his father, Clarence Ray.

"He said Connie freaked when he started shooting people, and when she freaked, he had to hurry up and as he was running out of the store he lost Connie, and that was when he was wounded."

"By the neighbor?"

"He said as he was running out, the neighbor was coming over a fence and shot him. The neighbor shot him in the foot evidently, because he pointed to his foot, and I looked down but it was too dark and I couldn't see nothing on his feet. He kept looking around like he was looking for the other person that was supposed to pick me up and then he said, 'Where's your partner that's going to take you?' I said, 'There's no other partner. I'm taking the Comet and I'm going to go back into town.' He said, 'I can't let you take the car.'"

"Why did he say that?"

"Well, evidently, it was hot, 'cause from where we were, you could see the helicopters over the market. I saw him drive straight out toward Herndon and then I got back in the Comet and drove off back to Fresno. Then I drove home and told my wife we were gonna have to get rid of the car. Then I took the Comet over to the people's house and parked it in their garage. I told them I just repossessed it and that I would sell them the car for two hundred dollars. My wife drove up and she picked me up."

I looked around. Nobody had more questions. Allen's son had given us his father. We had Hamilton in custody. Now, we knew that from inside prison walls Clarence Ray Allen had conspired to kill witnesses from the Kitts' case, and we knew that he had sent Billy Ray Hamilton to do it. He had made his son and his daughter-in-law accomplices to murder.

What Allen had done was retaliate against people who had simply done their duty. Most people are nervous about testifying; they worry about criminals getting even. They worry about their families. But the killing of witnesses just doesn't happen. That is what law enforcement officers tell people every day. We tell them that, not just because we need their cooperation, but because it's true. It doesn't happen, except on television. What Clarence Ray Allen had done was tell every witness in the country that it could happen to them, because he had made it happen.

We had one piece of evidence we were saving. It could wait until we needed a sharp stick.

34

The End of the Slow Dance

October 7, 1980
Fresno, California

The Comet was right where Kenny said it would be. When we examined it, we were not surprised to find blood on the steering wheel and the floor mats. We knew even before the results came back that the blood smears would match the sample of blood drops we had taken from the floor of Fran's Market and the blood we had drawn from Hamilton.

We used Clarence Ray Allen's handwriting exemplars from the Kitts trial to establish that the letters from Allen to his son were indeed written by him. Clarence Allen's poetic paeans to himself had again caught up with him, just like they had in the Kitts trial when we used them to prove the existence of the "Allen Gang."

Prisons keep track of who associates with whom within the prison, so it wasn't hard to establish that Allen and Hamilton were associates while in Folsom Prison. Just as he had when he was on the outside, Clarence Ray Allen was able to convince people of weak character to follow him, and he had no difficulty in finding those people inside Folsom Prison. The difference was that the people inside Folsom were there because they were the worst of the weakest and many were also the worst of the vicious. Allen had found his soul mates. We moved Kenny Allen to the Mariposa jail, which was a small jail without a significant criminal population. He would be safer there, while we prepared the cases against Hamilton and Barbo and put together the final aspects of the case against Clarence Allen.

We knew Kenny hadn't told us the whole truth, just bits and pieces as he tried to limit his own involvement. Bill kept in touch with him, trying to make sure he would go forward with testimony against Hamilton and Barbo—and his father. As the time grew near for the preliminary hearing, Kenny was smart enough to know that he would have to tell us where the shotgun that Hamilton used had come from.

On October 7, 1980, the day before the scheduled preliminary hearing for Hamilton and Barbo, we brought Kenny down from Mariposa. On the trip down, he decided to tell us that he had some additional information. We took him to the district attorney's office, where Bill, Kenny Badiali, and I sat down with him.

Bill had already checked with Kenny Allen's attorney to make sure we could talk to him. His attorney didn't mind; his client was our witness. Kenny had an agreement that as long as he cooperated with us, he would only be prosecuted on the drug charges. It was possible that he didn't fully comprehend that he had confessed to legal responsibility for the Fran's Market murders as an aider and abettor, but he did understand that he had to tell us the truth and he had to testify. Bill had played him like a violin and now he was scared. Now, he was ready.

It only took a minute. Again, Bill advised him of his rights. We wanted to make sure that if he folded on us, we could use everything against him. He didn't give it a moment's thought before he said he understood his rights and would talk. Bill got right to the point.

"Mr. Allen, I'll let you go ahead and give me the additional information you have. I understand that there is possibly information regarding some weapons or something of that nature?"

Kenny looked around as if he were providing us with something that we hadn't thought of, and he was delivering it to us gift-wrapped. The only reason he would do that is because he knew we would eventually get it, and he wanted to make sure that he had covered all his bases regarding immunity. My supposition is that his attorney had told him that he needed to tell us everything or his immunity deal might fall through, and that as long as he told us the truth, we couldn't go back on the immunity deal. That was true, but, more importantly to us, he only had immunity for everything he told us *if he testified in the trial of his father*. If he backed out, it would all be on his head as an aider and abettor to first-degree murder. Giving us what we expected only drew the noose tighter around his neck. However, Kenny just couldn't see that far into the future.

Kenny still had that little smirk on his face that I so detested. "Okay, I provided Billy Ray Hamilton with a sawed-off, twelve-gauge shotgun to go out to Fran's Market with. And I also gave him a .32 caliber revolver." Kenny sat back and waited for a reaction. I suppose he thought we would be surprised. We weren't. It wasn't hard to figure out; he had already admitted giving Hamilton the shells. We just needed for him to say it. Now he had. He waited a minute and decided to go ahead with the rest. Hamilton was supposed to burn the shotgun and Kenny was sure Hamilton had it with him when he took Kenny's Cadillac the night of the robbery.

Then Kenny said the one thing that had never been put into words. We had never considered it, perhaps because it had simply never crossed a logical mind. When he uttered this comment, he was almost casual. "You might well want to know also that this was just the starting of six other homicides that were supposed to have been taking place. Everybody that testified against my father allegedly was going to be hit. That way, whenever he came back up for his appeal, *there wouldn't be no witnesses.* That way, he got a better shot at getting out."

So, that was it. Sherlock Holmes was right. You eliminate the impossible and what you have left is the truth. But Holmes was wrong about one thing. To eliminate the impossible, you have to realize that it is a possibility; otherwise, it doesn't even cross your mind. We had considered vengeance, although even that didn't make a lot of sense when it came to killing Bryon or Ray Schletewitz. Certainly, the list made vengeance a probability. But we hadn't considered the elimination of witnesses as part of a scheme for a retrial. In retrospect, that motive might make sense *if you didn't realize that killing witnesses would accomplish nothing.* We had the trial testimony from the Kitts trial and could reuse it even if any witness was unavailable, and there was no realistic possibility of a retrial except in Clarence Allen's imagination.

Clarence Allen thought that by eliminating the witnesses he would somehow get another trial. It was about getting even with the witnesses, but it was also about setting up his appeal. He would rob more people of having a future of their own, while eking out a bit more future for himself on the outside. It only made sense in the twisted logic of Clarence Allen. The only reality was those kids lying on that floor and the fact that

Clarence Allen was still able to influence others to kill for him. The most frightening realities of all were what kind of a man he was and what he could still do.

I remember sitting there, quietly trying to conceptualize the callousness and depravity of all of it. I don't know if *evil* is the right word. Perhaps St. Augustine was right. It was more like the absence of good, without character or remorse or guilt—no thought given to the catastrophic harm or the magnitude of agony he would cause.

But there was more pain to come for one more human being, even as sad an excuse for a human being as Kenny Allen was, one last knife thrust from his father, Clarence Ray Allen, that we would inflict; we had to. We still held that in our file, waiting for the moment that was still a breath away. Bill shook his head and asked Kenny, "Who was going to do the rest of the hits Allen had in mind?"

"Billy Ray Hamilton was going to do every one of them. I was told this by my father."

"Did you ever see a list of people who were to be killed?"

Kenny shook his head no. "No."

This slow dance was drawing to an end. We had waited until the right time, holding onto our sharp stick. We had decided it was time to share some additional information with him, as well.

Bill took out a copy of the assassination list that he had placed on my desk the day after Hamilton's arrest. We had never shown it to Kenny Allen and we had a reason. Now, we would play the last card. Bill handed the list to Kenny. "Would you take a look at that, please? Do you recognize those names?" Bill's voice came out softly, almost gently. He knew what was about to happen and even Bill had a fleeting moment of empathy.

Kenny read the names aloud, as he made his way down the list. He stopped suddenly. He stared at the paper. We all knew why. The words came out in a mumble. "They crossed out mine and my wife's name."

It was a statement. I am sure it was a shock to see his name and know that his father had selected the names.

Bill waited for a moment, letting the thought sit there in Kenny's mind. "Mr. Allen, this is a list of people whom you say were to be killed and your name is on here. But it's scratched off. I wonder why your name was on there?"

Kenny was shaken, but Bill persisted. "Did you know your name was on there?"

"No." Kenny was still staring at the paper. I almost felt sorry for him. His father had put his own son's name on an assassination list. Kenny's face sagged. What color there was left washed away. There was no remnant of rodent-like cunning, no smirk. What little inner-strength Kenny Allen ever possessed was sapped. His words were uttered in the voice of a defeated man, a man who realized that his actions had betrayed anything of value he had ever held onto. He was completely alone. "The last time I was at Folsom. That was everything I heard—'Shirley Doeckel's going to change her testimony so that's going to be one witness I'll have on my side.'"

Kenny looked at me. I don't know if he was searching for sympathy or just human contact from the person he believed held his life in his hands. The tone of his words did not suggest that it was mercy he was seeking. I think it was humanity. I'm not sure he saw any in my face. I do know that I felt a flicker of pity. We were all looking back at a man who realized his father had provided a list to Hamilton of who was to die. As the realization seeped into him, Kenny's voice came out in a whisper. "If everybody else is gone, he's just got the one witness."

Even Kenny Allen was smart enough to realize that if everything had gone according to plan, he and his wife would have been the only witnesses to what had happened at Fran's Market. His father didn't intend for there to be *any* witnesses when he had the list drawn. Allen had learned his lesson the last time.

Bill let the realization sink in. We wanted Kenny Allen to understand that we were it. We were all he had. There was no going back. Bill's voice was flat, emotionless. He sensed that there was no resistance left. The small piece of paper covered in a penciled litany of death had taken it all. "Okay, Mr. Allen. To avoid your having to keep coming back for interview after interview, is there anything else that you're holding back that you haven't told us?"

Kenny slowly shook his head. At that one moment, he had nothing left in him. "Not a bit this time. I provided the gun. I provided the car. I showed him the location. Him and Connie linked up together and I was left out of the picture. I didn't provide Connie with any weapons whatsoever."

Badiali waited quietly while Bill finished up and looked around to see if anybody had any more questions. Badiali had just one. "How did you get involved in this? I thought you said at one time that you didn't even like your dad anymore?"

Kenny Allen pursed his lips and stared up at the ceiling. "You can only say no for so many years and I said it for twelve. Then, this last time, it was just 'boom,' pushed upon me. I had no choice."

"Did you fear your dad?"

"I don't fear my dad, no. But I don't know who he's got in contact with up there in prison. And, I do know that no matter what he says, they may decide to do something else, 'cause they just got their own laws to go by and if I hadn't of sent Billy the money, I feared that my family would have been next in line. I really felt that." He never said another word, but his subdued tone and the crushing reality of that small slip of paper and the look on his face said it all: He was right.

It was as close to finished as we were going to make it. We had Clarence Ray Allen. He had used his own son to help him get revenge. Now, three kids were dead and one more would be maimed for life. There was no question in anybody's mind. Each of us was going to do whatever we could to put Billy Ray Hamilton and Clarence Ray Allen in the death chamber at San Quentin. At this point, it was personal for all of us. What none of could ever realize was how hard that would be or how many more years it would take.

I left the room, my mind a jumble of thoughts. There was no end to this. Allen was like some toxic poison seeping up from the bowels of the earth and contaminating everything and everyone he touched. Those names were on that list because they were the witnesses I had called. All my promises of their being safe from harm had meant nothing.

Bill followed me out of the interview room. As always, he could sense my mood. He found me in my office, staring at the desk that was finally clean. One thought kept going through my mind—four young lives wasted due to the malevolent selfishness of one man. No matter how I looked at it, the fact remained that Bryon had testified in my case after I had given him and his parents my promise. In the end, I had been the one who had to tell them that their son was dead. I knew they didn't blame me. They never blamed me.

Bill had a way of talking when he reached out to someone or felt they needed reaching out to. He could almost reach inside you. It is what made him such a skillful interrogator. He reached for me then. "Jim, bad things happen. We can't stop that. You can't stop that. All we can do is try to make sure they don't happen to somebody else." He was right. I wasn't to blame. But there is a difference between blame and responsibility. I thought I had stopped Allen. But I hadn't stopped him from killing again. Clarence Ray Allen had still been able to reach his hands through stone walls.

PART IV

RETRIBUTION

35

The Tentacles of the Past

January, 1981
Fresno, California

We had the preliminary hearings for Hamilton and Barbo. We didn't rush into the arrest of Clarence Allen. We knew where Allen was. He would be waiting for us at Folsom. He knew what was coming. Like I said, information travels into jails and prisons like jungle drums.

Hamilton and Barbo had a pre-trial evidentiary hearing, where just enough evidence was put forward to demonstrate a strong suspicion that they had committed the murders at Fran's Market. We needed to see how the case would hold together and it held together just fine.

As I said before, it is the investigation that makes a case for trial. All the prosecutor does is figure out how to get the evidence in and how to present it to the jury. We had the picture, we had the letters, and we had the list. And we had Clarence Ray Allen.

I had decided the year before to run for election to an open seat on the municipal court. By the time we reached the November election, I had survived the primary and had every reason to believe I would be elected. The new district attorney made the decision that I would handle the case through the preliminary hearing, but he needed to make sure a prosecutor would be ready to take it to trial. If I were elected, I knew that prosecutor wouldn't be me. My recommendation was a young prosecutor I had brought into the homicide unit, Jerry Jones. We worked intensely on the case so he would be up to speed. It wasn't easy to know I was going to hand the case over to him, but it was the right decision and I knew it.

Hamilton and Barbo were bound over for trial for capital murder, and shortly after that I was elected to the municipal court. I left the district attorney's office and left the case. The investigation was done. The case was as together as I could make it. It was time for me to walk away. But it was difficult. No matter how hard I tried, I knew that my relationships with my friends in the district attorney's office would change. There is an invisible barrier that draws itself in front of those who take the bench. I would see Bill and all of the men I had worked with through long hours in the night, but I would never again be with them when that call came. I would never be a hunter again. Now, I would watch from a distance, and when we gathered together, I would only be someone who once was one of them. Still, I had come to accept that the judiciary was my chosen path. For me, it was the right decision. But I would miss it. All these years later, I still do.

Clarence Ray Allen was served with a warrant of arrest while he sat in Folsom Prison. When told he was charged with three counts of murder, he showed no reaction at all. As always, he refused to make any statement.

There was an issue as to whether the district attorney's office would be recused from the prosecution of Clarence Ray Allen. His attorney in the Mary Sue Kitts trial was now the assistant district attorney of Fresno County. Because the Kitts murder would be central in proving motivation for the Fran's Market triple murders, the defense for Allen was arguing that the district attorney might somehow be given information by Allen's former attorney now that he had "changed sides." Everyone knew that the implication of potential unethical conduct was ridiculous. Allen's former attorney would never violate his attorney-client privilege, but it wasn't the reality of conflict we were arguing against; it was the perception of conflict. And, in the law, perception, as it is in politics, too often becomes almost as valid as reality. The district attorney would argue there was no conflict, but the state attorney general's office would have to come in. Allen's trial would have to wait. The trial for Hamilton and Barbo would go forward. I would put on a black robe. I was no longer a prosecutor. I was a judge.

I was present as an observer when Clarence Ray Allen was brought in for arraignment on the Fran's Market murders, simply as someone who sat in the audience and watched the drama instead of being a part of it. I couldn't stay away. It had been a little over three years since the conclusion of the Kitts case. Allen didn't look much different. He was still the same emotionless man that I remembered. His hair was a little grayer and he had fleshed up a bit, but he wasn't intimidated by the publicity or the accusation. As he looked around the courtroom, I think he actually enjoyed being the center of attention again. That was the last time I would see Clarence Ray Allen in person for over a quarter of a century.

I can say it was hard to walk away. I wanted to be in that courtroom and say "Ready for the People" on the day that Barbo and Hamilton were sentenced. Hamilton was tried by the Fresno County district attorney and prosecuted by Jerry Jones, who did the job as well as I had known he would do. Because of the publicity, Hamilton's case was granted a change of venue and was tried in Monterey County. I testified as a witness for the prosecution. Hamilton received the only judgment that he deserved— death. Connie Barbo received life without the possibility of parole.

Clarence Allen was tried by the California attorney general's office. Two young deputy attorneys general, Ron Prager and Ward Campbell, took over the case when the court determined there was a conflict with the Fresno district attorney. Because of the publicity, Allen's trial was held in the small northern California county of Glenn. Bill Martin said it was the biggest thing to happen in Glenn County that anybody could remember. One fact was evident to everyone however; Glenn County wasn't a liberal mecca. Glenn County was a place where if you rustled cattle, you better hope the sheriff got to you before the ranchers did.

I always knew that Clarence Allen's trial was going to be difficult. The investigation had put the case together against him, but it was still circumstantial and again it would be his word against everybody else's word. But there were the letters he had sent to his son that were no longer shrouded in ambiguity. Those letters were now placed in a context next to the death list that only he could have drawn. It was clear he had sent Billy Ray Hamilton to Fresno to begin a bloodbath of retaliation and revenge on those who had testified against him.

Kenny Allen made his decision. He had confessed to Bill and me to complicity in capital murder. For him to receive a lenient plea agreement, he knew he had to testify against his father. In the end he refused. I suppose that deep within himself he found some measure of what passed for him as character. Or, perhaps, it was just fear of his father. Only Kenny Allen knows the truth of that and he has a long time to think about it. He is now serving life without the possibility of parole in Corcoran State

Prison for his involvement in the Fran's Market murders. He is in good company. Corcoran houses Charlie Manson, Sirhan Sirhan, and a number of others who occupy their own place in the history of crime and murder. In the end, Clarence Ray Allen destroyed his son's life just as he had destroyed so many others.

Prager and Campbell did a tremendous job weaving together all the strands of evidence against Clarence Allen. Just as they had before, all the weak people he had manipulated testified against him in the end. And Bill Martin was there to hear the jury's verdict. Instead of being in the courtroom as the prosecutor, I received a phone call when the case was finished. The verdict was guilty of three counts of first-degree, premeditated murder. The judgment was death. At the time, I felt the tension of expectation begin to drain from me. What I did not realize, what I could *never* realize at that moment, was that the same tension of expectation would slowly fill me up again, but it would take twenty-six more years of my life.

Some might ask that after all that happened why I was not there to see Clarence Ray Allen sentenced to death. The answer is textured by experience. It was not the pronouncement of the sentence that mattered. It was the imposition. I knew that until that day came when there were no more appeals and the last plea for clemency was denied, when Clarence Ray Allen was finally called to account—that would be when justice would be served. What I did not know was how long that wait would be.

The years passed, but the tentacles of Clarence Ray Allen's existence never stopped reaching out. I never got away from the case. It would come up in the papers as it wound its way through the California Supreme Court and then descend into the morass that has become the federal system of habeas and appeals after a case was affirmed by the United States Supreme Court. I would get calls for my comments and I would stare at Allen's and Hamilton's faces, as they looked out from photographs and as I looked back at faces slowly aging with the years.

Through those years, I rose up through the judiciary, first as municipal court judge and then as a superior court judge. I moved to the California Court of Appeal in 1988 and then became presiding justice in 1994. I taught other judges how to try death penalty cases. I wrote decisions in criminal cases on appeal. Clarence Ray Allen and Billy Ray Hamilton would disappear from the news and then someone would ask what happened to them. The answer was always the same. They were still in San Quentin on Death Row and everyone was still waiting for the day they would finally be punished. The years dragged on. All of us got older. Nothing changed.

In California, a sentence of death does not present much threat of execution. I've heard it said that more people on San Quentin's Death Row die of old age or at the hands of their fellow inmates than die in the green room. But that doesn't mean they don't still reach out and pull people in with their claims of innocence and the petitions of well-meaning people who only see the face of the man on Death Row and not the blood-smeared faces of the people they killed.

Bill Martin retired from the district attorney's office. Nobody ever learned exactly how old he was. We kept in touch and each time we saw one another, even though it wasn't often, it was as if we were next to one another at a crime scene. When we saw one another, we would always talk for a moment about the Allen case. Bill never saw the case end. Allen and Hamilton had been sitting on Death Row for over twenty years when Bill died of cancer. Sadly, the man who helped put Allen and Hamilton on Death Row would not outlive them. I knew Bill was very ill and didn't have long. Bill asked another former D.A. investigator and me to go with him and make his funeral arrangements. It was one of the hardest things I've ever had to do.

At the last minute, Bill was not feeling well enough to go. Two of us picked out his coffin and his grave site. We took pictures back to Bill. We thought he had at least a few months left. That is what the doctor had said. The doctor was wrong. Three days later, I was in San Francisco on business when I got the call. I wouldn't make it home in time to be with him before he died.

I remember going off by myself, seeking a few minutes to be alone with thoughts of my friend, a man who had traveled with me through the years of my youth. He was a man who had been my partner and in the business we had been in, that was more than being just a friend, much more.

I spoke at his funeral, as did former sheriffs of Fresno County and tough cops who had shared his friendship. I cried and I wasn't the only one. I was one of the six men who carried Bill to his final resting place. I was the only attorney. All the rest were cops. At the gathering after Bill's service, all of the old investigators gathered around and we talked about

Bill and we talked about Clarence Ray Allen and Billy Ray Hamilton, both of whom both still lived on at San Quentin.

While Clarence Ray Allen walked the long, twisting path of the court process, he married Shirley Doeckel. The marriage only lasted a few years. I suppose incompatibility was a leading cause. Bill would have appreciated the irony. I know I did.

Allen continued to draw people into his cesspool of evil through the long years he sat on Death Row. In 2004, I was in a meat market in Fresno when I saw a man standing near the check-out line. He was looking at me like he knew me. I had to search my mind to recall what was familiar about him. He was disheveled. His pants were stained and so was his shirt. His hair wasn't combed and he was unshaven. He called my name. I am frequently recognized by people, but they certainly didn't look like this man looked. I've sent a lot of men and women to prison. Most of them bear me no ill will, but you never know. I hesitated before walking over to him. It was his voice that brought it home to me. It was Kenny Badiali. The detective that I had known years before who always smelled like soap and was always neat and well-pressed now looked like a derelict. I was stunned.

I have seen men come apart before and I've seen men hit the skids and go downhill. I had heard that Kenny had unraveled. I found out later he had been forced to retire from the sheriff's office, suffering from too much booze, too many bad memories. He had always been wrapped too tightly, but I really wasn't prepared for this image before me. He could see I hadn't recognized him immediately. He was embarrassed. I could tell. He said his name just as I said it—"Kenny?"

I could see something in his eyes that I could never remember seeing before. It was fear. Kenny told me that he had been trying to get hold of Bill Martin and Ross Kelly. He told me that informants had told him Allen had hired hit men from New York to come to California and kill him and the other witnesses from the second trial. I listened quietly as he gave a confused and rambling account of how all of this was going to happen very soon. The hit men were on their way. I told him that Bill was dead. His face reflected sadness at that news, but it also showed how out of touch he was. I told him how to get hold of Ross Kelly. He said I had to be careful. He was going home and he would be waiting for the hit men when they came through the door. He told me to stay in touch and how proud he was of me and what I had accomplished. I shook his hand and walked out of the market, shaking my head at the thought of the shell of the man I had known.

That night, Kenny Badiali shot and killed his roommate in a confusion of paranoia and alcohol. He was convinced his roommate was one of the hit men sent by Clarence Ray Allen. All those years later and the Allen case and his nightmares from the crime scene had triggered Kenny's descent into madness.

I testified for the defense at Kenny Badiali's trial for murder. The defense attorney asked me about the crime scene at Fran's Market. He was trying to establish the impact that night had on Kenny's mind and the indelible memory of what we all had seen. I said it was the most horrific thing I had ever seen. Twenty years later, I could close my eyes and see it spread out before me like the still-red pools of blood that never left my memory. I testified about the more recent scene at the meat market and the confused rambling of a man who was delusional. And I testified that Kenny had been a good detective, a homicide detective—top of the line for cops. I could see him swell with pride, even as he sat in that chair where he had put so many others.

I was later told that based in significant part on my testimony, Kenny Badiali was convicted of manslaughter. I am sure it was the right verdict. Kenny was no murderer, but the years had twisted his mind and his reality had become the persistent threat of Clarence Ray Allen. Perhaps, there comes a time when you have seen too much blood. Maybe, for Kenny Badiali, that time came when we all stood in a small room staring at those kids on the floor. I don't know.

When I left the courtroom with Kenny sitting in the defendant's chair, I felt the sting of tears in my eyes. It was almost a quarter century after the murders at Fran's Market. Clarence Ray Allen still sat on Death Row and Ken Badiali had now become yet another of his victims.

36

The Time of Retribution

San Francisco, California
January 16, 2006

I moved uncomfortably in my chair, trying to find a position that would relieve the tension coiled inside me. I stared at the hotel room walls, the bed, the carpet, the faux-wood doors on the armoire closet. Neither upscale nor low budget, the room was simply adequate to someone who had stayed in better but had seen worse.

Twenty-seven years ago, I gave up being the chief of homicide for Fresno County, California, and for the last twenty of those years I had been an appellate court judge. But on this day I was neither a prosecutor nor a judge—I was a witness, and like all witnesses in the legal process, I was waiting.

I looked out the window at the roof of a lower part of the hotel. My view was of air conditioning units and that gravelly white surface they put on commercial roofs to cover the tar paper. On this day, what was outside didn't matter; I would be leaving soon and wouldn't come back until dark. The next day, I would check out before morning light.

For me, this day in San Francisco simply did not move at all. I sometimes think life is about waiting—waiting to be born, waiting to find yourself, waiting for something to happen, and waiting for the end. Everything that happens in between makes time pass quickly or slowly. On this day, my life was about waiting for something that was supposed to happen years before, and the only thing that filled the passing minutes was time. I was here to see something few judges have ever seen. I was here to witness an execution.

I had already waited over a quarter of a century, but now the remaining hours and minutes seemed longer than any I could remember. There was nothing on this day that could hold my attention—too much coffee, too much adrenalin, and too little sleep. I waited. There was no choice.

I had witnessed evil many times, but this one man's evil had changed my life, and on this night he would change it again. St. Augustine would say that evil is the absence of good. Perhaps evil is simply that part of a person that is not filled with good. I have never found a man who is totally without some redeeming value, but I have found a few that do not have much of a reservoir of good. It has been my experience that all men are capable of doing that which is not good. But it has also been my experience that all men are capable of doing good in some measure, great or small. In my view, each person possesses some degree of evil and some degree of good, hopefully, mostly good. Tonight, I knew I would be touched by the essence of a man in whom I had never seen the good, only the evil. I didn't know what I would see this night, either in the man I watched or in myself.

I kept looking at the clock in my room. The digital clock just sat there freezing time while I watched it. It was the only thing that moved, other than the second hand on my watch. I sat in a chair and picked up a book, letting the pages lie unread on my lap. Across the bay at San Quentin Prison, I could easily imagine that another man was trying to hoard time. He was running out of it. It was his execution I was here to witness.

I hadn't seen the man whose life I was going to see end tonight for over twenty-five years, but he had been a part of my life for almost thirty years. He was always there in the recesses of my mind. The memories of who he was, of what he had done, and of how it affected my life were never buried deep. It was always there, just below the surface, and the name was a klaxon sound—Clarence Ray Allen—that startled me every time I heard it.

Sitting there, I had a lot of time to think about where I had started and where I was now. Why I would think of those things at such a time, I'm not sure. Perhaps, it's because the moment lent itself to introspection; in a matter of hours, I would watch the ritualized death of a man and accept the fact that I had played a direct role in that emotion-wrenched human drama.

I had not made the judgment that ordered this day's execution. That responsibility had fallen on another man. But I knew what went through his mind. I had pronounced the death sentence before as a trial judge. I had asked for the death sentence before as a prosecutor. I had taught judges how to try a death penalty case and how to pronounce the judgment. In that one moment, you weigh all the conduct for which the defendant stands convicted against all his good and his bad, all his human turmoil and scars, all of his attempts to justify himself as a human being. You look to the aggravating factors and the mitigating factors. You think and you search. Then you decide. There is nothing easy about it. The reality is that despite all the appeals and labored process inherent in a death sentence, in the end the decision as to whether death will be the judgment comes down to one person in a black robe, and all the wisdom, experience, and gravity that one person can bring to the words that mark his judgment indelibly writ. That remains the sole decision of the one in the black robe who pronounces judgment. Everything else merely allows the process to go forward or to go backward.

Despite what people think, courts of appeal and supreme courts only determine if legal error was made. The sentence of death is a discretionary judgment pronounced by a single trial judge, who has balanced the scales of justice in his or her mind. Higher courts do not second-guess the wisdom or the verity of the words uttered by that single trial judge that death is the law's due.

But the responsibility for this final judgment was in part mine. In the panorama of Clarence Ray Allen's life considered by the sentencing judge, I knew I had played a direct role in bringing all of his venality to the light of day. Allen alone would confront the darkness of the judgment he would face after man's judgment was levied.

In recent months, his name had been a reverberating reminder on every news show and in every newspaper. The murder makes news. The trial makes news. The death watch makes news. The condemned's face peers out above the fold of every newspaper and from every newscast, staring at the curious, the angry, and the bored. But the long years that the victim's family waits for justice to be served never makes the news. It is not their picture the public sees when they open the morning paper. It is always so with executions.

It has always puzzled me that when there is an execution pending, so much angst pours out of well-meaning people, angst that is spent on the least-deserving who have performed the most abhorrent acts. But most of those who march and yell have never seen the ravaged faces of victims, nor have they ever smelled the coppery scent of life seeping onto the floor or the dirt or the street. I had seen those things too many times over the years. No, I did not share their outrage at the penalty, nor did I share other's hatred or desire for vengeance. What I had not shared with anyone was how I felt with the approaching end of a case that had taken half of my life.

I had at least another hour before I was to meet with the other official witnesses who I would join this evening. The law requires a specific number of official witnesses, and I was one of them. Nobody tells you in advance who the other official witnesses will be. You meet when it is time to go across the bay to San Quentin. Then, there would be more hours of waiting for everyone to gather. And the passing of those hours would affect each person differently. Later, after the event, we would each go on with our lives—except for one person.

I had struggled with my emotions all day. Did I really need to be there? It wasn't opposition to the penalty itself. It was a reservation about what seeing it might do to me. I didn't need to be there to know it was being done.

Through the years, I had watched the grinding stone that is the justice system as it milled every last particle out of the issues in this case and ground down the victims, their families, and everyone associated with the man who was about to pay the law its due. On this night, after twenty-five years, Clarence Ray Allen was going to have to walk into a glass-enclosed, green room and at last it would be his time. I was going to go because I had the responsibility of a commitment I made long ago, and, for me, responsibility weighs heavy.

It was time. I stood and put on my coat. I walked to the room where I was to meet the others.

Two hours after meeting with the other witnesses, I sat in the front seat of the car as my driver followed a caravan across the Golden Gate Bridge. In California, if you are an appellate court judge, particularly a presiding justice, when you travel in your official capacity you have personal security, provided by the California Highway Patrol. My security officer, Mike

Higgins, was driving me now. It was highly unusual for a person in my position to witness an execution. As far as I know, very few modern-day judges have ever done so, even though we sign warrants of death, and even though we review judgments of death. But the very fact that I was coming and would be watching the execution was well known to all who were waiting at the prison, including, I assumed, the man who would be looking out from the inside of the green room.

I kept looking out the window, my breath fogging the cold glass. We wound our way along the road that leads to the back entrance to the grounds of San Quentin. Highway patrol officers stood at the back gate to keep away the protesters. But there were no protesters here; there were no television cameras here. The jumble of protesters and reporters were at the front entrance gate, the one you see on television. The front entrance gate is several hundred yards away from the walls of the prison and the main door. No one could come through the main door, unless authorized. All the protesters could do was watch from a distance and all they would see would be walls. No one moved on the grounds except prison personnel. San Quentin was in lockdown. When an execution is in its process, all prisoners are confined to their cells. An execution is a time when the prison has to have absolute control.

We waited until the guards cleared us through, examining our identification cards and shining a light into our faces to see if we matched the pictures on our ID cards. We drove down a hill and parked the car. Officer Higgins came to the passenger side, but I had already opened my door. We walked around the corner and there it was—the front wall of San Quentin Prison, the lights shining on it making the beige wall glow white in the darkness. The massive slab of concrete rose from the ground and confronted you like some monolithic barrier, thick and impenetrable.

I had been here before. There is only one entrance to San Quentin if you are a visitor. There is a separate entrance to San Quentin if you are a prisoner. From the inside of maximum security housing, all you can see are walls. From the inside, there is no outside except the main yard, and the main yard is inside the walls. When men are brought into San Quentin, they arrive by via a California Department of Corrections bus. There is one exception—a condemned prisoner is brought by himself in a car or a van. I know this because I made that journey once with a condemned prisoner who I had prosecuted, a different man than the one facing his sentence this night.

I remember walking across the main yard with the condemned man, who was wrapped in a belly chain and leg irons, his wrists handcuffed to the chain that ran around his waist and then between his legs and down to the leg irons that limited his stride to short, mincing steps. He shuffled across the vacant yard. All the inmates cleared the yard as a guard intoned, "Condemned man coming through." That was almost thirty years ago.

I remember walking with a guard across the main yard to a door in a stone wall. The path through the door led to the area known as Death Row. As I walked through the steel door, the first thing I saw was a gurney with a body bag on it. To the right was the steel door that led to the holding cells next to the execution chamber. To the left was the elevator to Death Row. There was no question that he had known where he was; his chest was heaving as he walked through the wire-caged man-trap that led to the cells on what the condemned men called "the Row." I never forgot that image. It was the only time I ever saw a man's heart beating so hard that I could see his shirt move with his heartbeat. All those years ago, and that same man was still here, waiting and, I assumed, watching as the man I came to see, Clarence Ray Allen, walked off the "Row" for the last time.

San Quentin hadn't changed, but I had. I was older. My dark-brown hair was now streaked with gray. I was no longer a young man filled with dreams. Most of my youthful dreams had come true. I still had the good fortune to be able to make new dreams, but they had become increasingly fewer and less dramatic.

As I stared at the walls, I could hear the protesters out by the front gates of the prison. Some were protesting that the execution was taking place, and some were protesting that it had already taken too long. I caught the breath of the bay as the fog rolled in. I looked out across the blackness of the water that edged the prison. I was only a few hours from keeping a commitment I made on another night so long ago, a commitment not just to the families of the victims, but also to myself.

The memory of that night twenty-six years ago and its aftermath surged from the recesses of my mind. I remembered the commitment. Now, I was going to keep it.

The highway patrol officer waited while I stopped and looked at the walls of the prison. Finally, I turned and we walked along the edge of the wall to the main door. It wasn't quite as I remembered it. I don't know if they had changed the entry door or if my memory just hadn't held the details as firmly as I would have thought. I walked through the door with the investigators who had worked with me many years ago, Tommy Lean, Harry Massucco, and Ernie Duran. We were all older men now, each of us here for our own reasons. We hadn't discussed why. I know we were glad to see one another, but we didn't talk about much of anything as we followed one another inside the prison. Behind us, the sound of the protesters receded as we walked through the portal, surrounded by the stone walls of San Quentin.

The brightly illuminated waiting room was crowded with official witnesses, as well as people who were going to be unofficial witnesses. I was an official witness. I had some idea of what that meant, but it still hadn't been well defined for me.

There was a large table in the middle of the wood-paneled room. I moved toward the back and removed my overcoat. I was already feeling the heat of the room and I was fighting fatigue. Normally, I wouldn't consider drinking a cup of coffee after three in the afternoon. But the first thing I reached for was a cup from the urn labeled "Regular."

Some people think they have an image of what this process is like, if only from movies and television, or from their own imaginations. I didn't have an image of the whole process, but I did have an understanding of what the execution chamber would look like. I had been inside it many years ago. When we had brought that condemned prisoner in twenty-eight years before, they had given us a tour and removed the chains from the door. I had walked in at the urging of some of the same people who were with me tonight. There were two chairs, labeled "A" and "B," sitting in the middle of the chamber. I remember that at the time it struck a chord of dark humor in me that they would label the chairs. What was the chance of confusion? I also remember the sound that the steel door made when it was slammed shut. I'm not claustrophobic, but I wanted out right then. The only thing that had kept me quiet was the realization of what I would have to face from my investigators if I had exhibited any panic. Peer pressure can overcome a host of human preferences.

I knew the chairs were gone. California no longer used the execution room as a gas chamber, but it remained a steel-walled chamber of death. Lethal injection would be used. Silent needles had replaced the hiss of poison gas. The chairs had been replaced by a gurney. But the glass-walled chamber remained, a room where death was its only purpose. On this night, I would be outside that glass-walled room, looking in.

The spokesperson for San Quentin Prison entered the room. Vernell Crittendon was a handsome black man who didn't fit the image of a prison guard, but it was apparent that he did fit the image San Quentin wanted to convey. He was confident and well-spoken. He took charge of the room and quieted everyone down. San Quentin had prepared a full meal for us and it was to be served in an adjoining room. The execution would take place after midnight. I looked at the clock on the wall and at my watch. We had almost two hours to go. I didn't have an appetite.

Crittendon told us that we would be taken into the inmate visiting room that would be entered off to the left of the main entrance. There, prison officials would configure us in the same way that we would be placed in the witness room. The warden would speak to us. There were no stays. The execution was expected to proceed on schedule. The condemned prisoner's family and chosen witnesses were in a different room, as was the press. All had been provided with the same meal. Crittendon asked if there were any questions and he answered each of them professionally and succinctly. The few questions were strikingly mundane and subdued, and the nervousness of the questioners was betrayed in the sound of their quiet voices.

The rest of the evening crawled by. I kept looking at the clock on the wall, knowing that in the holding cell outside the execution chamber Clarence Allen had to be looking at the clock, as well. I wondered what he was thinking as he was finishing his last meal. I knew that the day before a scheduled execution, they moved the condemned prisoner down to a holding cell in the area behind the execution chamber. I wondered if that gurney with the body bag was still kept outside the back entry to those holding cells. I looked at the clock again. It had barely moved. I could only speculate that the minutes would not be passing slowly for him. I went back to the room where the prepared meals sat, congealing in steam trays. They had cheesecake, usually my favorite. I just couldn't muster an appetite.

I grabbed another cup of coffee and walked back outside to get some air and be alone with my thoughts. Several guards were stationed outside, and they greeted me. It was clear they knew who I was. It didn't surprise me. The presence of someone like me at an execution was more than unusual, but they left me alone. I walked fifteen or twenty feet away from the wall and listened to the sounds of the protesters and the cadence of what sounded like a drum. I knew what was out there—people with strongly held convictions for and against execution; or, worse, there were those with little or no convictions who merely had a morbid sense of simple curiosity and a desire to be where something was happening. And there were people like me, who had a reason to be there, but would share it only in their own time. I could see the bright lights from the television news cameras. I could imagine that several hundred yards away, young reporters were trying to convey a sense of urgency to the situation and give people who watch news at eleven some sense of the moment.

I didn't need a sense of the moment. I understood the burden of a judgment of execution. I was an appellate judge. I had been a trial judge. I understood that across the bay in San Francisco, justices of the California Supreme Court were sitting in the conference room of the chief justice, prepared to make any last-minute orders. They would listen to the process over the telephone lines, speaking in muffled voices that conveyed nothing of the moment except its reality when they were told it was over. They had never seen what I would see. They would never feel what I felt. Justices of the United States Supreme Court were sleeping fitfully, waiting for any last-minute application for a stay. Though it had taken twenty-six years, I understood the finality of the sound a gavel makes when it falls at a judgment of death.

Of the tangle of thoughts and feelings rushing through me, I knew only that I had a strong desire not to be there. Even when I had written to the warden asking for permission to be present, I had been of two minds.

I walked down the cement pathway and looked briefly at the steel door in the wall of the prison. I knew where it led and I knew I would soon be walking through it with the other witnesses. Down near the water's edge, I stopped and thought about what I had said to the small group of other witnesses who gathered in the room at the hotel before crossing the bridge to San Quentin. I had stood off in the corner, away from the family members who were the other official witnesses. It wasn't that I didn't want to be with them. It was because they all shared a unique sense of loss. I didn't have the same sense of loss that they shared. I could never presume to feel their pain. For me, there was something else.

The deputy attorney general, Jonathan Raven, who was in charge of victim relations, had set up the meeting of the witnesses in the hotel room in San Francisco. He took me aside and told me that it meant a lot to the family members that I had come. It made me feel a little better about being there. They had pizza and soda available for everyone, but nobody really ate. We all just looked at one another uneasily. Most of us were looking at faces that had been changed by twenty-five and thirty years—familiar, but in some cases, not immediately recognizable. It was a bit like attending a thirtieth high school reunion and trying to match faces in the room to pictures in a graduation album.

The deputy A.G. explained what was going to happen over the course of the evening and asked if we had any questions. There had been no questions, just tired, strained, blank faces that stared back at him. He then asked the witnesses if they had anything they wanted to say. Some people thanked the members of the attorney general's staff for their kindness. A few explained why they were present. Bryon's sister was there, as were his niece and nephew, who hadn't even been born when Bryon died.

But the years had taken their toll. Ray and Fran Schletewitz had both died in the last two years. Clarence Ray Allen, their child's murderer, had outlived the parents of his victim, their only son. Josephine Rocha's brother and sister were there. Allen had outlived one of Josephine's parents, and the other was too infirm to attend the murderer's execution. Douglas White's aunt and uncle were there. Similar to the parents of Josephine, Allen had outlived one of Douglas' parents, and the other was also too infirm to come. Jack Abbott, who still carried pellets in his body from Hamilton's shotgun blast, was there. And I was there.

Clarence Ray Allen had lived longer fighting the sentence of death than the children whose killing he had orchestrated had been alive. He had lived longer fighting the sentence of death than all but two of the parents of the children he had murdered. Those who were gathered that day were all that were left to see him serve his sentence. In the end, he had drawn all of the people in that room through years of frustration and pain. And he had condemned the families of Josephine, Douglas, and Bryon to a sentence that they were still serving—a sentence that for their parents was a lifetime of grief.

I had remained in the corner of the hotel room while everyone spoke. I didn't intend to say anything. I had my reasons for being there and they were mine alone. I had shared them with no one, not even my family and friends. I just wanted to do what I had to do. I didn't want to be the center of attention. My thoughts were focused on the emotions etched on the faces of the family members more than they were on the spoken words. Then, quite suddenly, I realized everyone's eyes were fixed on me. Deputy Attorney General Raven said that perhaps I would like to say something to the witnesses. The truth was I didn't. I had indulged myself with the notion that I could stand to the side and remain in a private capacity. As I looked around the room at the faces staring at me, I realized that I had to do what was expected of me as a public official, as a judge, and as the one person who had been there from the beginning.

I make my living with words and decisions. I knew what was expected of me. I knew that it was important that I represent the judicial system and, at the same time, communicate what *the others* were thinking. I understood; everybody needed to know that they all shared some of the same feelings.

I took a few steps away from the corner wall where I had been standing and moved my eyes slowly around the room. I could sense the expectation in the expressions of those who had gathered in the circle that had formed around me. And I understood—really for the first time—their hope that I would say something that would be meaningful to them. I hadn't planned on speaking, nor had I had time to reflect on appropriate remarks or to jot down notes. So, I just talked until I was finished and that was when I couldn't talk any more. What I said that night came straight from my heart, without hesitation or preconceived thought. But the words are imprinted on my mind as indelibly as they would be on a piece of paper.

"When I handled the Mary Sue Kitts case, I was a young man with dark-brown hair and only one chin. Now I am a middle-aged man with graying hair. I didn't expect to say anything here tonight. I didn't lose a loved one, as all of you did. All of us have our own reasons for being here. I will explain mine in just a moment. I want to say to each of you that I am sorry that it has taken so long to bring you and your families to this night. I am sorry that the appeals and judicial process have taken so many years that now parents are no longer alive to see the punishment of their child's killer, or they are so infirm that they couldn't make the trip. As a member of the criminal justice system, I have an understanding of why this has taken so long. I understand the concerns about executing innocent people. I understand the process of the law. I understand the motivation of individuals who work both for and against executions. But regardless of the process of the system, there is no excuse for it having taken this long. I can only say I am sorry. I can only ask that you consider that there are people in this room and at San Quentin right now who have worked almost their entire careers so that you might see justice in this case. I ask you to remember those people and how hard they have worked when you think about the system. They are part of the system, too.

"More than anyone in this room I know what happened in this case. I have been here from the very beginning. I was there when we arrested Clarence Allen for the murder of Mary Sue Kitts. I was there when I promised Ray and Fran Schletewitz that nothing would happen if they cooperated, and if Bryon cooperated. I was there the night your loved ones were murdered. I saw Josephine, Douglas, and Bryon lying on that cold, cement floor. For as long as I live, I will remember that night. I will not talk further of what I saw. I *will* say that I will never forget it as long as I live. All I can say to you and your families is that I did my best.

"I said I would tell you why I was here and I will. I confess to you that I've had feelings of ambivalence about coming. I suppose that may be hard for you to understand. It's not due to either my opposition or approval of the penalty. It goes deeper than that and I have difficulty understanding it myself. I almost didn't come at all. Even today, I debated with myself. I have pronounced this sentence as a judge and I have asked for this sentence as a prosecutor, but I have never had any desire to watch it being carried out and I have no desire to watch it tonight. I hope for each of you this sentence brings some closure, but to be honest with you, I doubt that it will. I can only say to you that after tonight you need to go on with your lives and close this door behind you. I hope this sentence brings you and your families some measure of peace."

I paused, studying the expressions of those around me. I could see in their eyes that they were still reaching out for something more from me. The room, the building emotion, all of it was closing around me—and them. I reached as far inside me as I could. I searched for words and spoke slowly, trying to give them what I sensed they needed. Maybe, it was what I needed, too. It was time for me to try to explain what I had not been willing for so long to put into words.

"I told Ray and Fran and Bryon that nothing would happen to them if they cooperated. That is what prosecutors say to witnesses. They say it because it's what they believe. They say it because it is true. It's what I believed."

I looked around the room and I could see police officers in the room nodding. They understood what I was saying. It had seemed such a logical and reasonable thing to tell people that they would be safe. Things like this weren't supposed to happen. I felt like I had to say more, but I knew that there was nothing I could say that would undo the harm caused by this man. Still, I tried to convey what I was feeling. "Retaliation against witnesses is not something that you see except on television and in the movies and in organized crime. I truly believed that Bryon would be safe. I think about that frequently. I have thought about it daily as we began to get closer to this night. To each of you here tonight, I can only say that Josephine and Douglas were simply innocent victims who were in the wrong place at the wrong time, and Bryon was a young man who died as a result of doing his duty as a citizen, a duty that I asked him to do. I never believed anything would happen to him. I was wrong. Your family members died that night because Bryon did what I asked of him. I can only say to you that I am sorry. I wish there was something else I could say, but there isn't.

"I will tell you now that I am here because Ray and Fran couldn't be. I saw them a number of times over the years and I know that seeing justice done was something that was important to them. I was proud that they became my friends. When they died, I felt like somebody had to be here for them. I am here because I made a promise to myself that I would be here for them because they couldn't be. I am here for Ray and Fran."

I remember that I stopped talking because I couldn't talk anymore. Many family members were nodding. Some were crying. I was struggling to control my emotions. For the first time in my life, I realized that Allen had made me a victim, too.

Now, standing outside the walls of San Quentin, I considered what all of this would mean for me in the days and years to come. I wasn't here to find out what an execution was like. I had spoken truthfully when I said I was here for Ray and Fran, but what I hadn't shared with anybody was how deeply I was troubled by the assurances I made to people that they would be safe and years of living with the realization that what I had so confidently assured would turn out to be wrong. *That* was why I was here. It was about responsibility—Clarence Ray Allen's and my own. Tonight, I would watch one man accept responsibility with his final breath, and I would accept my own and see this case through to its end, whether I wanted to watch it or not.

I looked across the bay at the glow of San Francisco and the reflections of light that came off the water. The sound of the protesters was muffled, but they were there and so was that drumbeat. In a few hours, they would go home. In a few hours, I could go home. After twenty-five years, I hoped it was almost over. Certainly time was growing short for Allen. Soon, it would be over for him and he would meet whatever judgement the next life held for him. But I knew that it was never going to be over for the families and it wasn't going to be over for me. For the rest of my life, the rushing waters of the Piedra Canal and the cement floor of Fran's Market would be part of my memory. As I stood alone outside the walls of San Quentin, all that kept going through my mind was the echo of my own words explaining to people, who were locked in grief, why I was there among them. In the last few hours, I had come to the realization that I grieved because they did and I could not detach myself from my role in their grief. All I could do was stand in for those who could no longer be there.

I looked back at the guards standing a respectful distance away. I was next to one of the most beautiful bays in the world, its water lapping up against the stone walls of one of the most secure prisons in the world. From beauty to the belly of the beast and all that separated them was gently rising bluff. In my career, I sent a lot of men and women to prison, and many of those men were still inside San Quentin. Some were still inside other walls in other prisons. Others were men sitting in special cells who I had asked to be condemned or that I, as a judge, had condemned. Even the man I had brought to San Quentin when I was a young prosecutor was still sitting up on the Row. I wondered what he thought when they moved Allen down to the holding cell and he saw him walk off the Row for the last time.

I could feel the guards looking at me as I walked back inside. I nodded. What was there to say? When I got back to the waiting room, I stood around with the others and we talked quietly, looking at the clock as it edged toward midnight. I wondered if Allen had a clock that he could see.

At 11:15, the prison officials asked us to walk into the visitor waiting room. There were chairs lined up in clusters that matched the locations where we would be sitting or standing at the time of the execution. They seemed to know who we were and we were quietly directed to specific chairs. There was very little talking. Mostly, there was the sound of shuffling feet. The tension in the room was building and the emotions of the family members were rising. I looked over as Josephine's sister began to cry, her emotions overflowing. I turned away. The waiting was beginning to fray the nerves of everyone.

I looked around at the walls and the chairs. This was where the inmates visited their families. There were vending machines and plastic-backed chairs. There was very little talking and even that was whispered. Mostly, there was silence, the occasional cough, and the low, broken sound of quiet grief. People kept to themselves and looked at the clock on the wall as it ticked closer to midnight.

Ward Campbell was sitting next to me. He had been the deputy attorney general who had helped prosecute Allen when the Fresno district attorney's office was disqualified. Ward had handled Allen's appeals all the way to the United States Supreme Court. For twenty-five years, this case had been his mission and tonight he would see it through to the end. He had done an incredible job. People don't realize the dedication it takes to do what Ward had done. Like me, he would be there to the end. Campbell nudged me and pointed at the walls. There were murals on the walls that had been painted by an inmate. The painting showed talent, wasted talent. It took me a while before I saw the name and realized that the artist had the same name as another man whose murder case I had handled when I was a prosecutor so long ago. He was still there, too. The mural took on a whole different perspective for me as I remembered seeing the bodies of the two young people he had murdered. Images of crime scenes pushed themselves into my mind, but I pushed it all back. I didn't want to think of those things now.

The warden came in and spoke to us. He said that when we were asked to enter the witness room, everything would be ready to begin. The designated legal witnesses would be taken in first. Everyone else would follow us. He was professional and businesslike, but like everyone else in the room, you could see the strain on his face.

I turned my head when I heard the sound of rapid footsteps. A man dressed in a suit came in, some kind of prison official. He was clearly agitated and I remember thinking that something had gone wrong. Maybe, there was a last-minute stay. I didn't want to think about sitting here like this, waiting endless hours for the rest of the night for another appointed time to arrive.

The official walked over to Crittendon and said, "It's time." His voice had a tone to it, a pitch that was startling. It was oddly discordant in a way. I realize now he was pulled into the emotion of all of it, just as we were. Somebody must have told the person at the end of the group to stand up, because everyone began to get up. We walked out of the room in single file. I didn't look behind me to see who was following me in the line.

The guard in front led us outside and we walked along the high stone wall. The cement walkway echoed a hollow sound as shuffling feet moved down the wall. I knew what to expect. I had walked down this path many years before. At the end of the walkway was a steel door that led into the witness room that looked into the semi-circular steel-and-glass walls of the execution chamber. As we turned the corner into the recess in the wall that led to the door, I could see a phalanx of guards standing at attention. They lined the last few yards of the walkway. Each of them was smartly dressed in his uniform, with jackets fastened tightly at the waist. I remember a woman guard looking at me and nodding slightly. For some reason, her face communicated everything I know she meant to say. She was doing her duty and she was acknowledging that we were doing ours. I nodded back and kept walking. There was a growing sense of ritual.

The door was as I remembered it—a simple steel door, not elaborate or massive, in the outside wall of the prison. It was open and low light from the interior filtered out. We walked in. There it was in front of us, with a drawn curtain around it. It was the same sickly green color that I remembered, the window frames sharply outlined against the institutional beige of the walls. The light in the room had a certain softness to it, almost like candlelight. There was enough illumination to allow one to see, but the detail was lost in the dimness. Around the perimeter of the room was a stepped-up area of risers for people to stand in tiered rows. Around the curtained execution chamber, there was a steel railing. In front of the railing, chairs had been positioned, less than three feet from the chamber Those were the seats for the official witnesses; everyone else would stand on the risers. We walked in file in front of the chairs, and Ward Campbell took the seat next to me. A voice from behind us told us to be seated. No one said anything. The stillness was thick. You could feel the silence. You could almost hear your own heartbeat. I kept my eyes fixed on the curtain. I couldn't take my eyes off it.

Behind me, I heard the shuffling of feet as the other witnesses filed in behind us. The press took up stations on the riser steps to the far end of the room—the right side as you faced the chamber. The other witnesses were directly behind us. You could sense the movement, but only by the sound of the grind of shoes scraping against the wood of the tiered steps. Then there was silence, broken only by the sound of breathing and the occasional cough. I looked to my right and caught sight of reporters. I didn't look behind me.

The silence was broken again by the movement of more people walking in—some of Allen's family and his chosen witnesses, including his spiritual counselor, who had spent Allen's last hours at his side. I looked over my left shoulder. I remember thinking about the sensitivity of the guards escorting the family. I recognized one of Allen's chosen witnesses. I had interrogated her many years before. I know she saw me. We didn't exchange anything more than a momentary locked stare. Kathy Allen, Clarence Allen's daughter in law, just looked older, her face a tight, hard mask as she looked at me. For a fleeting moment, I saw her sitting in the interrogation room. The flash of recognition was unexpected for me—and probably for her as well.

My gaze was drawn once again to the curtained chamber, with the drape still waiting to be drawn open. The emotion in the room took on an oppressive weight. I could feel it pressing down on me like some invisible massive burden. It was almost suffocating, closing in on me, and I felt the sense of others next to me and behind me, their feelings adding to mine, bearing down on all of us, each of us distinct as people but merged into some shapeless emotion-drenched mass—waiting, breathing, waiting. And then, suddenly, the wait was over. Two guards walked along the rail to the center of the closed drape. They pulled the curtain to the edges of the chamber and tied the drape back.

Three panes of windows, set into angled walls, pushed out into the room where we were seated. I was less than five feet away from the window on the right side, and through that window I could see the execution chamber, brightly lit by a single, wire-shrouded bulb. The focal point in the room was a greenish gurney, like a surgical table, with straps attached. The room was encased with riveted plate-steel, with darkened windows at the back of it. On the back left side was a window covered by blinds. I knew that was where the official executioner stood, concealed from view. There was not a sound in our rooms, as all eyes were fixed on the gurney and on the steel door that led into the chamber. A slight movement caused me to swing my head slightly to my right. I saw a small circle of steel swing aside, opening a hole in the door at the back of the witness room. A piece of paper was handed through the hole in the door. Whoever slipped it through was standing in the area behind the back of the entrance into the execution chamber and the holding cell area for condemned prisoners on their last watch. I knew what was happening now. Allen had been read the order of execution. He was standing outside the closed door to the chamber, waiting for the order to be read to us.

The guard who took the order was a woman. When she spoke, it startled me. Her loud, firm, deep voice unexpectedly broke the silence. She read the order of execution and the name of the judge who had issued the judgment. Her voice reverberated throughout the room, the words clear and clipped, ringing with the finality and clarity of a gavel striking the bench.

As the clock approached midnight, the door to the chamber finally opened. Two guards stepped inside the chamber and turned back toward the figure who stood just outside the door. After twenty-five years, there was Clarence Ray Allen—standing, outlined by the light, which faded to black behind him. There was no way to tell if there were people behind him, supporting him, as the two guards reached through the door and each took one of his arms. They weren't supporting him, but they were steadying him, as he stepped over the six-inch threshold into the chamber.

There was no cascade of competing images or emotions. My mind wasn't a jumble of thoughts. I was surprised by the clarity of it all, particularly by how gentle the guards were with Allen. But most of all, I was struck by the fact that he was just an old man. He was nothing like I remembered. He was just a paunchy old man. I had anticipated what I would feel next—a brief flicker of pity. I couldn't help it. He didn't deserve any pity, but I couldn't help it. I suddenly had an urge to leave. If it hadn't been for the fact that everybody in that room knew who I was, I am not sure what I would have done. How odd it seems that I didn't feel any rush of emotion. I wasn't anguished by the sight of a man stepping into the steel death chamber. It wasn't that it was unbearable for me—I just didn't want to watch it. Even now, so long removed from that room, I can't explain it any better than that. I think now that the passage of years had detached me from the anger, from the resentment, and from the sense of righteousness that sustains a desire for retribution.

I can only surmise that I needed to feel a sense of justice being served to take me past the sight and sense of a man dying in a deliberate and sterile manner. I needed that anger to watch. I wanted that anger because I could feel myself wavering and I needed the emotion of retribution to justify my watching. I had to remind myself of what he had done. I had to force myself to picture those three young people lying on the floor in pools of their own blood. I had to force myself to think of Mary Sue, now so long a part of the sand and rubble of the Piedra canal. I realized I was struggling.

More than any other person in that room, I understood the justice of this case. I had stood on the edge of that canal looking down at that frigid water. I had been there that night at Fran's Market in that small killing ground. I had pursued this man relentlessly. I had called this man to account. And yet, I was struggling. I had asked of others what I had no right not to expect of myself. It was duty that kept me sitting quietly. It was duty that the guards in that green room accepted and it was duty that brought me to that chair in that room, watching as an official witness. For the others in that room, I do not know what was in their minds. I only know what was in mine.

Allen was wearing new prison clothing, the yellow prisoner lettering on the sides of his pants still shiny and sharply stenciled. His blue work shirt hung loosely and various monitor lines dangled from beneath his shirt, having been attached before he came into the room. He stepped over the threshold and looked at the gurney that was directly in front of him, dominating the small room. If he had any thoughts, I couldn't detect them on his face, or in the jowls and lines which were now those of an old man, the skin bleached by the darkness of sunless rooms. But I could see he was breathing heavily, his chest pushing his shirt out in rapid, jerky movements.

Allen was carrying a feather attached to some kind of handle. It was obviously some kind of Indian religious talisman. In his last years, he had claimed his part Indian heritage as his ethnic identity. I could see the white of his knuckles as he held the feather tightly against his chest. He looked at the gurney, green and shiny under the light. I did not know what goes through a man's mind when he looks upon the bed on which he knows he is going to die. I still do not know, as Allen's face betrayed nothing.

He took the few steps toward the gurney and sat down first, then lay down while the guards supported him, removing the feather from his hands as they finished their task. His head was pointed toward the witness room and his feet were toward the door at the back of the chamber. Guards moved around him and strapped him down. One then carefully laid the feather on his chest. I remember thinking that they gave his religious object the same consideration that would have been given to a crucifix or to a Star of David or to prayer beads.

In some ways, the simple gesture of laying the feather on Allen's chest was singularly moving, the compassion and sensitivity of the guards was evident as they performed their duty. It struck me that some of them had probably spent twenty-five years with this man, talking to him and moving him around. He wasn't a stranger to them. He raised his head slightly and spoke. From the outside of the chamber, it came as a soundless gesture. You could hear nothing. The feather moved up and down, carried by the rhythm of Allen's rapid breathing.

I sat quietly in my chair, watching the methodical and efficient movement of the guards as they inserted needles into Allen's arms. My eyes followed the lengths of plastic tubing that draped down from a hole in the wall of the chamber. It was through those tubes that the chemicals would flow to put him to sleep, to stop his respiration, and to stop his heart. I had the impression of tentacles reaching out from the steel walls. The heart monitors were attached to other lines running out of the chamber. There wasn't a sound in the witness rooms, not even the breathing from those gathered.

Then the guards were finished. Allen said something to them, his mouth moving silently. There was no response that I could see. The guards attached the tubes to the needles, then most of them moved out of the chamber. The last two guards checked and tightened the restraints and moved the gurney around so that his feet faced toward the area where his family was. The side of Allen's head was no more than five feet from me, his profile etched sharply against the white light of that naked bulb. These were his last moments given to him by the State to frame his final thoughts, to say his final goodbyes, to see the living through the eyes of the living, and to make his peace.

It was more consideration than he had ever given to those whose lives he had taken. It was just a few minutes before midnight, and it happened to be Clarence Ray Allen's birthday. He was 74.

Allen turned his head to the side and looked directly at me. If there was any recognition in his face didn't betray it. He held my gaze for just a moment and then his head turned down the row of witnesses, stopping briefly in the middle. He kept turning his head until he was looking at his family. I saw one of his family members wave to him. She was young and there was anguish on her face. Her arm moved back and forth, like a willow swaying briefly in a gust of breeze. I looked back at Allen. He raised his head slightly, as much as the restraints allowed. His lips were moving. There was no mistaking his words even in silent movement. We had all said them at one time or another as we said goodnight or goodbye. He told his family, "I love you." I remember thinking that Allen had loved ones, too. In retrospect, that seems like a naive revelation, but I had spent so many years thinking of him as the man who shattered the lives of young people and their loved ones that he had become entirely one-dimensional to me. In these final moments, I saw some depth of feeling there that tried to touch me. My only reaction was that Allen had also made his loved ones victims, because what brought him here to this place and time would also be the legacy he would leave to them.

The execution was ordered to proceed. The scene before me was sharply defined. The slightest movement was immediately noticed. Allen lay there quietly. His tongue passed over his lips and he kept his eyes open. I saw one of the tubes move, rhythmically undulating as liquid came through the intravenous tube. There was no movement from him, no twisting or resistance. He just yawned and went to sleep. Then, he stopped breathing. There wasn't a sound in the room except this tiny squeaking noise that sounded like a pump methodically working. I thought it was probably the pump pushing in the chemicals. I don't know. I just remember that squeaking sound and watching the tubes undulate one after another as chemicals continued to be pumped in. Then it was over.

We sat there for several minutes in silence, looking at this old man lying on the gurney, brightly lit by that single bulb. He had been given a peaceful and painless end to his life. You had to remind yourself that he had been responsible for the premeditated, brutal, and painful murders of four young people and the shattering of the lives of those who loved them. My mind held the image of that cold, gray floor in that storeroom so many years before, juxtaposed against the stillness of the old man lying in front of me, his eyes closed and his breath silenced. Whatever waited for him on the other side, he was now there.

Holding my thoughts deep inside myself, with nothing but silent emotion surrounding me, I realized why I had struggled, why I didn't want to watch. What was it whispering inside me? It wasn't mercy or compassion. He didn't deserve mercy, and any compassion I felt was separate from mercy. There was no darkening blood or scent of violence. This was not death at the hands of another as I had known it nor death as his hand had meted out. There was no terror, no pain, no last blood-bubbled gasp for air. For death as I knew it, you would have to stand in the street and in the alleys and on blood-stained floors. This was an execution. And, deep inside me, I knew—I had had enough of the many signatures of Death. I simply could not watch it anymore.

The guard read the announcement that the order of execution had been complied with and Clarence Ray Allen was pronounced by the State to be dead. The guards closed the curtains around the execution chamber, and his family filed out. After a period of time, we followed. There was no talking; everyone was lost in his or her own thoughts. As for me, the punishment was so far removed from that night in 1980 that I was detached from my own outrage. The clarity of retribution, the righteousness of it, the moral force of it had become blurred, the sharp lines of justice obscured by the ambiguity of time.

I didn't want to feel sorry for Allen. More than almost anybody there, I knew what he had done. I had been there since the beginning. But I did feel a moment of pity. I couldn't help it. That will be hard for some to understand, and it's hard for me to understand. It just is what it is and, I guess, I am what I am. Certainly, this night had drawn me deeper into my perceptions of myself. I kept reminding myself of what he had done. I could imagine that someday my name as sentencing judge would be read in that room as another warrant of execution was intoned. It was a sobering thought.

As we moved slowly past the curtained execution chamber, the only sound was the shuffling of feet against the linoleum. We walked out of the witness room, outside the thick walls of San Quentin, where the damp chill of the air rolling in off the bay provided sharp contrast to the warm and closely held air of the room we had just left. I looked at the people walking out behind me. In the end, Clarence Ray Allen had left a trail of victims behind and many of them were here walking along in silence. For most of them, I don't think it was over or would ever really be over. But there is one thing I know for sure. The length of time that all of the proceedings took as the case moved at its glacially slow pace through the judicial system added to the layer of pain that these people had endured. That was wrong.

The deputy attorney general moved beside me, speaking quietly. The press would very much like a statement from me. I shook my head, "No statements. I have nothing to say." I kept walking, following the line of people before me.

I wanted to go home. I had been there from the beginning and now I had been there at the end. I could hear the sounds from the main gate as protesters registered their final outcry, the drumbeat still faintly audible in the night air. My only thought as I walked to the car was whether it was really the end. Clarence Ray Allen had been behind walls of concrete and steel, and yet he had still been able to send a messenger of death. He had still been able to put his hands through those stone walls.

Epilogue

My driver waited for me and for the men who had been my investigators as we walked from the prison to my car. I nodded and said we were ready to go back to the hotel. He asked me about the press. Apparently, he had been told they were waiting for me. I told him I didn't have anything to say, and I just wanted to go home. It was a quiet ride across the bridge. Tom Lean, Ernie Duran, and Harry Massucco sat in the backseat.

Tommy had left the sheriff's office years before and was now an instructor and supervisor at the community college training new peace officers. Ernie was about to retire from the state department of justice and go into private security work for a major car rental company. Harry had left law enforcement altogether and was now a partner in an executive job placement and headhunter firm. We had all moved on with our lives and yet we hadn't quite finished with the past. Nobody said much of anything as we rode back across the bridge. We just looked out the window, watched the lights of San Francisco, and thought whatever thoughts we had.

When we reached the hotel, it was almost 1:30 in the morning. We talked about having a drink, but the bars were closed. It was just as well. Drinking wasn't really what we wanted anyway. We went back to Ernie's room and sat for a few minutes in silence. I remember looking at those three men and feeling a kinship of spirit that I can only describe as something like the feeling you have for men you have been through battle with. We knew too much about one another—our strengths and our weaknesses—to waste time trying to impress one another. We were middle-aged men who had started as young men and taken a journey together across the span of our lives. What we had seen, we had seen together. What we had done, we had done together. And now, that night, it was fitting that we had together seen a part of our lives through to the end.

We pulled a bottle of wine from the bar in the room. I have no idea how long it had been there, but I do know the cork was almost impossible to remove. It took each of our efforts. Ernie finally got the cork out, but we knew it was only because the rest of us had loosened it for him. We passed the bottle around and drank from plastic glasses.

We didn't talk about what we had seen. We only talked about why we were there. Ernie and Harry had worked on the Allen cases while they were sheriff's detectives, and both had become investigators for me in homicide when they came into the district attorney's office. Both men had been out digging through rubble beside the Piedra Canal. They both said the same thing: They wanted to see it through to the end both for themselves and for all the old guys who had gone before them, like Art Tabler, who had passed on, and Art Christenson, long retired but still a legend. Tommy just said, "I came for Mary Sue Kitts."

And me? I said I came because I had made a promise to myself that I would see it through to the end for Ray and Fran, who didn't live long enough to see the punishment of the man who had taken so much from their lives. We nodded, as each of us spoke in turn. We understood one another and we all knew we each understood. We talked about where we were with our lives. We finished a second bottle of wine and said our goodbyes, each of us returning to our separate worlds, but forever joined by what had led us to be together that night. It was a sharing of a singular moment and each of us knew when we left the room that we would never again experience the words and the feelings that we had in those hours before we again went on our separate ways. We drank a toast. It was a toast to Bill, our very good friend and brother in all that we had done. It was fitting that he, too, would be part of our time together this night. We had also seen it through to the end for Bill.

And what of Billy Ray Hamilton? His appeals dragged on after Allen's execution. I was told the night I walked out of San Quentin that Hamilton had killed three more men while he waited on Death Row. The prison staff couldn't prove it, but they knew he did it. Everybody in the prison was afraid of him, and everybody hated him.

When Hamilton's time finally came to meet his judgment day, it would not be in the green room of San Quentin. A year and a half after Allen's execution, Hamilton died in a hospital in Bakersfield, California, chained to a bed. Bladder cancer poisoned his body, instead of the chemicals that should have ended his life years before. Billy Ray Hamilton, murderer of children, destroyer of lives, and servant of Clarence Ray Allen lived longer in prison than the length of time Josephine Rocha, Douglas White, and Bryon Schletewitz had lived from birth to their death at his hands. He died on a clean bed with clean sheets, cheating the executioner.

Allen's appeal and writ process had taken over twenty-five years. He had outlived the parents of most of his victims. What toll had they paid during their long years of waiting? Much of the publicity the last weeks before Allen's execution had been about public and legal reaction concerning executing such an aged inmate. In the end, Allen's health had been stronger than that of the parents of the victims. Where was the outrage at that?

Nobody wants to execute an innocent person, but sometimes the judicial system loses sight of the pain that it inflicts by its lumbering movement. The system sometimes seems to forget that its responsibility doesn't only involve the defendant. No one wants to make a rush-to-judgment, but neither should the system simply consume time without regarding the consequences. The system has another responsibility—to the victims—the people who died and the families they left behind.

We are the means of justice for those whose lives are shattered. We are the rational and dispassionate forum that keeps people from seeking their own justice. We need to remember that our work is not only about justice for the defendant; it is also about justice for the victims.

We have to remember that the passage of time eats at people's souls. Without an ending, their anger can consume them. Over twenty-five years had passed in this case, and yet, for me, the emotions at the end of it were remarkably detached from the emotions at the beginning. Justice should not be imposed in anger, but neither should it be delayed so long that we have trouble remembering why we seek it. It had been so long since the acts for which this man was condemned that it was difficult to place the execution in the context of his crime. So many years had passed that the murder victims' faces had become merely memories and photographs from the past, and Allen's aged face had become the present. For the families of those who died, I wonder if the long wait had left only bitter dregs of emotion that final judgment could no longer stir.

I don't know if I left the prison with any answers. But I know that somewhere in this country today or this week or next month, there will be a young prosecutor looking at anguished parents or wives or husbands and saying, "Don't worry. You are going to be safe and the system will take care of you. We will get justice for you."

I hope that is true. I have devoted my entire professional life to that assurance. I would like to believe that in the end, we did right by the parents of those kids who lost everything. I know I will think about that for a long time, and I know I will never be sure.

But there is one more thing of which I know I will never be sure. The morning after the verdict for the murder of Mary Sue Kitts, I walked into my office and sat at my desk. The phone rang. I picked it up and caught the hesitation in the woman's voice at the other end. She asked if I was the Allen prosecutor and if I would talk to her about something that she needed to tell somebody. You often get calls like this after a big case, from people who want to share their conspiracy theories with you. But occasionally there is someone who really does have something to say. I always gave them a few minutes. You never know what's coming and you can't tell much by the voice, except in this case the woman sounded frightened. I could tell that almost immediately.

She wouldn't give me her name, but she did tell me that she was a medical professional. She wanted to tell me something that had happened to her involving Clarence Allen. She needed somebody to listen to her, to believe her. She said that she showed horses, and several years earlier she had been to a horse show near San Luis Obispo, California, on the Central Coast. For some reason, she had to go to Allen's trailer and give him some papers. She knocked on the door and then walked in without waiting for an answer. She saw Allen kneeling on the floor, shirtless. There was a rifle on the floor in front of him. He was wearing a headband and he had a string of blue beads around his neck. She said he looked at her in a way that simply scared her to death. He stood up and told her that if she ever told anyone what she had seen he would kill her, that he had killed before. She ran out of the trailer and never went back. She never told anybody what she had seen. But it had haunted her to the point that she wasn't sure any more what was reality and what was fantasy. She needed reassurance that she wasn't crazy.

What she wanted to know was whether I believed her and would she be safe now? I told her she would be safe and I told her I believed her, just as I had told Bryon that he would be safe and that I believed him. I hung up the phone and took a deep breath. I didn't tell her I believed her just to get rid of her. I believed her because there was something that very few people knew. Allen had told some of the people he kept around him—his gang—that he was a hired killer. He told them that he was part Choctaw Indian and that when he was going to kill somebody, he would go through a ritual where he would kneel and pray to his ancestors. He told them that his Indian spirit would take over his body and he would become one with the stealth of an Indian warrior. When I had heard this story, I laughed. However, there was one other thing that I knew about Clarence Allen that nobody, except a few people steeped in the investigation, knew. When he went through that ritual, he wore a headband and a string of blue beads.

I picked up the phone and called the San Luis Obispo sheriff's department. I couldn't erase the memory of Mary Sue Kitts from my mind. Maybe there was another family out there wondering why their loved one never came home. I didn't know. They had missing people. There are always missing people. They had nothing to go on. Neither had we, until somebody talked. But sometimes, nobody talks. And sometimes, families wait through the years and only hear silence. I had to make that call. I had to make sure it was over.

Three years later, I walked through a small room in Fran's Market awash in blood. And now, twenty-six years later in another small room inside stone walls, I had seen it through to the end. Now it was finally over.

Principal Characters

INVESTIGATORS

Willie "Bill" Martin, District Attorney Investigator, Fresno County

Jim Ardaiz, Chief Deputy District Attorney, Homicide, Fresno County

Ken Badiali, Detective, Fresno County Sheriffs Office

Arthur "Blade" Christenson, Detective, Fresno County Sheriff's Office

Thomas "Tommy" Lean, Detective, Fresno County Sheriff's Office

Art Tabler, Detective Sergeant, Fresno County Sheriff's Office

Ross Kelly, Detective, Fresno County Sheriff's Office

Ernie Duran, District Attorney Investigator

Harry Massucco, Detective, Fresno County Sheriff's Office

Bill Lehman, Detective, Fresno County Sheriff's Office

Ray Schletewitz

Fran Schletewitz

Hon. Robert Z. Mardikian, Judge of the Superior Court, County of Fresno

VICTIMS

Mary Sue Kitts, Murder Victim, July, 1974

Bryon Schletewitz, Murder Victim, September, 1980

Josephine Rocha, Murder Victim, September, 1980

Douglas White, Murder Victim, September, 1980

Joe Rios, Attempted Murder Victim, September, 1980

"ALLEN GANG" ASSOCIATES, MURDER OF MARY SUE KITTS

Clarence Ray Allen

Barbara Carrasco

Eugene Leland "Lee" Furrow

Carl Mayfield

Shirley Doeckel

Charles "Chuck" Jones

Roger Allen

FRAN'S MARKET MURDERS

Kenneth "Kenny" Allen

Kathy Allen

Connie Barbo

Billy Ray Hamilton

Ronald Prager, Deputy Attorney General

Ward Campbell, Deputy Attorney General

Jack Abbott

Timeline

June 29, 1974	Burglary of Fran's Market
July 15, 1974	Mary Sue Kitts disappears
Dec. 8, 1976	Robbery of liquor store, Sacramento, California
Dec. 10, 1976	Barbara Carrasco gives statement to Sacramento sheriffs detectives
Dec. 16, 1976	Detective Christenson and Detective Lean interview Barbara Carrasco at Alderson Federal Women's Penitentiary, Alderson, West Virginia
March 17, 1977	Robbery of Kmart, Visalia, California
March 24, 1977	Arrest of Clarence Ray Allen for Kmart robbery
March 26, 1977	Arrest of Eugene "Lee" Furrow
March 30, 1977	Arrest of Carl Mayfield
March 31, 1977	Arrest of Shirley Doeckel
March 31, 1977	Discovery of stepping stone
April 1, 1977	Arrest of Chuck Jones
April 5, 1977	Arrest of Clarence Ray Allen for murder of Mary Sue Kitts

Oct. 18, 1977	Trial of Clarence Ray Allen for the murder of Mary Sue Kitts
Sept. 5, 1980	Triple murder at Fran's Market
Sept. 9, 1980	Arrest of Kenneth and Kathy Allen
Sept. 11, 1980	Arrest of Billy Ray Hamilton for three murders at Fran's Market
Dec. 1980	Arrest of Clarence Ray Allen for three murders at Fran's Market
Jan. 16, 2006	Execution of Clarence Ray Allen

Index

ABOUT THE AUTHOR

James A. Ardaiz is a former prosecutor, judge, and Presiding Justice of the California Fifth District Court of Appeal. From 1974 to 1980, Ardaiz was a prosecutor for the Fresno County District Attorney's office. In 1980 Ardaiz was elected to the Fresno Municipal Court, where he served as assistant presiding judge and presiding judge. Ardaiz was appointed to the California Fifth District Court of Appeal in 1988 and was named the court's Presiding Justice in 1994. Ardaiz retired from the bench in 2011.

Ardaiz has received many civic honors, including the Distinguished American Award presented to him in 2008 by the Japanese American Citizens League for his service to the Japanese American community.

Ardaiz's previous books include *Tears of Honor*, a novel that vividly depicts the experience of Japanese American soldiers serving in Europe during World War II, and *Fractured Justice* and *Shades of Truth*, the first two novels in Ardaiz's Matt Jamison mystery series.

Ardaiz's website is **jamesardaiz.com**.

CPSIA information can be obtained
at www.ICGtesting.com
Printed in the USA
JSHW010703051222
34238JS00004B/4